MODERN LEGAL STUDIES

Medical Negligence:
Common Law Perspectives

John Healy
BCL, Mlitt, Barrister-at-Law, Dublin

London

Sweet & Maxwell

1999

Published by
Sweet & Maxwell Limited of
100 Avenue Road London NW3 3PE.
http://www.smlawpub.co.uk
Typeset by LBJ Typesetting Ltd, Kingsclere
Printed in England by Clays Ltd, St. Ives plc

A CIP catalogue record for this book
is available from the British Library.

ISBN 0421 680601

No natural forests were destroyed to make this product, only farmed
timber was used and re-planted.

Acknowledgements

The author wishes to thank his editors and all responsible for publishing the book. Thanks also to my colleagues at University College Cork for their generous encouragement and friendship over the six happy years I spent there, in particular to Aine Ryall for many useful comments on drafts, and to Professor David Gwynn Morgan for advice and guidance in the early years; also to Professor William Binchy of Trinity College Dublin for encouraging me to develop a research thesis into its present form; and especially, love and thanks, as always, to my family and friends.

The author wishes to acknowledge permission to integrate copyright material in Chapter 5 of this book, earlier published by the author in (1998) Medico-Legal Journal of Ireland.

Contents

Table of Cases

Introduction

As a social concern, medical negligence touches upon many stimulating but delicate issues, and requires the lawyer's analysis to venture past the law's somewhat self-facing logic. In this book, I have drawn selectively but evenly from a range of disparate sources devoted to these issues, in part to assess the implications of the common law's various responses to the medical negligence action, and in part to capture the nuances of the doctor-patient relationship and the accusation of negligence. A vast number of cross-disciplinary studies has already been published in America, whose sheer scale and ambition quickly confirmed my sense that members of the public, members of the professions, students, and academics are naturally intrigued by the issues this legal action presents.

It is not an easy time to be a doctor. In an increasingly pressurised working environment, doctors must assimilate and balance more technical information than ever before, work longer hours, face tougher competition from their peers, and on top of this are now far less certain about the law's present demands and the future directions it may choose to take. To this extent, my own book may appear at first blush to contribute to their plight. I have attempted as best I can to avoid any bias, and certainly I began with none. Whilst I argue in many parts for liberalisation of the rules that continue to govern the courts' determination of medical negligence, in many cases the sought-for change is of a symbolic nature, argued from the perspective of a lawyer who has the advantage of knowing how the law generally operates within and beyond the tort of negligence.

From its structural inception, the medical profession has always acted quickly to minimise the bad publicity associated with litigation, whether threatened or actual. This tendency seems to persist today with the swift private settlement of strong, even border-line claims. Though practical and convenient, this encourages the sense that the medical negligence claim is notoriously unsuccessful—a sense that is further confirmed by the dramatically difficult obstacles faced by patients who choose to fight their case in the courts. Some of these obstacles inhere naturally in the subject matter of the action— typically, in proving the cause of the patient s injuries, considered in

1

chapter seven—but some of them are man-made, or shall we say judge-made. The obvious bone of contention, and one which has already generated mountains of heated criticism in England and abroad, centres on the rules that determine how the court assesses whether the defendant failed to abide by a standard of care owed by law.

For ordinary negligence actions, the standard of care is assessed according to the reasonable man, a vague construct which enables the court to consider basic levels of conduct apparently expected by and of members of society. In reaching its decision on this point, the court may seek guidance from the views of expert witnesses if their expertise is considered necessary to the determination, but as a general rule the court independently decides the standard or level of care required of the defendant in the given circumstances. For professional negligence actions, however, the common law traditionally binds itself to a principle that the defendant is not shown to be negligent where he has followed a practice or made a decision which broadly accords with a customary or approved professional practice testimonially endorsed by expert witnesses appearing on the defendant's behalf. In real terms, this confers a peculiarly high status on expert professional witnesses, and none more so than for expert medical witnesses. The unswerving application of the professional standard model in medical negligence cases is sometimes hard to justify, and it is my purpose throughout this book to highlight the anomalies it entails. It is directly responsible for the defence-centric nature of prevailing medical negligence rules, and for the pervasive sense that "[u]ndue judicial deference to medical opinion is a blot on English medical law".[1]

Dissatisfaction with the apparent lack of accountability of doctors is not a modern phenomenon. In Ancient Greece, Hippocrates observed that the lack of state penalties for bad medical practice had bred suspicion amongst observers and caused medicine to fall into the "least repute".[2] When one reflects upon the history of the medical profession and its ongoing calls both for exclusive rights to practice and for professional self-regulation, one is tempted to conclude that the common law tacitly acceded to many of those demands, to the extent that it developed a body of law whose

---

[1] Keown (1995), p. 32.
[2] Hippocrates, "The Canon: A brief note on the characteristics desirable in a student of medicine" (trans. 1950), p. 10.

conspicuous effect was to miminise the law's ability to censure the exercise of medical practice. The increasingly anachronistic nature of the professional standard model has been highlighted more recently by the informed consent action, which continues to attract attention in England and Ireland, perhaps because it was initially considered by the courts with a lack of intellectual rigour. Though anything but ideal in its phrasing,[3] *informed consent* has become a ubiquitous reference-point—notably canvassed in recent years by the World Health Organisation "WHO", the European Community, and the Council of Europe.[4] As a legal concept, informed consent properly refers to the civil action for damages taken against a doctor for failing to make full disclosure of relevant medical information prior to the patient consenting to and undergoing recommended treatment. Despite its classification as a subset of the medical negligence action and duty of care, the claim gradually earned specific consideration grounded in the right of a patient to govern what is to be done to his body, and in the correlative duty on doctors to provide information which safeguards that right. For instance, in its Principles of 1981, the Judicial Council of the American Medical Association asserted that the "patient should make his own determination on treatment . . . Social policy does not accept the paternalistic view that the physician may remain silent because divulgence might prompt the patient to forego needed therapy. Rational, informed patients should not be expected to act uniformly, even under similar circumstances, in agreeing to or refusing treatment". [5]

Since its emergence in 1972,[6] the doctrine of informed consent swiftly courted a keen critical scrutiny from a wide array of intellectual disciplines, perhaps because it seemed to embody an age-old dissatisfaction with the institutional detachment and intransigence of the medical profession. To many lawyers, it was a compellingly simple and timely development which recognised that the court is not justified in abrogating its determination of the standard of care to expert medical witnesses (effectively, the medical profession) where

---

[3] See Chapter 3, *infra*, p. 86, n. 99 and Chapter 4, *infra*, p. 125, nn. 53–54.
[4] The WHO, (*Promotion of the Rights of Patients in Europe* (Kluwer, 1995) at para a. proclaimed that "informed consent is a prerequisite for any medical intervention." According to Article 5 of the Convention on Human Rights and Biomedicine (April 4, 1997), to which member state representatives of the European Community and the Council of Europe agreed: "An intervention in the health field may only be carried out after the person concerned has given free and informed consent to it."
[5] *Current Opinions of the Judicial Council* (Chicago, 1981).
[6] *Canterbury v. Spence* 464 F.2d 772 (1972).

the issues facing the court were essentially non-technical. This view was succinctly expressed by Parker J.: "The general rule in medical malpractice cases is that the negligence of the physician or surgeon must be established by the testimony of medical experts . . . The reason for the rule is that laymen are not qualified by learning and experience to judge the medical aspects of such cases. When the reason for the rule ceases to exist, the rule no longer applies." [7] The leap in judicial logic was inherently a natural one to take, rooted in an appreciation that respect for the rights to self-determination, bodily integrity, and autonomy—whether dignitary or compensatory in effect—ought not to be subordinated within a legal analysis whose central focus is consistency of the alleged wrong with a prevailing professional custom.

The doctrine of informed consent has provided a valuable opportunity to critically evaluate and improve the subtle relations between doctors and patients, and to update archaic ethical imperatives, many of which were uncritically inherited by doctors from the writings of Ancient Greece.[8] Though it seems to lack the headline-grabbing sensationalism of other controversies, it has reasonably been argued that informed consent is:

> "*the* ethical issue in medicine today and that unless we sort out our views and determine what we really mean when we talk about the patient's right to give informed consent, we are imperilling our ability to make wise and humane decisions about all the other bioethical problems now facing us. . . . [S]triving to retain our moral integrity must always score higher than our quest for knowledge or other scientific achievements."[9]

Many other groups beyond lawyers and doctors have entered this debate, so much so that it is often now claimed, and sensibly so, that the study of medical law is obliged to draw from an array of cross-disciplinary sources rather than function in the abstract.[10] This is an

---

[7] *Block v. McKay* 126 N.W. 2d.808 (1964) at 810.
[8] So recognised by the U.S. President's Commission for the Study of Ethical Problems in Medicine and Biomedical and Behavioral Research, Vol. 1 (1982), p. 16.
[9] Faulder (1985), pp. 2–3.
[10] According to Callahan. (1973) p. 73), bioethics must be inter-disciplinary to survive. Ideally, analysis should embrace "sociological understanding of the medical and biological communities; psychological understanding of the kinds of needs felt by researchers and clinicians, patients and physicians, and the varieties of pressures to

approach I have been very willing to adopt, particularly in chapters one and nine, though the variety and weight of legal issues have necessitated a more legalistic analysis in chapters two to eight. In chapter one, I begin by assessing the ancient roots of health care in mysticism and spirituality, and the consequent exaltation of medical *judgment*. This strong cultural anchorage provides a compelling preliminary point of enquiry into the moral, ethical, and societal dimensions to medical health care, bridging millennia of history to the present day where we see the medical profession struggle to retain control of the reins in the resolution of current bioethical controversies, despite an increasingly more determined assertion by society of its own evolving values. An historical account of the organisation of health care practices reveals themes which have continually recurred from primitive to present times, and which also shed considerable light on the modern ethical practice of the medical profession. This will show the long struggle of doctors to cultivate reputation and exclusive recognition, and how success depended ultimately upon the development of ethics, collegiate loyalty and secrecy, the requirement of trust and faith on the part of patients, and the innovations which the scientific transformation of health care effected. I have attached much importance to this latter event, for it has been persuasively argued that though beneficial in its long-term effects and continually tantalising in its promises, the commitment to science marked a dramatic shift in focus from the patient to the disease—a break in tradition which throughout this century has caused doctors to lose sight of the palliative effect of dialogue, communication, and rapport with patients. In many ways, the doctrine of informed consent, particularly as developed by ethicists across the United States, represents a valiant attempt to repersonalise the doctor-patient relationship, at a time when litigation threatens most to depersonalise it. The development of the doctrine in the United States, its fate in other jurisdictions, and the special legal challenges raised by the disclosure action, will be considered in chapters four through to six, and by way of conclusion in my closing chapter.

---

which they are subject; historical understanding of the sources of regnant value theories and common practices; requisite scientific training; [and] awareness of and facility with the usual methods of ethical analysis as understood in the philosophical and theological communities".

Chapter 1

Culture of the Medical Profession

Ever since the dawn of organised health care, doctors and healers have laid claim to practise a skill which is intrinsically higher in kind, and which may not properly be appraised, censured, or influenced by outsiders unversed in its many intricacies. This concept of health care seems scarcely tenable in an age now keen to recognise the importance of safeguarding an individual's autonomy and freedom, an age for which transparency and information have become the *mots de jour*. Yet it endures vestigially—in the profession's proud, sometimes defiant defence of medical paternalism; in its resistance to calls for change to health care ethics and practice; indeed in the tort of medical negligence itself, which is constructed to enable the medical profession to shape, with an authoritativeness no other profession is permitted, the standard of professional care required by law. This state of affairs is not surprising when one considers that health care first took root in mythology, mysticism, divinity, and elevated status. Today's medical profession has come to inherit a unique culture and sensibility, constructed upon assumptions and themes which course through history, rendering health care a subject which cannot properly be appraised without reference to its accumulated traditions.

Origins and Moorings

The study and dating of ancient health care practices has naturally proven difficult, and it can never be certain to what extent the information discovered on surviving clay tablets and papyrus rolls reflects antecedent oral tradition.[1] It is clear from documents dated

---

[1] See generally: Bullough (1966); Carmichael and Ratzan (1991); Guthrie (1945); and von Klein (1905).

between 1000 and 612 B.C. that at least in the Ancient Near East, sickness was looked on as a form of divine punishment for impurity through the visitation of demons, each representative of a specific illness. It would seem to be the case that primitive societies each possessed a variant of the shaman healer, who tended to be priest, sorcerer, king, chief, or poet of his tribe. The healer's ability was based less on his competence to treat and heal than on his ability to communicate with the gods through visions and dreams.[2] Non-compliance with his therapeutic regimens—based mainly on water, oils, plants, and herbs—was considered offensive to the gods, and thus was rarely attempted.

We find evidence of the origins of modern medicine in ancient Greece, whose great advances were prompted by a rigorous intellectual *esprit* typified by its epochal contributions to logic and philosophy. Like the Egyptians before them, the Greeks developed specialised categories of doctors, and by the fifth century B.C. had established medical schools. Though this period marked a move towards a more secular approach to cures, it also laid the basis for the *divinity* of healing. In the myth of Aesculapius, the Greeks invested much of their dread of mortality, awe of immortality, and fretful respect for any mortal attempts to bridge the two. According to legend, Aesculapius had been the offspring of a God (Apollo, God of Truth) and a mortal.[3] Reared and educated by Chiron the centaur in a cave on Mount Pelion, Aesculapius surpassed each of Chiron's other charges, and proved anxious to learn the arts of healing, ultimately outstripping even his master. But because he "thought thoughts too great for man"—on one occasion reclaiming a body from the dead, the provenance of Hades—Aesculapius incurred the wrath of Zeus who duly slew him with a thunderbolt. On earth, the felled healer emerged a martyr, and with this a presumption that through death this hero had ultimately gained favour with the gods who now numbered him amongst their own as the God of Medicine.

---

[2] Bullough (1966), p. 6.
[3] See Hamilton, "The Myth of Aesculapius", reprinted in Carmichael and Ratzan (1991), pp. 33–35.

Throughout Greece, temples and statutes were erected in Aesculapius' honour, to which healers would come for inspiration and the ill for a cure. Like so many other myths cultivated by man, Aesculapius' unwittingly performed a valuable social function. Through its "identification with a deity", this myth equipped the first physicians with the status to treat and to innovate.[4]

Mythologising further enabled the first medical ethicists to mysticise the art and practice of health care, and in this way to legitimate an expansive conception of medical paternalism which implicitly viewed itself as transcendently impervious to external enquiry or censure. The writings of Hippocrates typified an emerging culture of paternalism and secrecy.[5] Our medical professions have inherited this tradition in a modified strain—though more recently it seems to have become something of an Achilles' heel, antagonistic to an increasingly rights-based culture yet vulnerable now to intellectual censure from an array of disparate disciplinary bases. Under the Hippocratic Oath, physicians swore by Apollo and by Aesculapius to do good and to avoid harm—otherwise known as the ethical principles of *beneficence* and *non-maleficence*—but also to "keep secret and never reveal all that may come to be known in the exercise of the profession."[6] In his texts, Hippocrates counselled doctors to work with cheerfulness and serenity, sometimes to reprove sharply, and to "reveal nothing of the patient's future or present condition."[7] Yet notwithstanding the perceived need to be secretive, it was sometimes acknowledged that therapeutic benefits could accrue when patients were informed of the details of their illness and more actively engaged in their treatment. Plato in his *Dialogues* urged doctors to

---

[4] Bullough (1966), p. 15.

[5] Though it has proved impossible to tell whether his commandments were universally accepted in the ancient world, or whether they consolidated earlier advances, the Hippocratic corpus attained with the passage of time and the benefit of unforeseeable historical developments, the status of solemn authority. The date of the basic Hippocratic Oath is variously believed to lie at points between the 6th century B.C. and the 1st century A.D. It has survived intact as a translated text, and remains the first point of enquiry for analyses of the ethics of Western modern medicine.

[6] Hippocratic Oath, reprinted in Mason & McCall Smith (1994), p. 429, Appendix A. It has been argued that this attempt to keep the patient under the physician's vigilance was partly rooted in an attempt to preserve *reputation* from the losses it suffered through the incompetent practice of quacks and charlatans. See: Faden & Beauchamp (1986), pp. 63-64; Pellegrino (1979), pp. 36; and Welborn (1977), p. 213.

[7] Hippocrates, *On Decorum* xvi, in *Hippocrates* (1923), p. 297.

elaborate and communicate with the patient, "at once getting information from [this] sick man, and also instructing him as far as he is able", on the basis that if the patient knew more about his illness, he would be better able to bring it under his control.[8]

The cult of paternalism prevailed, exalted by Greek society as flowing naturally from the *derivative* nature of the doctor's healing charisma. Though the power to heal was accepted to depend upon physical application, it was seen to converge in an ethereal concept of *judgment*. Hippocrates wrote that "[b]etween wisdom and medicine there is no gulf fixed; in fact medicine possesses all the qualities that make for wisdom. . . . In fact it is especially knowledge of the gods that by medicine is woven into the stuff of the mind. For in affections generally, and especially in accidents, medicine is found mostly to be held in honour by the gods."[9] One of Hippocrates' legacies was thus to ensure that henceforth, and indeed until the present century, medical ethics would be written by and largely for doctors, with a focus on the proper exercise of paternalism rather than on the rights or interests of others. Indeed by the end of the nineteenth century, Oliver Wendell Holmes could assure doctors, without fear of contradiction, that "your patient has no more right to all the truth you know than he has to all the medicine in your saddlebags . . . he should get only just so much as is good for him".[10] Injunctions against selective truth-telling were rare, and mostly expressed by disgruntled intellectuals who themselves felt victimised by it.[11] Throughout the history of medicine, doctors were encouraged to form judgments in a vacuum, uninfluenced by social, economic, or moral developments but primarily dedicated to the recipient of

---

[8] Plato, *Laws* (Law 720), Bury (trans) (1926), p. 309. See also Katz (1984), Chapter 1. Note that Plato limited this advice to the treatment of 'affluent' patients. There are indications that still today doctors are more likely to elaborate with patients who appear middle-classed, wealthy, or educated. See Chapter 5, *infra*, pp. 166–167.

[9] Hippocrates, *Decorum*, reprinted in Carmichael & Ratzan (1991), p. 36.

[10] Holmes (1883), p. 203.

[11] Samuel Johnson wrote: "I deny the lawfulness of telling a lie to a sick man for fear of alarming him. You have no business with consequences; you are to tell the truth. Besides, you are not sure what effects your telling him that he is in danger may have. It may bring his distemper to a crisis, and that may cure him. Of all lying, I have the greatest abhorrence of this, because I believe it has been frequently practised on myself." (Boswell s *Life of Johnson*, quoted in Beauchamp & Childress, (1983), p. 225.) See also Tolstoy, "The Death of Ivan Illich," in *The Death of Ivan Ilyitch and Other Stories* (1902).

their care.[12] Medical ethics failed to attract a significant measure of intellectual or philosophical curiosity until the twentieth century. Till then it remained discretely detached, falsely projecting a sense of internal consensus within the profession on key ethical values.[13]

Professionalisation

It is difficult to resist the conclusion that the medical community's traditionally uncritical homage to a collection of lofty but vague ideals had been strategically indispensable to its quest to assert itself as a homogenous profession with special claims to exclusive rights and privileges. The codification of medical ethics was crucial to its eventual professionalisation. According to Bullough, in order to "sell the public on the exclusionary tactics of the university trained practitioner, the need for regulation had to be couched in terms of ideals, but to gain the support of the would be professional it was necessary to emphasize self-interest. The result was a growth in medical deontology, a growth which coincided with institutionalization."[14] The various codes promulgated throughout the centuries consistently emphasised the need of university practitioners to maintain an honourable facade to counter any public apprehension of the degeneracy and inconsistency of health care practitioners.[15] The codes also emphasised collegiate loyalty within the medical community, so that doctors were discouraged from disparaging each other or whistle-blowing.[16]

Despite having cultivated codes of ethics, having delineated itself as referentially divine and vocational, and having begun its case for self-

---

[12] The 1963 World Medical Assembly, for instance, declared: "The moral, economic and professional independence of the doctor should be guaranteed . . . In the higher interest of the patient there should be no restriction of the doctor's right to prescribe drugs or any other treatment deemed necessary": as quoted by Henk Ten Have, "Ethics and economics in health care: a medical philosopher's view", in Mooney & McGuire (1988), p. 24.

[13] Ten Have, "Ethics and economics in health care: a medical philosopher's view", in Mooney & McGuire (1988), p. 25.

[14] Bullough (1966), p. 93.

[15] *e.g.* de Mondeville (1893) pp. 109 & 145.

[16] Mohr (1993), p. 121 writes that by the end of the 19th century, medico-legal experts were lionised for helping doctors out of legal entanglements, but not for promoting the exercise of their skill in a socially progressive manner.

regulation,[17] the process towards *professionalisation* of health care in Greece suffered an irreversible setback after the Roman conquest of the Mediterranean. Though the Romans achieved for the first time a wide dissemination of knowledge, they were responsible for demeaning the status of the physician whose occupation Rome regarded as suitable only for slaves, freemen, and foreigners. Professionalism received its worst blow when in the fifth century the imperial Roman Government fell into the hands of Germanic chieftains.[18] Marking in many ways a return to the amalgamated role of the shaman healer, the education and practice of medicine was brought under the influence of the Christian Church, which had the double advantage of having literate members who were symbolic agents of God's work. Priests were urged to visit the sick and to cure, encouraged by the example of Jesus Christ's missionary healing work. Though a good knowledge of Latin, which had been used little within the Roman Empire, enabled the clergy to translate and circulate early texts,[19] the process towards specialisation of medicine suffered significant losses. The early medieval monasteries made no obvious technical contribution to medicine, though they were responsible for humanising and christianising it as a healing and compassionate art. The sick and diseased were no longer looked on as sinful social inferiors, but instead as symbolic carriers of Christ's cross, partakers in man's earthly suffering.[20]

The *institutionalisation* of medicine began with the establishment of universities throughout the twelfth and thirteenth centuries, which encouraged the codification of past customs. This coincided with the growth of cities, challenges to the power of the clergy, and through the rediscovery of Aristotle, a re-secularisation of attitudes. Across Europe, as the religious hold weakened, particularly from the reign of Henry VIII on, close ties came to be forged between professors,

---

[17] Aristotle, himself a physician, argued that physicians should be judged by their peers because amongst other things they could be trusted to act in a manner which was not self-serving: Aristotle, *Politics*, Book III vi 8-13 (1950), p. 225-230. See, however, the cautions of Hippocrates against this, *supra*, p. 2.

[18] Bullough (1966), p. 32.

[19] Ancient Greek texts and principles retained their popularity. Though these texts invoked spent deities, they consistently emphasised do-gooding or beneficence and vocational zeal – virtues which subsequently became central to the Christian faith. Indeed, a surviving 12th century Byzantine manuscript inscribes the Hippocratic Oath into the shape of a Christian cross. See Carmichael & Ratzan (1991), p.24, colorplate 9.

[20] See Webb-Peploe, "The Medical Profession", in Scorer & Wing (1979), pp. 13–14.

lawyers, clergy, and physicians. These educated groups gained the ear of the King, then Parliament. They tended to support one another, and as one commentator would have it, became united in the "common pursuit of authority and power over ordinary citizens".[21] In Europe, the university was central to the eventual professionalisation of medicine by the end of the medieval period, a process which was endorsed by the papacy and complemented by advances in printing.[22] Stressing the dangers caused by quacks and charlatans, the university doctors petitioned the State to delegate control over medical licenses and practice. In 1518, Thomas Linacre successfully obtained from Henry VIII letters patent for a body of regular physicians which in 1551 became the Royal College of Physicians of London. These laws, under which the Bishop of London retained ultimate jurisdiction, decided who could practise in the city and within a seven mile radius thereof, forbidding unlicensed or domestic practice.

However, in Colonial America, members of the public preferred to trust unlicensed *domestic practitioners*, whose reputation was often more reliable. In post-revolutionary America, state legislators were less concerned with delimiting exclusive rights to practise health care than with ensuring that the various groups trained their practitioners to be competent and skilful. Indeed, the notion of stringent rules for admission and training followed by exclusive rights to practise, was repugnant to the fledgling democratic sensibilities of post-revolution America.[23] In the early part of the nineteenth century, a battle for recognition was fought out largely by three groups: allopathic (or university-trained), Thomsonian, and homeopathic healers.[24] Physicians struggled during this century for reasonable and consistent pay, and for social acceptance.[25] Significantly, the Thomsonian sect—whose therapy was based on the curative effects of herbs, emetics, and heat application—railed against what it saw as a deliberate befogging of medicine, an intentional deception and alienation of the public. Its founder, Samuel Thomson, declared that doctors "have learned just enough to know how to deceive people, and keep them in ignorance, by covering their doings under a language unknown to

---

[21] Katz (1984), p. 33.
[22] Bullough (1966), pp. 101–108.
[23] Katz (1984), pp. 35–36.
[24] See Kett (1968).
[25] For a historical account of the tension between empiricism and the rationalist tradition, see Harris L Coulter (1973). See also: Leach (1958); and Starr (1982).

their patients."[26] Steered as a crusade, it enjoyed significant popularity in the 1830s and 40s, eventually securing the repeal in New York of statutory penalties for unlicensed health care practice.

The success of the allopaths' struggle for professional supremacy was achieved largely by establishing more medical schools devoted to their practice, thereby gaining public and political visibility. At this critical juncture in its evolution, it chose to reject the scientific dogmatism of the homeopaths and to declare its allegiance instead to "free and open inquiry"—to observation, eclecticism, and clinical experience of patients on a case-by-case basis.[27] By this route, allopathic doctors came to seem more like the domestic practitioners they had consistently sought to conquer.[28] Yet what ultimately proved decisive in marking the shift towards allopathy was the "magical promise of science" and the emergence of significant scientific discoveries such as vaccination against the dreaded rabies, the discovery of the bacterial etiology of tuberculosis and of the plague, the invention of X-rays, and the anaesthetic properties of ethers.[29] Without questioning whether this necessarily represented a break in tradition, the university-trained allopaths emerged victoriously, armed now by a concomitant commitment to science.[30]

Science provided new means and opportunities that were denied the early physicians whose reliance on crude nonscientific processes must have been necessitated to a large extent by the shortfalls of their somatic cures. Only very few condemn the emergence of science in health care, and few would deny its inevitability.[31] Though carrying

---

[26] Thomson (1825), pp. 43–44.

[27] Katz (1984), p. 32.

[28] *ibid.*

[29] *ibid.*, p. 40.

[30] In its 1912 *Principles of Medical Ethics of the AMA*, Chapter 2, Article 1, Section 2, the AMA urged its members to join medical societies to promote "the advancement of medical science."

[31] In one of the most notorious attacks yet on the scientific rationalisation of medicine, Ivan Illich (1990), p. 254, argues that the "idolatry of science" has spawned overconsumption and overreliance on its illusory promises, which in the process has devastated the capacity of people to deal with their own mortality. This view is shared by Ian Kennedy (1983), p. 28, who eloquently selects the artificial respirator placed between doctor and patient as a central symbol of "Promethean eternity". Modern medicine, he writes, has too readily accepted the role of dispenser of cures, reducing the person into an assemblage of parts, until each disease and ill possesses a name, locus, and personality. This has resulted in an unnecessarily hospital-centric society whose focus is curative when it should be preventive, and in a disproportionate diversion of resources to fund costly technological machinery, a phenomenon that was remarked upon in the 1980 World Bank Report.

very particular benefits for health care and the treatment of diseases, the scientific revolution, which may be taken to have developed into the technological era of present times, was part of a larger social process—the rationalisation of epistemology, and the incremental displacement of the spiritual explanation in favour of the reasoned. It also facilitated the development of a discourse that was largely incomprehensible to lay persons from whom it required greater reliance and trust. This, it has been written, was "the key to the eventual emergence of medicine as a profession."[32]

The negative repercussions of the scientific rationalisation of health care are arguably most keenly felt in the exclusion of the patient from the discourse of health care.[33] Carmichael writes that during the Renaissance period, there emerged for the first time "a first-person authorial voice and the dominance of the human body as a principal focus of medical activity."[34] The paintings and writings of this time strongly reflected the loss of the patient from the traditional triangle of disease, doctor, patient, with the corresponding emergence of the hospital in the early nineteenth century.[35] The stethoscope neatly by-passed the need to elicit the patient's communicative version of where and how his chest pain hurt. Suddenly and abruptly there emerged the mechanical intermediation between doctor and patient of instrumentation and technology, and a cold authoritarian observation by medical staff.[36] The patient, in physicians' writings, became the adversarial *other* or the case-study.[37]

It has been argued that the scientific and technological transformation of medical health care dangerously eclipsed its psychotherapeutic

---

[32] Bullough (1966), p. 4.

[33] According to Frake, as cited by Waitzkin & Stoeckle (1972), p. 194, knowledge of diseases and diagnoses was distributed effectively amongst primitive societies to the extent that children could understand them.

[34] Carmichael & Ratzan (1991), p. 14.

[35] Hippocrates wrote in *Epidemica*, as quoted in Pellegrino (1979), p. 36: "The Art has three factors, the disease, the patient, and the physician. The physician is the servant of the Art. The patient must cooperate with the physician in combating the disease."

[36] See, for example, Chartan, *Laennec Listening with His Ear Against the Chest of a Patient at the Necker Hospital* (National Library of Medicine, Bethesda), reprinted in Carmichael & Ratzan (1991), p. 134.

[37] See for instance, Jenner, "An enquiry into the causes and effects of the cow-pox", in Carmichael & Ratzan (1991), pp. 131–33. Not until the late nineteenth century was the patient's discourse regained, mainly through the socially conscious literature of Dickens and Tolstoy, who both distanced themselves from prevailing literary concerns by highlighting the plight of the disenfranchised, the sick, and the ill, who traditionally had been viewed as menaces and burdens to society.

counterpart which up until then had been its primary source.[38] According to Katz, the persistent effectiveness of placebos today is symptomatic of an unresolved strain in the medical profession which extends back to the time when it chose the scientific cause as its legitimating claim to professional monopoly. Since then, the medical profession has chosen to stress "commonality of practice rather than diversity", uniting under the umbrella of MD degree disparate treatment philosophies.[39] These tensions have contributed in a large measure to "the much lamented modern demand for non-MD healers, even faith healers . . . . [so that] the centuries-old struggle between university-trained and domestic practitioners is covertly maintained, albeit now with both being part of the same professional group."[40]

The bid for public and State endorsement of the exclusive right of university doctors to practise was mirrored in Britain, though, without the structured rivalry that existed in America, it concluded somewhat earlier. Largely as a result of the British Medical Association's persistent campaigning, the Medical Act of 1858 finally granted the General Medical Council the power to control medical practice in Britain, limiting it to those enrolled on the Medical Register.[41]

The financing of medical health care also underwent radical changes. The availability of health care had been dependent on ability to pay; those unable to do so inevitably relied on services made available by government, philanthropists, the church, and by doctors themselves. The market-place soon ceased to be an effective economic system of rationing, mainly because medical technology and the drive for knowledge placed too great and unpredictable burden on the ill. Third party (governmental) payment became necessary. Though this inevitably led to tighter regulatory restrictions on the

---

[38] See Houston (1938), p. 1418: "in the large view we are forced to realize that [medical] learning was a learning in how to deal with men. Their skill was a skill in dealing with the emotions of men. They themselves were the therapeutic agents by which cures were effected. Their therapeutic procedures, whether they were inert or whether they were dangerous, were placebos, symbols by which their patients faith and their own was sustained." According to Stern ("The Specialist and the General Practitioner" in Jaco 1958), p. 357, the "bedside manner" is "acknowledgement that the way in which doctors handle their patients as personalities has an important effect upon the functioning of their physiological systems. Much of the 'art' of medicine has consisted in this type of psychotherapy which is a necessary accompaniment of all other therapy".

[39] Katz (1984), p. 41.

[40] ibid., p. 42.

[41] See: Smith (1994); and Turner (1982).

profession, it was generally favoured by physicians as a means of distributing more secure opportunities for remuneration.[42] Many developed nations such as Britain shifted from fee-for-service to "implicit rationing" through centralised budgetary procedures.[43] Under the National Health Insurance Act 1911 and the National Health Service Act 1946, central government budgeted fixed amounts for community medical services on a capitation basis and hospital services on a global basis.

Medical defence bodies developed in an attempt to protect licensed doctors and physicians from legal claims. Though there were as yet very few medical negligence actions, the problem immediately identified was that these few "hit the headlines and were discussed prominently in daily newspapers and medical journals."[44] The Medical Defence Union ("MDU"), founded by two solicitors and five 'gentlemen', was registered in Britain on October 23, 1885, under the Companies Act 1862.[45] In his history of the MDU, Hawkins writes that until the middle of the twentieth century, the MDU was responsible for an "authoritative and paternalistic approach" which tended to presume "the obstinacy and stupidity of the plaintiffs and the worthlessness of the allegations" made.[46] Priding itself on an ability to pool its resources in an ominous way, and no doubt assiduously served by their lawyers,[47] the MDU encouraged doctors

---

[42] Though the ongoing specialisation of medicine owes much to the developments of science and technology, it has been suggested that it is "also a political process bringing economic advantages and greater control over one's work and responsibilities": see Stevens (1971).

[43] See Mechanic, "The Growth of Medical Technology and Bureaucracy Implications for Medical Care", in Jaco (1979).

[44] Hawkins (1985), p. 13.

[45] Its declared objects were, *inter alia*: (1) to support and protect the character and interests of the medical profession; (2) to promote honourable practice and suppress unauthorised practice; and (3) to advise and defend its members in cases raising points of professional principle against them. It was eventually resolved—in *Medical Defence Union Ltd v. Department of Trade* [1979] 2 All E.R. 421—that the MDU did not come within the provisions of the Insurance Companies Act 1972 (which would have brought it under the control of the Secretary of State), mainly on the grounds that it is a non-profit-making defence association which exists partly to advise and educate its members: individual claims, for instance, do not result in higher premiums for individuals, and the costs and overheads are distributed evenly through standard annual rates.

[46] Hawkins (1985), p. 40.

[47] The medical profession received very bad publicity in the United States when it emerged that it had knowingly permitted the defendant in *Gonzalez v. Nork* 131 Cal. Rptr 717 (1976) to continue to practice incompetently for personal gain throughout nine further years. See also *Latson v. Zeiler* 58 Cal. Rptr 436 (1967).

to frighten off compensation-hunting patients by the counter threat of legal action against them. In its 1904 Annual Report, it expressed pride in the fact that "of the 383 cases undertaken within the last nine years on behalf of its members to vindicate and protect their professional honour and reputation, in only three have there been adverse verdicts against them".[48]

This unsympathetic defensiveness on the part of the medical profession may well have proved counterproductive, in fuelling rather than quelling contemporary interrogations of modern health care. The latter half of this century is marked by a revolution of secular, rights-based demands for greater freedom in a range of important activities over which the professions traditionally enjoyed provenance. This finds expression in the demands for greater transparency in the activities of the professions,[49] greater social and legal accountability for acts and decisions of professional judgment, the evolving resurgence of interest in alternative treatments, and the growing unwillingness of clients to blindly accept a professional's judgment.[50] These developments seem to represent an amalgamated attempt by members of society to withdraw from the medical community various powers it claimed throughout its evolution as a profession. The doctrine of informed consent is but one manifestation of these demands.

Historically, the demands the profession made for self-regulation and immunity from lay censure were assisted by a self-perpetuating image of its practitioners as engaged in a social calling which shared little in common with the business man's economic self-interest. This vocational character naturally begot an altruism and in turn the image of *economic disinterestedness*.[51] Professional altruism was bolstered by codes of ethics, and in the case of the medical profession, by its allegiance to the Hippocratic Oath with its mythological notions of

---

[48] Hawkins (1985), p. 41.

[49] The President's Commission for the Study of Ethical Problems in Medicine and Biomedical and Behavioral Research, *Vol. 1* (1982), pp. 123–124 recognised a growing demand by consumers for access to medical libraries, noting parallel developments in legal circles where clients increasingly assert their rights to fight their own case in small claims and divorce courts. See also Haug (1975), where it is argued that the public's increased access to and interest in medical knowledge will continue to undermine the power of doctors.

[50] Studies have revealed that public trust in professions has declined dramatically, one reporting a drop from 72% in 1966 to 43% in 1975: Harris Survey (1976). See also Burnham (1982).

[51] Parsons (1939), p. 458.

health care practice as *borrowed divinity.* Historical associations with the ruling religions enhanced these moral intonations.[52] It is this historical affiliation with divinity, the church, and social altruism which has perhaps most served to exalt medical judgment, and along with other factors to cushion the critical and litigious blows that medical paternalism has had to incur this century. In Katz's view, the "postulated intimate relationship between physicians, patients, and their God made any critical questioning of doctors' practices by patients difficult."[53] A shift in cultural focus has prompted much critical interrogation of the reality of this altruism or vocationalism. Talcott Parsons proposed in 1939 that the distinction between professional altruism and commercial self-interest was more "institutional" than "motivational".[54] More recently, Bullough argued that "the very fact that the growth of professionalisation has usually taken place in a business economy would tend to indicate that the stated contrast between business and professions, between self-interest and altruism, is not the whole story".[55]

Medical Ethics, Paternalism, and the Rights of Patients

The *discourse of rights* is something of a modern phenomenon, receiving little analytic attention before the middle ages. The seventeenth century social contract philosophers were responsible for popularising it within the politico-legal framework of *consent*, founded on the premise that man in society is governed by an implicit social contract with his governors.[56] In terms of the interest it has held for epistemology, and the challenges it continues to pose for society, one right in particular, the right to personal autonomy or self-determination, has become the right *par excellence.* Increasingly looked on as a genus of rights, autonomy has risen to prominence in current

---

[52] In its earliest definitional form, profession meant *"he who professes"*, which in turn meant he who "has taken the vows of a religious order". By 1675, this was secularised to that which "professes to be duly qualified" (*Shorter Oxford English Dictionary* definitions, as quoted by Hughes, (1963), p. 656.) Current definitions show signs of departing from reference to the three professions of divinity, medicine, and the law, yet retain reference to callings and vocations.

[53] Katz (1984), p. 9.

[54] Parsons (1939), p. 459.

[55] Bullough (1966), p. 2.

[56] Sabine & Thorsen, in Hinsdale (1973), p. 400.

philosophical and ethical debates, such that it can safely be asserted that the "history of the emergence of medical ethics as a special subject for study in the past 15 years is in many ways the history of concern for patient autonomy."[57] This dramatic shift of focus over to patients' rights must be regarded as partly due to the past failure of the medical profession to recognise the equality of these rights and to accord them a status distinct from its ethical commitments to *medical beneficence* and paternalism.

Some sense of the concept of autonomy is gleaned from its source in the Greek word *autonomia,* meaning "living by one's own laws". Though general and opaque enough to elude a monolithic definition, autonomy is best understood by reference to its actual and potential uses. Its attractiveness to modern society may well be due to its emphasis on *moral independence,* so that others must respect one as a moral end and must respect one's "moral goods": it is thus the "basis for moral enfranchisement, establishing my standing as an equal in the community and my liberty to pursue my own ends."[58]

John Stuart Mill's *On Liberty,* originally published in 1859, recently benefited from a revived interest in America, where it has been placed centre-stage in the socio-political assault on medical paternalism·and more particularly in the case for informed consent.[59] Mill's treatise called for the political and social freedom to cultivate one's own opinions and beliefs by recourse to one's own reason, to be free to act upon those beliefs even if the price to oneself is harm. It proposed that each society should make as its priority the fixing of the line between good and bad encroachments on the freedom of the individual, between "liberty and authority".[60] The single principle Mill asserted is that collective intervention is justifiable only for reasons of "self-protection" or "to prevent harm to others."[61] He further reasoned that no opinion is inherently true or false, nor any judgment infallible, and that "a large portion of the morality of the country emanates from its class structures and its feelings of class superiority".[62] In Mill's view, one best interprets experience through discussion with others: "Wrong opinions and practices gradually yield to fact and argument; but facts and arguments, to produce any effect

---

[57] Brody (1985), p. 380.
[58] Callahan (1984), p. 40.
[59] Mill (1956).
[60] *ibid.,* p. 3.
[61] *ibid.,* p. 13.
[62] *ibid.,* p. 9.

on the mind, must be brought before it."[63] With considerable argumentative verve, Mill countered the tendency of people to feel that others should act as they do or as they wish to act, by observing that "there is no parity between the feeling of a person for his own opinion and the feeling of another who is offended at his holding it, no more than between the desire of a thief to take a purse and the desire of the right owner to keep it."[64]

It is not difficult to appreciate the appeal of Mill in twentieth century analyses of the desired scope of medical paternalism, particularly with respect to the entitlement of patients to receive sufficient information to enable them to make informed decisions on treatment options whether or not those decisions converge with the course recommended by the doctor in his professional wisdom. In the bioethical context, Beauchamp and Childress write that autonomy is a

> "form of personal liberty of action where the individual determines his or her own course of action in accordance with a plan chosen by himself or herself. The autonomous person is one who not only deliberates about and chooses such plans but who is capable of acting on the basis of such deliberations. . . . A person's autonomy is his or her independence, self-reliance, and self-contained ability to decide."[65]

The attention which autonomy continues to receive in philosophical and legal circles has given rise to much vehement retaliation of the kind which attempts to reassert the primacy of the doctor's moral and ethical responsibilities. Callahan vividly argues against allowing autonomy to be "the controlling fulcrum in the obligations that I may owe to others", which he argues would be "hazardous to moral relationships".[66] This would "diminish the sense of obligation that others may feel toward us, and shrivel our sense of obligation toward others."[67] Society, he writes, must exist as *community*. It "requires constraints, limits, and taboos, just as it requires shared ideals, common dreams, and a vision of the self that is part of a wider collectivity. By bringing into the medical relationship the most sterile

---

[63] Mill (1956), p. 25.
[64] *ibid.*, p. 102.
[65] Beauchamp & Childress (1983), pp. 56–57.
[66] Callahan (1984), p. 41.
[67] *ibid.*

and straitened notions of an autonomous self, ethics has borrowed not from the richest portion of our tradition but from the thinnest."[68] In what Callahan says there is much anthropological authority. Society has existed as *community* for the greater part of its history; *individualism* is a relatively modern phenomenon, and one which Emile Durkheim cautioned against at the close of the last century when he drew the distinction between, on the one hand, the socially healthy differentiation of personality (individualism) and, on the other, the socially deleterious evolution of egoism (or cult of the individual).[69] The survival for so long of collective myths and precepts—such as the injunction to love one's neighbour—can be explained, at least materially, in terms of social function.[70]

But equally we may view this type of objection to the renaissance of autonomy as extreme, defensive, and unhelpful. Is it not the case that the principle of respect for autonomy would have averted innumerable atrocities and acts of tyranny had it been institutionally enforced throughout the centuries? Grave risks arise only if it is applied as the sole criterion for determining the propriety of human action or conduct, something which centralised states for obvious reasons do not favour. Its merits lie in providing us with a respectable modern counterpart against which we may appraise the validity and propriety of any of the mounting daily intrusions into our personal privacy and self-determination. In the medical context, autonomy, with its emphasis on self-governance, is by itself an inappropriate vehicle to forge compromise in the rights versus duties debate.[71] A rigid deference to autonomy may be tantamount in some cases to saying that the patient can go to hell if he so chooses. Yet people are not always the best judges of what best to do in their own interests under pressurised conditions, particularly when ill, and may be

---

[68] Callahan (1984), p. 41.

[69] Durkheim, *Le Suicide* (1897; 1952), pp. 246–252.

[70] Though Sigmund Freud was a psychologist and not a sociologist, he was aware and wrote briefly on the social perils of liberating the *individual*. In *The Future of an Illusion*, he warned that (1981), vol xxi, p. 6. "[c]ivilisation has to be defended against the individual, and its regulations, institutions and commands are directed to that task." He further believed that if the *ego* (one's controlling consciousness) fails to satisfy the *id* (one's unconscious or instinctual side), it becomes prey to neurotic anxiety arising from the strength of the instinctual drives; if it fails to satisfy the *superego* (one's socially developed conscience), it falls subject to moral anxiety: *New Introductory Lectures on Psychoanalysis* (1981), vol xxii, pp. 77–78.

[71] According to Thomasma (1985), p. 1, the doctor-patient relationship is generally regarded by both parties to it as a "special" one: it "seems to demand much more than a friendly handclasp between two autonomous beings."

temporarily weak-willed or emotionally defensive.[72] Indeed, medical research has suggested that the psychic trauma suffered after a serious accident can prompt a person to renounce his older goals and values.[73] The practice of health care is profoundly paternalistic, whether intrinsically so, culturally so, or in response to the implicit or explicit expectations of patients. Thus it may well be that the chief benefit of the autonomy principle is to encourage a softened, more justifiable exercise of medical paternalism.

Numerous philosophical arguments have been volleyed against the emergence of the autonomy principle in the medical context.[74] These typically claim that informed consent rests on false premises, wrongly presuming that patients *can* act autonomously when they are ill and dependent on health care. Yet most of the celebrated theories of autonomy and liberty did not envisage autonomy unbounded. Rather, they contextualised it, as did Mill, upon the wider canvas of social interaction and discourse. To this didacticism there are some refreshing antidotes. Katz reasons that man's diminished capacity for reason in the face of illness ought not be relied upon as a *justification* of medical paternalism; instead it should encourage doctors to confront and mitigate the emotional and psychological vulnerability into which patients may lapse.[75] Kao argues that gratuitous paternal tendencies within the medical profession have served to graft the *ism* on to the paternal. He attempts to reconstruct paternalism with 'maturity' (or holistic health) as its goal. Kao's conception of maturity is that of evolution of the person from childhood dependence, to adolescent independence, to adulthood interdependence (with the environment and with other persons). He argues that the dominant Western version of autonomy, most notably in America, has been the adolescent model. In contrast to adult interdependence, which tends to be "moderate, cautious, and flexible without losing individuality and integrity, freedom and autonomy", the adolescent model is reactive, rigid, and defensive.[76] In the medical relationship, *maturation*

---

[72] Wilkinson (1996), p. 433.

[73] Note (1976), p. 837.

[74] See Freidson (1970). See also Byrne, "Authority, social policy, and the doctor-patient relationship", in Dunstan & Shinebourne (1989), p. 229, where the author argues that the autonomy model, if taken to its logical extreme, will scarcely make it possible in future for doctors to make medical decisions, for "[i]t ignores the facts of weakness and dependence which frequently accompany being ill and it sets at nought the expertise of doctors which ought to come from their training and experience."

[75] Katz (1984), p. 108.

[76] Kao (1976), p. 183.

encourages dialogue and, in place of an aggressive rights and duties mentality, mutual respect: the "patient must be allowed to know, to ask, and to question as an autonomous person; the patient is not someone to be conquered, nor is the physician someone to be reacted against."[77]

As a concept, medical paternalism has been broken down into various sub-types, most commonly: pure and impure, weak and strong, active and passive acts of paternalism.[78] *Impure* paternalism, in contrast to its opposite, is paternalism which is justified by reasons which are partly extraneous, typically out of a concern for others. *Weak* may be distinguished from *strong* paternalism on the basis that the latter overrides a patient's wishes because it is felt that they are bad for the patient, whereas the former overrides the patient's wishes only because the patient suffers from some impairment to his decisional capacity. *Active* may be distinguished from *passive* paternalism on the basis that the former exists where the paternalist overrides the express wishes and/or values of the patient (even where these are shared by society and the reasonable man), and the latter exists where the paternalist refuses to carry out the wishes of the patient or to assist in a course of action. These tend to converge in the issue of consent—namely whether one can override a patient's consent or refusal to consent, and whether one can act when the patient is incapable of consenting.

Whether or not the common law is marked by a preference for consent or paternalism is naturally a matter of speculation for every generation.[79] The law, however, has made it clear that as a general rule subject to some exceptions, each competent adult has the right to refuse medical treatment for whatever reasons and with whatever

---

[77] Kao (1976), p. 183.

[78] Childress (1982), pp. 16–18.

[79] According to Prosser: "It is a fundamental principle of the common law that volenti non fit injuria—to one who is willing no wrong is done. The attitude of the Courts has not, in general, been one of paternalism. Where no public interest is contravened, they have left the individual to work out his own destiny and are not concerned with protecting him from his own folly in permitting others to do him harm." (as cited in Sommerville, (1980), p. 17.) The Law Commission in England, currently attempting to codify the criminal law, controversially identifies the common law's dominant principle in the area of consent to be "paternalism softened at the edges": Law Commission Consultation Paper No. 139, *Consent in the Criminal Law* 1985 HMSO, para. 2.15. For an argument against this assumption, see Roberts (1997).

consequences.[80] According to Lord Reid: "English law goes to great lengths to protect a person of full age and capacity from interference with his personal liberty. We have too often seen freedom disappear in other countries not only by coups d'etat but by gradual erosion; and often it is the first step that counts. So it would be unwise to make even minor concessions."[81]

Since the right to refuse treatment is not absolute, it may be prevailed upon by various public interests, in particular by the State's moral and social duty to respect and safeguard life, whether one's own or that of a third party placed at risk by one's course of action.[82] The right to refuse has been addressed more directly (and prospectively) in cases reviewing competent patients' refusals to undergo vital treatment.[83] The courts tend to attach much importance to the patient's prognosis and life expectancy, showing more obvious reluctance to uphold refusal rights where patients are young, or nonterminally ill but without treatment likely to die, than where patients are in their declining years or terminally ill.[84] For in the former type of case: "there is an opportunity to shape the future. The patient may be injured if permitted to refuse treatment, the decision lies in judicial hands, and patient choice gives way to the perceived greater good of saving a life."[85]

This line of thought has found favour recently in England. In *Re C*, a 68-year-old patient suffering from paranoid schizophrenia refused to allow medical staff amputate his leg, even though his

---

[80] *Sidaway v. Bethlem Royal Hospital* [1985] 1 A.C. 871, HL; *Canterbury v. Spence* 464 F.2d 772 (1972); *Reibl v. Hughes* 114 DLR 3d 1 (1980).

[81] *S. v. S.* [1970] 3 All E.R. 107 at 111.

[82] The range of extraneous interests which may from time to time be judged to override consent cannot be considered closed. Recently, in *Re R (a minor: blood tests)* [1998] 2 W.L.R. 796, the High Court ordered that a blood sample be taken from a 22-month-old child, in the process overriding her mother's refusal, on the basis that determining paternity was in the child s best interests.

[83] There has been a small cluster of *informed refusal* cases in America where patients claimed after the event that full disclosure would have led them to accept treatment, *e.g. Truman v. Thomas* 611 P. 2d 902 (1980). See Chapter 4, *infra*, p. 108.

[84] In *John F. Kennedy Memorial Hosp v. Heston* 279 A. 2d 670 (1971), the applicant hospital was authorised to give blood transfusions to a 22-year-old accident victim who had a long life to look forward to, despite his parents' resistance on religious grounds. That case was distinguished by the New Jersey County Court in *Re Robert Quackenbush* 383 A.2d 785 (1978), where the constitutional rights to privacy and self-determination of a 72-year-old eccentric reclusive patient were permitted to prevail over the State's interest in preserving life, even though without amputation of his leg the patient was expected to die within three weeks.

[85] Appelbaum, Lidz & Meisel (1987), p. 193.

chances of survival without amputation were assessed at 15 per cent.[86] The Court of Appeal upheld this refusal and resisted a test of his general competence, finding instead that despite his general mental impairment, he had shown the specific capacity to understand his predicament and decide what he wished to be done. The response of the same court was otherwise in *Re T*, where a young adult patient had pre-emptively signed a refusal to a blood transfusion (at a time when it was not needed) apparently due to religious belief. The circumstances of the case strongly suggested that she had been influenced by her mother, a devout Jehovah's Witness; the patient had not been baptised into that faith, though she had classed herself as an ex-Jehovah's Witness on the records held by her ante-natal clinic.[87] In authorising a blood transfusion to save the patient after she entered into a critical condition, Lord Donaldson recognised that the paramount concern was whether the patient "really did choose and, if so, what choice she made."[88] There was 'abundant evidence' to indicate that she had not exercised her power of choice independently: she had been drowsy, disoriented, and not fully compos mentis, and when she raised the issue of blood transfusions, it had been after seeing her mother.

There is some link between refusal of life-saving treatment and suicide or reckless self-destruction, to the extent that both may be believed maladaptive and resolvable through persuasion or therapy.[89] There is no satisfactory general theory explaining the urge to commit suicide. However, it has been proposed that the "underlying conviction is that the suicidal person suffers from a disease or irrational drive toward self-destruction and is, therefore, nonautonomously attempting to end his or her life."[90] This may account in part for the reluctance of medical staff to permit patients to take courses which put their health and life at unnecessary risk or (out of a fear of seeming to sanction euthanasia) to acquiesce to requests to permit incompetent patients to die naturally from their original pathology or injury. The common law traditionally regarded suicide as a wanton

---

[86] *Re C.* [1994] 1 All E.R. 819.

[87] *Re T (adult: refusal of medical treatment)* [1992] 4 All E.R. 649.

[88] *ibid.* at 652.

[89] However, note that in *Airedale NHS Trust v. Bland* [1993] A.C. 789 at 864, Lord Goff stated that such decisions are not suicidal, but are decisions to forego treatment which may or may not have the effect of prolonging life.

[90] Beauchamp & McCullough (1984), p. 95.

flouting of the sanctity of life and of God's Law.[91] Though the act of suicide is no longer a criminal offence in England or Ireland,[92] it remains an offence to assist in an attempt to commit suicide, so that to some extent a patient can *lawfully* choose to commit suicide but cannot suicidally consent to the actions of another.[93]

Some instances of impure paternalism have been defended by the common law on the basis that they sufficiently compromise the protectable interests of third parties or they present a threat to the common good for other extraneous reasons. For reasons of public health, the law from time to time imposes a duty on people to receive treatment where they suffer from a listed communicable disease.[94] Medical treatment may be enforced on people detained under mental health legislation.[95] In *Application of the President and Directors of Georgestown College*, the Columbia Court of Appeals granted an order to the hospital to administer blood transfusions to a patient against her will partly because compliance with her wishes would have been tantamount to the patient's abandonment of her young children.[96] There is some authority for the view that competent minors and pregnant women may be compelled to receive treatment where the consequences are likely to injure the minor[97] or the foetus[98] respectively.

---

[91] In *Hales v. Petit* 1 Plow. (1563) 253, 75 E.R. 387, suicide was stated to be "contrary to the rules of self-preservation, which is the principle of nature, for everything living does by instinct of nature defend itself from destruction, and then to destroy one's self is contrary to nature and a thing most horrible."

[92] Suicide Act 1961 and Criminal Law (Suicide) Act 1993 respectively.

[93] Under section 2 of the 1961 and 1993 Acts (*ibid.*), a person who aids, abets, counsels, or procures the suicide of another, or assists another in attempting suicide, shall be liable to criminal conviction on indictment. Indeed, where a patient is diagnosed or suspected of suicidal tendencies, doctors are under a heightened duty of care to ensure that the opportunity to commit suicide is minimised. See Chapter 2, *infra*, pp. 58–62.

[94] AIDS has been added to this list in England and Scotland, under the AIDS (Control) Act 1987.

[95] Mental Health Act 1983, s. 3.

[96] *Application of the President and Directors of Georgestown College* 331 F.2d 1000 (1964).

[97] The House of Lords' decision in *Gillick v. West Norfolk & Wisbech Area Health Authority* [1985] 1 All E.R. 533 seemed to usher in a judicial respect for adolescent autonomy, as did the Children Act 1989 which pledges respect for the rights of children and mature minors. However, recent cases have restricted these developments. See: *Re R (a minor) (wardship: consent to medical treatment)* [1991] 4 All E.R. 177, where the Court of Appeal overrode an unruly, wayward teenager's refusal to take anti-psychotic medication; *Re W. (a minor) (medical treatment)* [1992] 4 All E.R. 627, where the Court of Appeal overrode a minor anorexic's refusal to be fed by a naso-gastric tube; and *Re T, supra*, n. 87. Tomkin & Hanafin (1995), p. 40 doubt whether the Irish courts would reach a decision similar to *Gillick*, given the Irish

27

Paternalism in the patient's best interests has often arisen in the context of sterilisation of incompetents, as an instance of *weak* paternalism grounded in an appreciation that the patient suffers from some impairment to decisional capacity.[99] In *Re B (a minor)*, the Court of Appeal sanctioned the sterilisation of a mentally disabled minor, applying a best interests or welfare test.[1] The court accepted

---

Constitution's reference to the family as the necessary basis of social order (Art. 41.1.2) and the primary and natural educator of the child (Art. 42.1). The authors find further support in *G v. An Bord Uchtala* [1980] I.R. 32 at 56, where O'Higgins C.J. referred to the need to protect the child's unenumerated rights "to be fed and to live, to be reared and educated, to have the opportunity of working and of realising his or her full personality and dignity as a human being."

[98] See *Re S. (adult: refusal of medical treatment)* [1992] 4 All E.R. 671. A rather extreme example of paternalism endorsed by the common law is the unusual case of *Re AC* 573 A.(2d) 1235 (1990), where a pregnant patient suffering from cancer was forced by court order to undergo a caesarian section, despite evidence that neither she nor the baby would be likely to survive (as was ultimately the case). According to Nebeker J.: "The fundamental right to bodily integrity encompasses an adult's right to refuse medical treatment, even if the refusal will result in death. . . . The state's interest in protecting third parties from an adult's decision to refuse medical . treatment . . . may override the interest in bodily integrity."

The English Court of Appeal recently upheld the right of a pregnant woman not to receive medical treatment even if her life or the life of her unborn child requires it: *St George's Healthcare NHS Trust v. S.* [1998] 3 W.L.R. 936. The court reasoned that, though pregnancy increases the personal responsibilities of a woman, the unborn child is not a separate person, and his interests cannot be taken to override the mother's right to decide what is done to her body: in this light, the forced removal of the baby from her body constituted an unlawful trespass to her person. In Ireland, constitutional protection of the unborn under Art. 40.3.3 of the Constitution (as amended) would be likely to restrict the extent to which a pregnant woman could refuse treatment which would incidentally injure the foetus. However, the eighth amendment pledges respect for "the equal right to life of the mother". This had been respected by the law previously: the ban on abortion under the Offences Against the Persons Act 1861 had been interpreted not to apply to scenarios where it was "reasonably certain" that the mother would die in childbirth: *R. v. Bourne* [1938] 3 All E.R. 615 at 678, *per* McNaghten J. This was loosely reflected by the Medical Council in its *Guide to Ethical Conduct* (4th ed., 1994), p. 136, where it advised that doctors must be guided by a duty to "*preserve* life and health" (emphasis added) and that "it is unethical always to withhold treatment beneficial to a pregnant woman, by reason of her pregnancy." In the controversial case of *Attorney General v. X* [1992] I.R. 1, the Supreme Court accepted that abortion may be lawful where it is established as a matter of probability that there is a real and substantial risk to the life as distinct from the health of the mother which could only be avoided by abortion, and that such included the risk of suicide by the mother. This development has, however, suffered from the defeat of part of the proposed 14th constitutional amendment in 1992, leaving the relationship between the rulings in the *X case*, the eighth amendment, and the ethical theory and practice of the medical profession uncertain.

[99] See also Chapter 6, *infra*, pp. 176–178.
[1] *Re B. (a minor)* [1987] 2 All E.R. 206.

that: pregnancy would leave the girl disturbed; she would never possess maternal feelings nor understand the right to reproduce; contraceptive pills would adversely react with pills she was already taking for epilepsy and mental instability; and if her condition worsened she might have been deprived of the freedom she currently enjoyed in local authority lodgings. In *Re F*, the House of Lords exercised its "inherent jurisdiction" to sanction sterilisation of a mentally incompetent adult who had developed an attachment for a fellow patient.[2] In so doing, the House paternalistically employed a best interests, as opposed to rights based, analysis.[3]

Medical paternalism is rooted in ancient ethical injunctions characterised by the twin duties of nonmaleficence and beneficence referred to together under the Hippocratic Oath: "I will use treatment to help the sick according to my ability and judgment, but I will never use it to injure or wrong them."[4] The *Declaration of Geneva*, adopted by the WHO in Geneva in 1948, retains the Hippocratic Oath in updated modern terminology.[5] Though the duty to do no wrong is often said to be "the foundation of social morality",[6] the positive ethical duty on doctors to do good distinguishes medical paternalism from other types of professional paternalism, and is rooted in a particular concept of the doctor's role within society. Thus is explained the ethical fervour with which doctors typically seek to ensure in the patient's

---

[2] *Re F (mental patient: sterilisation)* [1990] 2 A.C. 1.

[3] The dangerously wide scope of a test based on *best* interests was evident recently in *Re Y (mental patient: bone marrow donation)* [1997] 2 W.L.R. 556, where the court sanctioned a bone marrow transplant to be taken from a mentally incompetent woman for the alleviation of her older sister's pre-leukaemic bone marrow disorder. Connell J. reasoned that it was in the woman's best interests, emotionally, psychologically, and socially, that her sister live.

[4] As quoted in Beauchamp & Childress (1983), p. 106. In other translated versions, this reads: "I will prescribe regimen for the good of my patients . . . and never do harm to anyone": reprinted in Mason & McCall Smith (1994), p. 429, Appendix A.

[5] Declaration of Geneva (as amended at Sydney, 1968), reprinted in Mason and McCall Smith (1994), p. 430—under which doctors further pledge that the health of my patient will be my first consideration." The four basic ethical principles, which have attracted a consensus amongst American bioethicists and are now enshrined at federal level in the Belmont Report, are beneficence, nonmaleficence, justice, and autonomy: National Commission for the Protection of Human Subjects of Biomedical and Behavioural Research (1978). There is considerably less agreement on the rules which may be said to be derivative from these principles; however, most of the leading accounts recognise the rules of veracity, fidelity, confidentiality, and privacy: Beauchamp & Childress (1983), p. 221. See also Gillon (1986), Chapters 14–15; Mooney (1980), p. 179; Newdick (1995), p. 106–108; and Postema (1980), p. 68.

[6] Beauchamp & Childress (1983), p. 106.

best interests that their recommended therapy is agreed to and complied with. In a survey conducted for the President's Commission Report, doctors were asked whether they felt it was their duty to dissuade patients from not following their recommended treatment: 75 per cent felt that it was.[7] More recently, in a survey of doctors from 16 western European countries, only 25 per cent responded that they would give complete information to patients, and only 75 per cent accepted the right of patients to refuse treatment.[8]

It is the trust which medical practitioners have traditionally required of their clients that gives life to medical paternalism. Its dynamic has been subjected to close social scrutiny in recent years, ultimately because the spheres in which the profession and in turn its paternalism have traditionally assumed responsibility are spheres which intimately affect the lives and interests of individuals.[9] It has been said that what makes paternalism so morally interesting is that "the paternalist claims to act on a person's behalf but not at that person's behest".[10] Acting paternalistically on another's behalf necessarily requires the violation of some moral rule such as deceiving the person or depriving him of the opportunity to decide something for himself, where that violation is morally justifiable. To this end, it is necessary that the paternalist believes that: (1) the action is for the other's good; (2) he is qualified to act on the other's behalf; (3) some moral rule with regard to the other is violated; (4) he is justified to act on behalf of the other independently of the other's past, present, or future consent; and (5) he generally knows (perhaps falsely) what is for the other's good.[11]

Contemporary philosophy has argued for some time that the Hippocratic-based ethical code is an insufficient basis for medical

---

[7] President's Commission for the Study of Ethical Problems in Medicine and Biomedical and Behavioral Research, *Vol. 2* (1982), p. 200, Tables 6–8.

[8] Vincent (1998).

[9] The professional practice of law, by contrast, may be taken to affect the workings of *society* far more directly than it does the *individual*. The individual may expect to be entangled in the legal process, or to need a lawyer, far less than he will require health care or doctors. For this reason, the professional paternalism of lawyers has survived fewer attacks with less injury to it; ethical analysis of the practice of law has been slim, and rarely undertaken by outsiders. For instance, in *Nelson v. State*, the client's claim that he had a right to insist that his counsel follow a particular courtroom strategy was met with the following ruling, as quoted in Beauchamp & McCullough, (1984), p. 101: "One of the surest ways for counsel to lose a lawsuit is to permit the client to run the trial. . . . If such decisions are to be made by the defendant, he is likely to do himself more harm than good."

[10] Childress (1982), p. 4.

[11] Gert and Culver (1976), pp. 48–50.

decision-making, and that any analysis of the universal principles on which such codes are based must be accompanied by analysis of the *process* of medical judgment, how it should prioritise the various principles, morals, and beliefs before a paternalistic decision is formulated. It is further argued that medical ethics in its institutional form has unreasonably ignored the issues of veracity, truthfulness, autonomy, and disclosure to patients. Recognising, for instance, that the chief function of professional codes "is to promote trust and confidence within professional relationships so as to encourage professional activities performed for socially valued ends", Beauchamp and Childress in their landmark account argue that these codes have traditionally had much to say about the doctor's duties of beneficence and nonmaleficence, but little about modern concerns such as autonomy.[12] To this end, philosophical ethics and political morality have valiantly sought to inform and modernise the theory and practice of medical ethics.

Analyses of medical ethics and patients' rights tend to draw both from deontology and consequentialism.[13] Deontology features in the informed consent debate as the categorical principle of respect for patient autonomy. Being *a priori*, it does not depend upon proofs or justification for its validity. In an age grown sceptical of lofty unsubstantiated absolutes, the consequentialist model offers more

---

[12] Beauchamp and Childress (1983), p. 10.

[13] The first of two basic theories of ethics, *deontology* is derived from the Greek word *deon*, meaning "duty" or "binding". A deontological approach argues that a certain course, being normatively *right*, must be taken irrespective of its consequences. For instance, Paul Ramsay (1977) argues along deontological grounds that children should never be used as research subjects in non-therapeutic contexts; for to do so would be to violate their integrity in circumstances where they cannot give an informed consent, and would be to treat them as means to an end. The bases for deontology tend variously to be Divine Law (as revealed by God for example in the Ten Commandments), Natural Law, or innate moral intuition. The second dominant form of ethics, *consequentialism*, assesses the rightness or wrongness of an act primarily by its consequences. Thus, morally right action is determined by its nonmoral values. Beauchamp and Childress (1983), pp. 15–16, address the attempts by contemporary philosophers to identify criteria for identifying moral and non-moral considerations in disputes. The conditions which have gained most favour are: (1) the consideration must have a supreme or overriding quality for the individual or for society; (2) the consideration must possess *universability*, that is, all relevant similar cases must be treated in a similar way; and (3) the consideration must have some direct reference to the welfare of others. The first two conditions are formal; the third introduces a moral *content* which is designed to exclude egoistic reasoning.

scope for reinforming medical ethics.[14] The consequential model, since it depends on justification and consequence, encourages dialogue and progress, in many ways playing the paternalist at his own game.[15] Further, deontology may encourage an uncritical, automatic preference for prescribed courses of action. For instance, a deontological approach to the disclosure of information may prompt a ruthless, inflexible, and ultimately bureaucratic obedience to a perceived imperative, whereas disclosure should ideally be tailored to the desires and needs of the patient. Though each *rational* person may be expected to wish to retain decision-making provenance for himself, the emergence of illness and loss of mobility may evoke in some the contradictory wish to surrender, at least at some point, to the professional wisdom and authority of the expert other: "One patient may be respected by demanding that he or she resist a desire to capitulate, while another may be respected by lifting the burden of decision from a wearied and tortured soul in need of rest. There can be no single, general answer, substantive or procedural, to the utterly unanswerable and all too general question, "Who should decide?"[16]

The duty to disclose or to actively promote the dissemination of knowledge has at most tentative roots in morality and ethics.[17] Of considerably more force is the duty not to lie or actively deceive others. This duty becomes stronger in ethics and in law the more foreseeable it is that the other will rely on what is communicated, and the closer and more special the relationship is between the two.[18]

---

[14] Contemporary defences of disclosure and informed consent favour the consequentialist discourse, as it is likely to be taken more seriously – of which many examples are given in Chapter 9, *infra*, pp. 266–271. However, Edmund Pellegrino (1979), pp. 49–50, argues in a deontological vein that a patient's moral agency is at risk when he is ill, and that the doctor has a *special obligation* to protect and facilitate this wounded agency. He does this only partly by curing the patient's ailment. That must further be "complemented by disclosure of the information necessary for valid choice and genuine consent and by guarding against manipulation of choice and consent to accommodate to the physician's personal or social philosophy of the good life. A first requirement, therefore, is to remedy the patient's information deficit as completely as possible. Information must be clear and understandable and in the patient's language. He must know the nature of his illness, its prognosis, the alternative modes of treatment, their probable effectiveness, cost, discomfort, side effects, and the quality of life they may yield. Disclosure must include degrees of ignorance as well as the knowledge and the physician's own limitations."

[15] Buchanan (1978), p. 370.

[16] Beauchamp and McCullough (1984), p. 74.

[17] Beauchamp and Childress (1983), p. 205.

[18] Recognised also as a general legal principle in decisions such as *Hedley Byrne v. Heller* [1964] A.C. 465.

One of the most socially *special* of these is the fiduciary relationship, of which the relationship between doctor and patient is said to be one of the clearest examples.[19] Fiduciary relationships are characterised by trust, dependence, and good faith between both parties.[20] This element of trust, flowing from the patient, has in the past sanctioned the doctor's prerogative to determine whether or not to disclose. Advocates of informed consent, however, go far to expose the double standards in relationships which demand so much trust with such little faith in turn. According to Faulder, doctors trade in *trust*, and their jobs are dependent upon it; all too often, they insist upon the trust of patients, yet in the same breath explain that "white lies" are often necessary.[21] Trust has been a core concern of doctors since the dawn of health care, when blind faith was integral to the charismatic healing process. This therapeutic energy flowing from the physician retains some expression in the contemporary use of placebos for therapeutic and research purposes. Placebos raise questions of ethical propriety in the light of the requirement of veracity, given that their success depends wholly upon the use of deception or at least (in the case of double-blind research tests) incomplete truth-telling.[21] Childress argues that ethical problems do not arise where action is taken for the welfare of the patient.[23] Others choose to argue that the use of placebos, as deceptive alternatives to prescribed medication, may engender dependency on drugs[24] and that a more moral alternative would be to discipline patients into understanding that medication does not exist for every ill.[25] There is also the related argument,

---

[19] The fiduciary character of the medical relationship has been stressed by the U.S. courts. See: *Berkey v. Anderson* 1 Cal. App. 3d 790 (1969), 82 Cal. Rptr 67; and *Hunter v. Brown* 4 Wash App 899, 484 P. 2d 1162 (1971). However, in *Sidaway v. Bethlem Royal Hospital* [1984] 1 All E.R. 1018 at 1033–1034 (CA), Browne-Wilkinson L.J. rejected an attempt to extend the legal concept of *fiduciary trust* beyond its settled application to property rights.

[20] James Childress (1982), p. 137 writes that the two most common forms of paternalistic action are force and deception, since both attempt to influence the other's will, and the "very fact that paternalism so often thrives in families and in other relationships of closeness and dependence has a special effect on the choice between manipulation by force and by deception. These relationships require more trust than others, and over a long period of time."

[21] Faulder (1985), p. 25.

[22] Under a double-blind research trial, both doctor and patient know the range of placebos and non-placebos which may possibly be administered to an array of patients, but not exactly which one will be given to whom.

[23] Childress (1982), p. 137.

[24] Bok (1974).

[25] Faulder (1985), p. 93.

consequentialist in tone, which argues that deception serves instead to undermine relationships of trust, making it less likely that patients will in the future accept what doctors say or recommend to them.[26]

The medical profession's *beneficent* approach to disclosure has often driven a wedge between its concept of *patient's best interests* and society's. Coinciding with an earnest social enquiry into the power of the professions and other collectives, the disclosure issue has forced the medical community to re-evaluate the basis of its commitment to beneficence, and to justify its application by reference to more specifically drawn principles and rules for ethical conduct. If one accepts, as one must, that a physician's commitment to beneficence is not an absolute duty, but that it gives him a right in certain circumstances to act paternally in the patient's best interests, one must further accept that it is not enough that paternalism be justified on the basis only that it is permissible or that for instance, it is possible that disclosure will harm the patient: it must also be premised on a reasonable judgment that "giving information . . . will do greater harm to the patient on balance than withholding the information will."[27] This is to say that it has become necessary "to distinguish *motivating* reasons and *justifying* reasons" for medical beneficence, "without implying that they may not be identical in many instances."[28]

Regrettably, heated resistance within the medical community to this critical intrusion by interested parties persists. One of the most vibrant current debates, accelerated if not ignited by the prospect of informed consent, surrounds the extent to which external forces such as philosophy and social mores may modify or restrain the exercise of ethical and moral medical judgment. Against this prospect, Dunstan rails against the contemporary emergence of rights-based arguments, arguing that "doctors are themselves the responsible moral agents in their respective areas of practice."[29] Similarly ill-tempered, the editors of the Institute of Medical Ethics Bulletin in England have in the past adopted a blandly sarcastic anti-American tone, scorning an "aggressive bioethical imperialism" partly on the basis that the rise of bioethics in America has run parallel to the rise in patients' rights.[30]

---

[26] See: *Hunter v. Brown, supra* n. 19; *Sard v. Hardy* 379 A 2d 1014 (1977) at 1020; and *White v. Turner* (1981) 120 D.L.R. 3d 269 at 290.

[27] Buchanan (1978), p. 377.

[28] Childress (1982), p. 39.

[29] Dunstan, "The doctor as the responsible moral agent", in Dunstan and Shinebourne (1989), p. 1.

[30] Editorial (1986), pp. 1–2.

Many doctors and academics, some armed by a training in philosophy, have constructed counter-theories that variously justify and exalt medical paternalism; these are at times as aggressive as the rights-based arguments they react against.

It is not always clear whether doctors who theoretically encourage paternalism favour the view of paternalism as *permissible* under medical ethics, or as binding *duty*. In the present climate of scepticism, the latter view is less often articulated than the former,[31] though Dunstan may be illustrated for his conviction that the doctor's "relevant experience, knowledge, and skill ought to be used "ethically", that is, in pursuit of ends reckoned altruistic and good and in the avoidance of ends reckoned inordinately self-regarding and bad."[32] In terms of attaching weight to a patient's legal or moral rights, he proposes that the doctor "has therefore to decide, not only what are genuine rights and legitimate interests matched by corresponding duties, but also what wishes and interests are being presented *in the language of rights*, and how far he should go to serve them, *if serve them he should*."[33] This conception of the doctor's role as moralist continues to command a high level of support, certainly amongst ethicist doctors. According to Byrne, practising doctors both reflect and forge social morality.[34] For instance, a doctor may choose to manage a terminally ill patient's dwindling condition notwithstanding that it may amount in the technical sense to an act of indirect euthanasia (by omission): "Some of the decisions relating to not prolonging or terminating life appear, then, to be no more than the tacit application of accepted notions about justified homicidal acts. . . . Doctors, it might be said, have for years been making clinical decisions of this sort without hindrance or social condemnation."[35] This is echoed by St John-Stevas who writes that the "problem is best regulated not by the clumsy instrument of the law but by the medical profession itself."[36] Similarly, Gillon argues that accounts "of what the law stipulates . . . do not in themselves provide moral justification for a moral claim" but at most "can be used as part

---

[31] For instance, Allen Buchanan (1978), p. 377 presumes the implicit view to be that beneficence is *permissive*, finding this more "intuitively plausible".

[32] Dunstan (1989), p. 1.

[33] *ibid*. p. 3.

[34] Byrne, Authority, social policy, and the doctor-patient relationship , in Dunstan & Shinebourne (1989).

[35] *ibid*. p. 239.

[36] St John-Stevas, in Various (1968), p. 56.

of a moral claim that there is a general presumption that it is a good thing to obey just laws."[37] This does not square with his earlier remarks that in his experience doctors tend to be uncritically reluctant to confront medico-moral issues, and that the following three approaches by doctors tend to predominate: pontification, abstention, and scepticism.[38]

It may be worthwhile to consider the view that some doctors "conceive it to be their duty to force their advice upon everyone, including especially those who don't want it. That duty . . . is born of vanity, not of public spirit. The impulse behind it is not altruism, but a mere yearning to run things".[39] A rather vivid example of the medical profession's unhealthy resistance to external views was experienced recently in Ireland. It arose out of an application by a family to discontinue a system of extraordinary medical intervention which had kept their daughter artificially alive in a comatose state for over 23 years.[40] Members of the Irish medical profession rigorously contested the application, and according to the ward's mother, subsequently refused to assist the family in their efforts to take the patient home to die naturally and with dignity.[41] In an official response to the Supreme Court's decision approving the family's request, the Irish Medical Council merely affirmed its principles as formerly set down in its *Guide to Ethical Conduct and Behaviour*, asserting that: "Medical care must not be used as a tool of the State to be granted or withheld or altered in character under political pressure. Regardless of their type of practice, the responsibility of all doctors is to help the sick and injured. . . . The Council sees no need to alter its Ethical Guide."[42]

---

[37] Gillon R (1986), p. 116.

[38] *ibid.*, p. vii.

[39] Mencken, Christian Science (1927), reprinted in Mencken (1956), p. 342.

[40] *Re a Ward of Court* [1995] 2 I.L.R.M. 401, SC.

[41] Some months after the Supreme Court's decision, the ward's mother published a poignant account of her family's plight, in which she claimed that throughout the harrowing 23 year period in which her daughter remained in a comatose state, the medical and nursing staff alienated themselves from the family who were "ignored and fobbed off, day after day and week after week . . . [T]he first time I saw these doctors was when they were pointed to me in the Round Hall of the Four Courts . . . This ability to close ranks made us begin to realise the immense power of the medical profession": "The mother of the woman in the 'right-to-die' case tells her story", *Irish Times*, February 24, 1996, p. 10.

[42] Medical Council, "Statements of the Medical Council and An Bord Altranais on the Ward case" 1 *Medico-Legal Journal* 60 (1995).

Despite this resistance, medical ethics and practice has for some time attracted fervid critical analysis by interested outsiders, typically philosophers, lawyers, journalists, and academic doctors—a process which seems to have paralleled more general cultural developments, in particular the scrutiny of social and political power bases, and the growing demand by members of society for a return of some of the vital personal interests over which these collectives traditionally assumed authority. It is hardly very surprising that the study of medical ethics has become something of a growth industry. Fox proposes that medicine has entered a "new evolutionary stage" which is marked by organised concern about ethical and existential matters.[43] The involvement of non-medical groups suggests "a new rapprochement is taking place in the profession and . . . society. The overweening emphasis on scientific and technological phenomena that has characterized modern medicine, and its insistence on separating these so-called objective considerations from more "subjective" and "philosophical" orientations towards health and illness, life and death, seem to be giving away to a closer integration between the two dimensions."[44] According to Ten Have, this has caused "the gradual emergence of a new conception of medical ethics, namely that of an activity or process of systematic and continuous reflection on the norms and values guiding medical theory and praxis, as part of a more encompassing health care ethics."[45] It has also served to revitalise modern philosophy, according to Warnock, encouraging it to turn away from the abstractions of epistemology to the concrete challenges that medical and clinical practice readily present.[46]

The most problematic stumbling block in the bioethical debate has thus far proved to be the perceived opposition between the rights of patients and the ethical duty of doctors to act paternally in the best interests of the patient and sometimes society. This may be blamed in part on the aggressive pitch at which patients' rights were initially championed under the banner of autonomy, which may in turn be blamed on the fact that successive codes of medical ethics overlooked the rights issue until recent social and intellectual challenges forced some critical response. Yet it may also be blamed on the stubborn

---

[43] Fox, "Ethical and Existential Developments in Contemporaneous American Medicine: Their Implications for Culture and Society", in Jaco (1979), p. 437.

[44] *ibid.*

[45] Henk Ten Have, "Ethics and economics in health care: a medical philosopher's view" , in Mooney & McGuire (1988), p. 27.

[46] Warnock, "Philosophical Foreword", in Fulford (1989), p. vii.

traditionalism with which many prominent doctors at the forefront of the debate have continued to insist on the transcendence of medical ethics as a self-evident justification for medical paternalism.

Chapter 2

Negligence in Diagnosis and Treatment

Sir William Blackstone was apparently the first to use the word medical *malpractice*, when he wrote in 1768, "it hath been solemnly resolved, that *mala praxis* is a great misdemeanour and offence at common law, whether it be for curiosity or experiment, or by neglect; because it breaks the trust which the party had placed in his physician, and tends to the patient's destruction."[1] This was written at a time when the common law had not yet distinguished negligence as a separate tort from intentional trespasses to the person. Medical malpractice is now largely synonymous with the medical negligence action, though it may be taken to cover the much fewer cases of intentional trespass to the person or assault and battery on patients, discussed in chapter six. Medical negligence law is generated chiefly by civil actions. The crime of "gross negligence manslaughter" has survived but is rarely prosecuted, much less in the health care context,[2] and it would otherwise appear that instances of gross negligence are swiftly settled by the profession in private to minimise bad publicity.

The tort of negligence chiefly operates under a model of *fault* liability, which is broken down into various components of proof.

---

[1] Blackstone, 3 Bl. Comm. 122.
[2] *R. v. Bateman* (1925) 19 Cr.App.R. 8 decided that gross criminal negligence constitutes action that is in disregard for the life or safety of another to the extent that the remedy of compensation is inadequate and the act ought to attract punishment as a crime. This was refined in *R. v. Seymour* [1983] 2 A.C. 493 to refer to conduct amounting to an "obvious and serious" risk of death. The contemporary status of this crime was confirmed recently by the House of Lords in *R. v. Adomako* [1995] 1 A.C. 624, which favoured the rather vague and circular logic of *Bateman*, namely that gross negligence (or involuntary manslaughter) relates to conduct which falls so far beneath the expected level of care as to appear criminal. New Zealand rather exceptionally imposes criminal liability, under its Crimes Act 1961, for failure to exercise "reasonable knowledge, skill and care" in the treatment of patients.

The plaintiff must prove that in the circumstances: the defendant owed him a duty of care; that the defendant breached that duty by failing to meet a standard of care required by law; and that the defendant's breach of duty *caused* the plaintiff to suffer injury or harm for which compensation may be recovered at law. Notwithstanding, the linchpin of fault liability is in all respects the concept of *reasonableness*, which permeates each component of fault liability to the extent that it could be considered a rather circular analysis hooked to an array of inherited rules and principles. It would seem that proof of each ingredient, in particular causation, "merely extends the ambit of the allegation of fault."[3] For instance, in determining whether a defendant owed a duty of care to the plaintiff, the courts will often phrase the question as whether in the circumstances it was "reasonably foreseeable" that the plaintiff would be injured; when it considers proof of causation, "reasonable foreseeability" of injury becomes a critical factor in considering whether as a matter of law the defendant's proven breach of duty was a *proximate cause* of the plaintiff's loss.[4] The circularity of the fault analysis was highlighted recently in *Bolitho v. City & Hackney Health Authority*, where the professional standard of care or *Bolam* test was controversially applied by the House of Lords in considering whether causation was proved.[5] Lord Browne-Wilkinson accepted that this was exceptional but necessary where proof of causal link between the defendant's omission and the plaintiff's injury requires the court to assess what would have happened had the defendant not breached his duty to act (and in this case attended the patient). To ascertain as a matter of likelihood how the defendant would have acted in the hypothetical event of

---

[3] *Joyce v. Merton, Sutton & Wandsworth Health Authority* (1996) 7 Med. L.R. 1 at 20, *per* Hobhouse L.J.

[4] The link was exemplified by Lord Denning in *Roe v. Ministry of Health* [1954] 2 All E.R. 131 at 138. A nurse had innocently jolted an anaesthetic ampoule creating a crack invisible to the eye, which in turn caused contamination of the anaesthetic and ultimately paralysis of the plaintiff. The court was asked to consider the decision in *Re Polemis* [1921] 3 K.B. 560, allowing recovery for injury caused *directly* as opposed to *forseeably*. Denning considered that the *Re Polemis* rule was of limited application, and depended on two preliminary conditions. First, there must be a duty of care, which inevitably involves an element of foreseeability: "There is no duty of care owed to a person when you could not reasonably foresee that he might be injured by your conduct". Secondly, the act must be a cause, and causation involves questions of foreseeability. The chain of causation can be broken by an unforeseeable intervening factor; the latter can be disregarded only where the negligence is the "immediate and precipitating cause of the damage".

[5] *Bolitho v. City & Hackney Health Authority* [1998] A.C. 232.

having attended the patient, it was necessary to consider the relevant approved medical practice which one would have expected him to follow.[6]

The flexibility of the torts analysis is one reason why in the health care context the common law is reluctant to assess a defendant's alleged failure to employ reasonable care as a matter of *contractual* duty. There are numerous other reasons. The imposition of vicarious liability on hospitals for the tortious acts of their servants is preferred chiefly for reasons of policy and administrative convenience. It is often difficult and artificial to imply terms into contracts. Hospitals and patients are typically in unequal bargaining positions, especially in situations where patients are rushed to hospital in emergencies.[7] Interpreting terms of the medical contract as guarantees is inappropriate: "*A physician is not a warrantor of cures. . ..* [Otherwise, doctors] would have to assume financial liability for nearly all the 'ills that flesh is heir to.'"[8] If however, a patient's health care is privately and contractually arranged, the plaintiff may sue the private clinic or doctor exclusively for breach of the contractual duty of care, a term which is either implied by the common law or by statute,[9] or may sue concurrently for this breach and commission of the tort of negligence.[10]

The Duty of Care and Allocation of Liability

Until relatively recent times, hospitals were immune from liability in negligence, this chiefly because hospitals began on a non-profit basis and enjoyed a charitable immunity from suit.[11] This partly explains the ongoing reluctance of the common law to hold hospitals directly liable for the negligence of their doctors. The courts prefer to address the individual negligence of the doctor instead of the institutional responsibility of his employers, though in practice the loss is

---

[6] *Bolitho v. City & Hackney Health Authority* [1998] A.C. 232 at 239.

[7] *Yepremian v. Scarborough General Hospital* (1980) 110 D.L.R. (3d) 513, Ont., CA.

[8] *Ewing v. Goode* 78 F.442 (1897) at 443, *per* Taft J.

[9] *e.g.* Supply of Goods and Services Act 1982, s. 13, (U.K.).

[10] Concurrent liability is generally accepted throughout the common law, though doubts have been expressed by the House of Lords, albeit in a commercial context: *Tai Hing Cotton Mill Ltd v. Liu Chong Hing Bank* [1986] 1 A.C. 80.

[11] In the U.S., a ruling by the Columbia Court of Appeals in *President of Georgetown v. Hughes* 130 F.2d 810 (1942), marked the death-knell of immunity.

ultimately borne by the institution as the doctor's employer under vicarious liability. In theory, the party who has been deemed vicariously liable for the plaintiff's injuries is entitled to seek indemnification from the party whose negligence caused the injuries, though this power is not exercised in practice. An unsuccessful attempt was made by the Clinton Administration in 1993 to abolish the individual liability of doctors under negligence law and replace it with a model of enterprise medical liability under which statutorily identified health care plan organisations would bear and channel the loss.[12]

However, depending on the facts of the case, it may be more appropriate to hold a hospital directly liable for breach of a duty of care which it personally owed to the plaintiff. That hospitals may owe certain duties and be directly liable for their breach was confirmed by Denning L.J. in *Cassidy v. Ministry of Health*, where he explained that once hospital authorities undertake a certain task "they come under a duty to use care in the doing of it, and that is so whether they do it for reward or not."[13] In *Ellis v. Wallsend District Hospital*, the New South Wales Court of Appeal recognised that when a hospital offers a complete range of medical treatment, it thereby assumes a personal duty to ensure that the patient receives careful treatment at the hands of its staff.[14] Responsibility for compliance with these duties is usually non-delegable.[15] A plaintiff may on occasion attempt to fix direct liability on a hospital where vicarious liability is difficult to establish—for instance, where the doctor's professional relationship with the patient is independently arranged, in which case the doctor acts not in his capacity as hospital employee but in his capacity as independent contractor (in a self-employed, freelance sense). The attempt failed in the *Ellis* case on the basis that the relationship

---

[12] See Abraham & Weiler (1994). The proposal was ultimately defeated after intense lobbying from insurance groups and the American Medical Association which had belatedly begun to fear the consequences of exchanging the threat of lawyers for the threat of insurers.

[13] *Cassidy v. Ministry of Health* [1951] 2 K.B. 343 at 360. More recently, Browne-Wilkinson V.-C. ruled in *Wilsher v. Essex Area Health Authority* [1986] 3 All E.R. 801 at 833 that "a health authority which so conducts its hospital that it fails to provide doctors of sufficient skill and experience to give the treatment offered at the hospital may be directly liable in negligence to the patient." See also *Bull v. Devon Area Health Authority* (1993) 4 Med. L.R. 117, where a breakdown in the hospital's split-site servive caused delay, leading to asphyxiation of the patient and brain damage.

[14] *Ellis v. Wallsend District Hospital* (1990) 2 Med. L.R. 103 at 128, drawing from Fleming (1987), p. 346.

[15] *ibid.*

between the patient and the hospital was not sufficiently special or close to generate a personal and non-delegable duty to ensure that treatment was conducted by the doctor with all reasonable care. The patient had specifically approached the consultant and not the hospital for medical treatment.

Common law jurisprudence on employers liability has consistently recognised the following personal non-delegable duties on employers, for which they may be held directly responsible to their workers—these are the provision of: competent staff, a safe system of work, and appropriate equipment.[16] In the health care context, this means that hospitals are under a duty to employ suitably qualified and competent workers,[17] to ensure that staff and work are adequately directed and supervised, to provide the equipment and back-up support appropriate to the relevant skill, and to provide a competent and safe system of work.[18] Though broad, these are specific limbs of the general duty of care borne by hospitals both as employers and the providers of medical health care. It is clear that the common law has striven to limit their ambit to administrative and organisational duties.[19] However, these duties may not be as peripheral as they at first seem. It has already been accepted in a related context that the pressures of working excessively long hours may cause medical staff to fall physically and emotionally below par[20]; the possibility that this type of argument might emerge in the malpractice context cannot be ruled out.[21] In Ireland, a recent challenge was made to a common hospital practice whereby casualty officers are empowered to countermand a written request by a general practitioner that a patient be admitted to casualty.[22] Though it is a practice whose merits are anything but self-evident, the High Court upheld it chiefly because it is a practice adopted also in the United Kingdom. Yet its implication

---

[16] *Wilson & Clyde Coal Co. v. English* [1938] A.C. 57 at 78.

[17] *Yepremian v. Scarborough General Hospital, supra,* n. 7.

[18] *Osburn v. Mohindra and St John Hospital* (1980) 66 A.P.R. 340; *Ogden v. Airedale Health Authority* (1996) 7 Med. L.R. 153. In some U.S. states, this has been extended to reviewing the treatment provided by doctors to hospital patients, and to ensuring that doctors personally examine patients and review their medical records prior to their discharge. See respectively: *Darling v. Charleston Community Memorial Hospital* 11 N.E. 2d 253, 383 U.S. 946 (1966); and *Polischeck v. United States* 535 F. Supp. 1261 (1982).

[19] *Wilsher v. Essex AHA, supra,* n. 13.

[20] *Johnstone v. Bloomsbury Health Authority* [1992] Q.B. 333, where the court accepted that the plaintiff's contract of employment with the NHS was unlawful.

[21] See Chapter 8, *infra,* pp. 233–234.

[22] *Collins v. Mid-Western Health Board,* Irish High Court, unreported, May 14, 1996.

is that "the portal of entry for most citizens into the hospital system is controlled by some of the most junior—rather than the most senior—personnel in that system".[23]

Duty of Care: When and to Whom Owed?

A duty of care of some kind is owed to a patient once a hospital or doctor assumes responsibility for that patient or undertakes to exercise professional skill on his behalf. The extent to which this undertaking must be formalised or structured before it may be taken to exist is still uncertain. Medical ethics clearly requires doctors to provide medical assistance where it is needed; this reflects the vocational dimension of health care traditionally emphasised in successive codes of ethics and inherited concepts of *beneficence*.[24] The common law has for some time demanded less of doctors, out of a reluctance to impose positive legal duties on bystanders to administer emergency aid to strangers, even where to do so would create no risk to the bystander.[25] Accordingly, Fleming observed in an earlier edition of his work that a "doctor may flout his Hippocratic oath and deny aid to a stranger, even in an emergency like a road accident".[26] This reluctance stems in part from the lack of a proximate relationship (and thus duty of care) between the two parties, but also presumably because once a volunteer takes active steps to help a stranger, he unilaterally assumes certain obligations that require the exercise of reasonable care; thus if he bungles the job, he may be liable for causing or aggravating the stranger's injuries.[27] There was

---

[23] Binchy & Craven (1998), p. 20.

[24] In *Medical Ethics: Its Practice and Philosophy* (1993), p. 180, the British Medical Association advises doctors that they have an ethical duty not to drive past the injured on the road; in an emergency "all doctors would be expected to offer assistance, but the extent of care provided will depend on the nature of the emergency". A similar duty is recognised in Ireland by the Medical Council. In its *Guide to Ethical Conduct and Behaviour* (5th ed., 1998), p. 14, it provides that doctors "must provide care in emergency situations unless they are satisfied that alternative arrangements have been made" and must "also consider what assistance they can give in the event of a public disaster, a road traffic accident, fire, drowning or other similar occurences."

[25] *Grange Motors (Cwmbran) v. Spencer* [1969] 1 All E.R. 340. As an exception to this, general practitioners are often required by law to offer medical assistance to emergencies that occur within their practice area.

[26] Fleming (1987), p. 135.

[27] *Harrison v. British Railways Bd* [1981] 3 All E.R. 679.

also the fear in America of being sued for abandonment—a cause of action that may emanate from a doctor's assumption of assistance and subsequent failure to render the assistance or to deliver the patient into the care of another who can assist.[28] Mindful of the dangers of deterring rescuers through the threat of liability in malpractice and battery, and on the other hand of attracting bunglers, 49 North American states had by 1980 followed the lead of California in recognising an affirmative duty to provide emergency help, the potential liability for which is reduced to instances of gross, wilful, or wanton negligence. The courts have construed these provisions broadly in favour of the physician.[29]

Australian law, increasingly courageous in the field of medical negligence, has recently departed from common law tradition by imposing a positive duty on doctors to administer emergency assistance to strangers with whom the doctor previously had no professional relationship.[30] In *Lowns v. Woods*, a general practitioner refused an urgent request to attend a boy who was in epileptic seizure, insisting that an ambulance bring the boy to him. Due to the prolonged seizure, the boy suffered severe brain damage rendering him quadriplegic, a result that could have been avoided had the boy been administered valium. In holding the defendant liable, the New South Wales Court of Appeal was influenced by the fact that the legislature had already recognised that such a failure by a registered general practitioner can amount to professional misconduct.[31] The future scope of the *Lowns* duty is unclear, given that the court's finding of liability was dependent to varying degrees on the presence of physical proximity (the boy was 300 yards away), circumstantial proximity (there was no real obstacle to the defendant attending the boy), and causal proximity (an adminstration of valium would have arrested the fit before serious brain damage was incurred).[32]

Within the hospital context, a general duty of care arises once the hospital expressly or impliedly undertakes to assist a patient. It is rare in medical negligence cases that the existence of any duty of care, or assumption of some undertaking, is rigorously contested; most cases hinge on establishing that the defendant did not live up to a standard of care required in the circumstances (the scope of which will

---

[28] See *Restatement (Second) of Torts No. 324* (1965).
[29] *e.g. McCain v. Batson* (1988) 760 P. 2d 725.
[30] *Lowns v. Woods* [1996] Aust. Torts Reports 81–376.
[31] Medical Practitioners Act 1938 s. 27(2)(c), (NSW).
[32] McDonald & Swanton (1996), p. 689.

inevitably be qualified by the resources available to the hospital, though the courts are reluctant to develop this reasoning).[33] The existence of a duty of care in the hospital context is more likely to arise as an issue in cases where the patient presented himself to the casualty department of a hospital for urgent treatment and was left untreated. In *Barnett v. Chelsea & Kensington Hospital Management Committee*, Nield J. was tentative in proposing when a duty might definitely arise.[34] He accepted that on the facts of the instant case, where a patient presented himself to casualty complaining of severe stomach pains, a duty clearly arose to examine and treat the patient. He did not, however, go so far as to rule that a duty always arose when a patient presented himself to casualty staff, and considered that a duty might not arise where the patient's complaint or injury is minor and can be properly treated by a nurse without calling on the casualty officer, or where the patient presents himself for a second opinion. It would be more accurate to propose that a duty of some kind arises in all cases where a patient presents himself at casualty, but that the duty is merely to assess with due diligence and competence whether or not the patient requires hospital treatment and whether or not his treatment should be arranged on a casualty or an out-patient basis.[35]

The duty of care is owed to the patient, with whom the physician has entered into a relationship of professional trust governed both by ethics and legal rules. A duty of care may be owed in fewer instances to third parties. Past examples include failing to diagnose a contagious disease, causing the patient to infect another,[36] failing to warn third parties forseeably placed at risk by a patient's contagious disease,[37] and failing to warn about the side-effects of medication, causing the patient to lose consciousness when driving and to crash and injure others.[38] If the strict ingredients of the nervous shock action are

---

[33] The relative independence of health authorities in determining the allocation of scarce resources in hospitals was affirmed recently in *R. v. Cambridge HA, ex parte B* (1995) 6 Med. L.R. 250. The Court of Appeal upheld the defendant's decision not to fund a £75,000 chemotherapy treatment, which carried a 10 to 20 per cent chance of success and without which the patient would have six to eight weeks to live.

[34] *Barnett v. Chelsea & Kensington Hospital Management Committee* [1969] 1 Q.B. 428.

[35] Suggested in *Collins v. Mid-Western Health Board, supra* n. 22.

[36] *Hofmann v. Blackmon* 241 So. 2d 752 (1970).

[37] *Davis v. Rodman* (1921) 227 S.W. 612; *Wojcik v. Aluminium Co. of America* (1959) 183 NYS 2d 351. The existence or scope of this duty may now be questioned in light of the generally accepted public interest of preserving the confidentiality of HIV and AIDS diagnoses.

[38] *Kirk v. Michael Reese Hospital* 483 N.E. 2d 906.

proved, a third party may recover damages for psychiatric injury caused by witnessing the effect of the defendant's medical negligence on a close family member or friend. The claim failed in *Taylor v. Somerset Health Authority* on the basis that the plaintiff had not witnessed her husband's death at the time nor incurred her shock in the immediate aftermath of the death.[39] However, it succeeded in *Tredget v. Bexley Health Authority* where the plaintiffs had observed the death of their new-born baby caused by the defendants' negligent delivery.[40] The court was influenced by the fact that: there was proximity of relationship between the parties (parents and child); the shock was reasonably foreseeable since neo-natal death is known to give rise to psychiatric disturbance; the injury suffered by the parents was more than grief or distress, but was a recognised form of psychiatric injury; and what unfolded around the parents at the time of the birth constituted a "horrifying external event".

Thus far, the most litigated third party scenario involves psychiatrists. The courts have been asked to determine the extent to which liability should be imposed for injuries caused by mentally ill patients who were negligently deemed non-dangerous and released prematurely into society.[41] The issues are as complicated as they are unpalatable. On the one hand, there is a natural fear by psychiatrists of wide if not indeterminate liability, and on the other hand an appreciation that detaining patients out of a vague and unsubstantiated belief that they may be dangerous or aggressive would severely undermine the advances gained in recent years in the area of civil liberty.[42] There is also of course the impossibility of predicting with any degree of certainty that a psychiatric patient is likely to cause harm to others.[43]

In a leading case, *Tarasoff v. Regents of Univerity of California*, the Supreme Court of California pronounced that psychiatrists owe a duty of care to protect third parties who are "forseeably" at risk of violence or injury.[44] This duty, it felt, could be discharged by warning or notifying the third parties who are placed potentially at risk. The instant case was a clear example of a failure to alert an obvious and foreseeable target: the patient had told his psychiatrist that he

---

[39] *Taylor v. Somerset Health Authority* (1993) 4 Med. L.R. 34.
[40] *Tredget v. Bexley Health Authority* (1994) 5 Med. L.R. 178.
[41] See generally Johnson (1991).
[42] *ibid.*, p. 440.
[43] See Chapter 3, *infra*, pp. 79–80.
[44] *Tarasoff v. Regents of Univerity of California* 551 P. 2d 334 (1976).

intended to kill his girlfriend, which he did two months later. In these circumstances, the psychiatrist breached a duty to warn the third party of the patient's apparent intentions, which overrode the professional duty of doctor-patient confidentiality, for the "protective privilege ends where the public peril begins". *Tarasoff* has been affirmed in many states of America, rendering psychiatrists potentially liable to third parties who are the reasonably foreseeable victims of a psychiatric patient's violent disposition.[45] Some courts have imposed liability where the patient made no specific threats against the third party; that is for indiscriminate injury caused by a widely dangerous patient.[46] Other courts have restricted the pool of potential claimants to specifically foreseeable victims, out of a policy fear of indeterminate liability (to which the common law is traditionally averse).[47]

Usually, the psychiatrist has known that the patient was dangerous, but not to what extent. The defence has often argued that the epistemological inability to accurately predict the extent of dangerousness compels the conclusion that the defendant was not negligent in failing to appreciate the risk in particular cases. The argument has not always met with success.[48] Some courts have conceded the point, but concluded that it should not bar recovery.[49] Other courts, notably in New York, have sensibly enquired into whether or not the defendant made a good faith analysis based on generally agreed signs and symptoms.[50]

---

[45] *Lawson v. Wellesley Hospital* [1978] 1 S.C.R. 893, where liability was imposed for negligently releasing patients with a known propensity for violence. See also the recent English decision in *Osman v. Ferguson* [1993] 4 All E.R. 344, where the court accepted the possible existence of liability for injury caused by a man to the father of a son he had stalked, where the man had earlier told the police that he "might do something insane".

[46] *McIntosh v. Milano* 403 A. 2d 500 (1979); *Jablonski v. United States* 712 F. 2d 391 (1983); *Williams v. United States* 450 F. Supp. 1040 (1978); *Cain v. Rijken* 700 P. 2d 1061 (1985).

[47] *Hasenei v. United States* 541 F. Supp. 999 (1982) at 1011 (denying recovery to the victims of a car crash involving the patient); *Furr v. Spring Grove State Hospital* 454 A. 2d 414 (1983) (denying recovery for the murder of a child); *Brady v. Hopper* 570 F. Supp. 1333 (1983) (denying recovery for injuries sustained by President Reagan during the assassination attempt by John Hinckley).

[48] *Schuster v. Attenberg* 424 NW 2d 159 (1988).

[49] *Lipari* 497 F. Supp. 185 (1980).

[50] *Bell v. New York City Health and Hospitals* 456 NYS 2d 787 (1982).

Medical Misadventure and Errors of Judgment

Across the common law, the courts have emphasised that errors of judgment and instances of medical misadventure do not necessarily afford proof of negligence.[51] The distinction recognises that in the course of medical diagnosis and treatment, mistakes will occur, judgment calls will later be proved wrong, without the defendant having acted incompetently or negligently. For instance, in *White v. Board of Governors of Westminister Hospital*, the surgeon accidentally cut the plaintiff's retina whilst performing a highly delicate and precise operation on the eye; this, the court concluded, was mischance and not negligence.[52] *Maynard v. West Midlands Regional Health Authority* was a classic challenge to a bona fide exercise of professional judgment.[53] The plaintiff's symptoms had indicated a diagnosis of tuberculosis, in which case surgery would not be necessary; on the other hand, certain symptoms suggested the possible existence of a carcinoma which, if not caught at an early stage by a highly risky operation, would probably have killed the plaintiff. In the event, the consultants embarked on the operation, which ultimately resulted in permanent paralysis of the plaintiff's vocal chords. It later transpired that the plaintiff had tuberculosis and not carcinoma. Upholding the defendant's appeal, Lord Scarman ruled that the trial judge had erred in law by expressing a preference for the plaintiff's expert evidence, and he dismissed the claim of negligence on the ground that: "in the realm of diagnosis and treatment, negligence is not established by preferring one respectable body of professional opinion to another. Failure to exercise the ordinary skill of a doctor (in the appropriate specialty, if he be a specialist) is necessary."[54]

Whilst on the surface the distinction appears to make good sense, appealing broadly to one's sense of fairness to the professional man, it

---

[51] *Hodges v. Carter* 80 S.E. 2d 144 (1954); *Scardina v. Colletti* (1965) 211 N.E. 2d 762. In *Whitehouse v. Jordan* [1980] 1 All E.R. 650 at 658, Lord Denning's remark that "in a professional man, an error of judgment is not negligent" was corrected by the House of Lords to the following, *per* Lord Edmund-Davies [1981] 1 W.L.R. 247 at 276: "To say that a surgeon committed an error of judgment is wholly ambiguous for, while some such errors may be completely consistent with the exercise of professional skill, other acts or omissions in the course of exercising 'clinical judgment' may be so glaringly below proper standards as to make a finding of negligence inevitable."

[52] *White v. Board of Governors of Westminster Hospital*, *The Times*, October 26, 1961.

[53] *Maynard v. West Midlands Regional Health Authority* [1984] 1 W.L.R. 634.

[54] *ibid.* at 639.

is not necessarily a workable one within the particular context of the medical malpractice claim. It seems to require the plaintiff to prove in many cases that not only did the defendant commit a critical error, but that the error was utterly indefensible. How can the court ever realistically know when an error amounted to negligence and not merely misadventure? Too often the defendant can hide behind an array of statistics indicating that in a remote number of cases, non-negligent misadventure was likely to occur. When the precise means by which the plaintiff's injuries were caused is unfathomable, the plaintiff's difficulties reach herculean proportions. A rather typical example of this arose in the Irish case of *Russell v. Walsh & Mid-Western Health Board* where the allegation was that a hysterectomy had been negligently performed.[55] Initially the plaintiff claimed that a suture had been negligently placed by the defendant, and that the plaintiff's ureter had got caught in it. Subsequently by amendment, it was claimed that a clamp had been negligently misplaced causing the ureter to rupture and sever, and in the alternative that certain tissues were negligently tied back by sutures causing loss of blood to the ureter. An expert witness for the plaintiff testified to having performed 1,150 such operations successfully, strongly implying that the defendant had incompetently performed his. That witness was, however, needled to admit under cross-examination that though damage should not result if a hysterectomy is competently performed, damage may be expected to result without negligence in one quarter to a half per cent of cases. As the defendant doctor testified to having already performed about 3,800 such operations without damage, it is hardly surprising that the plaintiff was judged to have failed to prove his case.

Duties Owed at the Diagnosis and Treatment Stages

As a general rule, in assessing whether or not the defendant negligently misdiagnosed his patient's condition, the courts will consider the patient's symptoms, his age, and the rarity of his condition.[56] Doctors are not generally held liable for mere errors of judgment; the law requires that they exercise due diligence and

---

[55] *Russell v. Walsh & Mid-Western Health Board*, Irish High Court, unreported, April 3, 1995.

[56] *Huse v. Wilson* (1953) 2 B.M.J. 890.

competence, not that they achieve 100 per cent accuracy in each case.[57] A doctor should not make unsubstantiated assumptions about the patient's condition.[58] Before diagnosing, he must conduct an adequate *anamnesis*. This entails a thorough physical examination of the patient.[59] The patient's own medical history is an integral part of the diagnostic process, whether the history emanates from medical records or the patient himself. According to White J. for the South Australia Supreme Court: "Modern aids to diagnosis no doubt assist the medical practitioner in varying degrees depending upon the circumstances, but they can hardly take the place of listening to the patient's history."[60] Efforts should be made to elicit candour from the patient, though if a patient's response to questions are inaccurate, the physician who assumes them to be true in the absence of any contraindications is not negligent.[61]

Plaintiffs frequently come undone when they claim that they presented themselves with particular symptoms before the defendant. The courts tend overwhelmingly to accept the defendant's records as the most accurate account of what occurred. This is especially so for disclosure actions, considered later. In *Gordon v. Wilson*, a Scottish court decided that if the plaintiff had presented himself, as he said he did, with symptoms of left-sided deafness and problems of balance, the doctor had come under a duty to refer him to a specialist; ultimately, however, the court accepted the defendant's report of the plaintiff's headaches, and deduced that the absence of any reference to the patient's deafness in the doctor's notes arose from the plaintiff's failure to properly communicate this information to the defendant.[62] Diagnosis by telephone has become a significantly litigated area. Case law has emerged in support of the proposition that a general practitioner who has been presented with worrying symptoms by phone may have to ensure that the patient is physically examined,[63] or that the patient attend his office or a hospital emergency department as soon as possible.[64] It has also been decided that doctors are under a duty to ensure that the prescriptions they

---

[57] See *supra*, p. 50.
[58] *Barnett v. Chelsea & Kensington Hospital Management Committee, supra*, n. 34.
[59] *Wood v. Thurston, The Times*, May 25, 1951.
[60] *Giurelli v. Girgis* (1980) 24 S.A.S.R. 264 at 276–277.
[61] *Leadbetter v. Brand* (1980) 107 D.L.R. (3d) 252.
[62] *Gordon v. Wilson* (1992) 3 Med. L.R. 401.
[63] *Cavan v. Wilcox* (1973) 44 D.L.R. (3d) 42.
[64] *Dale v. Munthali* 16 O.R. 2d 532 (1977), aff'd 21 O.R. 2d 554 (CA 1978).

write are legible and accurate and do not "reasonably permit misreading", though pharmacists shoulder some responsibility in this context to ensure that the prescription is accurate.[65]

Diagnosis is not a discreet event; it permeates the doctor-patient relationship. The doctor must monitor the progress of the patient's response to medication and treatment, and must refine or alter his diagnosis to reflect any relevant developments.[66] An initial diagnosis of a patient's complaint may subsequently appear overly optimistic.[67] Underestimation of a patient's illness has become a significant source of litigation. In *Sa'd v. Robinson*, a general practitioner was held negligent for underestimating a child's injuries sustained from sucking hot tea from a teapot spout, and for failing to appreciate that this could have caused steam to enter and inflame the baby's throat without causing visible burns yet ultimately resulting in an anoxic fit and consequential brain damage.[68] In one case, the patient's symptoms were diagnosed as psychosomatically induced, whereas in fact the patient suffered from a form of brain damage.[69] Underestimation may be the result of the doctor's overconfidence in his ability to treat the patient at the level of specialisation actually required.[70] General practitioners, in particular, are expected to be able to identify symptoms that indicate the necessity of a more expert or specialised assessment.[71]

In numerous cases, plaintiffs have sued for loss sustained as a result of the defendant's negligent failure to diagnose a condition on time. A high proportion of these cases relate to the detection of cancer; where the cancer was terminal, for the most part these turn on the question of causation—whether the disease or the doctor's negligence could be said to have caused the patient's death.[72] Some cases have prayed recovery for the negligent failure to diagnose a pregnancy in time for the patient to procure a lawful abortion.[73] In a recent decision by the New South Wales Court of Appeal, it was

---

[65] *Prendergast v. Sam & Dee Ltd* (1989) 1 Med. L.R. 36.

[66] *Bergen v. Sturgeon General Hospital* (1984) 28 C.C.L.T. 155; *Judge v. Huntingdon Health Authority* (1995) 6 Med. L.R. 223.

[67] In *Bova v. Spring* (1994) 5 Med. L.R. 120, a second appointment would have revealed that the patient's condition was not minor, but was in fact urgent and critical.

[68] *Sa'd v. Robinson* (1989) 1 Med. L.R. 41.

[69] *Hungerford v. United States* (1962) 307 F. 2d 99.

[70] *Gordon v. Wilson, supra* n. 62; *Dale v. Munthali* (1976) 78 D.L.R. (3d) 588.

[71] *Gordon v. Wilson, ibid.*

[72] See Chapter 7, *infra*, pp. 215, 222–223, 225.

[73] See Chapter 5, *infra*, p. 154.

accepted that the plaintiff's hypothetical abortion would probably have been unlawful unless the pregnancy had placed the woman in serious danger to life or physical or mental health.[74] The court reasoned that in cases of hypothetical abortion, it is not possible to rule on the lawfulness of an actually contemplated abortion, nor can the court be sure that in the circumstances the doctor and not the patient (for whom knowledge of unlawfulness is essential) might be guilty. For this reason it resisted denying recovery, but felt that the possibility that the abortion would have been deemed unlawful should be reflected in the damages awarded.

A doctor ought not to treat a patient unless he possesses the necessary skill and expertise to do so[75]—though there is authority for the view that he may not have to disclose his lack of past experience (where it is reasonable nonetheless that he conduct the treatment).[76] If he lacks this expertise, he ought to refer the patient's case to someone who is suitably qualified in the relevant specialty.[77] It may be the case that the hospital lacks the back-up expertise or resources to assist the patient should the operation give rise to complications, in which case depending on the circumstances, the doctor may be under a duty to refer the patient to a hospital that can, or if this is not possible to discuss the range of remaining options before the patient chooses whether or not to proceed with the treatment.[78] If the patient requires referral to another hospital or consultant, it becomes vital that all the relevant details of the patient's medical case (records, details of medication or treatment to date, and responses thereto) are communicated from one institution or doctor to the other.[79] Where necessary, the doctor must impress upon the patient the need to attend a certain hospital or doctor and ought to ensure effective written correspondence to the second hospital or doctor.[80] This duty applies equally to general practitioners who, depending on the circumstances, may have to make considerable effort to ensure that a

---

[74] *CES v. Superclinics (Australia) Pty Ltd* (1995) 38 N.S.W.L.R. 47, considering Crimes Act 1900 s. 83 (NSW).

[75] *Nickolls v. Ministry of Health, The Times*, February 4, 1955; *Fraser v. Vancouver General Hospital* [1952] 2 S.C.R. 36.

[76] *Lepp v. Hopp* (1979) 98 D.L.R. (3d) 464.

[77] *Payne v. St Helier Group Hospital Management Committee* [1952] C.L.Y.B. 2442; *Buck v. United States* 433 F. Supp. 896 (1977).

[78] *Lepp v. Hopp, supra*, n. 76.

[79] *Coles v. Reading and District Hospital Management Committee* (1963) S.J. 115; *Welch v. Frisbie Memorial Hospital* 9 A. 2d 761 (1939).

[80] *ibid.*

patient agrees to go to a hospital.[81] In the United Kingdom and Ireland, a general practitioner's written request on the patient's behalf for hospital treatment may be overriden by a casualty officer following examination of the patient.[82] In this context, it would seem logical that where a general practitioner is clearly of the view that medical treatment is urgently needed, he is under a heightened duty to communicate this fact to the hospital staff.

Negligence may arise from the defendant's *choice* of treatment, which often intersects with disclosure issues—whether or not the defendant furnished adequate information to the patient regarding the pros and cons of the recommended treatment and the existence of alternative methods.[83] However, the overwhelming majority of cases relate to the *performance* of the treatment undertaken by the defendant and consented to by the plaintiff. Sometimes the mistakes will be obvious, such as injury caused to another part of the patient's anatomy during treatment[84] or the failure to remove foreign articles from the patient's body.[85] The more difficult the treatment—such as spinal or brain surgery, or administration of anaesthetics—the higher the standard required of the doctor in his specialty such that it may not be reasonable to delegate the task in question[86] or to leave the operating theatre while surgery is still being performed.[87] Extreme care is required with respect to injections. Doctors have been held liable for injecting narcotics into a vein instead of an artery,[88] and for injecting a lethal form of cocaine instead of its harmless procaine equivalent.[89] The defendant must familiarise himself with the side-effects of any medication prescribed.[90] He should verify that the patient is complying with his treatment regimen and taking the prescribed medication. In one Canadian case, the doctor was deemed one third at fault when his patient continued to take his medication beyond the prescription time-limit.[91] The patient must be fully

---

[81] *Reeves v. Carthy and O'Kelly* [1984] I.R. 348.
[82] *Supra*, pp. 43–44.
[83] See Chapters 4 & 5, *infra*.
[84] *Guillen v. Martin* 333 P. 2d 266 (1958).
[85] *Karderas v. Clow* (1972) 32 D.L.R. (3d) 303; *Marshall v. Curry* [1933] 3 D.L.R. 260; *Gerber v. Pines* (1934) 79 S.J. 13.
[86] *Williams v. St Claire Medical Center* 657 S.W. 2d 590 (1983).
[87] *DeChamplain v. Etobicoke General Hospital* (1985) 34 C.C.L.T. 89.
[88] *Caldeira v. Gray* [1936] 1 All E.R. 540.
[89] *Collins v. Hertfordshire CC* [1947] 1 All E.R. 633.
[90] *Reynard v. Carr* (1983) 30 C.C.L.T. 42.
[91] *Crossman v. Stuart* (1977) 5 C.C.L.T. 45.

examined after treatment to ascertain the extent of recovery and whether or not post-operative care is necessary.[92]

The plight of junior members of staff was considered in *Wilsher v. Essex Area Health Authority* where junior doctors failed to monitor a baby's arterial oxygen tension and negligently administered extra oxygen.[93] The defence argued that it was in the public interest that hospitals engage junior doctors who must learn 'on the job', and that the law should not impose on them a standard of care as high as that owed by experienced doctors. Mustill L.J. was of the view that doctors must meet the standard of care ordinarily attached to the relevant medical specialty, however junior or senior the doctor. Similarly, Glidewell L.J. believed that a doctor's inexperience does not affect the standard of care that he owes. The result seems harsh: a successfully litigated slip-up in one's first year at a hospital seems a damning start to a professional career in which many years, much expense, and resources have already been invested. It is hoped that this decision does no more than ensure, as Glidewell L.J. intended, that junior doctors seek out assistance from senior colleagues wherever it is necessary, or that tasks are not delegated to junior doctors who have had incomplete instruction.[94]

There is a duty on doctors to keep abreast of ongoing developments as published and disseminated, particularly where relevant to their specialty. It is not, of course, clear how soon a doctor must learn or act upon recent developments, nor how extensive his assimilation of information ought to be. In *Crawford v. Board of Governors of Charing Cross Hospital*, Denning L.J. considered that the defendant was not at fault for neglecting to read an article published in *The Lancet* that expressed doubts on the safety of a technique the defendant seven months later adopted to his patient's physical detriment.[95] The decision seems of dubious status now. First, Lord Denning's notoriously pro-defendant crusade throughout the corpus of medical law is treated by many today with suspicion and aversion. Secondly, *The Lancet* is a high-profile publication, ubiquitous within the profession. Thirdly, a doctor—like a lawyer, who must inform himself of relevant case precedents and statutory changes—is obliged to update his knowledge continuously; it might indeed be said that

---

[92] *Momsen v. Nebraska Methodist Hospital* 313 N.W. 2d 208 (1981).

[93] *Wilsher v. Essex Area Health Authority, supra,* n. 13.

[94] Such delegation may amount to negligence on the part of the doctor or hospital: *Wimpy Construction U.K. v. Poole* [1984] 2 Lloyd's Rep. 499.

[95] *Crawford v. Board of Governors of Charing Cross Hospital, The Times,* December 8, 1953.

this is all the more so for doctors, since contemporary medical health care is based on science, and scientific theory constantly evolves at a dizzying pace.

However, doctors may rely on the state of medical or scientific knowledge at the relevant time, so long as their reliance on it was reasonable in the circumstances. In *Roe v. Ministry of Health*, the plaintiffs suffered permanent paralysis from the waist down as a result of the administration of an anaesthetic that had become contaminated by its phenol solution. Because the state of knowledge had not by the time of the alleged negligence advanced to an appreciation of this risk, it was not negligent of them to fail to foresee the risk of contamination and consequent medical injury. However, the court took pains to stress that doctors would in the future have to watch out for invisible cracks by using dye solutions: "If the hospital were to continue the practice after this warning, they could not complain if they were found guilty of negligence."[96]

A doctor is under a continuing duty to update his knowledge of the latest advances in his specialty. Where new drugs appear on the market, doctors are under a duty to acquaint themselves with the manufacturer's literature. They may have to do more. American courts have consistently expressed alarm at the medical profession's over-reliance on promotional material supplied by pharmaceutical firms.[97] Waltz and Scheuneman reason that doctors must be under a duty to *discover* risks, particularly where the treatment is innovative or experimental, and that it is not enough to disclose risks that are known.[98]

The health care which a patient naturally expects to receive is of a *therapeutic* quality. This ordinarily involves the application of conventional and approved methods which have commanded a wide level of support within the medical community. However, where there is no known cure for a condition, or where conventional medication has successively failed, the doctor may wish to recommend a course of treatment which has not thus far attracted general support. Clearly, innovative or experimental treatment should be used only as a last resort where other treatment has failed and where there is a better than even chance that it will yield better results.[99] A doctor would be

---

[96] *Roe v. Ministry of Health, supra,* n. 4 at 139, *per* Denning L.J.
[97] *Holley v. Burroughs Welcome Cpy* 348 S.E. 2d 772 (1986).
[98] Waltz & Scheuneman (1970), p. 631.
[99] Curran (1978).

negligent in deciding to treat by innovative means what he could have treated by adopting an approved course that promised equal success with less risk to the patient.[1] On the other hand, it would be difficult to establish that a doctor was negligent for failing to recommend an innovative therapy, given that the defendant can rely in his defence on the fact that he followed general or approved practice.[2] Unlike a case of pure experimentation conducted as part of a clinical trial for research purposes, the doctor is in a professional relationship of care with the patient, whose recovery from illness is the doctor's primary ethical and legal goal.

The key to successfully negotiating the tricky ethical and legal pitfalls that arise in this context will in most cases lie in the disclosure that the doctor makes to his patient. If an innovative treatment has been ineffective in the past, the doctor must surely disclose this fact along with information on the possible consequences of a bad result. Courts have not shied away from recognising a greatly heightened duty of disclosure where the treatment is to any degree experimental.[3] This is all the more so in view of the dangers presented by conflicts of interest.[4] According to Stevenson C.J.: "The risk of the interest in the experiment conflicting with the interest in the patient's welfare must necessarily be considered when a doctor is prescribing *his* new process as distinct from the objectivity that is presumed in the use of someone else's new process."[5]

Issues of disclosure apart, there will be cases where the defendant was never justified in recommending a new treatment, in particular where the treatment is highly risky and has not yet attained scientific validation. This was the case in *Hepworth v. Kerr*, where the defendant adopted a novel hypotensive anaesthetic technique that necessitated keeping the plaintiff's blood pressure at a hazardously low level for an excessive length of time, ultimately causing the plaintiff to suffer a spinal stroke.[6] By contrast, the relationship of the plaintiff with the doctor may be that of researcher/scientist and volunteer/subject,

---

[1] Giesen (1988), p. 554.

[2] Giesen (1988), p. 558 proposes, however, that a doctor is under a duty to keep abreast of scientific and medical developments, and where conventional medical actions offers no hope to the patient, he may be obliged to try out innovative treatment even where it is currently untested.

[3] *Cryderman v. Ringrose* (1978) 89 D.L.R. (3d) 32; *Hepworth v. Kerr* (1995) 6 Med. L.R. 139.

[4] See Chapter 4, *infra*, pp. 114–115.

[5] *Cryderman v. Ringrose, supra*, n. 3 at 42.

[6] *Hepworth v. Kerr* (1995) 6 Med. L.R. 139.

where the plaintiff agrees to participate in a research trial. These trials are designed to test hypotheses about what will change if certain conditions are altered.[7] Where the volunteer is also a patient in need of treatment, the constraints of the scientific protocol adopted for the trial may significantly restrict or impede that patient's recovery. The doctor may have to adhere to a chronology of steps—such as trying out different medications sequentially—and may have to ignore that these are inappropriate in the patient's case. Where the plaintiff had agreed to participate in a randomised trial—necessary where controlled studies are unhelpful or unfeasible—the patient inevitably loses the right to choose from the range of possible treatments. In this regard, medical researchers must inevitably tread a difficult legal minefield which disclosure may be the sole means of defusing. Once disclosure is complete and the patient has understood the implications of the trial, much is ethically and legally acceptable.[8] However, a subject's consent may be interpreted to have been secured on the basis that a genuine scientific uncertainty needed to be clarified. If that is the case, where at any stage in a trial the specific uncertainty is removed (for instance that the treatment is clinically beneficial or not), the trial should be discontinued.[9]

A duty may arise to prevent or minimise opportunities for the patient to cause himself harm.[10] This is typically the case where the patient is diagnosed as suffering from a mental or psychiatric illness, though it may also arise where the patient has been given a sedative[11] or an epileptic patient is in imminent danger of suffering a seizure.[12] The phenomenon of suicide, and its sheer scale, has finally started to attract attention.[13] The common law has faced a barrage of suicide cases over the past few decades, many of them prison suicides, and has generally recognised that a heightened duty of care exists to protect a suicidal patient from himself, where in the circumstances it

---

[7] Fromer (1981) p. 276.

[8] Appelbaum, Lidz, and Meisel (1987), p. 240. However, see Chapter 4, *infra*, pp. 112–115.

[9] Mason & McCall Smith (1994), pp. 354–355 propose that this should be decided according to the balance of probabilities.

[10] See generally: Jones (1990); Weit (1998). For liability to third parties, see *supra*, pp. 46–48.

[11] *Beatty v. Sisters of Misericordia of Atlanta* [1935] 1 W.W.R. 651.

[12] *Dowey v. Rothwell* [1974] 4 W.W.R. 311.

[13] Such that "suicidology" has emerged as an independent discipline. The second annual conference of the Irish Association of Suicidology (November 1, 1997) noted that an estimated 2,500 people world-wide commit suicide each day.

is reasonably foreseeable to the authorities that the patient is a suicide-risk. There is now of course an appreciation that many suicides are the result of long or short term depressions or psychiatric illness, though there is yet no satisfactory general theory explaining the urge to commit suicide, and it is impossible to predict with any degree of certainty that suicidal patients will carry out their expressed intentions.[14] However, in considering compensation claims by relatives of the deceased, the courts more often than not adopt the view that a life has unnecessarily been lost or injuries unnecessarily sustained because of the suicide, and that to employ the language of a patient's right of self-determination—choosing in Hamlet's words, whether to be or not to be—is inappropriate. This manifests itself in the courts' reluctance to find the suicidal patient contributorily negligent.[15]

In assessing the proper scope of the duty of care towards suicidal prisoners and patients, the courts have had to resolve the constraints placed in particular by two time-honoured common law principles, *ex turpi causa non oritur actio* and *novus actus interveniens*. *Ex turpi* is a rule that traditionally has prevented the courts from 'lending aid to a man who founds his cause of action upon an immoral or illegal act'.[16] In *Hyde v. Tameside AHA*, one of the first cases to consider the liability of a hospital for injuries sustained during a suicide attempt, Lord Denning invoked the doctrine to restrict the future development of this action.[17] He observed that, though suicide was no longer a criminal offence since the Suicide Act of 1961, it was still an ecclesiastical transgression and it was wrong to place the burden of self-inflicted injuries on the community. In *Kirkham v. Chief Constable of Greater Manchester Police*, the Court of Appeal accepted that the *ex turpi* principle extends beyond crimes (which attempted suicide no longer was) and embraces activities that amount to an affront to the public conscience. It felt, however, that the decriminalisation of suicide reflected a shift in public attitudes and a sympathy towards the plight of the suicidal. The approach taken in *Kirkham* to the *ex turpi* plea was followed recently in *Reeves v. Commissioner of Police of the Metropolis*.[18]

---

[14] See Chapter 1, *supra*, pp. 26–27.
[15] *e.g. Armstrong v. Eastern Health Board*, Irish High Court, unreported, October 5, 1990, where Egan J., rather understatedly, commented that the plaintiff "was not really in control of her thoughts when she jumped from the balcony".
[16] *Holman v. Johnson* (1775) 1 Cowp. 341 at 343, *per* Mansfield C.J.
[17] *Hyde v. Tameside Area Health Authority* [1981] C.L.Y. 1854.
[18] *Reeves v. Commissioner of Police of the Metropolis* [1998] 2 W.L.R. 401.

More recently, in *Clunis v. Camden and Islington HA*, the Court of Appeal was asked to consider *ex turpi* in the context of a claim for damages by a mentally ill patient who following his discharge from the defendant institution, fatally stabbed a man.[19] The plaintiff had earlier pleaded guilty to manslaughter by reason of diminished responsibility, and had been sent to a high security hospital. At this action, he claimed the defendants breached a duty of care to treat him with due professional care and skill, which should have caused them to continue to detain him. Judgment was given by Beldam LJ, whose review of *ex turpi* confirms that the doctrine is predicated on the assumption that the plaintiff knew what he was doing at the relevant time *and* that his actions were unlawful.[20] The learned judge was reluctant to propose that the doctrine applies in all cases where the plaintiff's responsibility was diminished by reason of a mental disorder. His decision against the plaintiff was based on his view that the plea of diminished responsibility does not remove liability for criminal acts.[21]

The second principle invoked in suicide cases is *novus actus interveniens*, by which the injured party's conduct may sometimes be regarded as having severed the causal connection between his injury and the defendant's breach of duty. Its application was rejected by Tudor-Evan J. in *Kirkham v. Chief Constable of Greater Manchester Police*, on the basis that the deceased's suicide was the very thing the defendants were shown to have a duty to avert.[22] Clearly, the *novus* principle is inappropriate in cases where the defendant's intervening act (availing of an opportunity to kill himself) was a reasonably foreseeable consequence of the defendant's breach of duty. In the *Reeves* case, a prisoner was known to be a suicide-risk but had been deemed sane by a visiting doctor who as a precaution removed the prisoner's belt from his cell.[23] Shortly after the assessment, the prisoner hanged himself after threading his shirt through a hatch in the cell door via a spy hole above it (both exposed contrary to standing orders). In finding the defendants liable, the court largely bypassed the *novus* plea and the causation issue. According to Buxton

---

[19] *Clunis v. Camden & Islington Health Authority* [1998] 2 W.L.R. 902.

[20] For example in *Burrows v. Rhodes* [1899] 1 Q.B. 816, the rule was not applied because although the plaintiff had acted intentionally, he had been duped by the defendants into believing that the acts were lawful.

[21] Approving *Gray v. Barr* [1971] 2 Q.B. 554.

[22] *Kirkham v. Chief Constable of Greater Manchester Police* [1989] 3 All E.R. 882 at 889.

[23] *Reeves v. Commissioner of Police of the Metropolis, supra*, n. 18.

L.J., once a duty of care had been established, causation became irrelevant—a conclusion that rightly has been decried as "nothing short of dotty".[24] No less surprisingly, Lord Bingham was of the view that the prisoner's apparent sanity was also irrelevant, on the basis that there is no sharp line of demarcation between mental normality and abnormality—which Weir interprets to mean that "we are all to be treated as mad because some are marginally madder than others."[25]

Reeves is currently being appealed to the House of Lords, and it is likely that the issues glossed over by a majority of the Court of Appeal will form the basis of the House's decision. The dissenting views of Morritt L.J. may yet prevail. His lordship decided the case largely on the basis of *novus actus interveniens*, and a sense that it is inappropriate to complain of acts which one has deliberately engineered. In other words: "the voluntary, deliberate and informed act of a plaintiff . . . intended to exploit the situation created by the defendant albeit in breach of duty precludes a causative link between the breach of duty and the consequences of the plaintiff's action."[26] Whether consciously or not, the availability of resources is likely to affect the verdict of the appeal as it has done in past cases, where the tendency has been to adopt a proportionality analysis alongside an enquiry into whether or not the suicide was reasonably foreseeable in the circumstances.

For example, in *Thorne v. Northern Group Hospital Management*, Edmund Davies J. found for the defence on the basis that though a higher standard of care is owed to suicidal patients, it does not require a constant vigil.[27] The judge was influenced by evidence that the patient had been determined to kill herself, and that shortly before she was due to be transferred to an outside neurosis unit, she had snatched an opportunity and swiftly committed the deed. By contrast, in *Selfe v. Ilford & District Hospital Management Committee*, Hinchcliffe J. found for the plaintiff on a risk-detriment analysis, concluding that to "leave unobserved a youth of 17 with suicidal tendencies and an unlocked window behind his bed was asking for trouble."[28] In *Knight v. Home Office*, it was not possible to place the prisoner in the prison's hospital wing—which would have given him

---

[24] Weir (1998), p. 243.
[25] *ibid.*, at 244.
[26] *Reeves v. Commissioner of Police, supra*, n. 18 at 418.
[27] *Thorne v. Northern Group Hospital Management* (1964) 108 S.J. 484.
[28] *Selfe v. Ilford & District Hospital Management Committee* (1970) 4 B.M.J. 754.

constant supervision—because he was a threat to the safety of others.[29] A special system had been set in place for him, giving him supervision every second 15 minutes period. In exonerating the defendants, the court accepted that the availability of resources is a factor which must affect any determination of the standard of care owed in the circumstances. In *Hyde v. Tameside Area Health Authority*, the patient had been in hospital for the relief of shoulder pain.[30] Having convinced himself that he was dying of cancer, he attempted suicide by jumping from a third floor building. The court reversed a first instance judgment in the patient's favour on the basis that it was not reasonably foreseeable for the medical staff that this patient, who had never been diagnosed by psychiatrists as a suicide-risk, should suffer mental distress to that extent; the case, it was felt, merely concerned a forgivable failure to achieve a standard approaching perfection.

A duty to eliminate, rather than minimise, the opportunities for committing suicide may be too exacting and impractical a duty—yet this would seem to be the implication of *Reeves* thus far, where a prisoner had "so determinedly seized the brief and unobvious opportunity afforded to him" to end his life.[31] Alongside the resources issue, the common law ought to factor into its analysis the epistemological inexactitude of psychiatric predictions and the implications of a practice that might begin defensively to favour hospitalisation and involuntary committal in all but the clearest cases.[32] These issues were sensitively addressed by the Ontario High Court in *Haines v. Bellissimo*.[33] A decision had been made not to commit a patient who had had a long history of chronic schizophrenia and who had recently purchased a gun. It was made on the basis that the patient had not evinced suicidal tendencies and had been content to hand over the gun. In defending the decision not to hospitalise the patient (who shortly after had killed himself), Griffin J. reasoned that observation and restriction of a patient's freedom may, if too rigid, work counter-productively, aggravating the patient's sense of worthlessness. The judge proposed that doctors should continue to opt for hospitalisation only if there is a real risk of suicide.

---

[29] *Knight v. Home Office* [1990] 3 All E.R. 237.
[30] *Hyde v. Tameside Area Health Authority, supra*, n. 17.
[31] Weir (1998), p. 242.
[32] See *supra*, pp. 47–48.
[33] *Haines v. Bellissimo* (1977) 82 D.L.R. (3d) 215.

Chapter 3

The Professional Standard of Care

The tort of professional negligence rests upon a set of principles which apply generally to the professions. What most distinguishes it from generic negligence law is the *extent* to which the defence of general and approved or customary practice may be successfully invoked. This type of defence avails non-professionals, as *persuasive* evidence of the appropriate legal standard of care.[1] By contrast, the courts are content to permit *professional* general practice to act as their touchstone when evaluating the standard of care required by law of professional practitioners. This approach is predicated on various assumptions of the professions. For instance, professional customary practice is assumed to be more co-ordinated, and to act upon ethical principles as opposed to wholly financial concerns. Members of the professions are called on to apply professional *judgment*, a process which draws both from learning and experiential wisdom, so that accordingly they "are not to be held responsible for results, but only for the kind of service rendered by them."[2] A professional holds himself out to possess at least the qualification, skill, and competence ordinarily expected of members of his profession. In other words, in professional cases unlike commercial cases, it may be assumed that the defendant has implicitly given an undertaking "only to employy

---

[1] *Morris v. West Hartlepool Steam Navigation Co. Ltd* [1956] A.C. 552; *Cavanagh v. Ulster Weaving* [1960] A.C. 145; *Hughes Dairies v. Kennedy* [1989] I.L.R.M. 122.

[2] *Block v. McKay* 126 N.W. 2d 808 (1964) at 811, *per* Parker J. According to Tindal C.J. in *Lanphier v. Phibos* (1838) 8 C. & P. 475: "Every person who enters into a learned profession undertakes to bring to the exercise of it a reasonable degree of care and skill. He does not undertake, if he is an attorney, that at all events you will gain your case, nor does a surgeon undertake that he will perform a cure; nor does he undertake to use the highest possible degree of skill."

customary treatment methods."[3] Although "a higher degree of skill is required of him than of one who does not profess to be so qualified by special training and ability",[4] the scope of the defendant's skill is to be understood primarily in terms of the profession that trained and updates the skill. Thus it is that a "doctor is not guilty of negligence if he has acted in accordance with a practice accepted as proper by a responsible body of medical men skilled in that particular art."[5]

This type of assessment may conveniently be referred to as the *professional standard*, since for the most part it determines the standard of care owed by professional defendants according to rules and guidelines set and followed within the given profession. Though it evolved for legitimate reasons (part of which must be understood by reference to the history and culture of the professions, discussed in chapter 1), the consistent experience of common law jurisdictions has been that the medical negligence model *when applied* is markedly weighted against plaintiffs. This is chiefly due to the impenetrability of the defence of approved medical practice, which tends to rest upon enthusiastic collegial support and (where the issues relate to diagnosis and treatment) upon a range of complex technical issues which the court is comparatively unequipped or disinclined to censure with the rigour it elsewhere displays.

Rules and Provisos

English medical negligence law takes its lead rather regrettably from a first instance decision, now some three decades old, reached in the case of *Bolam v. Friern Hospital*.[6] The plaintiff had suffered fractures in the course of electro-convulsive therapy which he had agreed to undergo at the defendants' advice to alleviate a mental illness. The patient coupled a claim of negligent administration of relaxant anaesthetics with a further claim that the defendants had negligently failed to warn him of the risk of injury. In a pithy decision which continues to endear itself to the sensibilities of English judges as *the*

---

[3] Linden (1973), p. 33.
[4] *Crits v. Sylvester* (1956) O.R. 132 at 143, CA, aff'd [1956] S.C.R. 991. See also *Ashcroft v. Mersey Regional Health Authority* [1983] 2 All E.R. 245: the more skilled a person is, the more he may be expected to exercise care.
[5] *Bolam v. Friern Hospital Management Committee* [1957] 2 All E.R. 118 at 122.
[6] *ibid.*

Bolam test, McNair J. went to great lengths to ensure not only that the defendants were fully exonerated, but that the bulk of subsequent malpractice claims would flounder. In a rather cold analysis of the relevant negligence law principles, the learned judge emphasised that "[w]hen you approach the case and consider whether it has been proved against the defendants that negligence was committed, you have to bear in mind the enormous benefits which are conferred on men and women by this form of treatment".[7] Further, the dependence of society on an effective health care system, unhampered by the threat of litigation, required a different approach to proof of negligence, according to which a "doctor is not guilty of negligence if he has acted in accordance with a practice accepted as proper by a responsible body of medical men skilled in that particular art . . . Putting it the other way round, a doctor is not negligent, if he is acting in accordance with such a practice, merely because there is a body of opinion that takes a contrary view."[8]

The English courts have often remarked that the *Bolam* test implicitly contains within itself its own quality control system, since it is subject to the caveat that expert medical opinion must be "respectable and responsible".[9] In *Bolitho v. City & Hackney Health Authority*, its most recent analysis of the standard of care, the House of Lords defended the professional standard test by highlighting McNair J.'s references in *Bolam* to the defendant's need to show that he followed a course regarded as proper by a *"responsible"* body of medical men or *"a competent reasonable* body of opinion."[10] The use of these adjectives suggested to Lord Browne-Wilkinson in *Bolitho* that "the court has to be satisfied that the exponents of the body of opinion relied upon can demonstrate that such opinion has a *logical basis"*; further, that in assessing whether this is the case, the judge must ascertain whether "the experts have directed their minds to the question of comparative risks and benefits and have reached a *defensible* conclusion on the matter."[11]

Bolitho has since been interpreted as a partial attempt to reclaim some of the power unwisely delegated in the past to the medical

---

[7] *Bolam v. Friern Hospital Management Committee, supra*, n. 5, at 120.

[8] *ibid.* at 122.

[9] *Hills v. Potter* [1984] 1 W.L.R. 641 at 653, *per* Hirst J.

[10] *Bolitho v. City and Hackney Health Authority* [1998] A.C. 232 at 241. The House was further influenced by Lord Scarman's reference in *Maynard v. West Midlands Regional Health Authority* [1984] 1 W.L.R. 634 at 639, to a "respectable body of professional opinion."

[11] *Bolitho, ibid.* at 242 (emphasis added).

profession, although its reference to "logical basis" seems unnecessarily narrow.[12] Ostensibly under this model, the court's central point of enquiry becomes whether the professional practices upheld by the defence's experts are "truthfully expressed", "honestly held", or supported by "distinguished medical men"—words used by Lord Scarman in *Maynard v. West Midlands Regional Health Authority*, where he stressed on appeal that "in the realm of diagnosis and treatment negligence is not established by preferring one respectable body of professional opinion to another."[13] That this in fact never affects how the *professional standard* test is seen to apply is obvious by the complete absence of case examples of any such enquiry.[14] In real terms, it enables the court in all but extreme cases to assume a less hands-on approach to the malpractice claim—a state of affairs hinted at by Dillon L.J. in *Bolitho* when he proposed that the court will only reject medical opinion as testimonially endorsed if it appears "*Wednesbury* unreasonable".[15] His Lordship's incorporation of the well-known administrative law concept[16] was unexpected, if somewhat telling, serving to emphasise that only in very exceptional cases will the court override the stated views of expert medical witnesses; and it is well-known that the Court of Appeal queried its merits on a later occasion.[17] Yet the *Wednesbury* analogy may well afford the most truthful account of the standard of care as currently assessed by the English courts in medical negligence cases. The courts remain highly reluctant to be seen to censure expert medical opinion. Indeed, Lord Browne-Wilkinson admitted in *Bolitho* that in the "vast majority of

---

[12] McKeown (1998) p. 249; Teff (1998).

[13] *Supra,* n. 10, at 639.

[14] In a rare instance of judicial comment on the proper conduct of expert testimony, Lord Wilberforce observed in *Whitehouse v. Jordan* [1981] 1 W.L.R. 246 at 256–257, that whilst "some degree of consultation between experts and legal advisers is entirely proper, it is necessary that expert evidence to the court should be, and should be seen to be, the independent product of the expert, uninfluenced as to form and content by the exigencies of litigation".

[15] *Bolitho v. City and Hackney Health Authority* (1992) 13 B.M.L.R. 111 at 132, CA.

[16] This was a reference to the doctrine laid down in the case of *Associated Pictures Houses Ltd v. Wednesbury Corporation* [1948] 1 K.B. 223, for the purposes of judicially reviewing exercises of discretionary powers delegated to agents of the state. The House of Lords opted for a highly restricted concept of reasonableness, preferring to focus instead on the process employed by the defendants in reaching their decision. It was later explained in *Chief Constable of the North Wales Police v. Evans* [1982] 1 W.L.R. 1155 that this inheres in an awareness that to intrude any further into delegated powers would be to usurp important public decision-making functions.

[17] *Joyce v. Merton, Sutton & Wandsworth Health Authority* (1996) 7 Med. L.R. 1 at 20, *per* Hobhouse L.J.

cases the fact that distinguished experts in the field are of a particular opinion will demonstrate the reasonableness of that opinion".[18] In this context, "it will seldom be right for a judge to reach the conclusion that views genuinely held by a competent medical expert are unreasonable."[19]

The professional standard model, by its terms and wording, is constructed to restrict the court's freedom to critically evaluate the defendant's conduct beyond the context of professional approved practice.[20] This was vividly demonstrated in a pivotal Irish decision, *Dunne v. National Maternity Hospital.*[21] An obstetrician engaged by the plaintiff child's mother had conducted his instructions for the plaintiff's delivery over the phone to a nurse and doctor on duty at the hospital. A scan revealed the mother to be bearing twins. The nurse informed the obstetrician that one foetal heart beat had been identified, and later that labour was very slow. He recommended that the mother take walking exercises, and later that she be put on a drip. When subsequently the plaintiff incurred foetal distress and was born permanently brain damaged through lack of oxygen to the brain, the crucial question became whether it had been negligent of the doctor to be satisfied with the location of only one heart. An army of experts testified, and showed clear division on the merits of locating a second heart and on the cause of the plaintiff's brain damage. The trial judge directed the jury that it was to determine, amongst other things, whether the obstetrician should have identified both heart beats, and whether he should have taken a scan and then delivered the twin by caesarian section. The jury answered in the affirmative to each question, and damages in excess of £1 million were awarded against the hospital. The defendants appealed to the Supreme Court, challenging the set of issues identified for the jury. In upholding the appeal and directing a retrial, Finlay C.J. decided that the court is restricted to considering whether the evidence for the plaintiff is capable of sustaining his allegations—but not whether the court prefers one body of testimony over another. Thus, the trial judge was not entitled to direct the jury to decide whether or not an obstetrician was negligent in actually arranging to locate only one of two foetal

---

[18] *Bolitho v. City and Hackney Health Authority, supra* n. 10 at 243.
[19] *ibid.*
[20] e.g. in *Maynard v. West Midlands Regional Health Authority, supra*, n. 10, judgment was reversed because the trial judge had wrongly favoured one body of expert medical opinion over another.
[21] *Dunne v. National Maternity Hospital* [1989] I.R. 91.

hearts when the patient was bearing twins. At most it was empowered to consider whether the doctor had been "guilty of such failure as no medical practitioner of equal specialist or general status and skill would be guilty of if acting with ordinary care."[22]

Finlay C.J. further explained that even where the plaintiff seeks to establish negligence by pointing to a departure by the defendant from customary practice, the plaintiff must further establish that the course he took was "one which no medical practitioner of like specialisation and skill would have followed had he been taking the ordinary care required from a person of his qualifications."[23] This approach to departure from orthodox medical practice is evidently rooted in the courts' unwillingness to condemn "an honest difference of opinion between eminent doctors, as to which is the better of two ways of treating a patient".[24] In practice, it translates to mean that the plaintiff must invoke testimonial proof that the defendant's decision was utterly *indefensible*. In the post-*Dunne* case of *Edwards v. Jenkins*, O'Hanlon J. seemed for the most part to favour the views of the plaintiff's expert, a practitioner and academic from England who had voiced strong disagreement with the defendants' decision to drain the plaintiff's post-natal infection conservatively using "wicks" and antibiotics.[25] However, the learned judge felt compelled to conclude that this divergence in views was not enough because the alternate method had "not been shown to have obtained anything like *universal* acceptance in the medical profession as *the only method*, or *the best method* which can be adopted for the treatment of such cases."[26]

This approach has alternately been justified on the basis that if "a deviation from ordinary professional practice [were] necessarily evidence of negligence . . . all inducement to progress in medical science would then be destroyed".[27] It is a view that has understandably attracted criticism on the basis that once a departure from

---

[22] *Dunne v. National Maternity Hospital* [1989] I.R. 91 at 109.

[23] *ibid*. This did not mean that a defendant must systematically be exonerated if he has the support merely of one reputable doctor (an unlikely state of affairs, at any rate, for a medical negligence case that has not thus far settled). Though the defendant may rely in his defence upon a practice which falls short of universal support, he must establish that that practice is "approved of and adhered to by a substantial number of reputable practitioners holding the relevant specialist or general qualifications."

[24] *Daniels v. Heskin* [1954] I.R. 73 at 85.

[25] *Edwards v. Jenkins* Irish High Court, unreported, January 20, 1989.

[26] *ibid*. at 20–21 (emphasis added).

[27] *Hunter v. Hanley* [1955] S.C. 200 at 206, *per* Clyde L.

customary practice is proved, it should be prima facie evidence of negligence requiring explanation by the defence.[28] According to Professor Linden, "if most are already complying with a custom, it must be practicable for those who are not yet conforming thereto."[29] There is indeed good reason to adopt this stance where the defendant is shown to have recommended an unnecessarily high-risk procedure or treatment that is novel, innovative, or experimental (a fact which must be disclosed to the patient[30]). There is, on the other hand, a real danger that applying such a rule would exasperate a natural tendency amongst doctors to behave defensively, and moreover that this would breed the worst type of conservatism, where a new advance—be it treatment or the recommendation of medication—is resisted for no other reason than that it is *new*.

A more sensible solution to the inequities of the professional standard model would surely lie in a reformulation of the standard of care, a restructuring of the words that compose this test, whereby the court is encouraged and is seen to preside more vigorously over the expert testimony produced by either side. Evidence of compliance with general and approved practice ought to be accepted as naturally persuasive evidence that the defendant was not negligent, and no more. When a defendant is shown to have departed from orthodox medical practice, the case for liability naturally becomes stronger, though the higher courts seem reluctant to concede this point lest it be mistaken for a general principle. Illustrative cases, as one might expect from this body of law, are few. In *Clark v. MacLennon* the defendant performed a post-natal operation four weeks after birth where approved practice was to wait until three months after birth. Peter Pain J. found for the plaintiff on the basis that the defendant had not adduced adequate justifications for his departure from general practice.[31] In *Hepworth v. Kerr*, an anaesthetist was found negligent for adopting an innovative and insufficiently tested procedure that involved reducing the patient's blood pressure lower than the accepted level, ultimately causing the plaintiff's stroke.[32]

Under the current model, customary practice has been artificially elevated as determinative in most cases of no negligence—even in

---

[28] Linden (1973), p. 35. This view is shared by Professor Fleming (1987), p. 109.
[29] Linden (1973), p. 34.
[30] So affirmed by the Alberta Court of Appeal in *Zimmer v. Ringrose* (1981) 16 C.C.L.T. 51.
[31] *Clark v. MacLennon* [1983] 1 All E.R. 416.
[32] *Hepworth v. Kerr* (1995) 6 Med. L.R. 139. See also *Cryderman v. Ringrose* (1978) 89 D.L.R. (3d) 32.

instances (such as disclosure practices) where the existence of a consensus sufficient enough to merit the epithet *general, customary,* or *approved* is unlikely to exist.[33] Below, I consider the full implications of a system of law that surrenders such a vital part of its decision-making process to expert medical witnesses. For now, it is necessary to identify the exceptions, qualifications, and provisos that have emerged in this increasingly categorical field of law.

In England, much critical attention has been devoted to the literal scope of qualifications to the professional standard test as they appear to arise, and for a time it appears to have been the view of some that the professional standard or *Bolam* test was utterly unqualified, and that the court was bound whether it liked it or not, by strongly expressed expert medical opinion. Lord Diplock's resonant and unqualified endorsement of the professional standard in *Sidaway v. Bethlem Royal Hospital* may be accused of having perpetuated this myth.[34] Thus the felicitous surprise when a Court of Appeal decision in the 1968 case of *Hucks v. Cole* was rescued from obscurity in the *Bolitho* case,[35] until finally it was seen to have emerged as a chink in the gilded armour of the *Bolam* test.[36]

In *Hucks v. Cole*, Sachs L.J. had justified imposing liability on the defendant for failing to treat the plaintiff with penicillin, on the basis that

> "[w]hen the evidence shows a lacuna in professional practice exists by which risks of grave danger are knowingly taken, then, however small the risks, the court must anxiously examine that lacuna—particularly if the risks can be easily and inexpensively avoided. If the court finds . . . that, in the light of current professional knowledge, there is no proper basis for the lacuna, and that it is definitely not reasonable that those risks should have been taken, its function is to state that fact and where necessary to state that it constitutes negligence . . . [And even where] other practitioners would have done the same thing as the defendant . . . . [t]he court must be vigilant to see whether

---

[33] See *infra*, p. 77.

[34] *Sidaway v. Bethlem Royal Hospital* [1985] 1 A.C. 871 at 890–895 (HL). See chapter 5, *infra*, pp. 141–142.

[35] *Hucks v. Cole* (1993) 4 Med. L.R. 393 in *Bolitho v. City and Hackney Health Authority*, *supra*, n. 10.

[36] Harpwood (1996).

the reasons given for putting a patient at risk are valid in the light of any well-known advance in medical knowledge, or whether they stem from a residual adherence to out-of-date ideas".[37]

Here at last, English law was perceived to have forged the legal basis for a genuine "qualification" to the otherwise all-prevailing professional standard—though not without the suspicion that Sachs L.J. had intended to limit his ruling to cases not involving two rival medical schools of thought, or to cases where experts testify that "they would have acted or might have acted in the same way as the defendant did for reasons which on examination do not really stand up to analysis."[38]

Judicial timidity and legalese are ubiquitous throughout medical negligence law. This belies the fact that for some time (though rarely in the *medical* negligence sphere) the courts have recognised the institutional reality that they retain at the very least a residual power to override expert opinion, even where that opinion unanimously supports the defendant's propositions. The Irish courts, considerably more pragmatic in this regard, have repeatedly acknowledged this to be so. In *O'Donovan v. Cork County Council*, Walsh J. for the Supreme Court observed that "the fact that [a practice] is shown to have been widely and generally adopted over a period of time does not make the practice any the less negligent. Neglect of duty does not cease by repetition to be neglect of duty."[39] In this regard, the learned judge was merely repeating a truism articulated some six decades previously in an English case (albeit in a different context) by Lord Tomlin in *Bank of Montreal v. Dominion Gresham Guarantee & Casualty Company*.[40] A principle of this nature amounts to no more than a reaffirmation of a power the courts already possess, indeed a power the courts are constitutionally obliged to exercise. In this context, the principle serves to remind the medical community that ultimately the rule of law applies to doctors as equally as it applies to solicitors or engineers, and that in any case the courts are entitled to hold liable a defendant

---

[37] *Hucks v. Cole, supra*, n. 35, at 397.
[38] *ibid.* at 399.
[39] *O'Donovan v. Cork County Council* [1967] I.R. 173 at 193.
[40] *Bank of Montreal v. Dominion Gresham Guarantee & Casualty Company* [1930] A.C. 659 at 666: in condemning as negligence the defendant bankers' system of issuing unauthorised cheques, his Lordship ruled that "[n]eglect of duty does not cease by repetition to be neglect of duty."

whose adherence to general practice has been blind, lax, or inherently negligent.[41] In doing so, the court indirectly transmits a precedential warning to the profession, a useful deterrent that serves to remind it that it must take care to ensure its standards are updated and that its primary professional duty is to the individual client.[42]

For too long now it has been assumed that the legal standard of care owed by doctors is governed by expert testimony on appropriate medical practices within the profession. This blanket assumption forecloses assessments of the weight of such testimony in individual cases, and divorces the rule from its rationale. By contrast, the following observation by Parker J. endears itself more naturally to legal logic:

> "The general rule in medical malpractice cases is that the negligence of the physician or surgeon must be established by the testimony of medical experts. . . . The reason for the rule is that laymen are not qualified by learning and experience to judge the medical aspects of such cases. When the reason for the rule ceases to exist, the rule no longer applies."[43]

This principle has been applied from time to time in relation to matters not involving diagnostic or clinical skills, on which an ordinary person may presume to sensibly pass judgment. Thus in *Corn v. French*, Badt J. of the Supreme Court of Nevada could justify his verdict in favour of the plaintiff, despite the latter's failure to adduce countervailing expert medical evidence, on the grounds that the court may independently apply its "common knowledge of physical facts and of the natural laws that govern physical life".[44]

Though the professional standard model exists for valid reasons, the weight it attaches to expert medical evidence seems increasingly anachronistic, particularly in the context of the disclosure action, where again too tentatively the English courts have begun to recognise qualifications, of which perhaps the most favoured has been Lord

---

[41] *Roche v. Pielow* [1986] I.R. 189.

[42] *e.g. Helling v. Carey* 83 Wash. 2d 514 (1974), finding that ophthalmists ought to routinely examine patients for primary open angle glaucoma on the basis that though the condition is rare, testing is harmless, speedy, and inexpensive, and further that the condition if not detected at an early stage could become irreversible.

[43] *Block v. McKay, supra,* n. 2 at 810, *per* Parker J.

[44] *Corn v. French* 289 P. 2d 173 (1955), citing with approval *Burris v. Titzell* 189 Iowa 1322 and *Agnew v. City of Los Angeles* 82 Cal. App. 2d 616.

Bridge's in *Sidaway v. Bethlem Royal Hospital*. There, his Lordship acknowledged that even when expert medical testimony endorses the defendant's conduct, the court "might in certain circumstances come to the conclusion that disclosure of a particular risk was so obviously necessary to an informed choice on the part of the patient that no reasonably prudent medical man would fail to make it."[45] The disclosure action raises essentially non-technical issues which are readily comprehensible to the court; as such it exerts considerable pressure on the professional standard model to justify itself. Before evaluating what might and what ought to be the rationale for the professional standard, it is useful to consider the implications of a model that relies so strongly on expert medical witnesses.

The Expert Medical Witness

Perhaps the greatest challenge currently faced by our medical malpractice laws is how best to subdue the excesses of the professional standard model which, in theory and to an appreciable extent in practice, has served to exalt expert medical testimony at the expense often of common sense and impartiality. The practical implication of the professional standard enquiry is that the plaintiff fails to prove his case where the defendant produces credible expert opinion to support the course he took in the given circumstances: for, no matter how stridently the plaintiff's expert witnesses condemn the defendant's actions, the courts are disinclined to find negligence where there appears to be an honest difference of opinion between doctors (so long as each view seems to represent an approved or respectable strand of medical thought). It is thus usually the case that the *defendant's* expert medical testimony is pivotal if not determinative of the action. Before considering possible cures, it is necessary to identify the ills of this system, virtually all of which adversely affect the plaintiff.

In one rare instance of judicial candour, Justice Carter of the Supreme Court of California eloquently observed that "physicians who are members of medical societies flock to the defense of their fellow member charged with malpractice and the plaintiff is relegated, for his expert testimony, to the occasional lone wolf or heroic

---

[45] *Sidaway v. Bethlem Royal Hospital, supra*, n. 34 at 900, HL. See Chapter 5, *infra*, pp. 138–140.

soul, who for the sake of truth and justice has the courage to run the risk of ostracism by his fellow practitioners and the cancellation of his public liability insurance policy."[46] That is to say that inevitably, members of the medical profession are institutionally and socially collegial.[47] One research survey of medical professionals revealed that in the hypothetical (and grossly negligent) scenario of a doctor who mistakenly removes a patient's good kidney instead of his diseased kidney, merely 31 per cent of specialists and 27 per cent of general practitioners expressed a willingness to testify on behalf of the plaintiff patient.[48] This problem is compounded further by an undeveloped assumption that the plaintiff is required in every medical negligence action to advance some expert medical evidence in support of his case.[49]

Potential medical experts for the defence are readily steered into a persuasive mentality by counsel whose primary aim is to successfully defend. The tendency of experts to be partisan, whether or not consciously, is stoked by the gladiatorial or adversarial nature of the trial which is the hallmark of common law procedure. Describing her experiences as an expert medical witness, Dr Yolande Lucire observes that when "perceived to be useful, the medical practitioner is wooed in the most flattering of tones, but when advice is inimical to the issue at hand the medical practitioner is subjected to insults in an attempt to rile and to discredit by causing the doctor to lose her cool".[50] This, of course, stems from the nature of the adversary

---

[46] *Huffman v. Lindquist* 234 P. 2d 34 (1951) at 46.

[47] According to Belli (1956), p. 255: "There's a camaraderie among doctors that doesn't exist among lawyers. They bloodlet, figuratively and literally, with each other. They sleep, not together, but with each other. They break bread together, and their school esprit de corps is high. Their professional ties are much more subtle, secret and esoteric than lawyers'. There's a morale that makes it unthinkable for one doctor, knowing the vagaries of his profession and the uncertainties of human life, to say that he could have done better than his fellow practitioner."

[48] Referred to in *Morris v. Metriyakool* 309 N.W. 2d. 910 (1981).

[49] This is suggested by the wording of the *Bolam* test, which emphasises (*supra*, n. 5 at 121) that the "true test . . . is whether [the defendant] *has been proved* to be guilty of such failure as no doctor of ordinary skill would be guilty of if acting with ordinary care." The court was presented with an untypical scenario in *Thake v. Maurice* [1984] 2 All E.R. 513 at 521–522 QB. On the one hand, the plaintiff had failed to produce expert testimony; on the other, the defendant admitted that he erred in failing to give a warning. In these circumstances, the court felt that to raise the *Bolam* argument against the plaintiff would be to turn an "utterly artificial argument" to mere "tactical advantage". This was endorsed by the Court of Appeal in *Thake v. Maurice* [1986] 1 All E.R. 497 at 506.

[50] Lucire, "The Expert Witness Self-Examined", in Winfield (1989) p. 89.

system, "a variant of hand to hand combat of selected gladiators, within the most rigidly formal and structured conditions."[51] On occasion, the judges have recognised this problem. In *Abbey National Mortgages Plc v. Key Surveyors Ltd*, Hicks J. observed that "expert witnesses instructed on behalf of parties to litigation often tend, if called as witnesses at all, to espouse the cause of those instructing them to a greater or lesser extent, on occasion becoming more partisan than the parties."[52] Though medical experts are unlikely ever to "wilfully misrepresent what they think, . . . their judgments become so warped by their regarding the subject in one point of view, that even when conscientiously disposed they are incapable of forming independent opinion."[53] Though potential work as an expert medical expert is unlikely to tempt a doctor consciously to serve the side that calls him, the tendency to evaluate the medical issues in a partisan light must to some extent be encouraged by the certain knowledge that expert witnesses are immune from subsequent actions in negligence grounded in their court-room testimony or pre-trial work.[54]

There is another dimension which one is compelled to identify somewhat more reluctantly, fearing to insult the integrity of the many experts for whom it is not an issue. An "expert is not like an ordinary witness, who hopes to get his expenses, but he is employed and paid in the sense of gain, being employed by the person who calls him . . . Undoubtedly there is a natural bias to do something serviceable for those who employ you and absolutely remunerate you."[55] Moreover, work as an expert witness can be a lucrative side-line to a professional career. The director of the Action for Victims of Medical Accidents in England ("AVMA")—which holds a database of about 2,000 potential experts for plaintiffs—has stated that it is "the best paid Saturday job on the market."[56] The extent to which experts can unwittingly become hired guns for one side of a dispute, and the

---

[51] Lucire, "The Expert Witness Self-Examined", in Winfield (1989), p. 89.

[52] *Abbey National Mortgages Plc v. Key Surveyors Ltd* [1996] 1 W.L.R. 1534 at 1542.

[53] Taylor (1931), p. 59.

[54] *Sutcliffe v. Thackrah* [1974] A.C. 727. Extended to the pre-trial preparation of a report in *Stanton v. Callaghan*, [1998] N.L.J. 1355.

[55] *Lord Abinger v. Ashton* (1973) 17 L.R. Eq. 358 at 374, *per* Jessel M.R.

[56] Cited in Bawdon (1996), pp. 1742–1743. The AVMA has revealed that experts can charge up to £200 for preparing a report and up to £1,500 for attending court. Nearly half of those surveyed admitted that they undertook this work whilst taking a day off work with pay.

damaging implications this may have for the integrity of the profession they represent, was recently highlighted by a study of 500 psychiatrists for the Institute of Psychiatry in England.[57] 25 per cent of those surveyed conceded that they had been asked to alter or edit their reports. 50 per cent of these agreed to make crucial changes even to their conclusions. In many instances, selective editing had been performed by lawyers: indeed 90 per cent of the requests to amend had been made by solicitors. In a recent test of claims against the Workers' Compensation Board of New York, it was found that while 99.5 per cent of doctors consulted by claimants concluded that their claimants were suffering a disability, only 24 per cent of doctors for the insurers reached the same conclusion.[58]

It is also the case that defendants, better placed to corral support within the medical profession, tend often to dominate the trial with a display of numerical supremacy. This tendency to flood the court with "big battalions of expert witnesses" has occasionally been criticised by judges.[59] Nonetheless, it persists. Indeed, one judge recently decided, albeit with some reluctance, that the court lacks the power to deny expert evidence or to limit the number of experts even where it feels that expert evidence is not strictly necessary.[60]

According to Jackson and Powell, the expert witness has two broad functions in court.[61] First, he attempts to decode and explain the technical issues as far as possible in layman's language; in the medical context, this will involve explaining the plaintiff's original condition, the type of treatment recommended, the effect of treatment on the plaintiff, and the nature of his resulting injuries. This strand was explained by Finlay C.J. in *Dunne v. National Maternity Hospital*—a decision as influential in Ireland as *Bolam* is in England—on the basis that medical "facts are incapable of being established by direct evidence of actual observation. Instead they fall necessarily to be proved by inferences drawn from, or analyses made of, diagnostic signs [as] recorded . . . Such inferences and analyses . . . cannot be drawn or made by a layman, except by the acceptance by him of expert medical evidence sworn before him as to the conclusions to be drawn from diagnostic signs."[62]

---

[57] *The Sunday Times*, May 12, 1996.
[58] Haddad (1987).
[59] *Midland Bank Trust v. Stubbs & Kemp* [1978] 3 All E.R. 571 at 582, *per* Oliver J.
[60] *Rawlinson v. Westbrook, The Times*, January 25, 1995.
[61] Jackson and Powell (1987), pp. 308–309.
[62] *Supra*, n. 21 at 108.

Secondly, the medical expert may assist the court in determining the standard of care owed in the circumstances by the defendant doctor to the plaintiff patient. The expert may testify to general and approved medical practices, different schools of thought, and the state of scientific knowledge at the time of the incident. This second strand is considerably more controversial, being nakedly more judgmental than the first. It enables, if not encourages, the defence's experts to testify decisively on the propriety of the defendant's conduct, and in the vacuum of the trial to convince the court that the course adopted by the defendant was an approved and respectable one in the circumstances. One doctor, with many years' experience as an expert medical witness, criticises the pro-defendant bias of the professional standard test, and confirms the author's suspicion that "[e]nquiry will often indicate that the expert's evidence is not supported by his own clinical practice; nevertheless his evidence is generally accepted by the court without question."[63] In truth, the professional standard approach is far too absolutist; it overlooks the fact that in many instances, expert evidence of general or approved medical practices is simply inappropriate. This is especially so for the disclosure action. The following observations by Myers were directly incorporated into *Canterbury v. Spence*, the decision that would become the launch-pad for informed consent doctrine,[64] and it is difficult to cavil with their logic:

> [B]ecause a physician supposedly considers his patient's emotional and mental as well as his physical condition in deciding to disclose, and because each patient is mentally and emotionally unique, there can be no single established custom concerning disclosure; if there is one, it is so general as to be of little value. An expert witness, not bound in his testimony by an established custom, can testify in one of two fashions. He can say what he would have done under the circumstances, or he say what he thinks a reasonable doctor would have done under the circumstances. In either case, the physician is constructing a personal standard and is not really stating the custom of a professional community."[65]

---

[63] Harris (1992), p. 206.
[64] *Canterbury v. Spence* (1972) 464 F. 2d 772 at 783–784, *per* Robinson J. See Chapter 4, *infra*, pp. 91–93, 98–100.
[65] Myers (1967), p. 1404.

A current controversy in America concerns the extent to which a burgeoning specialisation of knowledge should be reflected in the types of expert evidence admissible before the courts. Liberal admissibility rules run the risk of obfuscating the issues in each case, further estranging the court whilst encouraging the exploitation of "junk science". In *Daubert v. Merrell Dow Pharmaceuticals Inc.*, the U.S. Supreme Court sought to impose new limits by requiring that to qualify as "scientific knowledge", the "expertise" must have validated its theory or technique by proper scientific methodology.[66] The specialisation of knowledge carries implications for the future scope of the professional negligence action, particularly in light of the common law's past failure to critically identify the criteria which entitle an occupation to avail of the special rules governing allegations of *professional* negligence.[67]

The trend of specialisation within the medical profession continues, and may in future cases pose difficult challenges to the courts, given that a defendant specialist will seek to be judged according to the specialty or subspecialty which explains his action in the most favourable light. In *De Freitas v. O'Brien & Connolly*, the plaintiff relied on the observations of Hirst J. in *Hills v. Potter*, that in every case the court must be satisfied that the standard contended for by the defence accords with that upheld by a substantial body of respectable and responsible medical opinion.[68] The defendant had initially trained as an orthopaedic surgeon, but had proceeded to specialise with considerable success in spinal surgery. At the trial he insisted that he be judged according to the standard of spinal surgeons—who numbered some eight or so in the country, out of about 1,000 orthopaedic surgeons. Approved practice within the spinal surgery community favoured surgery in the instant case; approved practice within the orthopaedic surgery community did not. In the event, Otton L.J. for the Court of Appeal concluded that the trial judge had not erred in judging the defendant by the standards of the spinal surgery community, which represented a responsible body of medical opinion. His Lordship clearly felt that *substantial* for the purposes of testing liability is a qualitative not a quantitative concept:

---

[66] *Daubert v. Merrell Dow Pharmacueticals Inc.* (1993) 113 S.C.T. 2786.
[67] The courts have addressed this mainly in the context of tax law, in determining the schedule under which a worker should be assessed, *e.g. Commissioners of Inland Revenue v. Maxse* [1919] 1 K.B. 647.
[68] *De Freitas v. O'Brien & Connolly* (1995) 6 Med. L.R. 108, citing *Hills v. Potter* [1984] 1 W.L.R. 641 at 653.

"The issue whether or not to operate could not be determined by counting heads."[69] However, he cautioned that if "it appears from the evidence that the body of medical opinion relied on by the defendant is both very small and diametrically opposed in its views to the conventional views of the vast majority of medical practitioners, the court should be vigilant in carrying out its duty to test whether the body of medical opinion relied on by the defendant is a 'responsible' body."[70]

The rules governing expert opinion testimony are, according to time-honoured authority, designed to enable "the opinion of scientific men upon proven facts [to] be given by men of science within their own science."[71] It has been argued that to properly qualify as expert testimony, the evidence must relate to a discipline which is consistent (though not necessarily uniform), methodical, cumulative, and predictive—of which medicine is usually proffered as the paradigm case.[72] The actual and potential limitations of expert science have been highlighted in recent years by the particular inexactitude of psychiatric evidence which has been accused by one as being "so unreliable and up for sale to the highest bidder that it is a national scandal."[73] Though psychiatrists are medical men and therefore men of science, there is a greater than usual difficulty in reaching consensus on key issues. Further, within psychiatry, "it is uniquely difficult to draw a line between matters of fact and matters of value"; the latter "may involve the tacit conveyance of a decision on principle and policy which it is not the province of the expert to make."[74] The courts have often relied on the expert evidence of psychiatrists to assess whether or not it could reasonably have been foreseen that a particular patient would have harmed himself or others.[75] Many theories have been constructed to explain aggressive or sociopathic behaviour: psychological experiences as a child such as exposure to adult violence; the biochemistry of the brain; the link between chromosomal abnormality and deviance.[76]

---

[69] *De Freitas v. O'Brien & Connolly* (1995) 6 Med. L.R. 108 at 115.
[70] *ibid*. at 114.
[71] *Folkes v. Chaad* (1782) 3 Doug. 157, *per* Lord Mansfield.
[72] Kenny (1983).
[73] Stanford, as cited by Kenny (1983), p. 214.
[74] *ibid*., p. 208.
[75] See Chapter 2, *supra*, pp. 47–48, 62.
[76] See generally: Diamond (1974); Megargee (1976); Monahon, "The Prevention of Violence" in Monahon (1976); and Shah (1978).

Many such as the chromosomal theory have been invalidated.[77] According to Diamond, the chief stumbling block in the path of predicting dangerousness is the lack of any clear-cut association between mental illness and dangerous behaviour.[78] He proposes that psychiatrists should emphasise the fact that they cannot with any certainty predict this dangerousness.[79] In exonerating a psychiatric decision to maintain on an out-patient basis a schizophrenic patient who shortly after committed suicide, Griffin J. for the Ontario High Court said: "Psychology and psychiatry are inexact sciences and the practice thereof should not be fettered with rules so strict as to exact an infallibility on the part of the practitioners which they could not humanly possess."[80]

The facility to call expert witnesses is a significant exception to the general evidentiary rule excluding opinion evidence, which rule is soundly predicated on the premise that it is for the court to form all the relevant inferences of fact and then to apply the law, anything else being a dangerous abrogation of the sovereign judicial function to develop and apply the law. Common law jurisprudence on the purpose and scope of expert testimony has for the most part concerned the expert in criminal trials, in which context the courts are considerably more vigilant to ensure that expert testimony does not purport to establish the very facts that the court is constitutionally obliged to establish to its own satisfaction.[81] This more muscular approach is exemplified by such rulings as that in *Davie v. Edinburgh Magistrates*, where Cooper L.J. asserted that the duty of experts "is to furnish the judge or jury with the necessary scientific criteria for testing the accuracy of *their own conclusions*, so as to enable the judge or jury to

---

[77] Center for Studies of Crime and Delinquency, National Institute of Mental Health, *Report of the XYY Chromosomal Abnormality* 33–34 (Public Health Service pub. No. 2103, 1970).

[78] Studies have revealed that mental illnesses which most often lead to dangerousness, such as schizophrenia and other psychoses, are not more prevalent in the criminal class than in general society. However, non-mental conditions such as sociopathy, alcoholism, and drug dependency have frequently been associated with criminality. See: Guze, Goodwin & Crane (1969); Guze, Tuason, Gatfield, Stewart & Ricker (1962); and Cloninger & Guze (1970).

[79] Diamond (1974), p. 452.

[80] *Haines v. Bellissimo* (1977) 82 D.L.R. (3d) 215 at 229.

[81] For example, in the Irish case of *DPP v. Kehoe*, Court of Criminal Appeal, unreported, November 6, 1991, O'Flaherty J. condemned as inadmissible the opinion of a psychiatrist on whether the accused intended to kill or was instead provoked; those inferences could only properly be formed, on the facts of the case, by the jury.

form *their own independent judgment* by the application of these criteria to the facts proved in evidence."[82] When experts express conclusions on issues of responsibility, they usurp the function of the court; yet experts are invariably asked to present their views on the defendant's culpability in medical negligence trials.

The disclosure claim has served to expose the weakness of the professional standard assessment of medical negligence, but also the increasingly central place which experts and specialists have come to occupy within society. From the latter half of this century, indeed from the second world war on, there has been an incremental assault upon the social powers wielded by the professions over vital human interests, and more generally against the so-called "tyranny of experts". This has been manifest in a growing transfer of allegiance to holistic and alternative remedies, and in the correlative demand by modern society for more transparency and access to information. It has gradually become recognised by many leading academics that excessive reliance by individuals and by society on experts may ultimately cause dysfunction. According to Freidson: "Faith which all men may possess and politics in which all citizens participate fade away before knowledge which only experts possess . . . The relation of the expert to modern society seems in fact to be one of the central problems of our time, for at its heart lies the issues of democracy and freedom and the degree to which ordinary men can shape the character of their own lives".[83]

There seems to be mounting support for the proposition that historically, the professions set out to obscure issues which were previously tangible to most lay-persons, and that the cultivation of an esoterically impenetrable discourse has been as much an aspiration of the professions as has been the development of an altruistic or vocational attitude.[84] The net effect of this process may well have been the dysgenic estrangement of the person from vital personal processes, culminating in correlative measures of fatalism and passivity:

---

[82] *Davie v. Edinburgh Magistrates* [1953] S.C. 34 (emphasis added). More recently, the English Court of Appeal in *R. v. Adams* [1996] Crim. L.R. 898 at 899 rejected an evaluation of evidence by means of scientific or mathematical formulae, favouring instead "the joint application of . . . individual common sense and knowledge of the world".

[83] Freidson (1970), pp. 335–336.

[84] See Bullough (1966); Carmichael and Ratzan (1991); Guthrie (1945); Katz (1984); Illich (1990); Kennedy (1983); and Leach (1972).

"The individual feels helplessly caught in a chaotic mass of data and with pathetic patience waits until the specialists have found out what to do and where to go. The result of this kind of influence is a twofold one: one is a scepticism and cynicism towards everything which is said or printed, while the other is a childish belief in anything that a person is told with authority. This combination of cynicism and naivete is very typical of the modern individual. Its essential result is to discourage him from doing his own thinking."[85]

Many post-war sociologists and historians turned their attention to the medical profession, in many ways an easy target. There is now much support for the argument that organised medical practice cultivated altruistic ideals, codes of ethics, and an esoteric professional dialect (from non-vernacular Latin in the fifth century to the lexicon of science in the early nineteenth century) as a strategy to ferment and then protect its own professional self-regulatory status.[86] The exaltation of medical judgment, rooted in the enduringly influential works of Hippocrates, was part of this process.[87] The inscrutable, transcendent nature of this judgment continues to be asserted by the medical profession, increasingly in a bid to maintain control over morally sensitive issues. Despite textual acknowledgment by numerous doctors of their localised resolution of such issues (for instance, passive euthanasia), the response of the medical profession to external decision-making, even if it be by the highest court in the land, is sometimes defensive, sanctimonious, and paternalistic in the extreme.[88] The independence of medical judgment and paternalism is usually implicit in defence arguments against disclosure in litigated cases, and it has largely been accepted by the higher English courts as part of their rejection of informed consent. [89] Yet that doctrine and other modern alternatives to the professional standard test reflect real changes in intellectual and societal attitudes which, it is submitted,

---

[85] Fromm (1942), p. 249–250).
[86] See Chapter 1, *supra*, pp. 11–15.
[87] See Chapter 1, *supra*, pp. 9–10.
[88] See Chapter 1, *supra*, pp. 34–38.
[89] Lord Diplock's speech in *Sidaway, supra*, n. 34 at 893, is paradigmatic of this view, particularly where he decides that the general duty of care on medical practitioners "is not subject to dissection into a number of component parts, to which different criteria of what satisfy the duty of care apply, such as diagnosis, treatment, advice (including warning of any risks of something going wrong however skilfully the treatment advised is carried out)."

will inevitably compel the very changes which the English judiciary currently resists.

Reconstructing the Professional Standard

Wherefore this deference which the common law has traditionally shown to evidence of customary medical practice? It must partly be understood by reference to the history and evolution of medicine as a profession[90]—partly also in terms of its close affiliation, historically, with the legal profession. It is one of the undoubted advantages of our time that it encourages continual re-evaluation and sometimes reform of the limitations variously imposed on the rights and freedoms of individuals. It is unsurprising, then, that the dominant contemporary justification for the professional standard assessment chooses in the main to emphasise, as it ought, the court's inability and lack of qualification to censure complex medical decisions and acts of judgment best comprehended by medical men.

In England, the customary practice defence was explained by McNair J. in the celebrated judgement he delivered at first instance in *Bolam v. Friern Hospital*, where he said that "where you get a situation which involves the use of some special skill or competence, then the test whether there has been some negligence or not is not the test of the man on the top of the Clapham omnibus, because he has not got this special skill. The test is the standard of the ordinary skilled man exercising and professing to have that special skill."[91] Somewhat tellingly, Finlay C.J. for the Irish Supreme Court put it that

> "it is not possible . . . for a judge of trial . . . to take upon itself the role of a determining, *scientific* authority resolving disputes between distinguished scientists in any particular line of technical expertise. The function which a court can *and must* perform in the trial of a case in order to acquire a just result, is *to apply common sense* and a careful understanding of the logic and likelihood of events to conflicting opinions and conflicting theories".[92]

---

[90] See Chapter 1, *supra*.
[91] *Bolam v. Friern Hospital, supra*, n. 5 at 121.
[92] *Best v. Wellcome Foundation* [1992] I.L.R.M. 609 at 626.

That this is often the unspoken benchmark dividing passive and active judicial decision-making is strongly suggested in Ireland by the fact that an overwhelming amount of the few successful malpractice suits in recent years related essentially to non-technical and administrative issues.[93]

One could conclude, certainly by force of contrast with solicitors' negligence, that a confident critical appreciation of the issues is more likely to prompt the court to exert its independence in shaping professional standards of care. Solicitors are frequently held liable in negligence by the courts, presumably because a shared professional dialect between judge and defendant considerably short-circuits the relevant factual and legal analyses.[94] The common law's response to *medical* negligence actions has always been marked by its invocation of extreme public policy interests (which I address in Chapter 8). The pronounced conservation of the so-called floodgates is continually evident in the courts' tendency to sensationally transform each *particular* allegation of medical negligence into the *paradigmatic*.[95] Yet these public policy interests are not as visibly applied to restrict other species of professional negligence. Indeed, in the case of *Midland*

---

[93] For instance: *Kelly v. Board of Governors of St Laurence's Hospital* [1989] I.L.R.M. 437, where the plaintiff should not have been taken off his medication before the defendants had fully ascertained the causes of his depression; *Armstrong v. Eastern Health Board* High Court, unreported, December 5, 1990, where a doctor failed to consult the plaintiff's hospital records before deciding not to give him a hospital bed (in which case, Egan J. overruled the sworn testimony of the doctor that, even if she had read the records of the plaintiff, she would still have felt obliged to send the plaintiff home); *O'Doherty v. Whelan* High Court, unreported, January 18, 1993, where a doctor failed to promptly arrange to take a urine sample from the patient; and *Healy v. North Western Health Board*, High Court, unreported, January 31,1996, where the defendants failed to make a proper pre-discharge assessment to ensure that the patient's depression was in remission.

Most of the winnable malpractice claims seem to settle out of court or, significantly, trigger off the doctrine of *res ipsa loquitur*. See: *Mahon v. Osborne* [1939] 2 K.B. 14; *Colins v. Hertfordshire County Council* [1947] K.B. 598; *Cassidy v. Ministry of Health* [1951] 2 K.B. 343; *Gray v. Mid Herts Hospital Management Committee* (1974) 118 S.J. 501; and *Saunders v. Leeds Western Health Authority* (1985) 129 S.J. 225.

[94] The courts have proved eager to shape the professional standard of care for solicitors. See, *e.g. Edward Wong Financial Co. v. Johnson Stokes & Master* [1984] A.C. 296, where the Privy Council deemed negligent a conveyancing practice which had been widely endorsed by solicitors in Hong Kong; and *Bristol & West Building Society v. Mothew*, CA [1996] N.L.J. 1273. Irish examples of solicitors' liability in negligence abound. See: *Taylor v. Ryan* High Court, unreported, March 10, 1983, *per* Murphy J; *Kelly v. Crowley* [1985] I.R. 212; *Roche v. Pielow* [1986] I.L.R.M. 189; *O'Connor v. First National Building Society* High Court, unreported, July 3, 1990, *per* Lynch J.; and *McMullen v. Farrell* High Court, unreported, February 18, 1992, *per* Barron J.

[95] See Chapter 8, *infra*, pp. 243–250.

Bank Trust v. Stubbs & Kemp, Oliver J. responded heatedly to the defendant solicitors' reliance on expert testimony of much the same character as that which is routinely relied on by doctors in disclosure trials.[96] The learned judge doubted not only the "value" but also the "*admissibility*" of "evidence which really amounts to no more than an expression of opinion by a particular practitioner of what he thinks he would have done had he been placed, hypothetically and without the benefit of hindsight, in the position of the defendants . . . that [being] the very question which it is the court's function to decide".[97] Of similar comparative interest is the Irish case of *Aro Road & Land Vehicles Ltd v. Insurance Corporation of Ireland*, arising from a decision by the High Court to defer to a general practice amongst insurers to treat non-disclosure of previous convictions as material to subsequent claims. The Supreme Court upheld the appeal on the basis that, in matters of "professional competence, a profession is not . . . permitted to be the final arbiter of standards of competence . . . [nor] to dictate a binding definition of what is reasonable."[98]

In this light, it is difficult to comprehend the ongoing reluctance of the English courts, and to a lesser extent the Irish courts, to dismantle the professional standard test as it applies to the disclosure action. That action requires the court to assess whether or not the defendant doctor ought by law to have divulged the existence of specific risk information to the plaintiff patient before the patient agreed to undergo the recommended treatment. The courts will naturally be reliant on expert medical evidence to comprehend the plaintiff's injuries and the range of risks associated with particular treatment options; but is it natural, sensible, or just that it should consider itself bound to entertain and in most cases to follow expert medical evidence that establishes (apparent) general practices not to disclose certain risks to patients on the grounds that generally it is not in the best interests of patients to be divulged this information? Disclosure issues are far more comprehensible to the court than issues arising from diagnostic or treatment decisions. Once expert testimony has enabled the court to assess the rough percentile risk of injury, the court is relatively unshackled by professional esoteria. Having listened to the opposing arguments, it may, if it chooses,

---

[96] *Midland Bank Trust v. Stubbs & Kemp, supra,* n. 59.

[97] *ibid.* at 582 (emphasis added).

[98] *Aro Road & Land Vehicles Ltd v. Insurance Corporation of Ireland* [1986] I.R. 403 at 412, *per* McCarthy J.

freely consider whether or not disclosure was required in the particular circumstances of the case. At this stage, it does not require a scholastic understanding of medical science or aetiology, but rather must consider as a matter of law where the rights and duties lie in the instant and in future case scenarios. It is this fact which prompted decisions in Canada, New Zealand, and much of North America to assess the disclosure action under *ordinary* negligence principles, tailored to the special nature of the disclosure action, by which the court is less formally restricted by expert medical evidence of the appropriate standard of care. The action was originally named *informed consent*, an appellation which itself generated much judicial and critical cavilling[99] but which endured chiefly for reasons of convenience. In many ways, the development was sustained by the awareness that it did not inherently *need* to be justified. It was, that is, a logical attempt to retrieve the power, and indeed duty, of the court to steer the course this type of dispute takes.

Quite clearly, prejudice against plaintiffs, or something like a presumption that findings of medical negligence will be exceptional, is implicit in the articulation of the rules that ultimately forged the professional standard model. The practical effect has been to disable the court, and at one time the jury, from passing judgement on any professional decision which accords with a legitimate school or practice within the medical profession. One view of these rules is that they were implicitly designed to reduce the extent to which a jury of lay-persons—exposed, unlike the judge, to medical negligence issues for the first time—could legitimately censure complex medical decisions which require years of professional training and experience to digest.[1] There must also have been a sense that juries are more likely to sympathise disproportionately with the (often irreparably afflicted) patient, and to pin liability on the deep pocketed defendant. The abolition of jury trials for the bulk of personal injury actions in England and Ireland might have been expected to lead to some relaxation of medical negligence rules, given that those rules seemed

---

[99] Its nomenclatural awkwardness (confusingly referring to *consent* in the context of a *negligence* claim) has caused many to criticise it as a guiding title. See: *Reibl v. Hughes* (1980) 114 D.L.R. 3d 1; *White v. Turner* (1981) 120 D.L.R. 3d 269; and *Rogers v. Whitaker* (1992) 109 A.L.R. 625. See also: Clements (1995); Katz (1977); Feng (1987); and Plante (1968).

[1] Healy (1995), pp. 196–197. See for example, *Whitehouse v. Jordan, supra,* n. 14 at 246, *per* Denning L.J.: "Medical malpractice claims [in the U.S.] are very worrying, especially as they are tried by juries who have sympathy for the patient and none for the doctor, who is insured."

contrived to surrender much of the jury's decision-making power to expert witnesses. Whether or not one accepts that malpractice trials by judge alone are necessarily fairer or more accurate, the arguments in favour of restructuring the legal tests, especially as they apply to disclosure whose issues are more palpable, would seem to be enhanced by the transition.

It has been the practice of judicial pronouncements in England, symbolically an unfortunate one, to continually emphasise that honest differences between doctors do not infer negligence, nor necessarily do errors or misadventures, and that the court is bound by affirmative expert testimony, subject to some few bewilderingly literal exceptions. These have been artificially elevated to the status of tests which are wrongly presumed to tie the court's hands. The professional standard rules ought to be interpreted to derive from the court's *inability* rather than *disinclination* to assess difficult esoteric medical decisions with the rigour it would otherwise display. What results is a surfeit of legal principle and qualification in a sphere that is not intrinsically more legalistic than others.[2]

Given that it has faced tremendous critical pressure in England for almost a decade, it is astonishing that the *Bolam* test has survived this far. It is, however, important to note that there are visible signs of détente. Numerous first instance decisions in England suggest a mounting dissatisfaction with the professional standard model, particularly as it applies to disclosure issues, and a willingness to preside more rigorously over the facts in issue.[3] For instance, in *Joyce v. Merton, Sutton and Wandsworth Health Authority*, Overend J. decided that when the court is faced with alternative bodies of medical opinion, it is not precluded from reaching an assessment of the standard of care that should have been exercised in the circumstances.[4] Rather, it must ascertain that the clinical practice followed by the defendant stood up to analysis and was not unreasonable: "It is not enough for the defendant to call a number of doctors to say that what he has done or not done was in accord with accepted clinical

---

[2] See, *e.g.* Carswell, Lord Chief Justice of Northern Ireland (1997). Carswell C.J. misinterpets the North American doctrine of informed consent as having endorsed liability in battery for non-disclosure. On this basis, he criticises the decision in *Sidaway* to adopt the professional standard approach to disclosure, when instead it should favour the application of regular negligence principles.

[3] See Chapter 5, *infra*, pp. 144–145.

[4] *Joyce v. Merton, Sutton & Wandsworth Health Authority* (1995) 6 Med. L.R. 60.

practice. It is necessary for the judge to consider the evidence and decide whether that clinical practice puts the patient unnecessarily at risk."[5] This was affirmed on appeal by the Court of Appeal where Roch L.J. added that any other interpretation would leave the question of negligence in the hands of the doctors, "whereas that question must at the end of the day be one for the courts."[6]

Greatly to be preferred is the approach taken recently by the Australian courts, which benefits from the freshness of first principles. In *F. v. R.*, King C.J. for the Supreme Court of South Australia asserted that the "professions may adopt unreasonable practices . . . not because they serve the interests of the clients, but because they protect the interests or convenience of members of the profession. The court has an obligation to scrutinise professional practices to ensure that they accord with the standard of reasonableness imposed by law."[7] Bollen J. observed that the English cases tend to concentrate disproportionately on the practice of the medical profession. *F. v. R.* was applied subsequently in *E. v. Australia Red Cross Society*, where Wilcox J. of the Federal Court of Australia observed that, whilst "evidence of the practice usually adopted by persons in the position of a defendant will generally be of great assistance, and often decisive, the way must be left open to a plaintiff to persuade the court that the practice does not ensure an adequate standard of care."[8] This approach has the advantage of treating evidence of approved medical practice in much the same light as it does evidence in any case where a defendant belongs to a particular category or activity which follows in-house practices and guidelines.

In its high-profile decision of *Rogers v. Whitaker*, the Australian High Court refused to follow English law, represented by the *Bolam* and *Sidaway* decisions, declaring that the disclosure action raises matters "of simple common sense" rather than technical expertise beyond the comprehension of the court.[9] Accordingly, the court, and not the medical expert, determines the standard of care required by law. More recently in *Lowns v. Woods*, the Court of Appeal for New South Wales interpreted *Rogers v. Whitaker* to have rejected the *Bolam* test in its application not just to disclosure but also to diagnosis and

---

[5] *Joyce v. Merton, Sutton & Wandsworth Health Authority* (1995) 6 Med. L.R. 60 at 64.
[6] *Joyce v. Merton, Sutton & Wandsworth Health Authority* (1996) 7 Med. L.R. 1 at 14.
[7] *F. v. R.* (1983) 33 S.A.S.R. 189.
[8] *E. v. Australia Red Cross Society* (1991) 2 Med. L.R. 303 at 329.
[9] *Rogers v. Whitaker, supra*, n. 99 at 635. See Chapter 4, *supra*, pp. 105–107.

treatment.[10] However, it recognised that where the defence shows that the defendant followed general and approved medical practice, a heavy forensic duty shifts to the plaintiff to establish that that practice did not conform with the standard of reasonable care demanded by law in the circumstances.

---

[10] *Lowns v. Woods* [1996] Australian Torts Reports 81.

Chapter 4

Jurisdiction and Scope of Informed Consent

Informed Consent Law

Though the notion of an *informed consent* had been identified some time earlier in America,[1] it was not until the celebrated decision of *Canterbury v. Spence* in 1972 that informed consent was fully articulated as a legal doctrine.[2] The *Canterbury* decision represents a milestone in the history and evolution of the pre-treatment duty to disclose medical information, largely because it clarified developments which had taken root at the turn of the century but which had begun to result in uncertainty and inconsistency throughout the States.

The 19-year-old plaintiff had been suffering shoulder pains. Suspecting that the cause of this was a ruptured disc, Dr Spence ordered a laminectomy, which entailed surgical removal of the bony arches of the patient's vertebrae to expose his spinal cord. After the plaintiff's mother was told that this was "not anymore serious than

---

[1] Rather ironically, the phrase *informed consent* was coined in an *amicus curia* (or friend-of-the-court brief) submitted by the American College of Surgeons to the California Court of Appeals in *Salgo v. Leland Stanford Jr University Board of Trustees* 154 Cal. App. 2d 560, 317 P. 2d 170 (1957). The phrase was not, as thought by some (*e.g.* Ormrod (1989) p. 7), plundered by American malpractice lawyers from the English translation of the 1964 Declaration of Helsinki (promulgated by the World Medical Association in response to the Nazi atrocities).

[2] *Canterbury v. Spence* 464 F. 2d 772 (1972). This District Court decision was immediately accepted as an authoritative launching pad for informed consent; yet it was not until *Crain v. Allison* 443 A. 2d 558 (1982) that the opportunity arose for endorsement by a superior court of Columbia.

any other operation", she signed a consent. Shortly after the operation, the patient fell from his bed and hours later experienced full paralysis from the waist down. His mother signed another consent form, and the patient was again operated upon, resulting in some improvement of his muscle control. At the time of the trial, he remained partially paralysed. It was argued on behalf of Dr Spence that disclosure of minute risks of complication was not sound medical practice since it potentially deterred patients from undergoing much needed surgery, and often caused adverse psychological reactions inimical to contemplated treatment. In a rather disingenuous attempt to justify this general policy, the defence instanced the treatment of cancers.

In agreeing with plaintiff's counsel that the one per cent risk of paralysis ought to have been disclosed, Robinson J. firmly rejected the assumption that the standard of disclosure ought to be assessed in the light of professional custom. The learned judge felt that on the contrary, the court should not be "shackled" by expert testimony of general disclosure practices within the medical community. That kind of evidence was "unnecessary to a showing of the materiality of a risk to a patient's decision on treatment, or to the reasonably, expectable effect of risk disclosure on the decision."[3] As a matter of logic, there is "no basis for operation of the special medical standard where the physician's activity does not bring his medical knowledge and skills peculiarly into play."[4] Instead, Robinson J. proposed that the court should assume the responsibility to decide whether or not a patient has been given enough information to enable him to make an intelligent choice between alternative courses of treatment. To this end, a doctor must disclose all risks which might *materially* affect the patient's decision. The court should assess materiality by how a "a reasonable person, in what the physician knows or should know to be the patient's position, would be likely to attach significance to the risk or cluster of risks in deciding whether or not to forego the proposed therapy."[5]

It is important to realise that this rejection of the professional standard test of disclosure was only partly rooted in the right to self-determination, although it is true that the rights of patients were boldly affirmed throughout the court's judgment: "Respect for the

---

[3] *Canterbury v. Spence* 464 F. 2d 772 (1972) at 792.
[4] *ibid.* at 785.
[5] *ibid.* at 787.

patient's right to self-determination on particular therapy demands a standard set by law for physicians rather than one which physicians may or may not impose upon themselves . . . [T]he patient's right of self-decision shapes the boundaries of the duty to reveal."[6] However, Robinson J. placed equal emphasis on logical justification, identifying numerous contradictions arising from the assessment of disclosure standards by reference to medical practices testimonially approved by expert medical witnesses. These included:

(1) the unlikelihood of there existing within the medical communities any meaningful "professional consensus on communication of option and risk information";

(2) (*contra* any argument that there actually exists any such general practices) the fact that "the myriad of variables among patients makes each case so different that its omission can rationally be justified only by the effect of its individual circumstances";

(3) the danger that "no custom at all may be taken as an affirmative custom to maintain silence";

(4) the very real danger that experts "may state merely their personal opinions as to what they or others would [disclose] under given conditions"; and (5) the inevitability that a professional standard would "arrogate the decision on revelation to the physician alone."[7]

Canterbury v. Spence was a relatively natural judicial response to malpractice developments that had tentatively taken root in America at the turn of the century but had continued in a confused and incoherent manner until that landmark decision.[8] The malpractice suit failed to present a serious threat to the medical profession until the early 1900s. This sluggish and reluctant start had its roots in various factors. The tort of trespass had been narrowly defined, and generally required proof of touching that was intentional, hostile, and

---

[6] *Canterbury v. Spence* 464 F. 2d 772 (1972) at 784–786.
[7] *ibid.* at 783–784.
[8] See generally: Appelbaum, Lidz, and Meisel (1987), Chaps 3–4; Faden and Beauchamp (1986), Chap. 4; Jaeckel (1975); Katz (1984), Chap. 3; McCoid (1957); Plante (1968); and Smith (1942).

nonconsensual.[9] Due to the comparatively fledgling state of the negligence action, there was an absence of what today we refer to as *compensation culture*. According to Konald, this state of affairs was encouraged by a strategic decision within the profession to conceal information which might raise questions or elicit suspicion, grounded in the belief that this was more likely to attract the trust and respect of the general public.[10] There was as yet no prevalent custom amongst the profession for the taking of consents or the making of disclosure.

Gradually, a stream of increasingly sophisticated consent-based cases began to test the precise authority of doctors to treat their patients in specific ways. The courts often seemed disinclined to consider whether the medical procedures, once shown to be technically unauthorised, were in intent or effect beneficial to the plaintiffs. In one of the earliest examples, *Mohr v. Williams* in 1905, the plaintiff succeeded in her action for trespass to her left ear, despite evidence that the defendant only discovered that the cause of irregular hearing in her right ear was a blockage in her left ear, at a time when the patient was being examined under anaesthetic.[11] Though the court recognised the concept of implied consent, it preferred to reason that in the absence of emergency conditions, the doctor should have suspended treatment to obtain a fresh consent. In *Rolater v. Strain*, the plaintiff authorised an incision into her toe and drainage of an infected joint, but stipulated that the defendant not remove any bones from her foot.[12] Under anaesthetic, the doctor discovered that it would not be possible to drain the joint unless the sesamoid bone was first removed (which fact could not have been discovered by external examination). His decision to remove this bone exposed him to liability in trespass, despite evidence that the bone served no useful function, and that serious consequences would have flowed from a failure to drain the joint. Various later decisions sought to embrace the right of doctors to presume that some procedures are impliedly consented to; many of these were grounded

---

[9] The novelty of litigation based on consent is strongly suggested by the curiosity value which attached to the 1848 case of *Delaware v. Gale* where the plaintiff unsuccessfully prosecuted the defendant male accoucheur for inappropriately *touching* her during childbirth: Faden and Beauchamp (1986), pp. 82–83.

[10] Konald (1962).

[11] *Mohr v. Williams* 95 Minn. 261 (1905) at 268, 104 N.W. 12 at 14. See also *Pratt v. Davis* 224 Ill 300, 79 N.E. 562 (1906).

[12] *Rollater v. Strain* 39 Okla 572, 137 Pac. 96 (1913).

in a growing awareness of the importance of exploratory diagnosis and treatment under anaesthetic.[13] Nonetheless, the courts continued to emphasise the importance of *express* authorisation and consent. In an influential decision of the New York Court of Appeals in *Schloendorff v. Society of New York Hospital*, Judge Cardozo memorably declared: "Every human being of adult years and sound mind has a right to determine what shall be done with his own body; and a surgeon who performs an operation without his patient's consent, commits an assault for which he is liable in damages."[14]

In many ways, these cases demonstrated the limitations of the trespass/battery analysis within the medical context. Those limitations are due fundamentally to the restricted nature of its *defences*, being qualifications to the narrow right not to be touched without consent. In the light of this marked judicial preference for express consent, it was not unreasonable to predict that future cases would seek to vitiate the patient's apparent consent by arguing that lack of knowledge, through incomplete disclosure, made it impossible for the patient to appreciate what had only been apparently or formally consented to.[15] One attempt to assert disclosure rights within the parameters of battery took the form of a proposition that the doctor had *misrepresented* the nature of the treatment by failing to direct the patient's attention to certain risks and possible outcomes. This argument succeeded in *Wall v. Brim*, despite evidence that the defendant had made a mistaken rather than misrepresented diagnosis at a time when he could not have been certain of the gravity of the plaintiff's condition.[16] Ignoring the requirement of intention and the traditional scope of the concept of misrepresentation, Hutcheson J. compared the giving of a consent to the formation of a contract—

---

[13] See *Bennan v. Parsonnet* 83 Atl. 948 (1912) at 951, where it was proposed that strict consent requirements might "paralyze the judgment of the surgeon and require him to withhold his skill and wisdom at the very juncture when they are most needed, and when, could the patient have been consulted, he would manifestly have insisted upon their being exercised in his behalf." See also *King v. Carney* 85 Okla. 62, 204 Pac. 270 (1922).

[14] *Schloendorff v. Society of New York Hospital* 211 N.Y. 125 (1914) at 129, 105 N.E. 92 (1914) at 93.

[15] Indeed, Frederic Cotton's instructions to his colleagues (1933), p. 589, reveal that doctors were sensitive to the possibility of something like informed consent emerging: "Signature of a paper stating the understanding of the kind of treatment proposed, the risks involved, the necessary limitations in case of success, even the chance of partial failure, seems to have no argument against it, though rarely used. It would seem wise as minimizing the chance of honest misunderstanding."

[16] *Wall v. Brim* 138 F. 2d 478 (1943).

presumably in an attempt to render the battery action more amenable to patients—and concluded that "a surgeon may not perform an operation different in kind from that consented to or one involving risks and results not contemplated."[17] Deploying this loose contract law speak, the courts began to insist more and more on the necessity of obtaining the patient's *understanding* of what was to be consented to.[18]

At this embryonic stage in the evolution of the duty to disclose, a celebrated essay by Professor McCoid in 1957 cast a timely critical gaze over the varieties of actions which now beset doctors.[19] McCoid observed that some courts had rejected the charge of battery where it had been coupled with a charge of negligent treatment, on the basis that the two were mutually inconsistent, the former depending on the lack of authority and the latter depending on the presence of it.[20] Others had shown themselves willing to classify a medical wrong as negligent injury to the person in order to rescue the plaintiff from the shorter statutory limitation period governing the trespass action.[21] Some courts had treated mistakes or inadvertent deviations from consent terms as instances of *unauthorised* treatments (attracting liability in battery) without finding any intention to do so on the part of the physician.[22] Others had treated such scenarios as actually or potentially falling under either battery or negligence.[23]

---

[17] *Wall v. Brim* 138 F. 2d 478 (1943).

[18] For instance, in *Corn v. French* 289 P. 2d 173 (1955), the plaintiff had signed a consent "for mastectomy and hemorrhoidectomy", not knowing what those words meant. However, she had persistently, and at all stages until unconscious, insisted that there be no surgical removal of her breast. Badt J. for the Supreme Court of Nevada found that the doctor's removal of the plaintiff's breast had been contrary to her express oral instructions and could not be protected by the plaintiff's formal written consent to same.

[19] McCoid (1957). McCoid observed (p. 434) that the courts had not adequately decided when a medical wrong should be deemed an unauthorised trespass and when it could be deemed a negligent action. This prompted his conclusion (which was unheeded) that since each amounts to improper action by a doctor, each should for consistency's sake be governed by a single basis of malpractice liability.

[20] As in *Cody v. Fraser* 122 Colo. 252, 222 P. 2d 422 (1950).

[21] This was permitted in *Physicians' and Dentists' Business Bureau v. Dray* (1941) 8 Wash. 2d 38, 111 P. 2d 568, where the defendant removed the plaintiff's uterus notwithstanding that the patient had consented only to examination under anaesthetic.

[22] *e.g.* the extraction of the wrong teeth in *Throne v. Wandell* 176 Wis. 97, 186 N.W. 146 (1922).

[23] As in: *Estrada v. Orwitz* 75 Cal. App. 2d 54, 170 P. 2d 43 (1946); and *Moos v. United States* 118 F. Supp. 275 (1954).

Some months after the publication of McCoid's article, Justice Bray of the California Court of Appeals decided in *Salgo v. Leland Stanford Jr University Board of Trustees* that a "physician violates his duty to the patient and subjects himself to liability if he withholds any facts which are necessary to form the basis of an intelligent consent by the patient to the proposed treatment."[24] Though the plaintiff's claim of unlawful non-disclosure had been bravely framed in negligence, the court considered that liability lay in battery, with one important distinction: whereas the well-established duty to explain the basic nature of the operation was absolute, this broader duty to disclose facts "necessary to an informed consent" was subject to "a certain amount of discretion" in doctors by which a decision to disclose may be guided by their apprehension of the "patient's mental and emotional condition".[25]

The battery analysis of informed consent continued to develop in several states, most notably in *Gray v. Grunnagle* decided by the Supreme Court of Pennsylvania.[26] In condemning the non-disclosure of a 15–20 per cent risk of paralysis—whose disclosure was general practice amongst the profession—Justice O'Brien proposed that strict requirements of consent usefully enable the courts to encourage deliberation by patients. Where *Gray* had justified the association of disclosure with consent (and thus battery) by reference to the contractual nature of the medical relationship, the California Court of Appeals justified it in *Berkey v. Anderson* by loosely equating non-disclosure with deceit and fraud capable of vitiating consent.[27] In this, the court was very much driven by the wish to eliminate the defence of general medical practice and the resulting pressures it placed on plaintiffs to provide numerous authoritative and favourable expert witnesses. The decision to assess the consequences of disclosure in battery seemed to be equally motivated by a more vigorous attempt to safeguard the right of a patient to make an informed and

---

[24] *Salgo v. Leland Stanford Jr University Board of Trustees, supra,* n. 1 at 180–181.
[25] *ibid.* at 181.
[26] *Gray v. Grunnagle* 223 A. 2d 663 (1966) at 669. Drawing from *Black's Law Dictionary,* O'Brien J. distinguished between "consenting and submitting. Every consent involves a submission; but a mere submission does not necessarily involve consent."
[27] *Berkey v. Anderson* (1969) 1 Cal. App. 3d 790, 82 Cal. Rptr 67 at 805 & 78: "We cannot agree that the matter of informed consent must be determined on the basis of medical testimony any more than that expert testimony of the standard practice is determinative in any other case involving a fiduciary relationship . . . . To hold otherwise would permit the medical profession to determine its own responsibilities to the patients in a matter of considerable public interest."

enlightened decision, "regardless of whether he in fact chooses rationally"—a conclusion reached by the Supreme Court of Pennsylvania in *Cooper v. Roberts*.[28]

Judicial attention gradually turned to negligence as a more flexible and acceptable forum for determining disclosure duties. Prompted by McCoid's article, the Kansas Supreme Court in the 1960 case of *Natanson v. Kline* embarked upon an adventurous but deeply flawed attempt to forge a definitive test.[29] Though this went some way towards curbing the dominance of expert testimony in disclosure trials, it amounted ultimately to a small step, for it retained the professional standard test where any degree of relevant disclosure had been made by the defendant. Other states similarly tinkered with the professional standard. In *Hunter v. Brown*, the Washington Court of Appeals decided that the court does not require expert testimony for its verdict where the necessity of information would be obvious to the layman.[30] In *Getchell v. Mansfield*, it was decided that expert testimony is not required to establish breach of the duty to disclose, but that in most cases the court would depend upon it to ascertain materiality of risk, whether there were feasible alternative treatments, and whether the plaintiff could have been advised of risks and alternatives without detriment to his well-being.[31]

Against this backdrop, *Canterbury v. Spence* injected a much-needed structure and clarity to an emerging body of medical malpractice law. The decision marked a well-founded attempt to dismantle the dependence of the law on expert medical opinion for the resolution of issues in which it had never possessed exclusive expertise. Instead, it proposed assessment of disclosure standards by the application of generic negligence principles tailored to the special exigencies of doctor-patient communication.

As its central edifice, it opted for an objective *reasonable patient* test of due disclosure. This, the court felt, was necessary so that doctors are not subjected to unreasonable standards which might cause them to constantly second-guess their patients, for the doctor "cannot know with complete exactitude what the patient would consider

---

[28] *Cooper v. Roberts* 220 Pa. Super 260 (1971) at 267, 286 A. 2d 647 (1971) at 650.

[29] *Natanson v. Kline* (1960) 350 P. 2d 1093. The decision ultimately caused more confusion by misapplying battery and negligence terminology throughout its two decisions. For discussion and criticism of this, see: Davis (1960–1961), p. 220; Jaeckel (1975), p. 71; Katz (1984), pp. 67–68; and Plante (1968), pp. 643–646.

[30] *Hunter v. Brown* 4 Wash. App. 899, 484 P. 2d 1162 (1971).

[31] *Getchell v. Mansfield* 260 Ore. 174, 489 P. 2d 953 (1971).

important to his decision, but on the basis of his medical training and experience he can sense how the average, reasonable patient expectably would react."[32] However, its conception of *material risks* was clearly intended to exert a pressure on doctors to ascertain what each specific patient might wish to know. For this reason, the court accepted that *materiality* is not a static concept, but that the statistically assessed severity and frequency of a risk must be evaluated by reference to the patient's own context. Thus, a "very small chance of death or serious disablement may well be significant; a potential disability which dramatically outweighs the potential benefit of the therapy or the detriments of the existing malady may summons discussion with the patient. There is no bright line separating the significant from the insignificant; the answer in each case must abide a rule of reason."[33]

With respect to the status of expert testimony, Robinson J. allowed that where disclosure is fraught with technical or "special" professional considerations, "prevailing medical practice must be given its just due."[34] In any event, the court may accept and consider expert testimony in a persuasive and non-determinative capacity and on the "specific criteria measuring challenged professional conduct and whether they have been met."[35] Further, physicians are "indispensable to identify and elucidate for the factfinder the risks of therapy and the consequences of leaving existing maladies untreated", and to ascertain the cause and extent of the patient's injuries. This is where the issues are not "resolvable wholly within the realm of ordinary human knowledge and experience".[36] Robinson J. further recognised that the views of medical experts will be required where the doctor attempts in his defence to justify non-disclosure on grounds of necessity (circumstances of urgency) or of therapeutic privilege, which both acknowledge that "as important as is the patient's right to know, it is greatly outweighed by the magnitudinous circumstances giving rise to the privilege."[37]

Certain other issues arising from *Canterbury* call for closer consideration. Two of these affect the disclosure action throughout the

---

[32] *Canterbury v. Spence, supra*, n. 2 at 787.
[33] *ibid*. at 788. In its formulation of materiality, the court drew upon proposals made by Waltz & Scheuneman (1970).
[34] *Canterbury v. Spence, ibid*. at 785.
[35] *ibid*. at 791.
[36] *ibid*. at 792.
[37] *ibid*. at 788.

common law, irrespective of the model broadly favoured in each jurisdiction. These will be addressed in later chapters: in chapter 6, the distinction between the obtaining of a basic consent (reviewable under trespass or battery law) and the disclosure of relevant information prior to undergoing treatment (reviewable under negligence law); and in chapter 7, proof of causation. A third issue is more specific to the informed consent model—its recognition of two defences—and will be considered further on in this chapter.

Canterbury v. Spence was swiftly followed by two other influential decisions, *Wilkinson v. Vesey* and *Cobbs v. Grant*, which collectively have been referred to as the informed consent trilogy since each developed hybrid models grafting a more patient-centric standard onto the professional negligence model.[38] Between 1972 and 1978, 10 jurisdictions followed *Canterbury*. A significant number of these breakthroughs were achieved by appellate courts who were less concerned with the issue of damages than with the restricted nature of the directions given by trial judges to their juries. However, a number of states, provoked largely by the medical malpractice insurance crisis of the mid-1970s, intervened via legislation.[39] Some, such as Arkansas, Idaho, and Texas, confirmed their courts' retention of the professional standard.[40] Others, such as Georgia, Louisiana, and Washington, confirmed the judicial adoption of informed consent.[41] Some altered the direction taken by their courts, mostly changing back from a patient to professional standard of disclosure or from a subjective to objective assessment of causation.[42] Some, such

---

[38] *Wilkinson v. Vesey* (1972) 295 A. 2d 676; *Cobbs v. Grant* 502 P. 2d 1 (1972). In *Wilkinson*, the Rhode Island Supreme Court proved far less willing to diminish the relevance of expert medical testimony, but nonetheless endorsed a subjective assessment of causation. In *Cobbs*, the California Supreme Court accepted the *Canterbury* model, but qualified that decision by identifying a minimum standard necessary for the obtaining of an informed consent, beyond which the professional standard would continue to apply.

[39] Though 37 U.S. states had eventually recognised the informed consent claim, more than half of these subjected the action to statutory limits. See: Giesen (1988), pp. 305–306; and Meisel and Kabnick (1980).

[40] Arkansas Stat Ann #34–2614(b)(1); Idaho Code #39–4304; and Texas Code Ann title 71 art 4590i #6.03(a).

[41] Georgia Stat #88–2906; Louisiana Stat #1299.40(A); and Washington Stat #7.07.050(1)(a).

[42] The North Carolina legislature reversed the effects of its Supreme Court's decision in *McPherson v. Ellis* 287 S.E. 2d 892 (1982) at 897, changing from an objective to a subjective test of causation and from an objective patient to a professional standard of disclosure: NC Gen Stat #90–21.13(a)(3); and NC Gen Stat #90–21.13 (a)(1).

as Hawaii, New York, and Pennsylvania, circumscribed the therapeutic privilege.[43] Some, such as Texas, delegated to a committee of
physicians and lawyers the task of specifying what risks must be
disclosed.[44] Many states legislated to ensure that patients received
certain information for designated treatments such as sterilisation,
electroconvulsive therapy, breast cancer treatments, and for the
administration of certain drugs.[45] These did not address financial
compensation, but instead targeted compliance by doctors so that
patients would undergo certain treatments only with full knowledge
of their benefit-risk ratios.

This retreat in some North American States from informed
consent seems not to have adversely affected its acceptance (albeit
qualified) in other common law jurisdictions. The Canadian
Supreme Court delivered a sophisticated analysis in its landmark
decision in *Reibl v. Hughes*.[46] Prior to that decision, vigorous standards
of disclosure had been sanctioned by law, the breach of which had
resulted in the finding of battery.[47] In *Reibl v. Hughes*, however, the
Supreme Court of Canada aligned itself with the negligence analysis,
though distancing itself from *informed consent* as a descriptive legal
concept on the basis that it tends to blur the legal distinctions
between trespass and negligence. Of that distinction (examined in
chapter 6), Laskin C.J.C. proposed that the battery action should be
restricted to cases where the defendant intervenes without or clearly
beyond a patient's consent, and that the duty to disclose medical

---

[43] For example: under Hawaii Rev Stat #671–3(c), where "the obtaining of consent is
not reasonably feasible under the circumstances without adversely affecting the
condition of the patient's health"; under New York Public Health Law #2805–
d(4)(d), where "the manner and extent of such disclosure could reasonably be
expected to adversely and substantially affect the patient's condition"; and under
Pennsylvania Cons Stat #1301.103, where "furnishing the information in question
to the patient would have resulted in a seriously adverse effect on the patient or on
the therapeutic process to the material detriment of the patient's health".

[44] Tex Rev Civ Stat Ann Art 4590i #6.03(a), 6.04(a), (d) (Vernon Cum Supp 1985).

[45] Sterilisation is subject to federal regulations in the Code of Federal Regulations 42,
Part 50, adopted under the United States Public Health Service Act. These require a
30 day waiting period between first consultation and treatment, and they specifically
demand that obstacles of language, understanding, culture, and handicap are
resolved on a case-by-case basis.

[46] *Reibl v. Hughes* (1980) 114 D.L.R. (3d) 1.

[47] In *Kinney v. Lockwood* (case-note) (1931) 4 D.L.R. 907 at 907, the Ontario Supreme
Court seemed to justify the battery analysis by explaining that a defendant "brings
himself within the field of liability" under this intentional tort where he "plainly and
knowingly minimises the danger of the treatment to induce the patient to proceed,
and plainly and knowingly refrains from explaining to the patient the advantages and
disadvantages of an alternative course well known to him".

information to patients more properly "arises as the breach of an anterior duty of care, comparable in legal obligation to the duty of due care in carrying out the particular treatment to which the patient has consented."[48]

Laskin C.J.C. rejected the professional standard approach to disclosure which, he felt, had been tantamount to surrendering to the profession the power to decide the scope of liability for non-disclosure.[49] Instead, the court's focus should be on "the patient's right to know what risks are involved in undergoing or foregoing certain surgery or other treatment."[50] In a factual dispute which was conducive to an affirmative result for the patient,[51] Laskin accepted the plaintiff's testimony, and ruled that it was not enough that the doctor told him that he would be much better off after the operation. Discounting the defence's statistical evidence of the effects of disclosure on patients, he insisted that the focus remain on the instant patient. The defence had adduced no evidence at the trial that the plaintiff was "emotionally taut or unable to accept disclosure of the grave risk".[52] There was here no emergency, nor any present neurological deficit. The risk of stroke was in the future, and "immediate risk would be from the surgery and not from foregoing it."[53] The defendant should have made thorough disclosure and given the plaintiff's difficulties with the English language, should have ensured that this was understood.

In most respects, *Reibl v. Hughes* differed little in substance from its American counterpart, except with respect to the vexed question of

---

[48] *Reibl v. Hughes, supra*, n. 46 at 10–11.

[49] Laskin C.J.C. (*ibid*. at 13) recognised, however, that expert medical testimony would be "relevant to findings as to the risks that reside in or are a result of recommended surgery or other treatment" and to a small extent on the analysis of materiality of risk.

[50] *ibid*.

[51] The defendant neurosurgeon had discovered a build up of plaque in the left carotid artery of the plaintiff's neck during the course of examining him for possible causes of his hypertension. This was unrelated to the hypertension, and did not then affect the patient's health. In four to five years time, however, there would be a 10% risk of stroke for each additional year the plaintiff would live with this condition. The defendant was strongly of the opinion that it should be remedied as soon as possible, to which advice the patient submitted, unaware that the corrective surgery carried this 10% risk of stroke or death. In the event, the plaintiff suffered a massive stroke, leaving his right side paralysed. He later claimed that he would not have undergone the surgery if disclosure had been made, since after about a year and a half, he would have been entitled to a life-time retirement pension from his employers.

[52] *ibid*. at 34.

[53] *ibid*.

causation. Laskin C.J.C. recognised, on the one hand, that a patient who sues will inevitably believe (or testify) that disclosure would have altered his decision to undergo treatment; therefore, by itself the subjective assessment is inadequate. However, on the other hand, a purely objective test is similarly problematic since it "would seem to put a premium on the surgeon's assessment of the relative need for the surgery and on supporting medical evidence of that need."[54] As a compromise between these two poles, Laskin advocated an approach which would take account of the reasonable patient *in the plaintiff's position*, so that "the balance in the risks of surgery or no surgery" is considered by reference to any special considerations which emerge "from the plaintiff's particular circumstances", but which are judged objectively: this might include the fact that the plaintiff asked questions, or that, as here, he had a short time towards his pension entitlements.[55] *Reibl v. Hughes* was closely followed by a forthright analysis of the causation requirement by Linden J. for the Ontario High Court in *White v. Turner*.[56] Linden J.'s interpretation of the causation test in *Reibl* was that it is not enough "for the Court to be convinced that the plaintiff would have refused the treatment if he had been fully informed; the Court must *also* be satisfied that a reasonable patient, in the same situation, would have done so."[57]

It was assumed by many that *Reibl v. Hughes* had ushered in dramatic revolutionary change. The General Counsel of the Canadian Medical Protection Association ("CMPA") stated in 1981 that "[n]o legal event in the last fifty years has so disturbed the practice of medicine as did the decision of the Supreme Court of Canada in *Reibl v. Hughes*".[58] These assumptions were not necessarily naive, given that the analyses in *Reibl* and *White* had been undeniably rigorous. Indeed, subsequent decisions displayed what appeared to be leniency towards plaintiffs. Statistically remote risks were often interpreted to be material, especially where the consequences were fatal or the treatment elective.[59] In applying the objective test of materiality—which assumes that the defendant knows or ought to

---

[54] *Reibl v. Hughes, supra*, n. 46 at 15.
[55] *ibid.* at 16.
[56] *White v. Turner* (1981) 120 D.L.R. (3d) 269.
[57] *ibid.* at 286.
[58] CMPA Annual Report 1981, p. 39. See also Picard (1981).
[59] *e.g.* in *Meyer Estate v. Rogers* (1991) 78 D.L.R. (4th) 307, it was ruled that a risk between 1 in 40,000 and 1 in 100,000 of fatal reaction to a contrast media dye was a material risk which ought to have been disclosed. The plaintiffs ultimately lost, however, after failing to sufficiently establish a causative link: see *infra*, n. 62.

know what a reasonable person in the patient's position would want disclosed—the courts often favoured the plaintiff's account, emphasising what the reasonable person in the patient's position would have wished disclosed and paying less heed to what the defendant knew or ought to have known of the patient's special characteristics.[60] The courts, moreover, were reluctant to accept the defence of therapeutic privilege, particularly where grounded in the patient's apparent emotional state[61]—a stance confirmed more recently in *Meyer v. Rogers*, where Maloney J. concluded that the privilege does not currently form part of Canadian law, and that the *Reibl* decision only very tentatively suggested its possible existence in borderline cases.[62]

However, some 10 years on, Gerald Robertson published an article demonstrating the minimal effects which these developments had had on the frequency or success of malpractice claims.[63] Only 11 per cent (or 13 cases) of the 117 malpractice cases since *Reibl* were grounded solely in the failure to disclose. In 81 per cent of the cases in which the plaintiff succeeded, the defendant was held negligent in treatment. In 56 per cent of these, the additional informed consent claim was dismissed, as it was for 82 per cent of all the cases in which it was made. This finding, similar to earlier ones in America,[64] suggests that informed consent tends to be used as an ancillary claim, appended at little extra expense to the malpractice claim. It also suggests that liability for non-disclosure is difficult to establish, even under a model such as *Reibl* which purports to be more lenient to plaintiffs.

Though the comparative leniency of the *Reibl* model lay, at least theoretically, in its articulation of the causation requirement—which was designed to mitigate the severity of both purely objective and subjective analyses—this element of proof remained the chief stumbling block for plaintiffs in Canada. Robertson writes that in 25 of the 45 cases (or 56 per cent) in which the defendant was held to have negligently withheld disclosure of material information, the plaintiff failed to sufficiently establish a causative link between breach and

[60] See *Reynard v. Carr* (1986) 10 B.C.L.R. (2d) 121, 38 C.C.L.T. 217.

[61] *Hajgato v. London Health Association* (1983) 44 O.R. (2d) 264.

[62] *Meyer Estates v. Rogers*, supra, n. 59. Note, however, that Picard and Robertson (1996), p. 148 doubt the correctness of this interpretation. The Canadian Law Reform Commission (1980) p. 16 has proposed that the therapeutic privilege should not be a "wide doctrine and probably only applies when to disclose the information would cause *recognized* physical and mental harm to the patient" (emphasis added).

[63] Robertson (1991).

[64] President's Commission for the Study of Ethical Problems in Medicine and Biomedical and Behavioral Research, *Vol. 1* (1982), p. 21.

loss. This was due to what appeared to be a working presumption by many Canadian courts that the greater the trust and confidence which a patient displayed in his physician, the less likely it is that a reasonable person in the patient's position would have declined treatment which that physician recommended.[65] Further, despite the strong scepticism expressed in both *Reibl* and *White* to statistical analogies, later courts were influenced by expert testimony of analogous clinical experience showing that patients typically choose to undergo recommended surgery even if informed of the relevant risks.[66] And in some cases, evidence that the plaintiff was informed of more serious risks than the one which later materialised was interpreted to enable an inference that the patient's decision would have been unchanged if full, aggregated disclosure had been made,[67] despite the very possible "cumulative effect which [multiple] risks can have on a person's decision with respect to proposed medical treatment."[68] On the basis of this, Robertson concludes that the newly formulated duty to disclose has not, as prospective patient plaintiffs hoped and the medical profession feared, opened any floodgates to numerous successful malpractice claims.

The Australian High Court received much attention recently for its rejection of English law in favour of a more rigorously pro-plaintiff model of disclosure.[69] In *Rogers v. Whitaker*, the plaintiff's right eye had been almost blind since an accident at childbirth. She was advised by the defendant ophthalmic surgeon to undergo an operation to improve her sight. The surgeon disclosed information of risks specifically in response to questions asked. These all related to the eye undergoing surgery; nothing was asked or communicated

---

[65] In *Diack v. Bardsley* (1983) 46 B.C.L.R. 240, a hypothetical dialogue between defendant physician and plaintiff patient was imagined, enabling the conclusion that a duly informed patient would still have accepted the defendant's recommendation. See also *Bucknam v. Kostuik* (1983) 3 D.L.R. (4th) 99.

[66] *Diack v. Bardsley, ibid.* and *Meyer Estates v. Rogers, supra.* n. 59. See chapter 7, *infra.*, pp. 205, 207, 209.

[67] See *Parkinson v. MacDonald* (1987) 40 C.C.L.T. 90.

[68] Robertson (1991), p. 435.

[69] *Rogers v. Whitaker* (1992) 109 A.L.R. 625. Indeed, this had been earlier predicted on the grounds that "at least, in legal developments, things that have happened in America tend to happen in much the same way a decade or so on" in Australia: Kirby, as quoted by Mahoney (1985), p. 121. The development had been more concretely hinted, however, by a decision reached nine years earlier in *F. v. R.* (1983) 33 S.A.S.R. 189 at 191, where the South Australian Supreme Court sided against the conservative approach of the English judiciary, tentatively arguing that the issue of disclosure falls primarily to the court to decide, and that "*real* risks of misfortune" must minimally be disclosed (emphasis added).

about the left eye, or of the 1 in 14,000 risk of sympathetic ophthalmia spreading loss of sight to that eye. The operation was conducted with all reasonable care and skill; but the risk of sympathetic ophthalmia materialised, and the plaintiff lost the sight of her other eye.

The High Court in a joint majority judgment dismissed the surgeon's appeal, rejecting the professional standard model typified in England by the cases of *Bolam v. Friern* and *Sidaway v. Bethlem Royal Hospital*.[70] It favoured instead the application of simple negligence principles.[71] In reaching its decision, the court combined the following two observations. First, the general duty of care on doctors can and must be sub-divided into distinct component parts, such as diagnosis and treatment on the one hand and disclosure on the other, between which there are fundamental differences. Secondly, medical experts are needed by the court because the court is not trained in medicine. However, disclosure of information involves no special skill: "Rather, the skill is in communicating the relevant information to the patient in terms which are reasonably adequate for that purpose having regard to the patient's apprehended capacity to understand that information."[72] This latter, according to Gaudron J., tends to be a matter "of simple common sense" which does not call for any technical expertise beyond the comprehension of the court.[73]

Though the court accepted the simple negligence or reasonable patient assessment of disclosure, it rejected as guiding labels both the doctrine of informed consent and the principle of self-determination, on the grounds that the former confuses negligence with a test of the validity of consent, and the latter "is of little assistance in the balancing process that is involved in the determination of whether there has been a breach of the duty of disclosure."[74] Expressing a preference for the Canadian decision in *Reibl v. Hughes* and Lord Scarman's dissent in *Sidaway v. Bethlem Royal Hospital*,[75] the court

---

[70] *Bolam v. Friern Hospital Management Committee* [1957] 2 All E.R. 118; *Sidaway v. Governors of the Bethlem Royal Hospital* [1985] 1 A.C. 871, HL.

[71] Though the court explained its aversion to the *Bolam* test in the particular context of disclosure, it did not specify whether it rejected *Bolam* generally as a test for medical negligence. This has been recently clarified by the Court of Appeal for New South Wales in *Lowns v. Woods* [1996] Aust. Torts Reports 81, which interprets *Rogers* to have implicitly rejected the *Bolam* test in its entirety. See chapter 3, *supra*, pp. 88–89.

[72] *Rogers v. Whitaker, supra*, n. 69, at 633.

[73] *ibid.* at 635.

[74] *ibid.* at 633.

[75] *Sidaway v. Bethlem Royal Hospital, supra*, n. 70.

ruled that a risk is material, and ought to be disclosed (subject to therapeutic privilege and presumably to circumstances of emergency) "if, in the circumstances of the particular case, a reasonable person in the patient's position, if warned of the risk, would be likely to attach significance to it or if the medical practitioner is or should reasonably be aware that the particular patient, if warned of the risk, would be likely to attach significance to it".[76] The wording of this statement differs to the formulation accepted in *Canterbury* and *Reibl*, to the extent that it places less emphasis on the objectified notion of the reasonable patient and gives equal weight to the actual patient and what is known or should be known about him.

The court referred to the majority decision by the House of Lords in *Sidaway* to qualify the professional standard rule to reflect the questions a patient has asked, interpreting this to expose the underlying flaws of the professional standard model. It accepted that where a patient asks certain questions, the standard of disclosure required of medical practitioners becomes more rigorous.[77] This patient had "incessantly" volunteered questions and expressed concern about her good eye, asking that it be covered throughout the operation as a precaution. By this route, through the expression of concern, a highly remote risk became a material risk whose disclosure the law required. The central concern of the *Rogers* decision was how the court should assess the standard of care in general disclosure cases and in the specific context of the patient who actively enquires after risk information. The court did not expressly consider the causation issue, though the factual outcome of the case and the court's past preferences[78] suggested that it favoured a subjective assessment. This was recently confirmed in *Chappel v. Hart*, whose appeal was fought squarely on causation issues.[79] The High Court's judgment in favour of the plaintiff was implicitly grounded in an acceptance of her assertion that, if informed of the remote risk of damage to the vocal cords, she would have postponed treatment for a later date.[80]

There have been few publicised advances in informed consent law since the *Canterbury* decision took the attractively simple step of

---

[76] *Rogers v. Whitaker, supra,* n.69, at 634.

[77] See Chapter 5, *infra*, pp. 139–141, 160–161.

[78] See: *H. v. Royal Alexandra Hospital for Children* [1990] Aust. Torts Rep 81; *F. v. R., supra,* n. 69; *Glover v. State of South Australia* (1985) 39 S.A.S.R. 543; and *Ellis v. Wallsend District Hospital* (1989) 17 N.S.W.L.R. 553, (1990) 2 Med. L.R. 103.

[79] *Chappel v. Hart* [1998] H.C.A. 55.

[80] See Chapter 7, *infra*, pp. 202–203.

deciding to assess disclosure according to generic negligence principles. In *Truman v. Thomas,* the Supreme Court of California recognised a duty on doctors to obtain *informed refusals,* and found a gynaecologist liable for the death of a woman who had refused to agree to a cervical smear which would have revealed her cancer at a treatable stage.[81] Bird C.J. emphasised the inequality of the doctor-patient relationship, the patient's reliance on the doctor for information and elucidation, and the resulting obligation on the physician to ensure that clinical decision-making is not made at arms-length. Disclosure of risks, he reasoned, includes disclosure of the risk of *not* being treated, and applies equally to diagnostic tests. Where the consequences for the patient are fatal, the standard is correspondingly higher. Though logically this amounted to a step *within* rather than *beyond* the parameters of established informed consent theory, the *Truman* decision attracted considerable attention, principally because it neatly illustrated the fact that breach of the duty to disclose, since grounded in negligence rather than battery law, is not dependent on direct physical contact or medical intervention between doctor and patient. More interestingly, however, this case shifted focus away from disclosure as an isolated right to a duty which is rooted in the doctor's own vocation.

Recent case-law has concerned itself with the type rather than extent of information which a doctor is required to disclose. In *Arato v. Avedon*, the Supreme Court of California controversially rejected a widow's claim that by failing to disclose her husband's life expectancy, the defendants had violated their duty to obtain his informed consent, which more specifically would have caused her husband to forego painful treatment and saved him significant economic losses by giving him an opportunity to put his business and financial matters in order.[82] Though the court reaffirmed the reasonable patient test, it ruled that there was no general rule mandating the disclosure of specific information "beyond that implicated by the risks of death or serious harm and the potential for complications": any additional or "non-medical" information (such as statistical life expectancy) fell to be assessed according to the professional standard.[83]

Recent decisions have addressed disclosure of information relevant to the doctor's performance ability, and it has been proposed that the

---

[81] *Truman v. Thomas* 611 P. 2d 902 (1980).
[82] *Arato v. Avedon* 23 Cal. Rptr. 2d 131 (1993).
[83] *ibid.* at 143.

duty to disclose may broaden to include all facts which might adversely affect a professional's judgment or performance.[84] Some U.S. state courts have ruled that doctors must disclose their alcholism,[85] others the fact of a doctor's HIV positive status.[86] Numerous cases have raised the issue of disclosing information related to resource-based decisions on choice of recommended treatment. This has arisen in the context of *managed care arrangements* entered into contractually by prospective patients with health maintenance organisations ("HMOs").[87] Under this type of arrangement, insured health care is circumscribed by coverage rules that explicitly constrain treatment or procedure options available to patients and physicians.[88] Health care options may further be delimited by arrangements between insurer and doctor whereby the doctor is given financial incentives to reduce the costs of treatment. Thus it is now felt that a physician's self-interest may cause injury to his patient, and that therefore the law ought to require the physician to make disclosure of any known fact which is likely to compromise his duty of care to the patient.[89]

There is little disagreement amongst commentators that doctors should disclose information explaining how financial incentives work within the patient's arrangement.[90] It has been queried whether this includes a duty to disclose the existence of more expensive treatment alternatives which though preferable are not being made available to the patient under the agreement. In response to the proposition that no such duty lies, given that doctors are not obliged to provide medical services for free (outside at least of emergency situations), it has been argued that this wrongly assumes that care may be denied when payment is unavailable, whereas the courts have in the past ruled that a doctor may be liable for abandonment of his patient where payment has not been forthcoming.[91] It has also been argued

---

[84] Hall (1997), p. 519.

[85] *Hidding v. Williams* 578 So. 2d 1191 (1991).

[86] *Estate of Behringer v. Princeton Medical Center* (1991) 592 A. 2d 1251. The New Jersey Superior Court (*obiter*) reasoned that informed consent law is not limited to disclosure of risks incidental to the contemplated treatment, but that it extends to all material risks associated with treatment as performed by the particular physician.

[87] Half of all privately insured subscribers in the U.S. belong to variants of the HMO, according to Iglehart (1994), pp. 1167–1168.

[88] See Hall (1994) and (1997).

[89] Bobinski (1994).

[90] Hall (1997), p. 521. See also: Levinson (1987); and McGraw (1995).

[91] *ibid.* p. 528.

that knowledge of the preferred but unavailable option—as opposed to right of access to that option—must be disclosed so that the patient is able to consider whether he wishes to raise the money for the treatment in another way, and so that he may consider changing doctors or health care plans.[92]

If corners are going to be cut and other valuable medical procedures or treatments not followed, the doctor should disclose this fact. In the Washington case of *Gates v. Jensen*, a doctor was held liable for failing to disclose that an alternative more accurate test for glaucoma was not being made available to the patient.[93] In *Martin v. Richards*, a significant recent decision by the Wisconsin Supreme Court, a physician was held liable for $5 million, for failing to inform the parents of a child who had suffered a head injury that they could have requested that a CAT scan be taken if they were not content with a physical examination of the child (which in the event wrongly diagnosed a mild concussion).[94]

The courts have all too rarely had the opportunity to consider negligence or disclosure law as it applies to medical research and experimental treatment. Indeed for a variety of reasons, biomedical research on humans has tended to by-pass legal analysis. This is an area dominated by conventions and codes of generally stated principles intended for application in a largely self-regulated context (in the United States by institutional review groups and in the United Kingdom by local research ethics committees).[95] The now famous Nuremberg Code was the emanation of a *sui generis* jurisdiction, and as such expressed universal principles of a legally unenforceable (though influential) nature.[96] The Code declared that experiments must be designed to yield fruitful results for the good of society; that they must be conducted so as to avoid all unnecessary physical or mental harm; and that they should where possible be based on the results of animal experimentation. Two of the ten sections of the Code deal with informed consent, and they emphasise the need to obtain a consent which is voluntary, free, and enlightened. There must be no force, fraud, deceit, duress, over-reaching, or other ulterior form of constraint or coercion, and the

---

[92] Menzel, cited in Hall (1997), p. 533.
[93] *Gates v. Jensen* 595 P. 2d 919 (1979).
[94] *Martin v. Richards* 531 N.W. 2d 70 (1995).
[95] See Chapter 5, *infra*, pp. 147–148.
[96] Reprinted in Giesen (1988), p. 727, App. A.

subject must be shown to possess sufficient knowledge and comprehension of the elements of the subject matter involved. More specifically, this requires knowledge of: "the nature, duration, and purpose of the experiment; the method and means by which it is to be conducted; all inconveniences and hazards reasonably to be expected; and the effects upon the health or person which may possibly come from his participation in the experiment."[97]

The consensus view amongst commentators is that disclosure must be "fuller than full" where a medical intervention is innovative or experimental.[98] A more rigorous requirement of disclosure to research volunteers was recognised with little hesitation by the Saskatchewan Court of Appeals in *Halushka v. University of Saskatchewan*.[99] The plaintiff student had volunteered to be tested for a new anaesthetic in return for $50 payment from a university hospital. He was told no more than that it was a safe test which would last only a couple of hours. This was false information, as the drug had not yet been tested. In the event, the plaintiff suffered a cardiac arrest that left him with permanently impaired mental ability. In upholding a finding both of battery and negligence on the basis that the information imparted to the plaintiff before securing his consent had been incorrect and misleading, Hall asserted that the duty on doctors engaged in medical research is "at least as great as, if not greater than the duty owed by the ordinary physician or surgeon to his patient. There can be no exceptions to the ordinary requirements of disclosure in the case of research as there may well be in ordinary medical practice. The researcher does not have to balance the probable effect of lack of treatment against the risk involved in the treatment itself."[1]

---

[97] *ibid.* s. 1.
[98] Giesen (1988), p. 573. For this view, see also: Appelbaum, Lidz, and Meisel (1987), Part IV: Beyleveld and Longley (1998); Brazier (1992), pp. 418–419; Faden and Beauchamp (1986), Chap. 5; Jones (1996), p. 379; Kennedy (1988) Chap. 10; Kennedy and Grubb (1994) Chap. 14; McHale and Fox and Murphy (1997) pp. 574–576; Picard and Roberston (1996), pp. 86–93; and Sommerville (1980), p. 23. Note, however, Mason and McCall Smith (1994), p. 365 are of the view that the *Sidaway* decision would apply with equal force to research procedures despite the special concerns this context raises.
[99] *Halushka v. University of Saskatchewan* (1965) 53 D.L.R. (2d) 436.
[1] *ibid.* at 443–444. More recently, the Supreme Court of Canada ruled in *Weiss v. Solomon* (1989) 48 C.C.L.T. 280 that in the research context, the doctor is under the most exacting duty possible, and that he must disclose all associated risks however remote.

Undoubtedly, scientific research is a public good, essential to the progressive fight against illness and disease. Since its subject is the human body, experimentation on humans is intrinsic to its advancement. Yet unchartered legal and ethical dilemmas abound. Many trials depend for their success on some element of deception or secrecy. For instance, the double-blind procedure requires that neither clinician nor subject knows what treatment has been assigned to each group of patients; this type of procedure is a perfectly valid one, designed to minimise a doctor's subjective preference for one drug over another. A trial may be conducted on the basis that subjects do not know whether they have received a placebo or a tested drug, in which case it would be counter-productive to tell the research-subject too much.[2] If this is the case, it seems uncontroversial to insist that the patient be fully informed of all the possible procedures which it may be necessary to adopt throughout the course of the clinical trial. If the trial depends upon the withholding of certain information, the patient should be told what *type* of information may be withheld and for what reasons. If accurately and sensitively obtained, the patient may be taken to have waived his legal right to full knowledge—though the applicability of waiver at all in the research context has been rejected by some commentators.[3] Appelbaum *et al.* advise that if a randomisation procedure is to be adopted, patients should be told that they will receive one of a number of treatments but that it will be selected by chance not because it is believed that it is better for the patient.[4] If placebos are involved, patients should be told that they may receive either medication or sugar pills with no pharmaceutical properties, and that this is necessary to test whether patients in similar circumstances benefit from active medication. If a specific protocol is being adopted, the patient should be told that it is necessary that a particular dosage of the medication must be maintained over a specific time and that it will not be lowered or increased even if it would be advisable to do so in the patient's case, unless the patient starts to suffer a severe reaction to the medication.

---

[2] Mason and McCall Smith (1994), p. 359 propose that placebos should not be used where the patient is in real pain, unless it is necessary to test experimental treatment alongside the placebo in relation to an illness for which there is as yet no cure (such as acquired immune deficiencies).

[3] Fromer (1981), p. 284; Giesen (1988), p. 576; Sommerville (1980), p. 23.

[4] Appelbaum, Lidz, and Meisel (1987), p. 252.

Disclosure, if rigorously and conscientiously made, may well prove to be an invaluable means of avoiding the many ethical and legal dilemmas which potentially beset researchers and their subjects. It has been proposed that full disclosure may deter volunteers, and frustrate the protocol adopted for the trial.[5] On the other hand, clinical evidence has been published to advance the view that the welfare of volunteers will be best protected where the key elements of the research protocol have been explained; further, that where careful communication has been made and doctor-patient rapport is good, patients and subjects are actually more likely to accept any unusual or unpleasant aspects of the research procedures.[6] It has also been proposed that enhanced disclosure, and the fostering of a collaborative relationship between both parties (wherein the subject appreciates the good he is doing for future patients), may appease the sense of guilt which researchers are apt to feel after they have compromised a subject's immediate health.[7]

A medical intervention may be undertaken for mixed motives, for instance where a new, unconventional, or innovative treatment is recommended to the patient on the basis that conventional methods are unlikely to cure the patient. Where this is the case, the doctor must disclose the fact that the treatment is novel or innovative, and that it has not thus far gained general support within the profession.[8] Further, he must not only disclose what alternatives are available, but must also ensure that the patient understands that these are at all times available to him; inversely, if the patient chooses instead the conventional treatment, he should be informed that the experimental alternative may if the patient so wishes be considered at a later stage. This is necessary to mitigate any sense of being coerced into participating in treatment which is only partly therapeutic or which is as yet innovative.[9]

The subject should also be told why the experiment is taking place, and what stake the researcher or investor has in the experiment. One cannot presume a comity of interests between the doctor-researcher

---

[5] In one case, subjects withdrew when they were informed that they would be volunteering for randomised treatment within a range of possible therapies: Lancher (1981). In another, the double-blind process was frustrated by the patient's knowledge of the side effects to various drugs: Brownell and Stunkard (1982).

[6] Park, Covi, and Uhlenhuth (1967).

[7] Epstein and Janowsky (1969); Park, Covi, and Uhlenhuth (1967).

[8] *Zimmer v. Ringrose* (1981) 16 C.C.L.T. 51.

[9] Sommerville (1980), p. 21.

and the patient-subject. The Supreme Court of California has accepted that experimental and innovative treatments may be made riskier by the eagerness of the research-doctor to promote scientific advances. It is thus necessary that the doctor disclose to the subject "any personal interests unrelated to the patient's health, whether research or economic, that may affect the physician's professional judgment."[10] This would seem to be more vital still where the experimental treatment is partly therapeutic. In this context, the doctor is likely to believe that he enjoys a measure of therapeutic discretion or privilege, and yet he may be no less driven by an investigative scientific enthusiasm.[11]

It is vital that the law unequivocally require disclosure of the precise motives and goals upon which a research trial is based. The Nuremberg Code was the first in a long line of international codes designed to ensure that medical and scientific experimentation operate within humanitarian limits.[12] Its bleak context was the post-war discovery of the extent of Nazi experimentation on Jewish captives and prisoners-of-war.[13] Yet despite the high-sounding principles enshrined in successive codes, flagrant abuses continued in secret. Henry Beecher, a distinguished Harvard anaesthesiologist, unearthed numerous disturbing experiments used to ground research findings in high-profile medical journals.[14] For instance in 1971, black men suffering from syphilis had deliberately been left untreated in six southern states for four decades so that the natural progression of the disease could be observed.[15] It has wisely been remarked that

---

[10] *Moore v. Regents of the University of California* 793 P. 2d 479 (1990) at 483.

[11] Mason (1990), p. 289.

[12] At the Nuremberg trials, military judges asked their expert witnesses to formulate universal ethical standards which the Nazis could be said to have breached. Andrew Ivy obtained the support of the American Medical Association for the following three basic principles of human experimentation: (1) the voluntary consent of the subject must have been obtained; (2) testing should first be on animals; and (3) the experiment must be performed with proper medical protection and management. These three principles became the foundation of the Nuremberg Code, and were incorporated by the judges in their final judgment against the Nazi physicians, *United States v. Karl Brandt*: in U.S. Adjutant's General's Department, *Trials of War Criminals Under Control Council Law No. 10 (October 1946–April 1949)*, Vol 2, *The Medical Case* (Washington, U.S. Government Printing Office, 1947).

[13] This included: the irradiation of gonads to enable mass sterilisation; the exposure of captives to low air pressure and successive extremities of cold and heat to observe the progressive death of the vital organs; and the amputation of bones for transplantation to others. See Meltzer (1975).

[14] Beecher (1966).

[15] Brandt (1978); Caplan (1992); Jones (1981).

one of the morbid lessons of history is 'not much evil is done by evil men, but most is done by good people who do not know they are not good.'[16] This is peculiarly relevant in the context of clinical trials. The investor for drugs trials is typically a pharmaceutical company with a vested commercial interest in increasing its share on the drugs market. The researcher has an incentive to reach an outcome whose findings may be published. Many have already succumbed to the temptation to falsify their research results, as highlighted recently in England.[17] Pharmaceutical companies, despite having a vested interest in obtaining accurate trial results, may unwittingly have encouraged this falsification by offering attractive remuneration packages, corporate junkets and freebies, to hospital "opinion leaders".

Exceptions and Privileges

Canterbury v. Spence recognised that in certain circumstances, disclosure which the law otherwise requires may to varying degrees be suspended under conditions of necessity or emergency, or through the operation of a therapeutic privilege.[18] Together, these have been aptly referred to as "an important vehicle for the interjection into the decisionmaking process of another set of values, those involving the societal interest in the health of the individual."[19] The exceptions seem to work on the presumption that the typical patient would wish to be cured and healed, and they may be seen to provide a necessary outlet for the discharge by doctors of their primary ethical duty to heal the ill. The effect which these exceptions have on the burden of proof in informed consent trials has been questioned.[20] Robinson J. proposed the following in *Canterbury*:

"The plaintiff must first make out a prima facie case—that the risk was material and undisclosed, and that he would reasonably

[16] Reinhold Neibuhr, quoted in Fromer (1981), p. 272.
[17] See generally: Smith (1991); Swan (1991); Dyer (1996); and Lock (1996).
[18] *Canterbury v. Spence, supra*, n. 2 at 788.
[19] Appelbaum, Lidz, and Meisel (1987), p. 67.
[20] This is to the extent that specific rules have not been laid down by state courts. In Colorado, for instance, once the plaintiff has established that disclosure was not made at the time consent was given, it then falls to the defendant to establish that the nondisclosure accorded with a prevailing professional standard: *Stauffer v. Karabin* 30 Colo. App. 357, 492 P. 2d 862 (1971). In Kansas, this shift only occurs where no disclosure of risks has been made; where some disclosure has been made, the plaintiff must establish that the disclosure made did not accord with the professional standard: *Natanson v. Kline* 354 P. 2d 670 (1960). See, further, Frantz (1978).

have declined the therapy if informed of that risk. Then the defendant must, if possible, make out a case that non-disclosure was privileged. This is because any evidence of this is in the hands of the physician, and because judicial policy dictates that he who seeks the shelter of an exception is more likely to be in possession of relevant facts."[21]

Katz argues that the effect of this is unclear. If the plaintiff's failure to advance expert rebuttal evidence leads to a directed verdict or non-suit, then the difference between informed consent and the professional standard model is negligible. Alternatively, if the opinions expressed by the defence's experts on the therapeutic privilege may merely be put to the jury or considered by the court alongside the plaintiff's testimony, they become descriptive rather than definitive of due care.[22] Though this was not explicitly addressed by the court in *Canterbury*, it seems more than reasonable to imply from the judgment as a whole, that the court favoured the second proposal. In its analysis of whether or not a privilege has been made out, the court will be *guided* but not ruled by expert testimony of a sort which is not specific to the patient.

Broadly, two types of *emergency* scenarios may emerge, making the task of disclosure or even the seeking of consent impossible or dangerously impractical. The first occurs where medical care may need to be given at the scene of an accident, or where a patient is rushed to hospital in a critical and unresponsive condition. Generally, the patient must be unconscious or without capacity to make a decision, where no other legally authorised person is at hand; time must be of the essence; there must be a risk of serious bodily injury or death; and it should fairly be believed that the reasonable man or, if enough is known, the instant patient would probably have consented to the emergency intervention.[23] The courts have resisted defining its scope more specifically. However, in *Cunningham v. Yankton Clinic* it was stated to embrace immediate (and not future)

---

[21] *Canterbury v. Spence, supra*, n. 2, at 791. See also *Cobbs v. Grant, supra*. n. 38, at 12, where Mosk J. of the California Supreme Court ruled that the plaintiff must prove the fact of non-disclosure, and that thereafter the burden shifts to the defence to prove if it can that the non-disclosure was justified.

[22] Katz (1977), pp.156–157.

[23] Skegg (1974).

threat to life or health;[24] and in *Sullivan v. Montgomery* it was justified where "suffering or pain [would] be alleviated" by the intervention.[25] Whether this exception is grounded in preservation of life and health or life alone, depends in turn on whether one interprets the exception to be rooted in the humanitarian duty of the medical profession[26] or instead in the intuitive sense that the representative reasonable patient would wish medical attention in the circumstances.[27] Any attempt to distinguish between *life* and *health* would seem, under ordinary conditions, to be a task of Herculean proportions, and in the heated circumstances of an emergency, quixotically unrealistic. Common sense, and indeed basic fairness to emergency providers of health care, would seem to demand that the focus ought instead be on the extent to which disclosure could not have been made at the given time. On the other hand, the problems posed by the emergency exception to informed consent spring from the limitations of the disclosure action, which in the main retrospectively assesses what should have been done after something in fact has gone badly wrong for the patient.

These themes were brought vividly to the fore in *Dunham v. Wright*.[28] The plaintiff's wife had undergone thyroidectomy surgery to cure an enlarged thyroid, and had not survived the operation. The defendant testified that she had been one of the most gravely ill women he had ever encountered, and that it had been explained to her that she urgently required surgery of a serious nature. He further testified that the drugs she had been given had begun to lose their effectiveness, that surgery was her only option, and that if she had not been operated on at that particular time, her condition probably would have become inoperable and she would have died with "mathematical certainty". In accepting this as a basis for an emergency derogation from full and detailed risk disclosure, Circuit Judge Adams of the United States Court of Appeals rejected the plaintiff's attempt to limit this exception to "a sudden or unexpected event

---

[24] *Cunningham v. Yankton Clinic* 262 N.W. 2d 508 (1978).

[25] *Sullivan v. Montgomery* 279 N.Y.S. 575 (1935).

[26] This view was accepted in *Marshall v. Curry* [1933] 3 D.L.R. 260 at 275, where it was stated that the "crucial test always is whether the physician acted 'in order to save the life or preserve the health of the patient' in accordance with the standards of a reasonably competent physician in all the circumstances."

[27] *Jackovach v. Yocom* 237 N.W. 444 (1931).

[28] *Dunham v. Wright* 423 F. 2d 940 (1970).

which creates a temporarily dangerous condition usually necessitating immediate or quick action".[29]

Seitz J. in his dissent argued that no emergency situation capable of diluting disclosure had existed, for the patient had been in hospital for 30 days and in all that time the only treatment contemplated for her was surgery: "The reality is that the defendants had procured a consent to the operation well before it was performed . . . Merely because plaintiff thereafter denied that the consent was an informed one does not warrant treatment of this case as though the events prior to the operation had not occurred."[30] These dissenting remarks are significant chiefly for two reasons. First, they represent an optimal approach to informed consent, whereby protection of self-determination and patient autonomy is paramount, and practical inevitability an inadmissible justification. Secondly, they shift the focus away from the irksome issues of life, health, and inevitability, towards the primary duty to disclose information *except where this cannot be done*. Seitz J.'s findings are more faithful to the intent of informed consent doctrine. However, the flip-side to a rigid circumscription of the emergency exception may be the general deterrence of emergency aid. As it is, the common law has rarely recognised a general duty on bystanders to administer emergency aid, even where to do so would create no risk to the volunteer, which reluctance has in the past been extended to doctors.[31] This is based in part on the potential liability which a rescuer may face if after taking active steps to help someone, he fails to exercise reasonable care.

A second type of medical emergency occurs when something unforeseeable arises during the course of treatment which requires remedial action. Where the complication is unforeseeable, it doesn't affect the adequacy of the disclosure made prior to the commencement of treatment. Whether or not it justifies immediate remedial action, without postponement to obtain a fresh consent and to make renewed disclosure, depends upon the threat the complication poses to the patient's life or health. However, in this the courts are concerned to give flexibility to doctors, out of an appreciation of the inexactitude of medical science and the often investigative nature of surgery under anaesthetic.[32] In this sense, the emergency exception

---

[29] *Dunham v. Wright* (1970) 423 F. 2d 940 at 947.
[30] *ibid.* at 948.
[31] See Chapter 2, *supra*, pp. 44–45.
[32] See *supra*, pp. 94–95.

implicitly recognises that to insist on obtaining an informed consent in some circumstances would be to yield to form over substance.[33] It also recognises that stalling proceedings to obtain a patient's informed decision may amount to a breach by the doctor of his ethical duty to provide health care when it is perceived by him to be most needed.

The *therapeutic privilege* is considerably more controversial, and must in Robinson J.'s own words, "be carefully circumscribed . . . for otherwise it might devour the rule itself."[34] His definition of the general scope of the privilege seems at first wide, recognising a discretion not to make full disclosure where that would pose "such a threat of detriment to the patient as to become unfeasible or contraindicated from a medical point of view."[35] This is, however, substantially qualified by the following: "The privilege does not accept the paternalistic notion that the physician may remain silent simply because divulgence might prompt the patient to forego therapy the physician feels the patient really needs. That attitude presumes instability or perversity for even the normal patient, and runs counter to the foundation principle that the patient should and ordinarily can make the choice for himself."[36]

On closer analysis, this distils down to a privilege justified by the doctor's opinion that his patient would be unable to make a rational decision grounded on the information in question: "It is recognized that patients occasionally become so ill or emotionally distraught on disclosure as to foreclose a rational decision."[37] However, when Robinson's various dicta are taken together, it is clear that they envisage that patients possess the right to *rationalise* and to form a decision on the basis of certain information which they have the right to receive, and that their right to do so is not in any way prejudiced by the possibility that they may make a decision which to the medical staff *seems* irrational or otherwise than in that patient's best interests. The failure of Robinson J. to expand on this point has enabled other American courts to tamper with the privilege to the extent that in some states, what resulted differed little from the professional standard model.[38] This lies in contra-distinction to the approach

---

[33] As observed by Meisel (1979), p. 436.
[34] *Canterbury v. Spence, supra,* n. 2, at 789.
[35] *ibid.*
[36] *ibid.*
[37] *ibid.*
[38] For instance, *Nishi v. Hartwell* 473 P. 2d 116 (1970), decided that "the doctrine

taken in Canada, where neither the therapeutic privilege nor waiver of disclosure can protect physicians from the adverse consequences which may flow from non-disclosure where the treatment in question is non-therapeutic or elective, the reasoning being that in this context it is in the patient's best interests to be alarmed by the prospect of failure and complication.[39] Indeed in the recent case of *Meyer v. Rogers*, Maloney J. concluded that the privilege "does not presently form part of the law of Canada."[40]

It is important to understand what it is that doctors are excepted or privileged from doing. One can easily accept that the circumstances which trigger off the emergency exception may often rule out the proper taking of a consent and/or making of disclosure. This will be a matter of degree: where possible (such as where a conscious patient is being conveyed on a stretcher for emergency treatment), the physician ought to seek a consent by briefly and simply explaining what he intends to do. By contrast, the circumstances which generate the therapeutic privilege are not inherently strong enough to make a case for suspension of the duties incidental to the obtaining of a basic consent.[41] Indeed, any argument that the patient could not have understood or coped with information relating to the basic nature and character of the treatment would seem to imply that the patient was not even basically competent to give a consent or assent. If the privilege does not apply to battery claims, then the logical inference is that doctors cannot withhold all information on therapeutic grounds,

---

recognizes that the primary duty of a physician is to do what is best for his patient . . . . [A] physician may withhold disclosure of information regarding any untoward consequences of a treatment where full disclosure will be detrimental to the patient's total care and best interest"; disclosure may further be withheld if it "might induce an adverse psychosomatic reaction in a patient highly apprehensive of his condition." See also *Williams v. Menehan* 379 P. 2d 292 (1963), where it was decided that disclosure must be suspended when it poses an unreasonable threat of harm to patients.

[39] *Kelly v. Hazlett* (1976) 75 D.L.R. (3d) 536. See also *Stamos v. Davies* (1985) 21 D.L.R. (4th) 507 at 521, where Krever J. accepted that the plaintiff was of a highly nervous and fearful disposition, but concluded that this could not by itself ground reliance on the therapeutic privilege where the operation was non-therapeutic and elective. Sommerville (1981), p. 773 doubts for similar reasons whether the therapeutic privilege could ever apply in the medical research scenario, unless the treatment is the patient's last hope and the other criteria for the privilege are met, though this must be subject to tight controls lest dying patients become prey to experimentation.

[40] *Meyer v. Rogers, supra*, n. 59, at 316.

[41] In *Kelly v. Hazlett, supra*, n. 39, at 563, the therapeutic privilege was stated to apply only to negligence claims.

but must disclose a certain amount of information which relates to the basic nature and character of the procedure.

The type of amplified disclosure and communication anticipated by informed consent is ruled out by the very nature of emergencies. By contrast under the therapeutic privilege, the amount of information which is tendered to the patient, over and above that necessary to obtain a basic consent, should be specifically tailored to the extent to which it is not likely to work counter-productively for the patient. Robinson J. acknowledged in *Canterbury* that where a privilege is invoked, the physician ought to make disclosure to a close relative "with a view to securing consent to the proposed treatment".[42] The argument for doing this is significantly stronger for the therapeutic privilege. Whereas the existence of an emergency situation is only in very few cases a contestable fact, the subjective assessment of the patient's psychological make-up, upon which the therapeutic privilege is founded, arguably cries out for corroboration, and this may valuably be given or rejected by relatives or friends who know the patient more intimately. An unwillingness to emphasise the usefulness of such corroboration does little to substantiate informed consent as something which is founded on the *duty of care* as opposed to *consent*. It has, for instance, been ruled that there is no requirement that disclosure be made to a relative since it is the patient's consent which is required in the first place. According to Marumoto J. for the Supreme Court of Hawaii: "If it should be the law that, if the patient could not be told, his spouse should be told, the necessary corollary of that requirement would be that the spouse could refuse her consent to the proposed treatment."[43] Though this makes some sense in the emergency context, it makes much less when applied to the therapeutic privilege.

The duty of care is owed to the instant patient, and the form it takes should be responsive to that patient.[44] That this is so is readily

---

[42] *Canterbury v. Spence, supra,* n. 2 at 789.

[43] *Nishi v. Hartwell, supra,* n. 38 at 122.

[44] It is not clear whether liability for the consequences of failure to make due disclosure is limited to the patient whose body has been treated or operated on. Since the duty to disclose is now anchored in negligence, and not consent, it would seem that liability may in future cases attach for economic loss suffered by third parties who should have been in *reasonable* contemplation of suffering as a result of the breach (*i.e.* not part of an indeterminate class). Though extensions of liability to third parties are likely to be extremely rare in this field, certain scenarios—such as where the bread-winner of a family dies after undergoing a high-risk and low-

apparent from the various rulings in *Canterbury v. Spence*, which consistently react against the collective, amalgamated presumptions upon which the professional standard had been based. This makes the case for a careful and specific rendering of the therapeutic privilege, at the level of theory and practice, all the more urgent, lest it be allowed to become a back-door entrance for the kind of medical paternalism against which informed consent first responded. It should, that is, be justified in a way which is specific to the patient and to the privilege itself. This was not the case in the British Columbia decision of *McLean v. Weir*, where the trial judge confused a general practice of non-disclosure due to low probability of risk with the defendant's exercise of therapeutic privilege. This fallacy was indulged by the Court of Appeal which accepted the defendant's practice not to disclose remote risks that "would serve only to make the patient anxious and apprehensive."[45]

Appelbaum *et al.* persuasively argue that:

> "the boundaries of the privilege ought to be defined in terms of the primary functions of the informed consent doctrine, rather than by reference to the harm that may be done to the patient by disclosure. Thus, if the doctrine exists primarily to promote patient participation in medical decision making and to promote rational decision making, information should only be permitted to be withheld if its disclosure would thwart one of these objectives."[46]

The focus ought to be on the patient's ability to choose and decide, rather than on the harm which may result from the exercise of that choice. The writers further argue that the abolition of the controversial therapeutic privilege would not be revolutionary in effect, given its huge potential overlap with waiver and incompetency.

---

benefit operation at the doctor's recommendation and in the absence of due disclosure – may conceivably benefit from the rules which govern economic loss suffered by third parties due to negligent misstatement. In a recent wrongful conception/pregnancy action in England, a third party (the lover of a patient whose vasectomy was unsuccessful) attempted to recover economic loss suffered by a negligent misstatement to the patient that his vasectomy had been successful: *Goodwill v. British Pregnancy Advisory Service* [1996] 1 W.L.R. 1397, CA. The court rejected the action on the basis that there existed no relationship of care between defendant and plaintiff which the law should as a matter of policy recognise, and it could not be said that the defendant knew or reasonably ought to have known that the statements would be acted upon by the plaintiff without independent enquiry.

[45] *McLean v. Weir* [1980] 4 W.W.R. 330 at 336.
[46] Appelbaum, Lidz, and Meisel (1987), p. 73.

To obtain a voluntary and informed waiver from the patient, the physician may choose to say: "There is some information about your treatment that you may wish to know, and I will tell you about it if you like. There's a chance that this information may upset you, and if you'd rather that I not go into detail, please say so. And if you'd like, I'll discuss it with your spouse [or other family member] instead."[47] This would shift responsibility to patients. According to Appelbaum *et al.*, the therapeutic privilege as formulated "overlooks the possibility that if patients were asked to make a prospective determination, they might decide that they prefer to be harmed by being informed than be harmed by having to make choices in the dark of non-disclosure. In contrast, waiver—operating in the manner previously described—permits patients to make this very determination."[48] Numerous difficulties could arise from excessive reliance by doctors on the patient's entitlement to waive his right to information. On the other hand, if properly used, it could play a pivotal role in both discharging the doctor's duty to make disclosure and in safeguarding the patient's right to information. Further, it could go a considerable way towards making the therapeutic privilege irrelevant and unnecessary. This is because both consent and waiver are subtypes of decision-making:

> "a waiver, properly given, is in keeping with the values sought to be promoted by informed consent because the patient remains the ultimate decision maker . . . Waiver permits patients to be protected from any harmful impact they believe disclosure might have upon them or from the possible anxiety that may accompany the decisionmaking process. Patients here, not doctors, determine that disclosure or decision making will be harmful. The case is otherwise for therapeutic privilege."[49]

If waivers are to be properly given, they must constitute a voluntary and intentional relinquishment of a known right. For this reason, printed waiver clauses signed by patients are treated with notable scepticism by the common law.[50] A patient must first know

---

[47] Appelbaum, Lidz, and Meisel (1987), p. 77.
[48] *ibid.*
[49] *ibid.*, p. 72.
[50] In a leading decision by the Californian Supreme Court, *Tunkl v. Regents of University of California* 383 P. 2d 441 (1963), one such waiver was invalidated on the following grounds: (1) health care is an activity which is better suited to public regulation, and

that there is a duty on the doctor to disclose further information, that he has a right to make an informed decision, that he can decline to opt for the recommended treatment, and that the doctor must obtain his informed consent before proceeding. Misrepresenting an operation as *relatively simple*, in order to shift the onus upon the patient to inquire after more information, would run counter to the spirit of informed consent, just as much as would *compelling* patients to receive information which the law merely *enables* them to receive.[51] The dangers inherent in the use of waiver in the clinical context chiefly concern the manner in which the physician expresses himself to the patient. The manner in which he conveys to the patient that it is his duty to disclose more information, and that it is the other's right to receive it though the right can be voluntarily waived, may force the patient to conclude that it would be much better that he be told nothing more. This short-circuiting of communication is certain to engender bitterness and conflicts of evidence at later stages. As such, waiver should be handled with care by doctors, and should not be used as an outlet to facilitate significantly less communication and understanding between doctor and patient.

Informed Consent Doctrine

The ongoing reference in *informed consent* to *consent* is a direct and unfortunate by-product of its roots in the early cases of trespass and unauthorised treatment. Indeed, one reason why the courts have consistently ruled that responsibility for negligent non-disclosure falls on the person who is to physically treat the patient, is this historical link with consent and trespass.[52] The nomenclatural confusion between *consent* (battery) and informed *consent* (negligence) has already been the basis of much criticism of *informed consent* as a

---

the service the defendants were supplying was one necessary to the public; (2) the hospital held itself out as performing a service which was open to any member of the public; (3) the hospital had greater bargaining power than the patient; (4) the waiver form was not such as could give patients the option of higher protection; and (5) the hospital controlled the risk of injury.

[51] Particularly in light of the fact that many patients forget or choose not to remember what the doctor discloses to them. See: Cassileth, Zupkis, Sutton-Smith, and March (1980).

[52] See: *Wilkinson v. Vesey* 295 A. 2d 676 (1972); and Chapter 9, *infra*, p. 275.

guiding label by critics[53] and courts[54] alike. Certainly, the distinction between informed consent on the one hand and consent on the other must be carefully maintained, if the former development is not to work counter-productively. The most obvious danger is that the informed consent process may become a bureaucratic extension of the obtaining of preliminary consents. The American experience reveals that lawyers and doctors have overwhelmingly believed that the main function of consent forms is to protect against liability.[55] Though consent forms evolved in response to early legal developments, and were often and sometimes still are described as "release of liability forms", they were not intrinsically required by the common law when it developed the principle that physical touchings must be consented to. In the face of widespread use by doctors of "informed consent forms", American courts and legislatures have wisely responded by insisting that at most they are only additional pieces of evidence for the court to consider, and that they do not raise a presumption of disclosure.[56] One court went so far as to rule that if such a form is relied upon by a doctor in his defence, it falls not upon the plaintiff but on the doctor to prove that adequate disclosure has been made.[57]

It is possible that forms, if used to accurately detail information as it has been disclosed and understood, could complement rather than subvert the negligence-based duties of disclosure, and indeed serve to

---

[53] See Clements (1995); Katz (1977); Feng (1987); Jones (1996), p. 337; and Plante (1968). Mason and McCall Smith (1994), p. 252, advocate reference instead to *intelligent* or *rational* consent. This, I think, is equally likely to obfuscate the action, to the extent that it would render proof of causation still more difficult for plaintiffs, and would enable doctors to justify non-disclosure on the basis of vague fears that the plaintiff was then incapable of making a sensible or rational decision.

[54] See *Reibl v. Hughes, supra,* n. 46, at 8–9 (1980); *White v. Turner, supra,* n. 56 at 282 (1981); and *Rogers v. Whitaker, supra* n. 69 at 633 (1992).

[55] See: Cassileth, Zupkis, Sutton-Smith, and March (1980); and Appelbaum, Lidz and Meisel (1987), pp. 176–183.

[56] The approach adopted by the Oregon state legislature is to encourage the use of the form as a summary of the important items of disclosure, bearing a statement to that effect and an acknowledgment that there are other less severe, infrequent problems that may emerge which the doctor would be willing to discuss if requested: Oregan Revised Statutes #677.097 (1977). A growing trend is to rely on written consent forms, outlining what risks were disclosed, as evidence raising a presumption of informed consent. These have been accepted for this limited purpose by some courts: *Hondroulis v. Schumacher* 553 So. 2d 398 (1988); *Cross v. Trapp* 294 S.E. 2d 446 (1982). Some statutes require that such language be written "in layman's language and in a language understood by the patient": Cal Health & Safety Code # 1704.5 (West 1990).

[57] *Estrada v. Jacques* 321 S.F. 2d 240 (1984).

minimise the evidentiary problems which tend to obscure the courts' attempts to determine what in fact had been disclosed by the defendant.[58] Yet they carry much scope for further estrangement of the patient from the decision-making process through excessive technicality and bureaucracy.[59] If allowed to replace communication, the informed consent process might become as isolated an event as the consent process, differing only in the degree of information imparted. The value of encouraging more realistic communication in the medical relationship has been exemplified by cases such as *Sard v. Hardy* where the plaintiff had required sterilisation partly to protect against potential physical injury to herself and partly for financial reasons. Despite this, she was not informed of the six types of sterilisation she could have had and their comparative risks and failure rates, nor that sterilisation was not absolute. Though functionally illiterate, she was subjected to a consent form 10 to 15 minutes before being wheeled into the delivery room for Caesarean section. Accepting informed consent into state law, Levine J. of the Maryland Court of Appeals emphasised that "the doctrine of informed consent takes full account of the probability that unlike the physician, the patient is untrained in medical science, and therefore depends completely on the trust and skill of his physician for the information on which he makes his decision."[60]

There is a growing tendency, particularly in Australia and Canada, to treat risk information in a non-statistical light, and this one suspects derives from a sense of the substantive differences between information associated with consent and battery and information associated with a duty of care under negligence law. In *Ellis v. Wallsend District Hospital*, Samuels J.A., spoke of the risk of paralysis being "slight, or remote", yet considered it a risk that should have been disclosed due to the severity of possible injury.[61] In *Haughian v. Paine*, Sherstobitoff J.A. of the Saskatchewan Court of Appeal

---

[58] See, *e.g. White v. Turner, supra*, n. 56 at 273 where the defendant claimed that "Mrs White may not have recalled this information because, like many patients, she was nervous and her memory may not have been as clear as it might otherwise have been."

[59] See *Jones v. Berkshire Health Authority*, QBD, July 2, 1986, discussed in Symmons (1987). Ognall J. took issue with the defendants' failure to devote part of their consent form to a statement personally signed by the patient acknowledging disclosure and explanation of the remote risk that the operation could fail and that she could become pregnant again.

[60] *Sard v. Hardy* 379 A. 2d 1014 (1977) at 1020.

[61] *Ellis v. Wallsend District Hospital* (1990) 2 Med. L.R. 103 at 117.

overrode the defendant's general practice not to disclose risks of less than 1 per cent frequency, and observed that "the issue of materiality cannot be reduced to numbers for all cases. Statistics are but one factor to be taken into account . . . One cannot make an informed decision to undertake a risk without knowing the alternatives to undergoing the risk."[62]

According to Appelbaum, Lidz, and Meisel, its leading proponents, informed consent doctrine protects the bodily integrity, self-determination, and right of patients to make their own health care choices, whilst further compelling physicians "to engage in a discussion with each patient . . . [and] to involve patients in decision making about their own care."[63] This dialogic or co-operative conception of informed consent was endorsed by the President's Commission, to which Lidz and Meisel had been appointed. It proposed that informed consent should strive to a state of affairs where "the physician or other health professional invites the patient to participate in a dialogue in which the professional seeks to help the patient understand the medical situation and available courses of action, and the patient conveys his or her concerns and wishes."[64] Appelbaum et al. sensibly recommend, partly to avoid confusion with consent and battery, that one speak instead of an *informed decision*, a proposal I fully embrace though with some doubts that it can replace at this stage its mythologically entrenched predecessor. *Informed decisions* by patients are essentially what informed consent doctrine seeks to achieve, as opposed to a more knowledgeable surrendering of authority to another to do a particular thing. Informed consent doctrine, as judicially and critically conceived, seeks as far as is practicably possible to ensure that patients take responsibility for ultimate decision-making over matters which carry potentially weighty consequences for their future health and lifestyle. Appelbaum et al. emphasise *understanding* and *voluntariness* as essential components of an informed *decision*, though arguably these ingredients apply equally to informed *consent*.[65] To the extent that a test of understanding and voluntariness converges in an analysis of the patient's right to make a decision on the basis of information he

---

[62] *Haughian v. Paine* (1987) 37 D.L.R. (4th) 624 at 643–644.
[63] Appelbaum, Lidz, and Meisel (1987), p. 46.
[64] President's Commission for the Study of Ethical Problems in Medicine and Biomedical and Behavioral Research, Vol. 1 (1982), p. 38.
[65] Appelbaum, Lidz, and Meisel (1987), pp. 57–62.

understands, or his right to make an irrational decision, they provide useful points to test the parameters of informed consent doctrine.

It is clear that *Canterbury v. Spence* envisaged as pre-requisites to an *informed* consent both the physician's imparting of information *and* the patient's understanding of that information: "The doctrine that a consent effective as authority to [per]form therapy can arise only from the patient's *understanding of* alternatives to and risks of the therapy is commonly denominated 'informed consent.'"[66] Despite this and the law's general requirement of understanding as the basis of consent, post-*Canterbury* cases have not troubled themselves with this issue. Appelbaum *et al.* argue that this is primarily due to an underlying uncertainty as to the roots and purpose of informed consent and to slack judicial language which fails to properly distinguish between "inform" and "disclose", and between "know", "understand", and "rationalise".

There has been a more heightened appreciation of the need to obtain an understanding of disclosed information in Canada.[67] In *Kelly v. Hazlett*, Morden J. explained that informed consent is necessary to obtain a patient's "awareness and assent".[68] In its progression from a consideration of consent (under battery) to a consideration of *assent* (under negligence), this case comes closest to the recognition of informed consent as informed *decision*-making. Though qualifying its findings with the proviso that the doctor does not have to "see into the minds of patients", it seems to require doctors to obtain an *apparent subjective understanding* of information disclosed. A purely subjective approach, it has been argued, would impose too onerous a duty on doctors, and would bypass the reality

---

[66] *Canterbury v. Spence, supra*, n. 2, at 780, f. 15. This is reinforced by numerous critical responses to informed consent doctrine. See for instance, Tulley (1992), p. 74: "Disclosure is a means rather than an end and its place in the doctrine of informed consent is a contingent rather than a necessary one."

[67] In *Kellett v. Griesdale* (June 26, 1985, transcript judgment Vancouver Registry No. C833053, at 11), the trial judge interpreted *Reibl v. Hughes* to require understanding and comprehension, and commented that: "[i]t may very well be that the defendant gave a warning but, if so, it did not make a sufficient impression on the plaintiff. The defendant was aware of the problem I mentioned earlier about patients tending to push aside any consideration of risk. That being so, it was incumbent on him to ensure that the plaintiff clearly understood the risk of significant hearing loss." In *Stamos v. Davies, supra*, n. 39 at 519, Krever J. acknowledged that the cause of this litigation was the "less than satisfactory physician-patient relationship arising out of the failure on the part of the physician to take the patient into his confidence and share with him information which as a matter of professional relations, if not law, the patient was entitled to have."

[68] *Kelly v. Hazlett, supra*, n. 39.

that many patients do not want to vigorously engage in the understanding process.[69] On the basis of this case, to succeed in an informed consent/decision claim on the basis of lack of understanding, the plaintiff would have to establish either than a reasonable patient in the plaintiff's position would not have understood, or that the defendant knew or ought to have known that the plaintiff did not understand. A higher standard would hardly be tolerated by the medical profession, though one may query whether a doctor's disclosure could attract liability in battery or negligence solely because it was made in an excessively obscure or technical manner. This is unlikely to be the case where there is no evidence that disclosure was made dismissively or in undue haste, and where the patient failed to volunteer questions or communicate a need to comprehend the information in simpler terms. Where it appears to a doctor that his patient has special difficulty understanding the English language, the doctor may come under a heightened duty to ensure that the patient understands the gist of what he tells him about the recommended treatment and its alternatives.[70] It is, however, worth noting Tulley's observation that, whereas a patient is likely to make it known to a doctor that he does not understand the French that he uses, he is considerably less likely to tell him that he does not understand the *English* he uses.[71]

It may next be queried whether a requirement of understanding implies that *rationality* must also be present. If employed as a means of limiting disclosure, such a requirement would sharply cut through much of the rhetoric upon which informed consent was originally constructed—principally *Canterbury*'s autonomy-based rejection of "the paternalistic notion that the physician may remain silent simply because divulgence might prompt the patient to forego therapy the physician feels the patient really needs."[72] However, it raises the corollary possibility of rendering a doctor liable where he decides to impart less information on the basis of the patient's apparently irrational mentality. This was evident in *Kelly v. Hazlett*, where the defendant had agreed to operate on the plaintiff to correct numbness and stiffness in her right hand and elbow respectively, but had initially refused to cosmetically remedy a deformity in her right

---

[69] Sommerville (1981), pp. 776–778.
[70] *Schanczl v. Singh* [1988] 2 W.W.R. 465.
[71] Tulley (1992), p. 77.
[72] *Canterbury v. Spence, supra,* n. 2 at 789.

elbow on the grounds that breaking and resetting a bone would be too dangerous for the patient. Shortly before the operation and after sedation, the plaintiff insisted on seeing the defendant and told him that she wanted the cosmetic surgery performed also; his attempts to dissuade her failed. In deciding that the defendant ought to have impressed upon his patient the additional risk of permanent stiffness of the elbow, Morden J. was influenced by the defendant's acknowledgment that the patient's renewed request seemed at the time "irrational" and "foolish" to him. Far from exonerating the doctor from disclosure, the judge felt that this perception should have alerted him to the possibility that the patient had missed some fundamental point and lacked an adequate awareness of the consequences.[73]

A presumption that the duty of disclosure is designed to ensure an independent rational decision by the patient—one which will assess the pros and cons *objectively*—seems, however, implicit in some Ontario decisions, where the duty to disclose alternatives has been restricted to the disclosure of objectively *beneficial* alternatives. In *Bonnell v. Moddel*, Griffiths J. of the Ontario High Court limited disclosure to cases where "in the opinion of the physician the alternative procedures offer some advantage and are reasonably likely to achieve a beneficial result."[74] This, he stated, is because the reasonable patient, under the *Reibl* test, is likely to reject alternatives with less beneficial prospects. While such rulings make little sense in the light of the goals which ostensibly guide informed consent, they are, as I will later discuss, the unfortunate by-product of this type of claim for compensation which crucially requires proof of causation.

A second integral ingredient to the giving of a consent and the making of a decision is that each has been done voluntarily and in the absence of force or duress. Whilst voluntariness or the absence of undue influence is an essential element in the making of a proper basic consent, and thus often a critical point of enquiry in the battery analysis, its role in the negligence analysis is less defined, and it is not likely to emerge as an issue once it has been established that an objectively thorough level of disclosure has been made, basic understanding has been achieved, and the patient's right to make a

---

[73] *Kelly v. Hazlett, supra*, n.39, at 562–564.
[74] *Bonnell v. Moddel*, February 5, 1987, transcript judgment No. 1399/82, at 31.

medically irrational decision has been safeguarded.[75] As a criterion to test the extent of a patient's informed consent and assent to treatment, it is made vaguer still by the legitimate ethical commitment of medical health carers to do what is best, what is most medically prudent, for their patients in the circumstances. That is to say that the law must not only tolerate, but must to some extent encourage, a reasonable degree of persuasive recommendation by doctors, if it is not to wholly outrage and alienate a profession which is ethically constructed upon the vocation to cure or heal in the specifically medical sense. Appelbaum *et al.* bemoan "the paucity of analytic thinking being directed" to the issue of voluntariness,[76] yet they have neatly provided the reason why this is so: "One aspect of the legitimacy of a decision based on pressure from another person is the legitimacy of the pressure itself."[77]

---

[75] The U.S. President's Commission, Vol. 1 (1982), p. 64, urged that patients be made aware that they have choices over their treatment. See also the courageous first instance English decision in *Wells v. Surrey Area Health Authority*, *The Times* July 29, 1978, p. 3. A woman had consented to sterilisation during the course of a Caesarian section, at a time when she was clearly exhausted. Though the court ruled that she had understood the nature and implications of the operation, and that the defendant was not guilty of battery, it awarded £3,000 in damages for failure to provide an opportunity in which to advise her of such an important step.

[76] Appelbaum, Lidz, and Meisel (1987), p. 62.

[77] *ibid.*, pp. 61–62.

Chapter 5

The Professional Standard Assessment of Disclosure

The earliest reported common law analysis of patients' consent arose from the 1767 English case of *Slater v. Baker*.[1] The court's decision that doctors must as a matter of law obtain consents from their patients was primarily influenced by an evidenced general practice amongst a nascent medical profession to do just that.[2] The decision was equally grounded on an acknowledgment that the success of operations is dependent on the co-operation of patients. Indeed, the court ruled that "it is reasonable that a patient should be told what is about to be done to him, that he may take courage and put himself in such a situation as to enable him to undergo the operation."[3] The decision strikes a curious note two centuries on. Spirited observations in defence of informing patients are now regrettably scarce in England. The courts continue to adhere to a professional standard assessment of disclosure—one of the few jurisdictions still to do so[4]—despite ongoing critical objections to the relevance and substance of expert evidence on general disclosure practices within the

---

[1] *Slater v. Baker & Stapleton* (1767) 2 Wils. K.B. 860. The plaintiff had hired the defendant doctors to remove the bandages from a partially healed leg fracture. Against the plaintiff's protests, they instead refractured his leg and encased it in an experimental apparatus designed to stretch and straighten his leg during rehealing.

[2] The court found (*ibid.* at 862) that "it appears from the evidence of the surgeons that it was improper to disunite the callous without consent; this is the usage and law of surgeons: then it was ignorance and unskilfulness in that very particular, to do contrary to the rule of the profession, what no surgeon ought to have done".

[3] *ibid.*

[4] Ireland is a notable other, though the courts have proved somewhat bolder in qualifying the extent to which it is bound to accept the views of experts on proper disclosure practice. See *infra*, pp. 145–147, 152–153.

profession. In this chapter, I propose to assess the development of English disclosure law against the mounting challenges which are likely, ultimately, to force changes to this body of law.

Non-Disclosure: A Very British Affair?

In the first case to test *negligent* pre-treatment non-disclosure, *Hatcher v. Black*, the plaintiff singer had been advised to undergo surgery to correct a toxic goitre.[5] When she asked whether there was a risk to her voice, she was assured there was none. In the event, her vocal cord suffered paralysis. At first instance, Denning L.J. sensationally likened the effects of litigation on a doctor's professional reputation, to a dagger through the doctor's body. In vindicating the defendant, he was influenced by the fact that it did not appear to be general medical practice to make such disclosure, and further by the defendant's opinion that the plaintiff would still have chosen to undergo the recommended operation if she had been fully informed of the risk.

In 1957, McNair J. delivered a first instance decision in *Bolam v. Friern Hospital* which has since dominated English law on medical negligence.[6] At its core is a stout preference for the professional standard model, whereby a "doctor is not guilty of negligence if he has acted in accordance with a practice accepted as proper by a responsible body of medical men skilled in that particular art."[7] This the learned judge extended to claims for non-disclosure of medical information. His directions to the jury—one must assume, consciously—made it very difficult for the jury to accept the plaintiff's claim on this point; it was told that it had to consider whether the defendant was not "competent" in omitting to "stress" a "minimal" risk to a "mentally sick" patient whom the doctor had a "strong . . . hope" of curing.[8]

The status and format of this emerging action was considered more fully in *Chatterton v. Gerson*, where the plaintiff suffered

---

[5] *Hatcher v. Black* [1954] C.L.Y. 2289. Negligent non-disclosure had earlier been considered in the context of the failure of maternity home owners to inform the plaintiff that a case of puerperal fever had recently occurred in their establishment: *Marshall v. Lindsey County Council* [1935] 1 K.B. 516.

[6] *Bolam v. Friern Hospital Management Committee* [1957] 2 All E.R. 118.

[7] *ibid*. at 122.

[8] *ibid*. at 124.

permanent loss of feeling in her right leg after two operations to relieve post-operative scar pain in the region of her groin.[9] The contested operation had involved injection of a phenol solution into the area of the spinal cord, spinal fluid, and nerve roots, with a view to destroying the pain conducting fibres. It had been a controversial choice to the extent that it was opposed by many specialists and widely considered a matter of last resort for the relief of unendurable pain. It carried the possibility of many complications, in particular the regeneration of pain, transmission of pain-causing functions to adjacent nerves, and numbness. The case was marked by a deep-seated conflict of evidence, which was ultimately resolved in favour of the defendant's version of events.[10]

In considering the plaintiff's alternate pleas of battery and negligence, Bristow J. proposed that battery law restricts itself to the question of whether the patient gave a "real consent", and is not concerned with the mere "failure of communication between doctor and patient".[11] Instead, non-disclosure is assessed as part of the doctor's duty of care under negligence law, and is thus governed by the *Bolam* test or professional standard. A doctor must ordinarily "explain what he intends to do, and its implications, in the way a careful and responsible doctor in similar circumstances would have done".[12] Whilst no expert witness positively supported the defendant's choice of treatment, each expressed the opinion that the risk was too unforeseeable to merit disclosure. In this light, Bristow J.

---

[9] *Chatterton v. Gerson* [1981] 1 All E.R. 257. This case succeeded *Chadwick v. Parsons* [1971] Lloyd's Rep. 49, QB, [1971] 2 Lloyd's Rep. 322, where the defendant admitted liability, and *O'Malley-Williams v. Board of Governors of the National Hospital for Nervous Diseases* [1975] 1 B.M.J. 635, QBD.

[10] The court had the benefit of reading a paper published by the defendant in which he had advocated that patients be disclosed the pros and cons of particular treatments on the basis *inter alia* that they could then choose between alternative courses and would be less likely to be aggrieved at a later stage. Though the defendant could not clearly recall what he had disclosed, he claimed that he would have followed his usual practice and told the patient the purpose of the operation, that it would lead to an area of numbness larger than the pain source which the treatment was designed to undo, and that it might cause temporary loss to muscle power. A nurse who worked with the defendant testified to his meticulousness in making disclosure to patients. Further, the plaintiff's version of events seemed distorted and failed to accord with the sensible picture drawn by the experts. According to Bristow J. (*ibid.* at 263), "her account of this, which she clearly now believes to be the truth, is entirely unreliable and results from trying to rationalise the cause of the grievous disability which followed."

[11] *ibid.* at 265. See Chapter 6, *infra*, pp. 181–183.

[12] *ibid.*

concluded that the defendant's warning had been adequate, and that a repeat explanation before the second operation had been unnecessary. Finally, he doubted the plaintiff's claim that, if informed, she would not have consented, concluding that the "whole picture on the evidence [was] of a lady desperate for pain relief."[13]

Another awkward conflict of evidence arose in *Hills v. Potter*, where the plaintiff was left permanently paralysed from the neck down after undergoing an operation to cure a deformity of her back.[14] The plaintiff based her claim solely on the failure of the defendant to disclose a general risk of paralysis inherent in the use of anaesthetics, pleading both negligence and battery. According to her version, the defendant had explained that the operation would incise certain neck muscles to prevent them pulling her neck down, that it was "a major operation with a small risk", that she would have to wear a collar for some time after, that she would not be able to move her neck right or left, and that as time was not of the essence she should consider the options with her family and general practitioner. She denied the defendant's version that he had identified certain outside general risks naturally incidental to any surgical operation under anaesthetic, such as death and paralysis, or that the operation was irreversible. She would, she said, never have agreed to an operation which could leave her without the capacity to walk. Experts agreed with the defendant that it was important not to scare such patients off by exaggerating general and remote risks, and that either version of what in fact had been disclosed would have accorded with the medical standard. Hirst J. at first instance concluded that disclosure had been adequate, accepting the defendant's evidence of what had in fact been disclosed.

Compendiously reviewing the available case-law, Hirst J. resisted the revived attempts by counsel to import into English law the "transatlantic doctrine of informed consent", believing that a distinction between *diagnosis and treatment* on the one hand and *advice* on the other is less stark than that doctrine presumes. *Informed consent*, he argued, is misleading if it suggests that the duty of disclosure is dependent upon it, for "it is quite clear . . . that on any view English law does require the surgeon to supply to the patient information to enable the patient to decide whether or not to undergo the operation".[15] Though he accepted that the doctrine of informed consent is

---

[13] *Chatterton v. Gerson* [1981] 1 All E.R. 257 at 267.
[14] *Hills v. Potter* [1984] 1 W.L.R. 641.
[15] *ibid.* at 652.

designed to raise the standard of disclosure, he refused to accept "that by adopting the *Bolam* principle, the court in effect abdicates its power of decision to the doctors. In every case the court must be satisfied that the standard contended for on their behalf accords with that upheld by a substantial body of medical opinion, and that this body of medical opinion is both respectable and responsible, and experienced in this particular field of medicine."[16]

The first (and so far the last) rigorous challenge to the professional standard assessment of disclosure emerged in 1985 with the case of *Sidaway v. Bethlem Royal Hospital*[17]—since described as "a classic case for the full application of the doctrine of informed consent."[18] After more than a decade of pain, 71-year-old Mrs Sidaway went to a hospital, was given a myelogram, and was subsequently told that her doctor had "decided to operate". The operation in question was on the plaintiff's cervical vertebrae, and inherently carried a less than one per cent risk of damage to her spinal cord, which was not communicated to the patient. This risk materialised and resulted in her permanent paralysis. Direct testimony by the doctor as to what had been disclosed, and on what grounds, was frustrated by the surgeon's recent death. Accordingly, expert medical evidence of the general practice he and others followed in like cases assumed a perceptibly more important role during the hearing. At first instance, Skinner J. accepted that the surgeon had, in keeping with his customary practice, probably explained the operation to the patient in simple terms, warning her of the possibility and consequences of damaging nerve roots (a one to two per cent risk)—an assumption that the plaintiff denied and Lord Scarman later expressed some surprise at. Though satisfied that the patient would not have undergone the treatment had she been informed of the risk, Skinner J. refused the plaintiff relief on the basis that disclosure of this risk had not been general and approved practice within the terms of the *Bolam* test. The plaintiff appealed to the Court of Appeal.

Dunn L.J. referred to the duty on doctors to give *advice* to patients, comparing this to the advisory functions of solicitors[19]—an analogy which has been rightly criticised on the basis that "[a]dvice giving is

---

[16] *Hills v. Potter* [1984] 1 W.L.R. 641 at 653.
[17] *Sidaway v. Bethlem Royal Hospital* [1985] 1 A.C. 871, HL.
[18] Mahoney (1985), p. 114.
[19] *Sidaway v. Bethlem Royal Hospital* [1984] 1 All E.R. 1018 at 1030, CA, citing *Saif Ali v. Sidney Mitchell & Co.* [1980] A.C. 198.

to a solicitor what diagnosis and treatment are to a doctor".[20] Browne-Wilkinson L.J. also made comparison with "the general duty of care which the law would impose on anyone who in the course of business has undertaken to give *advice*".[21] That his Lordship contemplated the provision of *information* more than advice is evident by his analogy with the failure of a hotel brochure to point out that the sea in which potential tourists are invited to swim is populated by sharks. His rejection of informed consent was finally, though inconsistently, justified by "factors peculiar to the medical profession".[22] More specifically, he felt that disclosure ought to be "a matter of professional judgment"[23] and that excessive disclosure might prejudice the doctor's chance of curing the patient by undermining confidence. The plaintiff's appeal to the Court of Appeal having failed, the House of Lords was presented with an opportunity to rule for the first time on the status of the duty to disclose. Since its decision has subsequently domineered for better or worse English disclosure law, each of its lordships' speeches merits individual attention.

The more temperate analysis offered by Lord Bridge (with whom Lord Keith concurred) has since attracted by far the most credit and support. The learned judge accepted that the doctrine of informed consent, as articulated in *Canterbury v. Spence*, aims to safeguard against the kind of medical paternalism which assumes that "doctor always knows best".[24] The doctrine is further pinned to the belief "that a conscious adult patient of sound mind is entitled to decide for himself whether or not he will submit to a particular course of treatment proposed by the doctor". In rejecting the informed consent development, Lord Bridge expressed the view that the professional standard model does not necessarily surrender determination of disclosure standards to the medical profession; the court retains the power to resolve conflicts between experts, and even where expert testimony unanimously supports non-disclosure in a particular case, the court "might in certain circumstances come to the conclusion that disclosure of a particular risk was so obviously necessary to an

---

[20] Kennedy (1988), pp. 182 and 183: according to whom the duty to disclose contemplates instead the provision of medical "*information* . . . about alternatives and consequences, including risks, thereby enabling the patient to judge for him—or herself."

[21] *Sidaway v. Bethlem Royal Hospital, supra*, n. 19, at 1033, CA.

[22] *ibid.* at 1034.

[23] *ibid.* at 1035.

[24] *Sidaway v. Bethlem Royal Hospital, supra*, n. 17 at 897 and 899, HL.

informed choice on the part of the patient that no reasonably prudent medical man would fail to make it."[25] Because this risk was statistically remote, the medical standard afforded a "complete defence" to the charge of negligent non-disclosure. Like Lord Diplock, Lord Bridge doubted the merit of distinguishing between general and specific risks, though he acknowledged that even under informed consent, there is no duty to disclose every conceivable risk, and that this is often justified on the basis that "the patient may be expected to be aware of such risks or that they are relatively remote."[26] However, he accepted with certainty that if a patient volunteers questions about risks, the doctor's duty is "to answer both truthfully and as fully as the questioner requires."[27]

Lord Bridge's response to the informed consent innovation is deeply flawed and uninformed in many respects. The learned judge expressed three concerns. His first is a defence of paternalism, that the doctor is best able to weigh the "wide variety of factors" that must affect his clinical judgment on "how best to communicate to the patient the significant factors necessary to enable the patient to make an informed decision whether to undergo the treatment."[28] As a principled observation with intended effect, this fails to attach any importance to the need to safeguard the future rights of patients to autonomous participation in decisions regarding their health care. It also underestimates the incestuous logic upon which the professional standard test of disclosure inevitably depends. On the one hand, that test enables the defendant to testify to having considered an array of vague criteria before deciding not to "alarm" the instant patient with gloomy imponderables, whilst then on the other hand it enables the defence's expert witnesses to express an opinion that it is not general practice to disclose outside risks whatever their likely effect on specific patients may be.

Secondly, Lord Bridge was of the view that informed consent would deprive the court of the advantages of receiving expert "medical opinion" (as opposed to "explanation of the primary medical factors").[29] On the contrary, it is common knowledge that informed consent doctrine does not purport to banish expert medical opinion from the court; rather it logically alters the capacity with

---

[25] *Sidaway v. Bethlem Royal Hospital, supra*, n. 17 at 900.
[26] *ibid.* at 897.
[27] *ibid.* at 898.
[28] *ibid.* at 899.
[29] *ibid.*

which the court accepts that evidence, transforming it from *compelling* evidence of the due standard of care to *persuasive* evidence of that standard.[30] Rather strangely, in his third objection, Lord Bridge felt that informed consent would introduce into law an uncertain judicial forum for assessing the requirements of the reasonable patient, *Canterbury v. Spence* being "so imprecise as to be almost meaningless."[31] In fact, the *Canterbury* decision presents a careful, meticulous analysis of the relevant rules and principles: the vagueness of which Lord Bridge complains is no more than the vagueness and generality which inevitably pervades negligence law.[32]

Lord Templeman elaborated on the nexus between disclosure of obvious/remote risks and questions volunteered by the patient. He argued that disclosure of the remote but serious risk of damage to the plaintiff's spinal cord would merely have "reinforced the obvious", that there is a "possibility of something going wrong in the course of a delicate operation performed in a vital area".[33] In the absence of direct questions from the plaintiff, the doctor was not required to identify this risk. He could legitimately have feared that too much or detailed information would distress and confuse her "at a time when she was suffering from stress, pain and anxiety."[34] Additionally, Lord Templeman asserted that doctors ought to disclose the presence of any "danger which by its nature or magnitude or for some other reason requires to be separately taken into account by the patient in order to reach a balanced decision".[35] Significantly, he instanced as risks which ought to be disclosed because they are "special in kind or magnitude or special to the patient", both the 10 per cent risk of stroke identified by Lord Bridge and the 4 per cent risk of death identified by *Reibl v. Hughes*.[36] Of this distinction between special and general risks, he proposed that if it is general practice to disclose a particular risk, then the court may presume that it is a special risk, so that the defendant will have to explain why he failed to disclose it. If experts are divided, it is for the court to decide whether the risk was of a general or special kind. More radically, his Lordship asserted that in the "case of a general danger *the courts must decide* whether the

---

[30] See Chapter 4, *supra*, p. 99.
[31] *Sidaway v. Bethlem Royal Hospital, supra*, n. 17 at 899, HL.
[32] See Chapter 6, *infra*, pp. 177, 180 and Chapter 9, *infra*, pp. 276–277.
[33] *Sidaway v. Bethlem Royal Hospital, supra*, n. 17 at 902, HL.
[34] *ibid.*
[35] *ibid.*
[36] *ibid.* at 903.

information afforded to the patient was sufficient to alert *the* patient to the possibility of serious harm of the kind in fact suffered."[37]

However, the learned judge qualified these points by drawing unexpectedly from contract law, a strange and potentially dangerous direction to take which goes against a pervasive common law preference for a torts-based analysis of doctors' duties and patients' rights. In his view, the doctor-patient relationship is essentially contractual in origin.[38] The doctor, in return for fees, performs a health care service, impliedly contracting to act at all times in the patient's best interests. He does not impliedly contract to provide the patient with all the information he has gained through his training and experience. An obligation of that nature could run counter to his other obligation to act in the patient's best interests, particularly where it is likely to cause the patient to "make an unbalanced decision" through being "made aware of possibilities which he is not capable of assessing because of his lack of medical training, his prejudices or his personality."[39]

Lord Diplock's response to the issues raised was uniquely pro-defendant. With few qualifications—save ambiguous references to ignorance, intelligence, and inquisitiveness in patients—he asserted that the general duty of care on doctors is indivisible. It cannot be dissected into component parts (such as diagnosis, treatment, and disclosure) for the purpose of applying different criteria to each.[40] With no critical justification of this hands-off approach to the medical negligence claim—except . to say that the prospect of defensive medicine haunts society, pointing out that many advances, such as the cures to smallpox and tuberculosis, were discovered in a climate which facilitated chances—he continued that just as much for the non-disclosure claim, "the court is not tempted to put itself in the surgeon's shoes; it has to rely upon and evaluate expert evidence, remembering that it is no part of its task of evaluation to give effect to any preference it may have for one responsible body of professional opinion over another, provided that it is satisfied by the expert evidence that both qualify as responsible bodies of medical opinion."[41] The *Bolam* test merely "brings up to date and re-expresses in

---

[37] *Sidaway v. Bethlem Royal Hospital, supra*, n. 17 (emphasis added).
[38] *ibid.* at 904.
[39] *ibid.*
[40] *ibid.* at 893.
[41] *ibid.* at 895.

the light of modern conditions in which the art of medicine is now practised, an ancient rule of common law".[42]

In his dissent, Lord Scarman sought to import into English law the doctrine of informed consent as formulated in *Canterbury v. Spence*. He was "disturbed" by the continued application of the professional standard to 'advice'[43]—for the "profession, it is said, should not be a judge in its own cause."[44] Informed consent, by contrast, is grounded on the basic human right already protected by the common law that a patient should be permitted to make his own decision. Acknowledging the inherent adaptability of the common law, and instancing *Donoghue v. Stevenson*[45] he proposed that if "it be recognised that a doctor's duty of care extends not only to the health and well-being of his patient but also to a proper respect for his patient's rights, the duty to warn can be seen to be a part of the doctor's duty of care."[46] His Lordship identified, beyond the humanistic pledge of informed consent to protect self-determination, various practical benefits, whereby it may enable each patient "to consider and balance the medical advantages and risks alongside other relevant matters, such as, for example, his family business or social responsibilities of which the doctor may only be partially, if at all, informed."[47] As a legal action, it also has the advantage of compelling doctors to first defend the charge of materiality of risk, and where materiality of risk and non-disclosure is established, to justify why disclosure was not made and whether it can objectively be defended under a therapeutic privilege. He further accepted the persuasive relevance of expert medical testimony in disclosure cases, and following *Canterbury*, expressed a preference for an objective test of causation on the basis that an inquiry into what the plaintiff would have decided would "be frustrated by the subjectivity of its aim and purpose".[48]

On the facts of the case, Lord Scarman ruled against the patient, despite accepting the trial judge's finding of fact that the plaintiff

---

[42] *Sidaway v. Bethlem Royal Hospital, supra*, n. 17 at 892.

[43] On a later occasion, Lord Scarman (1986) at 697 explained his conception of advice, which is "not limited to the recommendation which the doctor makes to the patient, but [includes] also advice about alternative courses of treatment, their advantages and disadvantages. That is to say, . . . information as to options as well as the doctor's recommendation."

[44] *Sidaway v. Bethlem Royal Hospital, supra*, n. 17, at 882, HL.

[45] *Donoghue v. Stevenson* [1932] A.C. 562.

[46] *Sidaway v. Bethlem Royal Hospital, supra*, n. 17, at 885, HL.

[47] *ibid*. at 886.

[48] *ibid*.

would not have undergone the operation had the risk been disclosed to her. He explained his decision on the basis that counsel for the plaintiff, despite pleading informed consent, had not established materiality of risk to the extent that the doctor ought to have known that the reasonable person in the patient's position would have considered the risk material. His Lordship was clearly influenced by the lack of evidence before the court, due to the doctor's recent decease, on the extent of the warning given but also his assessment of "the mental, emotional, and physical state of the patient . . . with especial reference to his view as to what would be the effect upon her of a warning of the existence of a risk, albeit slight, of serious personal injury arising from the operation".[49] His belief that such evidence was necessary to ascertain whether the doctor felt that disclosure would "frighten the patient into refusing [the recommended] operation"[50] suggests that Lord Scarman envisaged a fairly broad application of the therapeutic privilege.

The *Sidaway* decision unravelled a range of different views, and it is perhaps unsurprising that it evoked an unusually disparate critical reception—a fact that additionally suggests the kaleidoscope nature of negligence law which seems peculiarly apt to mean different things to different people in different contexts. Gillon believes that *Sidaway* "changed considerably" the law, since only Lord Diplock accepted the *Bolam* test without qualification.[51] Mahoney shares this view, attaching importance to Lord Bridge's majority decision to qualify the *Bolam* test of disclosure, which suggests that the courts might exercise a freer hand when considering whether to override the stated views of experts on customary disclosure practice.[52] Similarly, Kennedy declares that the "message of *Sidaway* is clear . . . Medical Paternalism has had its day."[53] By contrast, Teff argues that it is "difficult to read *Sidaway* as representing more than a slight divergence from the *Bolam* test, especially given the general tenor of the speeches and the clear rejection of 'informed consent'."[54] Similarly, Newdick proposes that any differences between Lord Diplock on the one hand and Lords Bridge, Keith, and Templeman on the other are "illusory".[55]

---

[49] *Sidaway v. Bethlem Royal Hospital, supra*, n. 17 at 876–877.
[50] *ibid.* at 883.
[51] Gillon (1986), pp. 116 and 117.
[52] Mahoney (1985), p. 119.
[53] Kennedy (1988a), p. 210.
[54] Teff (1985), p. 450.
[55] Newdick (1985), pp. 249 and 250.

The *Sidaway* decision has given rise to no greater consistency in the courts. In the Scottish case of *Moyes v. Lothian Health Board*, Lord Caplan aligned himself with the pro-paternalism sentiments expressed by Lord Diplock.[56] In his view, there was "nothing in the majority view in *Sidaway* which suggests that the extent and quality of warning to be given by a doctor to his patient should not in the last resort be governed by medical criteria."[57] Despite evidence that the plaintiff's allergy to iodine-based contrast media (which was known by the defendant) doubled the normal risk of stroke during an angiography, his Lordship decided at first instance that the defendant could not be held liable for failing to disclose that risk unless it was proper medical practice to have so warned. He further supported the view that in deciding whether or not to disclose, a doctor may choose to consider "the ability of the patient to absorb information about his station without adding damage to his health".[58]

However, recent first instance decisions display a readiness to adopt a more rigorous assessment of disclosure standards than would be possible were the *Bolam* or *Sidaway* tests strictly adhered to. These are best seen as mounting evidence of the unworkability of the professional standard approach to disclosure, and not merely deviations from the strict letter of the law. In *Smith v. Tunbridge Wells Health Authority*, the court with little hesitation held the defendant negligent for failing to disclose a risk that would not apparently have been disclosed had general and approved medical practice been followed: indeed, there was sufficient expert evidence to support the view that "a body of experienced competent surgeons" would not have disclosed the risk of impotence.[59] The High Court decided that this omission was neither "reasonable nor responsible", and that the defendant was negligent.

In *McAllister v. Lewisham and North Southwark Health Authority*,[60] the plaintiff underwent a brain scan and angiograph, after being strongly advised so to do, to correct a large arteriovascular malformation. She was told that there was a 20 per cent risk that the leg would get worse rather than better, but not that there were any risks inherent in brain surgery, nor that there was a specific risk of left-sided hemiplegia and a further risk that increased deficit would extend beyond the leg.

---

[56] *Moyes v. Lothian Health Board* (1990) 1 Med. L.R. 463.
[57] *ibid.* at 469.
[58] *ibid.*
[59] *Smith v. Tunbridge Wells Health Authority* (1994) 5 Med. L.R. 334.
[60] *McAllister v. Lewisham and North Southwark Health Authority* (1994) 5 Med. L.R. 343.

After the 24-hour operation, the patient incurred a complete hemiplegia which left her left arm wholly without voluntary movement, a condition which subsequently proved unresponsive to physiotherapy. Rougier J. expressed the view that the distinction between general and specific risks, as attempted by Lord Templeman in *Sidaway*, is a "distortion" of reality.[61] With commendable rigour, he assessed the merits of each expert's view of good disclosure practice, assessing the testimonial support of the doctor's non-disclosure in the context of each expert's estimation of the relevant risks. It seems clear that the learned judge felt that the fact that the choice of treatment was questionable made the need for ample disclosure all the greater. He concluded that the doctor "seriously underestimated" the risks: "Merely to say that there was a one in five chance of making her leg worse, and to leave her with the impression that there were really no two ways about the operation and that she had nothing to lose constituted an actionable breach of duty."[62]

Numerous other decisions suggest a growing dissatisfaction with the use to which expert evidence is put in disclosure trials. In *Gascoine v. Ian Sheridan & Co and Latham*, Mitchell J. observed that a group of doctors testifying to what they would and should have done in similar circumstances does not necessarily constitute an alternative school of medical opinion.[63] In *Newell & Newell v. Goldenberg*, Mantell J. held a doctor negligent for failing to disclose the risk of a sterilisation failing, observing that the "*Bolam* principle provides a defence for those who lag behind the times. It cannot serve those who know better."[64] And in *Lybert v. Warrington Health Authority*, the Court of Appeal concluded that the defendant had negligently failed to impress upon the patient the fact that the sterilisation operation might fail, despite an entry in the doctor's notes which suggested that a warning of this nature had been given.[65]

The Irish courts have faced similar challenges, though seem to have attained a greater measure of doctrinal certainty with respect to the court's power to override expert medical evidence on the due standard of care.[66] The Supreme Court had an opportunity to consider the evolving pre-treatment disclosure duty in the case of

---

[61] *McAllister v. Lewisham and North Southwark Health Authority* (1994) 5 Med. L.R. 343 at 352.
[62] *ibid.* at 351.
[63] *Gascoine v. Ian Sheridan & Co. and Latham* (1994) 5 Med. L.R. 437.
[64] *Newell & Newell v. Goldenberg* (1995) 6 Med. L.R. 371 at 374.
[65] *Lybert v. Warrington Health Authority* (1996) 7 Med. L.R. 71.
[66] See Chapter 3, *supra*, p. 71.

Walsh v. Family Planning Services.[67] The most troublesome aspect of the court's decision (no less indeed than the fate of the House of Lords' decision in *Sidaway*) is the various and inconsistent nature of its findings, making it difficult for jurists and courts to extract a majority judgment or clear set of principles for future cases. Finlay C.J., with scant regard for nomenclatural coherence, endorsed a professional standard test of disclosure, whilst also affirming the obligation on Irish doctors to "inform the patient of any possible harmful consequence arising from the operation, so as to permit the patient to give an *informed consent*".[68] At the core of his judgment is a qualification, similar in wording and effect to Lord Bridge's in *Sidaway*, which recognises that "it may be, certainly in relation to very clearly elective surgery, that the court might more readily reach a conclusion that the extent of warning given or omitted contained inherent defects which ought to have been obvious to any person giving the matter due consideration than it could do in a case of complicated medical or surgical procedures".[69] On the other hand, O'Flaherty J. (with whom Hederman J. concurred) expressly favoured assessment of disclosure standards "on the established principles of negligence"[70] and not according to the professional standard principles enunciated in *Dunne v. Irish Maternity Hospital*.[71]

The *Walsh* decision yielded a scattering of judicial dicta whose relative weightiness was unclear. Unsurprisingly, confusion in the High Court followed. Attention naturally focused on the judgments given by Finlay C.J. and O'Flaherty J. (The remaining two judgments by McCarthy J. and Egan J. were evasively limited to the special facts of the case.) Given that O'Flaherty J. had the support of Hederman J, one might have been pardoned for presuming that he delivered the majority decision—as indeed Geoghegan J. clearly felt in a subsequent High Court decision in *Bolton v. Blackrock Clinic*.[72] Though this issue does not seem to have been taken up by courts or jurists since, it appears that the bulk of O'Flaherty J.'s findings must be treated as *obiter dicta* (that is, as non-binding *opinions* of the law

---

[67] *Walsh v. Family Planning Services* [1992] I.R. 497.
[68] *ibid*. at 510 (emphasis added).
[69] *ibid*. at 511.
[70] *ibid*. at 535.
[71] *Dunne v. National Maternity Hospital* [1989] I.R. 91 establishes the principles of Irish medical negligence law, which operates a professional standard model subject to more decisively expressed qualifications: see chapter 3, *supra*, pp. 67–68, 71.
[72] *Bolton v. Blackrock Clinic* Irish High Court, unreported, December 20, 1994.

which were not actually applied by the judge to the facts of the case).[73] The learned judge had been of the view that Mr Walsh, "having made the case that *no* warning was given, and his case having been conducted on that basis, [could not now] argue in the alternative that if a warning was given it was insufficient."[74] When O'Flaherty J. considered at a more general level how the standard of disclosure should be assessed, he consciously expressed his findings in a hypothetical sense. This point is no longer critical to an assessment of current Irish law: during the appeal hearing for the *Bolton* case, Hamilton C.J. of the Supreme Court availed of the opportunity to affirm the professional standard test as articulated by Finlay C.J. in *Walsh*.[75] Therefore at its most basic, Irish law currently assesses the standard of disclosure by reference to general or approved medical practice, with the caveat that the courts are more likely to substitute its view of due disclosure for those stated testimonially by expert witnesses.

The English courts have so far attempted to assess disclosure issues as they relate to the therapeutic context, but they have yet to consider the disclosure rights of a patient or subject who suffers injury arising from research-based or experimental medical procedures. Throughout the common law, judicial regulation of biomedical research has been scarce, largely it would seem because the area has traditionally been governed by conventions and codes, but also because it is significantly more self-regulated by institutional review groups (in the United States) and local research ethics committees ("LRECs") (in the United Kingdom).[76] The practice in the United Kingdom seems to be that *ex gratia* payments are paid by the Medical

---

[73] See Healy (1998a), p. 27.

[74] *Walsh v. Family Planning Services, supra*, n. 67 at 534.

[75] *Bolton v. Blackrock Clinic, supra*, n. 72 at 7–10. This was also the view of O'Hanlon J. in his earlier High Court decision of *Farrell v. Varian* Irish High Court, unreported, November 19, 1994.

[76] In the U.K., there are as yet no statutory guidelines or controls operating on Local Research Ethics Committees in relation to projects that require experimentation on humans. According to Beyleveld and Longley (1998), where an LREC approves a clinical protocol, it does so on the basis that the proposed research is ethical, and not necessarily on the basis that the safety of subjects is assured. The authors argue that this fact should be explained to potential subjects, lest they misinterpret the function of the LREC's approval. The LREC has no specific legal status, nor does its approval render the clinical research lawful—so recognised by the Law Commission in *Mental Incapacity*, Law Com. 231, 1995, at para. 6.33. Decisions in response to research proposals may be judicially reviewed as an administrative decision: *R. v. Ethical Committee of St Mary's Hospital (Manchester), ex p. H.* [1988] 1 F.L.R. 512.

Research Council out of the NHS indemnity scheme to patients or subjects who suffer injury arising from medical research. According to one view, injured research subjects may find it difficult to recover for non-disclosure of risks following the *Sidaway* decision, given that the protocol adopted for the clinical trial will have been carefully considered and plotted by the LREC as a matter of general and approved practice within the relevant specialty.[77] This of course presumes that "*Bolam* as modified in *Sidaway* would be as likely to be followed in experimentation as in treatment".[78] According to the other view—which I am eager to endorse—*Sidaway* cannot and should not be interpreted to extend beyond the therapeutic context.[79] That decision is by now greatly at odds with developments in other common law jurisdictions. Its stubborn allegiance to the professional standard assessment of disclosure has been justified by the judges, rather tenuously at that, by reference to the doctor's paternalistic right to assess what the patient should know having regard to the fact that the patient requires the treatment to improve his health—a dynamic which is absent in the research context. The courts which have considered this question have concluded with little hesitation that disclosure should be heightened where a medical intervention is partly or wholly experimental, and in any case where the intervention is not *primarily* required for the patient's health care.[80] Indeed, the Convention on Human Rights and Biomedicine (1997), agreed by member state representatives of the European Community and the Council of Europe, provides by Article 5 that all medical interventions, whether therapeutic or experimental, "may only be carried out after the person concerned has given free and informed consent to it."[81]

---

[77] Mason and McCall-Smith (1994), p. 365. The authors propose that research subjects may have a cause of action in negligence against a research board or committee who approved a project without adequately and competently considering the risks to the subjects. They also argue that there is a strong case to be made for creation of a no-fault liability compensation scheme (not involving recourse to the court) for accidents due to medical research. This category of accident victims singled itself out to the Pearson Commission as meriting compensation for strict liability: Report of Royal Commission on Civil Liability and Compensation for Personal Injury Cmnd 7054, 1978, at para. 1341.

[78] Mason and McCall-Smith (1994), p. 365.

[79] See Chapter 4, *supra*, at p. 111.

[80] See further, Chapters 2 and 4, *supra*, pp. 57–58, 111; and Chapter 6, *infra*, pp. 185–186.

[81] Convention on Human Rights and Biomedicine 18, *Human Rights Law Journal* (1997) 135 at 135.

The various findings of the lawlords in *Sidaway* on the elective/non-elective divide, and the effect of questions asked by patients, have since been restrictively interpreted by the Court of Appeal in *Blyth v. Bloomsbury Health Authority* and *Gold v. Haringey Health Authority* respectively[82]—all the more surprising given that in recent years the Court of Appeal has proved readier than the House of Lords to embrace innovative developments in the law of torts.[83] The elective patient and the inquisitive patient each raises special concerns, and in their different ways they usefully expose the disingenuousness of the professional standard approach to disclosure. Each will continue to imperil that model and may ultimately quicken its demise.

Duties of Disclosure and Elective Treatment

The task of distinguishing between elective and non-elective (or *therapeutic*) forms of medical treatment is not without its difficulties. The most basic difference between the two in obvious cases is that an elective treatment is opted for by a patient *more* freely and *less* for reasons of medical necessity. It is a treatment which comparatively the patient can afford *not* to undergo. The two classic examples of elective treatment are cosmetic surgery and sterilisation. Cosmetic surgery may be sought to reshape "normal" structures of the body in an effort by the patient to enhance his physical appearance and self-esteem. Sterilisation may be sought by the patient to enable him to enjoy non-procreative sexual intercourse. Yet both these examples possess non-elective counterparts. The self-perceived need of a patient to undergo cosmetic surgery may be so deeply entrenched, psychologically, that the treatment has become something of a necessity for that patient. There is also, of course, the grey area which exists in some cases between cosmetic surgery and reconstructive surgery (that being a surgical reshaping of abnormal or damaged structures). Similarly, sterilisation procedures may be undertaken as a

---

[82] *Blyth v. Bloomsbury Health Authority* (1993) 4 Med. L.R. 151; *Gold v. Haringey Health Authority* [1988] 1 Q.B. 481.

[83] Two conspicuous examples include the loss of chance doctrine—see Chapter 7, *supra*, p. 224 and the emergent tort of unlawful interference with trade—see *Lonrho v. Shell Petroleum (No. 2)* [1982] A.C. 173, CA/HL and *Lonrho v. Fayed* [1989] 2 All E.R. 65, CA; [1991] 3 All E.R. 303, HL.

medical necessity, where for example the patient cannot safely bear (or financially afford) further children. Mixed motives in any case will inevitably affect the balance between therapeutic and elective components.

It is this writer's considered opinion that the prospect of mixed motives in many cases is not sufficient to diminish the working relevance of this distinction between the elective and therapeutic. The distinction has already been rejected by one English judge on the basis that it lacks any stable medical value—albeit in a decision that staunchly defends the professional standard assessment of disclosure.[84] Brazier similarly criticises it for being unworkable and artificial, instancing the scenario of a 37-year old woman for whom sterilisation has a therapeutic effect because further pregnancy might be complicated and harmful.[85] Taking this one step further, she asks whether vasectomy for this woman's husband is also non-elective. Can doctors be possibly expected to place medical treatments into legalistic pigeon-holes in advance of every instance of disclosure and of treatment? To which one may simply answer that yes, doctors are indeed capable of understanding the law (if it is clear) and have already done so. Moreover, the elective/ therapeutic distinction is essentially a medical or contextual one; it is not inherently legalistic. Doctors have for years striven to preserve their authority to pronounce on the scope of their duties at the level of ethics and to some extent the law. They retain the authority to interpret what in any given set of circumstances represents a *medical* component of a patient's wish to undergo a particular treatment. In all but exceptional cases, the extent to which that treatment is therapeutic or not is formed on an analysis of facts which are *or should be* readily known to a doctor after basic communication with his client. Indeed, the very fact that the elective-therapeutic balance will rarely be automatically obvious should strengthen the case for requiring doctors to discover what their patients expect or hope for, particularly where it is possible that the patient can well afford to do without the treatment, and certainly where an irreversible sterilisation, with its attendant emotional and psycho-symbolism, is concerned.

Because the professional standard model is constructed to defer to expert medical witnesses, it has become a pertinent concern in the jurisdictions that apply it whether or not the law should encourage

---

[84] *Gold v. Haringey Health Authority, supra*, n. 82 at 489.
[85] Brazier (1987), p. 183.

enhanced disclosure where the proposed treatment is wholly or mostly elective. For this reason, the distinction has featured highly in the few cases on the duty to disclose that have reached the English and Irish courts. In *Gold v. Haringey Health Authority* the plaintiff challenged the defendants' non-disclosure of two risks—a 0.26 per cent risk that her sterilisation could fail and lead to conception, and the comparatively safer 0.05 per cent risk of failure inherent in a male vasectomy.[86] She argued that if these risks had been disclosed, she would have foregone the procedure in favour of her husband obtaining a vasectomy. Fortunately for this plaintiff, and rather untypically, all the defence's experts conceded that they personally would have advised the plaintiff of these failure rates and alternatives. In theory, however, it was not general practice so to do, and one expert estimated that some 50 per cent would not so disclose. At first instance, Schiemann J. ruled that the general practice defence did not apply to disclosure of risks arising from non-therapeutic (or elective) treatments and procedures. According to the learned judge, the *Bolam* test "is different from the one generally applied in actions in respect of negligent advice. I see nothing in the reasons given for adopting the *Bolam* test in the sort of circumstances in *Sidaway* which compels me to widen the application of this exceptional rule so as to confuse it to apply to contraceptive counselling."[87] On appeal, Lloyd L.J. rejected Schiemann J.'s description of the *Bolam* test as "exceptional", and asserted that that test is "of general application whenever a defendant professes any special skill."[88] Placing considerable emphasis on Lord Diplock's deeply pro-profession ruling in *Sidaway*, Lloyd L.J. argued that the elective/therapeutic distinction does not modify the application of *Bolam*, nor should it, for to do so would introduce an arbitrary distinction into the law. "A plastic surgeon", he argued, "carrying out a skin graft is presumably engaged in therapeutic surgery; but what if he is carrying out a face-lift, or some other cosmetic operation?"[89] Rather, the *Bolam* "principle does not depend on the context in which any act is performed, or any advice given. It depends on a man professing skill or competence in a field beyond that possessed by the man on the Clapham omnibus."[90]

---

[86] *Gold v. Haringey Health Authority, supra*, n. 82.
[87] *ibid.* at 488 (as quoted by Lloyd L.J.).
[88] *ibid.* at 489.
[89] *ibid.*
[90] *ibid.* at 489–490.

The strange result of this for the plaintiff was that, though each expert witness personally endorsed disclosure of the relevant risks and alternatives, the defence succeeded because a crude estimate of general practice amongst the relevant sector of the medical community suggested that most doctors would not have disclosed this information. Though the House of Lords refused leave for appeal in the *Gold* case, it is better not to look on it as the final word in England. The Department of Health in its *Guide for Examination or Treatment* wisely draws doctors' notice to the speeches of Lord Bridge and Lord Templeman in *Sidaway* and not to Lord Diplock's.[91]

An unsuccessful vasectomy sensibly prompted the Irish Supreme Court to assert in *Walsh v. Family Planning Services* that where treatment can be inferred from the circumstances to be elective, the law requires more rigorous disclosure of the relevant pros and cons.[92] According to Finlay C.J., who favoured a watered-down variant of the professional standard rule, "it may be, *certainly in relation to very clearly elective surgery*, that the court might more readily reach a conclusion that the extent of warning given or omitted contained inherent defects which ought to have been obvious to any person giving the matter due consideration than it could do in a case of complicated medical or surgical procedures."[93] According to O'Flaherty J, who rejected the professional standard test of disclosure, "where there is a question of elective surgery which is not essential to health or bodily well-being, if there is a risk—however exceptional or remote—of grave consequences involving severe pain stretching for an appreciable time into the future and involving the possibility of further operative procedures, the exercise of the duty of care owed by the defendants requires that such possible consequences should be explained in the clearest language to the plaintiff."[94]

Irish and English case-law on elective treatment has for the most part concerned sterilisation procedures. The comparative frequency of the post-sterilisation claim and the special issues it raises, mark it out as a concern that merits the law's close attention.

Because an effective sterilisation is irreversible, the patient is usually counselled first. This typically involves a more amplified form

---

[91] Department of Health, *Guide for Examination or Treatment* H.C. (90) 22, as extracted by Kennedy and Grubb (1994), p. 187.
[92] *Walsh v. Family Planning Services, supra*, n. 67.
[93] *ibid.* at 511 (emphasis added).
[94] *ibid.* at 535.

of disclosure and discussion by medical staff. The fact that heightened disclosure already occupies a central role in this type of doctor-patient relationship makes it disingenuous of the doctor to subsequently excuse a failure to discuss relative success rates, complications, and the range of alternatives. Indeed, this was recognised by Schiemann J. at first instance in the *Gold* case when he attempted to banish the professional standard test from the duty to disclose to elective patients.[95] The learned judge accepted that where the patient is considering sterilisation, a more interactive form of counselling is required and tends to be given, by contrast with general medical counselling which is more concerned with what the doctor recommends ought to be done to cure or alleviate the patient's condition. He found evidence of this in numerous sources. The 1974 *DHSS Memorandum of Guidance on the Family Planning Service* recognised that it is "particularly important that the couple receive full counselling before deciding upon a sterilisation operation . . . so that they may be fully aware of its implications and of the alternative methods available".[96] More radically, a 1976 Medical Protection Society document urged that enough information must be given to ensure "a proper decision and . . . [an] informed consent", that this information ought to be tailored to the "individual case", and that no guarantee of success should be given.[97] The 1979 *Handbook of Contraceptive Practice* more particularly encouraged doctors to assess the patient's psychological response to sterilisation and genital symbolism, existing children, relationship with the other spouse, and economic circumstances.

Given that many patients choose to undergo obviously elective treatments—for instance, sterilisation—it is surely uncontroversial to assert that the law ought to *unambiguously* insist that amplified disclosure of all the relevant pros and cons of the contemplated treatment be made to this type of patient. In rare cases, sterilisation may lead to loss of sexual capacity. As McCarthy J. rightly acknowledged in the *Walsh* case: "Remote percentages of risk lose their significance to those unfortunate enough to be . . .. critically concerned with that risk."[98] Most of the cases turned upon non-disclosure of the risk that sterilisation would fail, in particular

---

[95] *Gold v. Haringey Health Authority* unreported, QBD, June 16, 1986: references are to extracts cited in Symmons (1987).
[96] *ibid.* at 58.
[97] *ibid.* at 59.
[98] *Walsh v. Family Planning Services, supra*, n. 67 at 520–521.

through recanalisation, a risk assessed variously to lie between 0.5 per cent and 2 per cent. That risk is common to most sterilisation procedures, whereby sterilisation becomes unexpectedly reversed through the workings of the body when the *vas deferens* (in the case of a vasectomy) or the fallopian tubes (in the case of a tubal ligation) regenerate allowing the passage of spermatozoa or ova. Given that in the event of a sterilisation failing, conception and pregnancy may follow, it seems bizarre that non-disclosure was justified to the extent that it was in the *Gold* case.

An unconvincing attempt was made at first instance in *Thake v. Maurice* to distinguish the risk of recanalisation from mainstream disclosure cases, on the basis that the former involves a duty to disclose a risk that the sterilisation which was "initially perfectly satisfactory" might be reversed in time by the effects of nature.[99] Against Peter Pain J.'s analysis, it may be recalled that the disclosure claim is independent of the presence of negligence in treatment. The sole difference between the scenario in *Thake* and mainstream disclosure claims is that in the former case the risk of failure eventuates later when nature strays down an unpredictable course and reverses the sterilisation. This difference will chiefly affect proof of causation. To establish a causative link between the non-disclosure and the damage (the unwanted child), the plaintiff may have to prove that she was aware of the pregnancy at a stage when it was too late to procure a lawful abortion. This was the conclusion at first instance and on appeal in *Thake v. Maurice*, where it was also accepted that the plaintiff would, if aware in time, have had an abortion.[1] The necessity of proving this fact depends ultimately on how the plaintiff's case is phrased. It is submitted, in this light, that a plaintiff could equally establish a causative link between non-disclosure and birth, in circumstances where she had been aware of the pregnancy in time enough to terminate it but chose not to because she was morally opposed to abortion.[2]

---

[99] *Thake v. Maurice* [1984] 2 All E.R. 513, QBD. The learned judge referred to the duty as a contractual one. This did not seem to materially affect his decision on the point: as noted by Kerr L.J. on appeal [1986] 1 All E.R. 497, CA, the plaintiff's claim was "pleaded both in contract and tort, *i.e.* what was for convenience referred to as 'contractual negligence' as well as negligence simpliciter resulting from the duty of care owed by a surgeon to his patient" which "for present purposes" the judge felt it unnecessary to distinguish between.

[1] *ibid.*

[2] Though, in Ireland, the 14th Amendment to the Constitution permits the dis-

The law ought also to consider whether enhancing disclosure before sterilisation may serve in its long-term effects to curb the present escalation in wrongful birth/conception/life actions, with minimal cost to health care resources.[3] A *wrongful birth* action may be taken by the parents of a disabled child for losses caused by the wrongful birth (typically where the defendants could have detected a defect in the foetus in time enough to permit the mother to lawfully abort).[4] A parent may take a *wrongful conception* action for losses suffered on foot of the birth of a healthy but unwanted child (typically, where the defendants failed to effectively sterilise the plaintiff and to warn the plaintiff of the possibility that the procedure would fail).[5] A *wrongful life* action may now be brought by or on behalf of a child for damages suffered by the failure of the defendant (doctor or parent) to detect deformity in time to lawfully abort.[6] It is thus clear that these actions may spring from incomplete disclosure and advice (or *counseling*) at pre-operative and post-operative sterilisation stages.

Swift advances in genetic technology appear to have heightened consumer demands for compensation when things go wrong. This is chiefly due to the increasingly predictive capacity of genetic technology (pre-conception screening, post-conception techniques such as *in utero* examination, genetic counselling, etc.), and consequential perceptions of genetic disability as avoidable burden. In an early

semination of information relating to the provision of abortion services in other jurisdictions, it is highly unlikely, despite the positivist nature of the Supreme Court's determinations in *Attorney General v. X.* [1992] I.R. 1, that the possibility of obtaining an abortion outside of Ireland would be tolerated to emerge as a counter-argument in a similar scenario.

[3] See generally: Robertson (1978), p. 135; Teff (1985b); and Donnelly (1996) and (1997).

[4] A recent attempt in England to obtain compensation from an obstetrician, who had negligently failed to detect that the plaintiff's foetus suffered deformities which later manifested themselves as disabilities, failed on the ground that even if the defendants had ascertained whether the irregularities on the scans indicated spina bifida, it would at that stage have been too late for the plaintiff to lawfully obtain an abortion. Though the Infant Life (Preservation) Act 1929 identified 28 weeks gestation as the period beyond which an abortion could not lawfully be performed, Brooke J. ruled that even if the defendants had acted on a contrary interpretation of the relevant law which was a "reasonable belief, shared by many of their colleagues", he would not have found them negligent. See *Rance v. Mid-Downs Health Authority* [1991] 1 Q.B. 587, [1991] 1 All E.R. 801.

[5] *e.g. Emeh v. Kensington Area Health Authority* [1985] 1 Q.B. 1012; and *Thake v. Maurice, supra.* n. 99, QBD/CA.

[6] Congenital Disabilities (Civil Liability) Act 1976 (for births after 1976) s. 1(2)(b), reversing *McKay v. Essex Health Authority* [1982] 1 Q.B. 1166.

influential article, Capron wrote that the "genetic counsellor will be expected to exercise reasonable care to supply an accurate diagnosis (or, when necessary, a tentative one, with whatever qualifiers are needed to explain the uncertainty), and an explanation of the hereditary basis, if known, and the range of available therapeutic options, preventive measures, and further diagnostic procedures."[7] Such has been the effect of these developments that some American courts have recognised the right to be born as a functional human being without the handicap of a serious genetic defect.[8] According to the Supreme Court of Washington in its unanimous decision in *Harbeson v. Parke-Davis*: "Parents may avoid the birth of the defective child by aborting the fetus. The difficult moral choice is theirs . . .. We believe we must recognise the benefits of these medical developments and therefore we hold that parents have a right to prevent the birth of a defective child and health care providers a duty correlative to that right. This duty requires health care providers to impart to their patients material information as to the likelihood of future children's being born defective. . . . Recognition of the duty will . . . promote societal interests in genetic counselling and prenatal testing, deter medical negligence, and at least partially redress a clear and undeniable wrong."[9] These developments have exerted unforeseen pressure on obstetric practice, rendering it more susceptible to suit. During the malpractice crisis of the late 1970s, a genuine fear developed that unless preventive statutory action was taken, there would be a real disincentive to becoming an obstetrician, that obstetric services would suffer, and that for defensive reasons, Caesarean sections would become widespread without regard to their medical efficacy.[10]

Many actions arising from failed sterilisation operations are couched and analysed in contractual terms. This is principally due to the

---

[7] Capron (1979), p. 627.
[8] *Curlender v. Bio-Science Laboratories* 106 Cal. App. 3d 811 (1980).
[9] *Harbeson v. Parke-Davis* 656 P2d 483 (1983) at 491.
[10] Wadlington and Wood III (1991). For this reason, state legislatures in Virginia and Florida recently enacted legislation designed to replace tort liability for severe genetic or congenital disability with "no-fault" compensation schemes. See: Va Code # 38.2–5000 et seq (1990 Repl Vol); and Flo Stat Ann # 766–302(2) (1989). In the U.K., strict statutory liability was created under the Congenital Disabilities (Civil Liability) Act 1976 for congenital disabilities caused by the negligence of obstetricians or obstetric attendants. See further Chapter 8, *infra*, p. 233 (n. 6).

fact that elective treatments are often performed by private practitioners, with whom a specific contract and remunerative consideration has been arranged. In this context, it is often claimed that by omitting to disclose the risk of sterilisation failing and leading to pregnancy, the doctor breached a contractual warranty by misrepresenting the effects of surgery or treatment, or that he breached a contractual promise to achieve a certain result (for which strict liability may attach without proof of failure to exercise reasonable care and skill).[11] Useful as an alternate plea, the contract action benefits from longer limitation periods within which the plaintiff may sue, and depending on the jurisdiction, from the unavailability of the defence of contributory negligence.[12] More significantly, establishing breach of express contractual warranty may well serve a plaintiff who perceives some difficulty persuading the court on the causation issue, namely that if he had been informed of the undisclosed risk he would not have undergone the treatment.[13] In *LaFleur v. Cornelis* a negligent "nose job" on the patient left her with scarring and a sight deformity. The plaintiff could establish a failure to warn of the risks of this eventuality, but could not establish that if informed she would have changed her mind. But because the doctor had drawn a picture of how her nose would look after the $600 operation, saying "No problem. You will be happy", Barry J. ruled that there had been a breach of a warranty, making sure to point out that the existence or absence of negligence in non-disclosure was irrelevant. $6,000 in damages were awarded, a large part of which was for non-pecuniary mental distress following a decision by the English Court of Appeal in *Heywood v. Weller* to award same for solicitors' negligence, thereby making this action a more worthwhile prospect.[14]

However, the common law is markedly reluctant to extend the contract law analysis to the medical context. This is due to a variety of reasons, such as: the institutional preference for vicarious liability of hospitals in negligence; the fact that the torts analysis better captures accidents caused by independent contractors and volunteers; the discrimination that would inevitably emerge if claims by private patients were assessed under contract law and claims by public

---

[11] See Mahoney (1985); and Shaw (1972).
[12] Some U.S. state courts have ruled that where tort and contract are pleaded together in this manner, tort law applies as thus does the contributory negligence defence. See: *Nelson v. Anderson* 72 N.W. 2d 861 (1955); and Belli (1956), p. 280.
[13] *LaFleur v. Cornelis* (1980) 63 A.P.R. 569.
[14] *Heywood v. Weller* [1976] 1 All E.R. 300.

patients under tort;[15] the difficulty and artificiality of implying terms into contracts; and the "unequal bargaining positions of hospitals and patients" especially in situations where patients are rushed to hospital in emergencies.[16] Chiefly for these reasons, the common law typically emphasises in response to contract-based claims by patients, that a physician does not ordinarily warrant a cure or guarantee a particular result, only that he will apply such professional skill and learning as is ordinarily possessed by similar professionals.[17] Beyond this, the plaintiff must establish that he entered into a special contract with the doctor. The common law is loathe to interpret apparent words of promise as contractual guarantees, instead interpreting them as "therapeutic reassurances", mainly because it appreciates that medical science and health care are fraught with uncertainty,[18] that the relationship between doctor and patient is usually based on oral exchanges which can easily be misinterpreted,[19] and that expressions

---

[15] *Hotson v. Fitzgerald* [1985] 3 All E.R. 167 at 176, QBD, *per* Simon Brown J.

[16] *Yepremian v. Scarborough General Hospital* (1980) 13 C.C.C.L.T. 105 at 174, *per* Blair J., Ont. CA.

[17] In *Eyre v. Measday* [1986] 1 All E.R. 488, it was decided that the court would not imply guarantees of success into sterilisation contracts either as contractual terms or collateral warranties, and that where a doctor emphasises that the operation will be "irreversible", he means not that it will be 100% successful never leading to pregnancy, but rather that the operative procedure is incapable of being surgically reversed or undone. In *Thake v. Maurice*, QBD, *supra*, n. 99, Peter Pain J. departed from received judicial wisdom in ruling that the defendant had breached a contractual guarantee to the plaintiff that a vasectomy would be irreversible. In overriding both the defendant's accepted lack of intention to guarantee 100 per cent success and general medical practice not to do so for this type of surgery, the judge employed the canon of interpretation by which uncertainty as to the meaning of contractual terms is interpreted against the party who draws up the contract. Peter Pain J's decision was overturned by the Court of Appeal (*supra*, n. 99, at 511, *per* Nourse L.J.) on the more orthodox basis that the practice of medical science is inexact and unpredictable, and that a doctor cannot be regarded as having contractually guaranteed any more than the application of reasonable skill and care. A guarantee of success could only be construed where such was conveyed by the defendant in clear and unequivocal terms: to presume otherwise "would be to credit him with an omniscience beyond all reason."

[18] In *Sard v. Hardy* 379 A. 2d 1014 (1997) at 1026, the court agreed with the trial judge in rejecting the plea of breach of express warranty, noting that "a physician is not an insurer of the success of his treatment and absent an express agreement, does not warrant or guarantee that he will effect a given result."

[19] The fear of opening up the flood-gates to unduly quarrelsome patients or patients prone to subsequent exaggeration was expressed by the court in *Marvin v. Talbott* 216 Cal. App. 2d 383 (1963), 5 A.L.R. 3d 908 (1963).

of support and encouragement are necessarily incidental to the palliative role of doctors.[20]

Duties of Disclosure and the Inquisitive Patient

The defence commonly attempts to justify non-disclosure on the basis that disclosure of a particular risk would have served no useful purpose and would more than likely have deterred the patient from undergoing recommended treatment. This proposition seems to gain more credence according to the degree to which that treatment is perceived to have been essential to preserve the patient's health or life.[21] To some extent, this may be taken to reflect the doctor's ethical duty of *beneficence* (to do good for his patient)—though one suspects that it equally stems from argumentative necessity within the adversarial structure of the hearing.

Historical accounts of beneficence show how it was often—at the level of theory and practice—achieved through a benign secrecy and duplicity.[22] This form of medical paternalism has come under considerable scrutiny in recent times, not least through the disclosure action and more generally through contemporary calls for greater transparency and accountability in the health care services. It is

---

[20] In *Sard v. Hardy, supra*, n. 117 at 1027, Levine J. for this reason refused to interpret a statement that the plaintiff would not have any more children as anything more than a therapeutic reassurance giving her hope of a good result. The courts tend to insist that to be elevated to contractual status, the promise must have been express (though written or oral) and there must have existed some *consideration* which is independent and above the consideration normally paid for the engagement of such a physician. In *Wilson v. Blair* (1922) 65 Mont. 155, 211 P. 2d 289, the alleged promise was made after the consideration was given and original agreement made, and no further consideration was made which could support the existence of a warranty to achieve the particular result. In *Sard v. Hardy* at 1027, Levine J. proposed that there must be proof of special consideration "only where the alleged warranty is made post-operatively. Where the warranty is made prior to the surgery or treatment, however, the patient may recover in contract by proving breach of an *express* warranty".

[21] The comparative necessity of the plaintiff's treatment greatly affects proof of causation. The more necessary the treatment and the gloomier the patient's prognosis without it, the more difficult it becomes for a court to accept a plaintiff's retrospective claim that full disclosure would have caused him to forego the recommended treatment. See: *Reibl v. Hughes* (1981) 114 D.L.R. (3d) 1 at 16, *per* Laskin C.J.C.; and *Stamos v. Davies* (1985) 21 D.L.R. (4th) 507. Against this, however, see *Chappel v. Hart* [1998] H.C.A. 55, and Chapter 7, *infra*, pp. 202–203, 209.

[22] See further Chapter 1, *supra*, pp. 9–11, 30–34.

scarcely justified where a patient volunteers questions and expresses a wish to know more about the risks and alternatives to the recommended treatment. Ethically then, the inquisitive patient exerts considerable strain on any commitment to the *therapeutic lie*. Legally, the status of the inquisitive patient, like that of the elective patient, is an issue mainly in those jurisdictions which apply the professional standard model of disclosure, within which it emerges as a possible exception to the weighty defence of customary medical practice.

In *Hatcher v. Black*, a decision which has not aged well, Denning L.J. sanctioned the "therapeutic lie" whereby doctors may in their discretion decide what to say to their patients—questions and inquisitiveness notwithstanding. The court, he proposed, "leaves this question of morals to the conscience of the doctor".[23] The law changed considerably when the House of Lords chose to consider inquisitiveness in *Sidaway v. Bethlem Royal Hospital*.[24] There was weighty if not unanimous support for the proposition that where questions are asked, a doctor ought to endeavour to answer *truthfully*—a proposition considerably more powerful than one which would assert merely that inquisitiveness merits *fuller* disclosure of information. Lord Bridge (with whom Lord Keith concurred) resolutely accepted that if a patient volunteers questions about risks, the doctor's duty is "to answer both truthfully *and* as fully as the questioner requires."[25] Lord Diplock expressed the view that if a patient asked questions "the doctor would tell him whatever it was the patient wanted to know".[26] Though unduly tentative on this point, it nonetheless seems that his Lordship did not envisage the application of the *Bolam* test to the inquisitive patient.[27] Lord Templeman ruled that *in the absence of direct questions* from his plaintiff, a doctor is not required to identify remote serious risks, of whose existence the doctor may otherwise presume the patient is vaguely aware. His Lordship reasoned that a doctor may legitimately fear that too much or detailed information would distress or confuse the patient "at a time when [he is] suffering from stress, pain and

---

[23] *Hatcher v. Black* [1954] C.L.Y. 2289.

[24] *Sidaway v. Bethlem Royal Hospital, supra*, n. 17, HL.

[25] *ibid.* at 888 (emphasis added).

[26] *Sidaway v. Bethlem Royal Hospital, supra*, n. 17 at 895, HL.

[27] In his parting words (*ibid.*), Lord Diplock took pains to ensure the continued application of *Bolam* to warnings and disclosure, but only where this relates to "unsought" information which the doctor may "volunteer" to give (in the absence of inquisitive requests for same).

anxiety."[28] So therefore, the patient cannot complain of a lack of information unless the patient asks in vain for more information".[29] If by this, as seems, Lord Templeman meant that the doctor could *never* properly withhold disclosure out of a fear of its effect on the inquisitive patient, then his findings are potentially far-reaching. Regrettably, the judicial opinions in *Sidaway* were later given an unnecessarily restrictive interpretation by the Court of Appeal in *Blyth v. Bloomsbury Health Authority*.[30] At first instance, Leonard J. had sensibly interpreted *Sidaway* to mean that "if the patient is making a specific enquiry, it would be right to tell her the whole picture".[31] On appeal, perhaps prompted by the unconvincing nature of the plaintiff's factual claims,[32] Kerr L.J. erroneously interpreted *Sidaway* to mean that the professional standard test is "all-pervasive in this context" and that the "question of what a plaintiff should be told in answer to a general enquiry cannot be divorced from [it], any more than when no such enquiry is made."[33]

The law is faced by numerous problems in this area. If for instance it decides that general enquiries do not trigger higher duties of truthfulness, but that specific questions do (however unlikely it is that a patient enquires about a remote risk which by chance materialises later), it introduces a wholly unworkable standard according to which doctors must predict the legal consequence of their responses to communicative patients. It was this likelihood which prompted the Australian High Court to rule in *Rogers v. Whitaker* that *general* inquisitiveness is sufficient to indicate to the doctor in question that the patient wishes to make a *more informed* decision whether or not to undergo the given treatment.[34] The fact

---

[28] *Sidaway v. Bethlem Royal Hospital, supra*, n. 17 at 902.

[29] *ibid.*

[30] *Blyth v. Bloomsbury Health Authority, supra*, n. 82.

[31] *ibid.* at 156.

[32] The plaintiff claimed that the defendants had negligently failed to fully disclose to her all the side-effects of an injection of Depo-Provera which had been used in conjunction with a rubella vaccination to ensure that patients did not become pregnant within the following three months. In light of the fact that the plaintiff was a professional nurse, the trial judge found it highly unlikely that she would have asked whether the drug caused "upsets in anyone at all" or that the doctor would have responded with a simple negative. There was also evidence by the midwifery sister that she would never have withheld information of known side-effects if asked for it. Given Kerr L.J.'s conclusion that the patient could not have asked the questions she claimed she did, it seems possible to restrict the judge's findings to *obiter dicta*, a view endorsed by Montgomery (1997), p. 246.

[33] *Blyth v. Bloomsbury Health Authority, supra*, n. 82 at 157.

[34] *Rogers v. Whitaker* (1992) 109 A.L.R. 625.

that a majority in *Sidaway* ruled that questions should truthfully be answered, irrespective of general practice, suggested to the Australian court that the professional standard model was inherently flawed. Indeed, its strict application in *Rogers v. Whitaker* would have worked a peculiar injustice. Before deciding whether or not to undergo an operation to improve the sight in her right eye, the plaintiff patient had "incessantly" asked questions. However, these had each been in relation to whether her sight in that right eye might further deteriorate as a result of the operation, and not whether there was a risk of damage to her good eye, a fact which the defence claimed did not cast any duty of truthfulness with regard to that other eye. The court rejected this argument out of hand. Through the patient's expression of concern, an otherwise remote risk—a 1 in 14,000 chance of sympathetic ophthalmia spreading loss of sight to the good eye—had become a *material* risk which ought to have been disclosed.

It has occasionally been suggested by commentators that the remedy for the inquisitive patient may lie valuably elsewhere. Professor Skegg has proposed that the tort of deceit should be used to supplement the allegation of professional negligence where a risk which later materialises has not been disclosed.[35] The plaintiff would thus seek to establish:

(1) that the defendant knowingly or recklessly made a false representation of fact (by omitting an important piece of information);

(2) that this was made with intention that the plaintiff should rely on it; and

(3) that the plaintiff in fact relied to his detriment on it.

Acknowledging that the biggest impediment to establishing deceit is that the plaintiff must establish that the defendant knew the representation to be false, Skegg suggests that the plaintiff couple the claim of deceit with a claim of negligence, given that the latter requires the defendant to establish that the nondisclosure was grounded in a general or approved practice and was therefore on his part *intentional*. This rather deft strategy is, however, unlikely to be countenanced by the English courts which have not so far had the opportunity to consider the tort of deceit in the clinical environment. Although this

---

[35] Skegg (1988), pp. 93–95.

tort only requires proof that the defendant intended that the plaintiff act upon the false statement, and not that he intended that the plaintiff suffer because of it,[36] it is submitted that its conception of true and false representation is too rigid to apply to the clinical environment where half-truths and therapeutic lies (by omission) are not actively discouraged by ethical codes or indeed by the judiciary. Nor is it likely that the tactical admission of a *false* statement in accordance with a general medical practice, would be intention enough for the tort of deceit which traditionally has required proof of willful deceit or fraud.[37]

It has also been mooted that a remedy may lie in negligent misstatement, along the lines of the decision reached by the New Zealand Court of Appeal in *Smith v. Auckland Hospital Board*.[38] Barrowclough C.J. likened the scenario to a professional transaction in which the plaintiff seeks information from a doctor of special skill. He cited *Hedley Byrne v. Heller*[39] as authority for the proposition that in a business or professional transaction, a duty to take care in making an answer may arise where:

(1) A seeks information from B who possesses the relevant knowledge or skill;

(2) the gravity of the question and importance of the answer is made apparent to B;

(3) B knows or ought to know that A will rely on the advice; and

(4) B has not renounced responsibility for the accuracy of his answer.

Though finding in favour of the plaintiff, Barrowclough C.J. acknowledged that a doctor is not always required to give a full answer, and that much will depend on the likely effects of the answer on the health of the patient. It is clear, therefore, that in applying the principle of *Hedley Byrne*, the court insisted as a matter of law on *careful* rather than *truthful* answering to questions asked. It was a

---

[36] *Edgington v. Fitzmaurice* (1885) 29 Ch.D. 459; *Brown Jenkinson & Co. Ltd v. Percy Dalton (London) Ltd* [1957] 2 Q.B. 621.
[37] Heuston and Buckley (1992), p. 382.
[38] *Smith v. Auckland Hospital Board* [1965] N.Z.L.R. 191.
[39] *Hedley Byrne v. Heller* [1964] A.C. 465.

surprising direction to take. Indeed, the court glossed over a vital distinction between the *Hedley Byrne* principle and the professional negligence model. The former springs from unique and special circumstances, whereas the latter is specifically tailored to a continuing and structured relationship between a professional (doctor) and a client (patient). A rule which requires carefulness but not truthfulness in a doctor is surely best assessed by a forum which is specifically devoted to that purpose.

The standard consent form favoured by the English Department of Health in its *Guide to Consent for Examination or Treatment* tells the patient that "[i]f there is anything that you don't understand about the explanation, or if you want more information, you should ask the doctor or dentist."[40] In theory, a patient may be held contributorily liable for not asking questions or seeking clarification, though the law is unlikely to impose this duty beyond exceptional cases.[41] This would be consistent with the plaintiff's later claim that he would have wanted to know material facts. It would also have the effect of reducing damages arising from nondisclosure, which many reasonably feel are disproportionately high for the type of wrong committed. It would also mitigate the severity of assessing this claim according to a patient's right versus doctor's duty analysis, serving instead to recognise duties on both doctor and patient: the law ought not to reinforce the passivity of the patient in the clinical environment by recognising duties only on doctors.

Critical response to the dilemmas posed by the inquisitive patient has been decidedly mixed.[42] Gerald Robertson argues that not to recognise a distinction between the inquisitive and the reticent patient "would be tantamount to a complete rejection of the patient's right to self-determination."[43] As a general principle, this, it is submitted, rests upon a naive conception of patient autonomy, which cannot be presumed always to make itself known in the clinical environment. Though one may expect that questions will feature more prominently where the patient is paying privately for health

---

[40] Department of Health, *A Guide to Consent for Examination or Treatment*, (1990), App. A.

[41] In *Brushett v. Cowan* (1991) 2 Med. L.R. 271, the plaintiff was found equally at fault by the Newfoundland Court of Appeal, on the basis that she was a registered nurse with experience in orthopaedics and as such should have asked questions about the proper use of her crutches.

[42] See Robertson (1981), Mahoney (1985), and Brazier (1987).

[43] Robertson (1981), p. 120.

care, or where the patient is about to undergo an elective procedure such as sterilisation or cosmetic surgery, one cannot comfortably found the application of a separate legal test, with wholly different consequences, on the apparent silence or curiosity of the patient. One patient might coyly say, "It isn't anything dangerous, is it, doctor?"; another might seem timidly to defer to what the doctor thinks it important to tell him. Yet both, if put to the test, might equally want the same level of disclosure and truthfulness from their doctor. Indeed, it has been observed that being silent, and not bothering the doctor, is part of British culture.[44]

A host of reasons may prevent a patient from expressing concern in a sufficiently vocal manner to attract the doctor's concern over the possible legal implications of his non-disclosure. There is little academic disagreement amongst psychologists and behavioural theorists in the view that patients, particularly those with fatal and dangerous illnesses, are *infantalised* by the hospital experience.[45] Illness disrupts one's natural equilibrium, one's perspective on life, and one's customary ability to translate will to action. It renders the person vulnerable; the temptation to exalt the one who potentially can help correspondingly grows. In a hospital ward, the patient is sartorially and behaviourally exposed. Bed-bound and bed-clothed, encompassed by sickness, the distinct scents of the hospital, and the dominant colours of white and blue, the patient is very much a person in alien surroundings, "a 'captive' who cannot leave the hospital without serious consequences to himself."[46] Society expects the ill to be *co-operative patients* and to get better; rebellion attracts severe criticism. It is also so that the psychologically ingrained image of the public hospital is that of "crisis institution" within which rights and demands are subject to the relative seriousness of ill health, and within which personalised supportive care is not generally felt to be essential.

There is the additional danger that inquisitiveness will be interpreted by doctors as evidence of a patient's superior intelligence and ability to handle fuller disclosure, when the inquisitiveness may merely, and probably in most cases, amount to no more than assertiveness. Indeed, in a survey of 739 randomly selected people

[44] Brazier (1987), p. 186.
[45] First identified in Szasz and Hollander (1956).
[46] Tagliacozzo and Mauksch, "The Patient's View of the Patient's Role", in Jaco (1979), p. 196.

who had recently been patients, Cartwright dispelled a common prejudice when she found that there was no differences between the middle and the working classes in terms of desire to know as much information as possible about their illness.[47] However, she also discovered that the proportion of those who wished to know the *details* of the illness as well as how it affected them rose from 24 per cent for unskilled people to 54 per cent for professionals. This suggested to Cartwright that working-class patients may be more diffident and less articulate when it comes to asking questions of doctors. The middle and professional classes seemed to be more competitive, have fewer inhibitions, and tended to prefer private treatment where wards were smaller and communication more thorough.[48] These findings are supported by numerous authorities.[49] Bernstein, for instance, discovered that middle-class people tend to employ what he calls an *elaborated code* of language wherewith "the speaker will select from a wide range of syntactic alternatives".[50] This code by its nature is more loquacious and inquisitive. The *restricted code*, dominant in working-class groups, has considerably reduced syntactic alternatives and vocabulary, and relies far more on non-verbal signs. Physicians, themselves employing an elaborated code, unreasonably expect that desire for information will manifest itself in elaborated verbal requests.

The propensity of judges, when assessing entitlement to information, to discriminate according to *apparent* intelligence has already been evident in past Irish and English decisions. In the Irish Supreme Court decision of *Daniels v. Heskin*, Kingsmill-Moore proposed that doctors remain free to decide what should be disclosed to patients on the basis of, *"inter alia"* their "character . . . social position . . . intelligence . . . and innumerable other considerations."[51] The judge accepted the defendant's non-disclosure on the basis that "husband and wife were of a class and standard of education which would incline them to exaggerate the seriousness of the occurrence and to suffer needless alarm".[52] Though the contemporary relevance of

---

[47] Cartwright (1964), Chap. 2.
[48] *ibid.*, pp. 189–196.
[49] See: Pratt, Seligmann and Reader (1957); Anderson and Helm, "The Physician-Patient Encounter: A Process of Reality Negotiation" in Jaco (1979); Bernstein B (1964); and Fisher, "Doctor Talk/ Patient Talk: How Treatment Decisions are *Negotiated* in Doctor-Patient Communication" in Fisher and Todd (1983).
[50] Bernstein (1964).
[51] *Daniels v. Heskin* [1954] I.R. 73 at 87.
[52] *ibid.*

those words were recently queried by the Supreme Court,[53] *Daniels v. Heskin* has regrettably been construed by the outside world as authority for the view that under Irish law, the "smaller the education and understanding of the patient the less the technical disclosure need be, because of the lesser capacity to absorb it".[54]

The dangers of setting a standard by which doctors are encouraged to make value-judgments upon the intelligence of patients are obvious, and studies in the United States have shown how such judgments are frequently made in the clinical environment, based upon scant and unreliable indicators.[55] Indeed, the judicial attempts in *Sidaway* to justify and ground rules on the apparent traits of patients were in the end comically varied. At one point, Lord Diplock controversially argued that "it is flying in the face of reality to assume that all patients from the highest to the lowest standard of education or intelligence are aware of the extent and nature of the risks which, notwithstanding the exercise of skill and care in carrying out the treatment, are inevitably involved in medical treatment of whatever kind it be but particularly surgical".[56] By contrast, Lord Templeman felt that disclosure of a remote serious risk to the instant plaintiff would merely have "reinforced the obvious", that is, the "possibility of something going wrong in the course of a delicate operation performed in a vital area".[57] Such distinctions fail to appreciate that the choice over what is to be done to one's body is one which ultimately each person has a selfish interest in to the exclusion of almost all others.

In disclosure trials, the defence invariably asserts that it is general or approved practice not to make disclosure of minimal or remote risks on the grounds that it would be likely to deter the patient from undergoing the treatment in question or would cause the patient to suffer anxiety and stress in a counter-productive manner. Yet neither elective or inquisitive contexts present any real opportunities for *post-hoc* justification of non-disclosure on these grounds. For example, where a treatment which is to some degree elective carries high risks,

---

[53] *Walsh v. Family Planning Services, supra,* n. 67 at 535, *per* McCarthy J.

[54] *Daniels v. Heskin, supra,* n. 51, is identified as such in Samuels (1982), p. 41, Skegg (1988), p. 129, and Tomkin and Hanafin (1995), p. 31.

[55] See Glaser, "Disclosure of Terminal Illness" in Jaco (1979), p. 227; Oken, "What to Tell Cancer Patients: A Study of Medical Attitudes" in Lockwood (1985), p. 112; President's Commission, *Vol. 2* (1982) p. 246 and Tables 8–8.

[56] *Sidaway v. Bethlem Royal Hospital, supra,* n. 17, p. 894, HL.

[57] *ibid.* at 902.

alarming the patient by discussing its full possible implications tends very much to be in that patient's *best* interests.[58] The legal dilemma of the inquisitive patient is muddied somewhat by the fact that it is as difficult to *promote* higher standards for the apparently inquisitive patient as it is to *defend* resisting fuller disclosure to inquisitive patients by an indifferent application of the professional standard test. The answer to this dilemma does not necessarily lie in the middle, for there still remains the vexing need to articulate rules by which doctors ought to be able to predict the legal consequence of their actions. Attempts by the English courts to identify exceptions to the professional standard test have proved unconvincing and unclear, serving for the most part to expose the defects inherent in that model.

It is submitted that to resolve these and other issues, the common law must aspire towards a test of disclosure which can treat inquisitive and elective factors as part of its internal assessment of due disclosure. Such a test must in its net effects encourage doctors to ascertain *naturally* what each patient wishes or is content to be told. In seeking to involve patients more in decisions which vitally affect their most personal interests, the doctrine of informed consent does not require that an overdose of information be inflicted on unwitting patients, nor that to justify disclosure of certain information the patient must manifest an ability to grasp dense esoteric details which doctors have spent a large part of their lives studying. Rather, it encourages a more *sensitive* communication to patients of information which has been distilled down from the technical jargon by which it is known within the profession, into language which is comprehensible to the lay-person and which is conveyed contextually and pragmatically, having regard to the relative scale of risks and success rates.

Jurisdictions which adopted the doctrine of informed consent have had little difficulty deciding that where a patient volunteers questions about risks and consequences, or where the treatment is for whatever reason elective, a higher standard of disclosure is due to the patient.[59] In both these contexts, the defence can make little use of the therapeutic privilege justifying non-disclosure on the basis that it was

---

[58] *Kelly v. Hazlett* (1976) 75 D.L.R. (3d) 536; *Stamos v. Davies* (1985) 21 D.L.R. (4d) 507 at 521.

[59] See: the American case of *Gray v. Grunnagle* (1966) 223 A. 2d 663; the Canadian cases of *Hopp v. Lepp* (1979) 98 D.L.R. (3d) 464 and *Sinclaire v. Boulton* (1985) 33 C.C.L.T. 125; and the Australian case of *Rogers v. Whitaker, supra,* n. 34.

for the patient's benefit.[60] Though it may avail of the privilege in some cases, the burden of proof on the defence is likely to be considerably higher. In practice, what most concerns the plaintiff is that he establishes (1) that the risk was not so remote that disclosure of it would have served no practical purpose, and (2) that if the risk had been disclosed, the patient would not have undergone the treatment (proof of causation).[61] The concept of materiality of risk, central to informed consent law, usefully avoids rules which perpetuate clumsy legal distinctions. It is constructed to vary more naturally according to the patient's specific context, encouraging the doctor to ascertain what the patient's goals and expectations are (and therefore to what extent the treatment is elective or the patient inquisitive). At the trial, evidence of inquisitiveness or electiveness becomes *further* evidence that the relevant risks and alternatives, however remote, were in the circumstances *material* to the given patient.[62]

---

[60] *White v. Turner* (1981) 120 D.L.R. (3d) 269 at 288.
[61] See *Sard v. Hardy, supra,* n. 117 and *White v. Turner, ibid.*
[62] According to the High Court of Australia in *Rogers v. Whitaker, supra,* n. 34, at 631: "Even if a court were satisfied that a reasonable person in the patient's position would be unlikely to attach significance to a particular risk, the fact that the patient asked questions revealing concern about the risk would make the doctor aware that *this patient* did in fact attach significance to the risk."

Chapter 6

Consent and Medical Malpractice

It would appear that *consent* has come to be seen by numerous commentators as the concept which best unites the many disparate legal issues arising from modern health care, welding consistency to a discipline which has rather miscellaneously evolved under the rubric of *medical law*.[1] It is certainly the most unifying thread this body of law at present possesses, providing a reference point to assist on the one hand in defining the proper scope of medical paternalism, and on the other to evaluate the control a person has over what is done to his body during and after his life. Though technically patients may sue for the negligent failure of a doctor to obtain a consent, good legal advice would scarcely recommend it, unless as an alternate plea, given that it is significantly easier to obtain damages for a non-consensual intervention (as a battery or trespass to the person) than it is for the negligence of doctors.

Consent becomes relevant to malpractice law when the issue concerns the information which a doctor ought to have imparted before his patient could be said to have given a proper consent to the medical intervention. The common law has made a distinction between the failure to obtain a patient's basic or real consent (attracting liability under the tort of trespass to the person, as a battery) and the failure to provide sufficient information to enable a patient to understand the broader implications of the proposed intervention (attracting liability under negligence law, as a breach of the doctor's duty of care).[2] Common to both scenarios is the imparting of information (albeit to different degrees), and as a result

---

[1] Evidence of which in: Canadian Law Reform Commission (1980); Davies (1996), Chap. 6; Skegg (1988); and Sommerville (1980).
[2] See Chapter 4, *supra*, pp. 101–102, 106–107.

the distinction between the two has become anything but clear-cut, a fact which often obscures one's sense of where the patient's true cause of action lies.

In the torts sphere, we refer to the actions for assault and battery as species of *trespass to the person*. An "assault" has been defined as "an act which causes another person to apprehend the infliction of immediate, unlawful, force on his person".[3] A "battery" has been defined as "the actual intended use of unlawful force to another person without his consent . . . or any other lawful excuse."[4] Instances of tortious assault or indeed criminal assault and battery are exceedingly rare in the health care context, whose concept of consent has been developed largely through the tort of battery. Before considering why and with what effect the law chooses to assess disclosure of information for the most part under negligence law, it is necessary to consider information in the context of consent and the tort of battery or trespass to the person.

Disclosure, Information, and Battery

Battery is the tortious child of the quasi-criminal writ of trespass to the person (which in turn draws an ancestry from the crime of mayhem). As traditionally conceived, it constituted an intentional touching of a harmful, hostile, or offensive nature, to which no consent or authority had been given either orally or verbally. As a legal description, "medical malpractice" once referred to the trespass action[5] until an independent action in negligence was disentangled from the tort of trespass and developed under the emerging theory of fault liability from the mid nineteenth century. Thereafter, the plaintiff who sued in trespass generally had to show that the battery was deliberate and intended. By contrast, for actions in negligence the physical contact (where present) was traditionally the unintended result of carelessness.[6] Because the paradigm battery is intentionally committed, with potential liability for the same act under the

---

[3] *Collins v. Wilcock* [1984] 1 W.L.R. 1172 at 1177, *per* Robert Goff L.J.

[4] *Attorney-General's Reference (No. 6 of 1980)* [1981] 1 Q.B. 715 at 718, *per* Lord Lane C.J.

[5] A person could be found liable in trespass for unintended, carelessly caused injury, *e.g. Weaver v. Ward* (1617) Hob. 134, where the defendant was found liable for accidentally shooting the plaintiff during an exercise of trained bands.

[6] *Wilson v. Pringle* [1987] 1 Q.B. 237 at 247, *per* Croom-Johnson L.J.

criminal law, the stigmatising effects of a battery verdict against doctors were and are hard to escape. Battery was ultimately abandoned by the American courts as the appropriate tort for medical non-disclosure, partly out of an appreciation that "assault and battery involves a defendant who is acting for the most part out of malice or in a manner generally considered as "anti-social". One who commits an assault and battery is not seeking to confer any benefit upon the one assaulted."[7] According to this view of the action, a *therapeutic battery* amounts to a contradiction in terms.

For some time, there was an assumption that the battery action required proof of hostile intent. This probably owed much to the domineering presence of "fraud" and "misrepresentation" in the battery discourse. It is, for instance, well established that if a doctor misrepresents a procedure to be therapeutic, or if the defendant has fraudulently held himself out to be a doctor, the patient's consent to the "medical" interference is illusory and has been vitiated by a misrepresentation or fraud, exposing the defendant to liability in battery.[8] The hostility assumption shows distinct signs of yielding to the modern view that "the intention need not be malicious, nor need it be an intention to inflict either a harmful or offensive contact without the other's consent or to put the other in apprehension thereof".[9] The logical extension of this perspective is that a battery may be caused by the intentional violation of a legally protected interest of another in his person. The courts seem increasingly willing to broaden the potential scope of the action in this manner. Though in *Wilson v. Pringle* Croom-Johnson L.J. on the surface favoured a retention of hostile intent, he qualified this by observing that hostility cannot be equated with mere "ill-will or malevolence"

---

[7] *Natanson v. Kline* (1960) 354 P. 2d 670 at 670.

[8] In considering liability for covertly testing a patient's blood sample for AIDS, the courts face numerous options. Given that the defendant's act is intentional, it is submitted that the courts should assess the case as raising a battery for the fraudulent concealment of the doctor's intention or indeed for fraudulently performing the test without consent and authority. Kennedy & Grubb (1989a) favour the negligence option largely on the basis that the plaintiff can establish a departure from approved medical practice, which currently disapproves of unauthorised testing and generally requires that the patient receives prior counseling. This approach is a precarious one, given that its efficacy is contingent on the current state of approved medical practice. Moreover, according to Keown (1989), p. 799, it may be the case that the bulk of the profession is opposed to a blanket requirement that the doctor inform the patient of the need and his intention to test the blood sample for HIV and AIDS.

[9] Harper & James (1956), pp. 216–218; cited with approval in Katz (1984), p. 68.

(which nonetheless would be strong evidence of hostility), but may rather be implied from the circumstances of the case. Moreover, it may be deemed to exist where someone acts contrary to the other's "*legal right* not to be physically restrained".[10] In *Re F.*, Lord Goff seized an opportunity to reject the hostility requirement as an unreasonable limitation on the action: "A prank that gets out of hand, an over-friendly slap on the back, surgical treatment by a surgeon who mistakenly thinks that the patient has consented to it—all these things may transcend the bounds of lawfulness without being characterised as hostile."[11]

There have been other high-profile attempts to disentangle the battery action from its traditional moorings, of which perhaps the most significant concerns the issue of possible defences to the action. This has always been of acute concern to doctors, given that they daily face the likelihood of being summoned to administer medical treatment under emergency conditions, where the patient is incapable or only partially capable of giving consent to the intervention. It is also the case that surgical intervention is intrinsically investigative or exploratory, in so far as what a surgeon has initially presumed to be the problem may prove otherwise when internal surgery is conducted under anaesthetic, and the surgeon may have to attempt to rectify the unanticipated problem as discovered, without postponing proceedings to obtain the patient's fresh consent.

The courts often assess this predicament in terms of the scope of the patient's original consent, reasoning that the patient can be presumed to have simultaneously given an implied consent to interventions that become necessary during the anticipated intervention.[12] In *Brushett v. Cowan*, for instance, the patient had given a written consent to a muscle biopsy right distal thigh procedure, and had signed a form that contained a residual clause giving consent to "such further or alternative measures as may be found to be necessary during the course of the operation".[13] The surgeon excised a portion of the muscle, but then observed an abnormality in the bone area and chose additionally to excise a portion of the bone. Overturning a decision that the residual clause was too vague to authorise the defendant's unanticipated intervention, the Newfoundland Court of Appeal preferred to reason that the patient had been

---

[10] *Wilson v. Pringle, supra*, n. 6 at 253 (emphasis added).
[11] *Re F. (a mental patient: sterilistion)* [1990] 2 A.C. 1 at 73.
[12] See Chapter 4, *supra*, pp. 94–95.
[13] *Brushett v. Cowan* (1991) 2 Med. L.R. 271.

referred to her doctor "for the purpose of investigating persistent problems associated with an injury" and that the biopsy had been part of a "continuing investigative process."[14] Marshall J.A. considered that the patient's *inviolable* right to choose his own medical treatment "must be interpreted in relation to the overall social interest of precluding undue hindrance of the physician legitimately acting within the scope of the consent actually given by adopting too narrow a view of its ambit."[15] Nevertheless, this interest has often been defeated by a requirement that there be an immediate risk of injury to the patient—in other words, that emergency conditions exist rendering it necessary to proceed without the patient's consent.[16]

In more recent years, the courts have departed from notions of implied and imputed consent, preferring instead to identify broad exceptions to the need to obtain a consent in the given circumstances. In the 1933 case of *Marshall v. Curry*, Chisholm C.J. pre-empted much later developments when he asserted that "it is not useful to strain the law by establishing consent by fictions", and that it is more helpful and realistic, particularly in emergency situations, to justify the defendant's intervention in terms of *necessity*.[17] Much later in *Collins v. Wilcock*, Robert Goff L.J. was prepared to recognise a general defence or exception for all battery cases, and proposed that the specific instances of implied consent identified by the courts over the years should now be considered "as falling within a general exception embracing all physical conduct which is a generally

---

[14] *Brushett v. Cowan, supra*, n. 13 at 275.

[15] *ibid.*

[16] See for example, *Murray v. McMurchy* [1949] 2 D.L.R. 442 at 444, where a doctor committed a battery when he tied the patient's fallopian tubes during a caesarian section: although the doctor reasonably feared for the patient's health if she became pregnant in the future, an emergency had not existed. The court emphasised that merely acting in the patient's *best interests* does not justify operating without the patient's consent: "No amount of professional skill can justify the substitution of the will of the surgeon for that of his patient"—citing *Bennan v. Parsonnet* (1912) 83 N.J.L.R. 20 at 26, per Garrison J. A similar scenario led to damages in *Devi v. West Midlands Area Health Authority* [1980] C.L.Y. 687.

[17] *Marshall v. Curry* [1933] 3 D.L.R. 260 at 275. Endorsed by Professor Skegg (1974), p. 514, where he writes that the doctrine of necessity "amounts to little more than the notion that the interest or interests protected by a particular law (such as the individual's interest in being able to decide for himself what is done to his body) must be qualified by more important interests."

accepted conduct of daily life".[18] In *Re F.*, Lord Goff observed that implying consents "can be regarded as artificial; and in particular, it is difficult to impute consent to those who, by reason of their youth or mental disorder, are unable to give their consent".[19] In that case, the House saw no difference between the treatment of the mentally incompetent and the treatment of a person who has been rendered temporarily incompetent and who needs emergency medical intervention; in both cases, the doctor is entitled to administer aid in the best interests of the patient so long as a consent cannot be obtained without jeopardising the patient's health, and this is not because the patient impliedly consents to this, but rather because necessity and public interest permits it.[20]

In the few cases when it is determined that a patient is incompetent to consent (whether temporarily or permanently), the doctor is usually entitled to treat him without consent if in the patient's best interests. Though in theory an official legal adjudication of incompetence is required by law, after which a person becomes known as a *de jure* incompetent, in practice informal arrangements tend to be made between family members (or *surrogates*) and the relevant doctors, particularly where additional delay or expense places the patient's health at risk.[21] There is significantly more support within the legal community for an assessment of a patient's *specific* competence or capacity as opposed to *general* competence or status. The parameters of capacity have been tested recently in England in the context of the emancipated adolescent and his parent. In *Gillick v. West Norfolk & Wisbech Area Health Authority*, the House of Lords vindicated the rights of the former, proposing that "save where statute otherwise provides, a minor's capacity to make his or her own decision depends upon the minor having sufficient understanding and intelligence to make the decision and is not to be determined by any judicially fixed age limit."[22] This specific competence or capacity test is more apt to

---

[18] *Collins v. Wilcock* [1984] 1 W.L.R. 1172 at 1177. Affirmed in *Wilson v. Pringle, supra*, n. 6 at 252 by Croom-Johnson L.J. on the basis that though it had been customary in the past to identify instances of implied consent, it is better now "to say that the surgeon's action is acceptable in the ordinary conduct of everyday life."

[19] *Re F. (a mental patient: sterilisation), supra*, n. 11 at 72.

[20] *ibid.* at 74–79.

[21] Appelbaum, Lidz, and Meisel (1987), pp. 81–91.

[22] *Gillick v. West Norfolk and Wisbech Area Health Authority* [1986] A.C. 112 at 188, *per* Lord Scarman (quoting from *R. v. D* [1984] A.C. 778). The *Gillick* principle was subsequently applied in *Re R. (a minor) (wardship: consent to medical treatment)* [1992]

uphold an adult's right to refuse.[23] If properly employed, it should provide heightened protection of the right to make irrational decisions, though it would seem that the courts are more reluctant to uphold irrational, injurious health care decisions where made by young adults with a long life expectancy.[24]

According to one view, the *extent* of a patient's competence will determine the degree of explanation that must be made: the greater the patient's capacity to comprehend, the greater is the need to disclose relevant medical information; but where a patient's comprehension is more restricted (whether through severity of illness, complexity of medical issues, or lack of intelligence or education) the duty to disclose is less.[25] The dangers of discriminating between patients on the basis of their apparent ability to understand medical data are considerable, and I have already discussed this in the context of the duty to disclose under negligence law.[26] If a test of *actual understanding* is employed, the issue of competence turns on what the patient is told.[27] This is clearly an unsatisfactory approach, attaching too much importance to what is medically prudent. In the United States, the American President's Commission ultimately rejected a test which would appraise competence and autonomy by reference to the *content* of a patient's decision, on the basis that this process would be vulnerable to the value-laden concepts of reasonableness and rationality. On the other hand, it rejected a test which would rely solely upon a person's "expressed preference", since this is unable to

---

Fam. 11 at 26, where the Court of Appeal sanctioned the overriding of a minor's refusal to take anti-psychotic medication, finding her to be mentally disturbed, often psychotic, and suicidal. Of *Gillick*, Lord Donaldson M.R. said: "What is really being looked at is an assessment of mental and emotional age, as contrasted with chronological age". This decision has been stridently condemned for "driving a coach and horses through *Gillick*": Kennedy, "Consent to Treatment: the Capable Person" in Dyer (1992) Chap. 3. For further criticism of this direction, see: Davies (1996), p. 145; and Mason and McCall Smith (1994), p. 229.

[23] On the other hand, this test is equally vulnerable to the interjection of paternalism and extraneous public policies. In the recent case of *Re MB (caesarian section)*, N.L.J., April 25, 1997, the Court of Appeal decided that a temporary impairment of mental functioning may entitle the doctor to act paternally against the patient's wishes. In this case, the temporary incapacity was a fear of needles which, it was felt, disabled the patient from agreeing to submit to a caesarian section.

[24] See Chapter 1, *supra*, pp. 25–26.

[25] Skegg (1974), p. 88, citing: *Crydernan v. Ringrose* (1978) 89 D.L.R. (3d) 32; *Male v. Hopmans* (1965) 54 D.L.R. (2d) 592 and (1967) 64 D.L.R. (2d) 105; and *Daniels v. Heskin* [1954] I.R. 73.

[26] See Chapter 5, *supra*, pp. 164–168.

[27] Kennedy and Grubb (1994), p. 121.

reveal impaired reasoning.[28] It advocated that one look instead for the presence of the following in the patient: "(1) possession of a set of values and goals; (2) the ability to communicate and to understand information; and (3) the ability to reason and to deliberate about one's choices."[29] This approach has much to recommend it, and has a firm basis in ethical and philosophical attempts to define or describe autonomy.[30]

Philosophers and ethicists have cautioned against the dangers of the all-or-nothing conception of autonomy, advocating instead a sliding scale that reflects a variety of differentiating factors.[31] According to this view, more account should be taken of the fact that when ill and particularly when hospitalised, patients are caused to lose much of what we associate with autonomy, and they are often prompted to make decisions for transient emotional reasons. Ackerman writes that though a patient's illness is likely to be the biggest obstacle to autonomy, the doctor can help by providing education and information, keeping the patient's spirits up, and alleviating the illness.[32] Information, explanation, and comprehension are being increasingly identified as potential keys to a more rounded appreciation of a patient's competence and capacity to make health care decisions. In this light, discussion of the relevant medical information is not something which may be suspended or restricted as a matter of course whenever a patient appears incompetent or irrational.[33]

In rejecting the battery action as the appropriate forum for the *post-hoc* vindication of patients' rights to disclosure, the courts are likely to

---

[28] President's Commission for the Study of Ethical Problems in Medicine and Biomedical and Behavioral Research, *Vol. 1* (1982), p. 61.

[29] *ibid.* at 57.

[30] *e.g.* Miller (1981), pp. 24–25, according to which, the optimal state of autonomy has four essential aspects, which represent an optimal state of autonomy: (1) free action, whereby one knows what one is doing and does so voluntarily, though this requirement cannot be too rigid if most of one's daily actions are to be regarded as autonomous; (2) authenticity, whereby one acts in character, consistent to one's own values and desires; (3) effective deliberation, whereby one rationally weighs up pros and cons, though the absence of this will not be crucial given that most patients undergo therapy because their doctor recommends it, or because friends underwent it in the past, or because it seemed the best thing to do; and (4) moral reflection, whereby one questions one's core beliefs and values, particularly if faced with terminal illness.

[31] Brody (1985); Burt (1979); Faden and Beauchamp (1986) Chaps 1, 7; and Katz (1984) pp. 106–118.

[32] Ackerman (1982). The President's Commission Report, Vol. 1 (1982), p. 61 reached a similar conclusion.

[33] Appelbaum, Lidz, and Meisel (1987), pp. 89–90.

have been influenced by a range of factors, some general and some particular to the medical context. An expanded form of battery liability for medical wrongs would place a considerable strain on health care resources. Where the defendant is found to have committed a battery, he is typically liable for all the adverse consequences which flow from that act, irrespective of the remoteness of risk of injury or the skill with which the patient was treated.[34] Thus it is said, successful battery suits against a doctor could ultimately leave a plaintiff with "free care, improved health, and financial compensation."[35] The courts may also implicitly have considered the typical unavailability of insurance cover for intentional wrongs.

The focus of battery law is much narrower, being on the plaintiff's right to freedom from unwanted intrusions, and as such it asks fewer questions and admits less in defence.[36] The resulting advantages are significant. First, the defendant is significantly less able to rely in his defence upon expert evidence that he complied with general professional practice—a fact which sometimes prompted the courts out of sympathy to choose to assess the plaintiff's claim as an instance of medical battery rather than negligence.[37] Secondly, whereas the plaintiff bears the full burden of proof of negligence, once the plaintiff establishes the fact of physical intrusion in a trespass case, it falls to the defendant to justify the intrusion by (in most cases) establishing that consent was given either explicitly or implicitly; thus in battery cases, if the evidence leaves the court in equal doubt as to whom to believe, the defendant loses.[38] Though case law on this is not uniform,[39] a belief that the battery action "casts upon the defendant the burden of proving consent to what was done" was articulated by Laskin C.J.C. in *Reibl v. Hughes*, and formed part of his reasons for abandoning battery as the cause of action for non-

---

[34] See *Allan v. New Mount Sinai Hospital* (1980) 109 D.L.R. (3d) 634, where the defendant disobeyed the plaintiff's express instruction not to touch her left arm, and consequently was held liable in full for all the unforeseeable damage which flowed from surgical injury to the arm despite a complete absence of fault on the doctor's part.

[35] Katz (1977), p. 145.

[36] The 'defences' to battery include consent, self-defence, ejecting trespassers, and exercising parental authority. Contributory *negligence* is traditionally not open to defendants, given that battery is an intentional act.

[37] See Chapter 4, *supra*, pp. 96–97.

[38] Sommerville (1981), p. 791.

[39] In *Freeman v. Home Office (No. 2)* [1984] 2 W.L.R. 130 at 141, McGowan J. reasoned that the plaintiff bears the burden of proving that there was consent.

disclosure.[40] Thirdly, the damage upon which the battery action is grounded is the unauthorised invasion of the plaintiff's body. The common difficulties of proving causation do not exist, for the plaintiff need only prove that a touching or intervention occurred without consent; in this context, the test of recoverability is the directness of the damage incurred. Where a medical intervention is shown to be non-consensual on the basis of insufficient or misleading information, causation-in-fact is satisfied merely by proving that the interference caused the damage; the plaintiff does not have to establish that "but for" the failure to explain or disclose certain facts, he would not have consented and thus would have avoided damage (elements he must prove for the negligence action).[41] Fourthly, the plaintiff does not technically have to prove damage beyond the fact of unwanted interference, since the tort of battery protects the invasion per se of one's dignitary interests (though needless to say, the courts usually award only nominal damages if no physical or psychological injury is proved to have occurred).

The concept of reasonableness has little application under the battery analysis, yet it pervades the common law's assessment of negligence, rendering negligence a tort more apt to juggle competing social interests. To this end, negligence has generated a more public policy conscious body of law.[42] As a distinct tort based on the notion of fault liability, the modern law of negligence was cultivated in the late nineteenth century, first as a response to a spate of accidental injuries sustained during an accelerated development of infrastructure and industry across the Commonwealth and United States.[43] Articulated memorably by Oliver Wendell Holmes at the close of the century,[44] negligence law developed as a means of compensating some accident victims, deterring risk-creating activities, and, where those risk-creating activities were socially desirable (through, for example, generating employment or providing valuable public services), retaining a crude balance broadly designed to ensure that those activities were not over-deterred or discouraged.

---

[40] *Reibl v. Hughes* (1980) 114 D.L.R. (3d) 1 at 9.
[41] *Pratt v. Davies* 118 Ill. App. 161 (1905), aff'd 79 N.E. 562 (1906). See Chapter 7, *infra*, pp. 201–215.
[42] Recent examples in the health care context include: the wrongful birth action, *Emeh v. Kensington Area Health Authority* [1985] 1 Q.B. 1012; and the nervous shock action, *Tredgett v. Somerset Health Authority* (1994) 5 Med. L.R. 178.
[43] Winfield (1926).
[44] Holmes (1881).

Given the monolithic focus of the battery analysis on freedom from unconsensual touchings, it is ill-suited to balancing the competing rights, duties, and policy interests which arise as a matter of course in the medical context. Because the negligence analysis is reluctant to assume a bias against an isolated result, particularly where the circumstances of the case are difficult, it enables the court to commit to alternate principles—such as that patients have a right to be treated carefully and skilfully, and on the other hand, that an error of judgment does not constitute medical negligence—pleasing both (at least theoretically), until it is *moved* to vindicate one at the expense of the other in the case at hand. The success of such a forum is easily appreciated in theory, if not always in practice. English judicial policy has consciously restricted the fuller development of the tort of medical negligence, largely through its ongoing recourse to a set of *guiding* principles and presumptions of good public policy lazily unchanged by the judiciary from decade to decade.[45]

Mindful of the reasons why negligence has ultimately come to be favoured as the dominant forum for assessing wrongs committed in the medical context, it is necessary now to consider how one may distinguish between events that generate a battery or a negligence claim in the context of non-disclosure of pre-treatment risk information.

Consent and Battery; Disclosure and Negligence

The common law requires the doctor to obtain a patient's consent (often called a *real* or *basic* consent),[46] verbally or in writing, to the contemplated treatment or procedure, in the absence of which the defendant's intervention may amount to a battery. This process will inevitably entail the disclosure of relevant medical information and the explanation of consent forms. The courts have consistently ruled that patients must understand that to which they are giving consent. In the English case of *Chatterton v. Gerson*, Bristow J. warned that "getting the plaintiff to sign a pro forma expressing consent to

---

[45] See Chapter 8, *infra* pp. 242–250.
[46] Reference to *real* consent is favoured in England, following *Chatterton v. Gerson* [1981] 1 All E.R. 257 at 265, *per* Bristow J. *Basic* consent is favoured in the U.S. and Canada: see Katz (1977), (1984); McCoid (1957); Robertson (1981); and Sommerville (1981).

undergo the operation 'the effect and nature of which have been explained to me', as was done here, should be a valuable reminder to everyone of the need for explanation and consent."[47] The consent form would not have provided a defence to battery "if no explanation had in fact been given" in which case the "consent would have been expressed in form only, not in reality."[48]

Yet throughout the common law, a distinction has emerged between the information that must be imparted and explained: (1) to ensure an adequate basic consent as a defence to the battery claim, and (2) to discharge the doctor's duty to disclose additional medical information (chiefly regarding risks and alternatives) under negligence law.[49] Laskin C.J.C.'s analysis in *Reibl v. Hughes* has been particularly influential on this point:

> "In my opinion, actions of battery in respect of surgical or other medical treatment should be confined to cases where surgery or treatment has been performed or given to which there has been no consent at all or where, emergency situations aside, surgery or treatment has been performed or given beyond that to which there was consent. . . . I can appreciate the temptation to say that the genuineness of consent to medical treatment depends on proper disclosure of the risks which it entails, but in my view, unless there has been misrepresentation or fraud to secure consent to the treatment, a failure to disclose the attendant risks, however serious, should go to negligence rather than to battery. Although such a failure relates to an informed choice of submitting to or refusing recommended and appropriate treatment, it arises as the breach of an anterior duty of care, comparable in legal obligation to the duty of due care in carrying out the particular treatment to which the patient has consented. It is not a test of the validity of the consent."[50]

This approach has found favour in England and Ireland.[51] In *Chatterton v. Gerson*, Bristow J. decided that the battery action is not

---

[47] *Chatterton v. Gerson, supra*, no. 46 at 265.
[48] *ibid.*
[49] This was adopted by the founding cases of informed consent, in *Canterbury v. Spence* 464 F. 2d 772 (1972) and *Reibl v. Hughes, supra*, n. 40. See Chapter 4, *supra*, pp. 101–102, 106–107.
[50] *Reibl v. Hughes, ibid.*, at 10–11.
[51] *Walsh v. Family Planning Services* [1992] 1 I.R. 496, *per* Finlay C.J. and O'Flaherty J.

concerned with the communication of risks and alternatives nor with the mere "failure of communication between doctor and patient", but is limited to the assessment of whether a "real consent" has been obtained through informing the patient "in broad terms of the nature of the procedure which is intended".[52] In *Freeman v. Home Office (No. 2)*, McGowan J. agreed that the issue of risk disclosure is a matter for negligence since it "arises as a breach of an anterior duty of due care", and that for "consent in battery, it is sufficient if the plaintiff knew in broad terms what he was consenting to, not because of any special doctrine but because otherwise his consent would not be real."[53]

Ultimately, the distinction would appear to be one of convenience, the logical corollary of having decided that non-disclosure in most cases raises issues of negligence. In this light, what "a plaintiff consents to in a case of alleged battery is not risk but a specific intrusion on his body."[54] Thus, since "risks, by definition, may not occur, it is not possible to find the required intention to touch in the manner which results from risks occurring simply by demonstrating their crystallisation."[55] In this light, to obtain a patient's basic/real consent, the doctor must disclose and explain the *inevitable consequences* of the intended touching, but no more.[56] However, if we examine the legal concept of consent more closely, it becomes clear that some risks of a more *probable* nature may have to be disclosed if the patient could be said to have properly given consent. Definitions of consent have classically insisted that consent "supposes a physical power to act, a moral power of acting, and a serious, determined, and free use of these powers . . . There is a difference between consenting and submitting. Every consent involves a submission; but a mere submission does not necessarily involve consent."[57]

The requirement that a consent be freely and fully given has been interpreted to mean that in ordinary circumstances, "the medical man, before obtaining consent, should give his patient a fair and reasonable explanation of the nature of the operation or treatment proposed, of its probable effects and of any unusual *risks* involved in it; for where an inadequate or misleading explanation has been given there is a danger that the apparent consent obtained will be held to be

---

[52] *Chatterton v. Gerson, supra*, n. 46 at 265.
[53] *Freeman v. Home Office (No. 2), supra*, n. 39 at 140.
[54] *ibid.* at 141, *per* McGowan J.
[55] Sommerville (1981), p. 750.
[56] *ibid.*, p. 746.
[57] *Black's Law Dictionary*, as cited in *Gray v. Grunnagle* 223 A. 2d 663 (1966) at 669.

ineffective."[58] The English Law Commission in its second Consultation Paper on *Consent in the Criminal Law*, defined consent as including "a valid subsisting consent to an injury *or to the risk of an injury* of the type caused".[59] The tort of battery is more expandable than is sometimes thought. In the areas of medical research and innovative treatment, for instance, the courts have not hesitated in declaring that more rigorous disclosure is called for when the exclusive purpose of the doctor's intervention is not the plaintiff's health but instead the advancement of science, and that a failure to discuss each associated risk may lead to a battery verdict.[60]

In practical terms, this popular distinction between inevitable consequences and mere risks marks an unspoken attempt to restrict the invocation of medical battery, with its condemnatory and stigmatising implications, to extreme cases.[61] In doing so, this inevitably compromises the clinical and legal reality that both events—the obtaining of an adequate consent and disclosure mandated by negligence law—are part of the same process, and that the attempt to disentangle them is inherently a legalistic one.[62] In America, before the negligence action came to be favoured for disclosure claims, the tendency was to assess non-disclosure of medical risks and alternative treatments in relation to the patient's basic consent with potential liability in battery.[63] In *Wall v. Brim*, for instance, it was proposed that before a patient gives his consent he must be able to weigh "the dangers and results incident to its performance . . .. [A] surgeon may not perform an operation different in kind from that consented to or

---

[58] *Nathan on Medical Evidence*, as cited in *Lepp v. Hopp* (1979) 98 D.L.R. (3d) 464 at 473 (emphasis added).

[59] Law Commission Consultation Paper No. 139, HMSO, 1995, para. 4.52 (emphasis added).

[60] *Halushka v. University of Saskatchewan* 53 D.L.R. (2d) 436 (1965); *Whitlock v. Duke University* 637 F. Supp. 1463 (1986).

[61] Battery verdicts against doctors have been scarce. See: *Cull v. Royal Surrey County Hospital* [1932] 1 B.M.J. 1195, where the defendant performed an hysterectomy instead of an abortion; *Michael v. Molesworth* [1950] 2 B.M.J. 171, where a surgeon performed an operation which was wholly different from that to which the patient had consented; *Hamilton v. Birmingham Regional Health Board* [1969] 2 B.M.J. 456, where a sterilisation was unconsensually performed during Caesarian section; and *Devi v. West Midlands Regional Health Authority*, CA, *supra*, n. 16, where the defendant performed a sterilisation in addition to the consented-to repair of the uterus.

[62] According to Bromberger (1983), p. 17, to "suggest that there can be a partial consent and that this equals consent is the same as suggesting that a female can be 'a little bit pregnant'."

[63] See Chapter 4, *supra*, pp. 94–98.

one involving risks and results not contemplated."[64] In *Lepp v. Hopp* a case decided a few years before *Reibl v. Hughes*, the Alberta Supreme Court granted judgment in both battery and negligence for non-disclosure of risk information on the basis that both actions share a common concern, that of ensuring that the patient is furnished with sufficient relevant facts to enable him to make an informed choice and consent.[65] In *Canterbury v. Spence*, the case that launched informed consent doctrine, Robinson J. referred to this series of battery cases to illustrate the point that a consent is not "worthy of the name unless the physician first elucidates the options and the *perils* for the patient's edification."[66]

It is trite law that a proper consent to a physical intervention must be *voluntarily* given. This would appear to logically entail the exercise of choice free from undue influence, pressure, or coercion, and untainted by misrepresentation or fraud by the person to whom consent is given. Though the presence of any of these defects may vitiate or negate a person's apparent consent, they will be hard to detect in the medical context for the simple reason that illness and hospitalisation by themselves diminish a person's ability to behave autonomously and freely. This is further compromised by the allegiance of health carers to beneficent paternalism, which may involve filtering information in a non-neutral manner.[67] For this reason, the courts are loath to equate incomplete disclosure with fraud, deception, or misrepresentation. This perhaps also reflects the view that in a profession which prizes above all the cultivation of professional prestige and dignity, the intentional commission of a tort or crime is an exceptionally rare event. It is also the case that in the clinical environment, time is often of the essence and vital resources typically stretched, so that a failure to explain some specific detail of the treatment is often non-intentional and due instead to oversight. Thus one cannot know for certain the *extent* to which misrepresentation or fraudulent concealment of relevant information may potentially be applied to non-disclosure of medical information.

In this respect, it is significant that the courts have not recoiled from equating non-disclosure of risks associated with research-based

---

[64] *Wall v. Brim* 138 F. 2d 478 (1943) at 481, *per* Hutcheson J.

[65] *Lepp v. Hopp, supra*, n. 58 at 484.

[66] *Canterbury v. Spence, supra*, n. 49 at 783 (emphasis added).

[67] See by way of exception, *Norberg v. Wynrib* (1992) 92 D.L.R. (4th) 449, where the Supreme Court of Canada regarded the patient's consent to sexual acts with the defendant physician as having been vitiated by a coercive, exploitative relationship in which he had given the patient drugs in return for sexual favours.

or experimental treatment with misrepresentation (in the sense of misrepresenting the intervention as less complicated than it actually is, by failing to disclose all the associated risks). In *Halushka v. University of Saskatchewan*, a relatively early decision that has become ubiquitous as an authority, the Saskatchewan Court of Appeals found that inaccurately simplified information given to a research volunteer vitiates the subject's apparent consent because it has misled him.[68] The perils for patients (or subjects) where an intervention is undertaken partly or wholly for the purposes of medical research are many. It is widely agreed by lawyers and ethicists that the presence of coercive elements peculiar to the research context may ultimately affect the validity of consent. Where following admission to hospital, a patient is asked to participate in treatment which is partly or wholly research-based, there is a significant danger that the patient might give consent out of a fear that to refuse it would be to threaten his relationship with the doctor, or the quality of his treatment.[69] A statement by the doctor that participation will result in better care or the provision of services which the doctor would otherwise not make available to the patient similarly could amount to powerful evidence of coercion.[70] The doctor should ensure that the patient is left in no doubt that refusal to participate will have no impact on the quality of health care made available to him. The payment of a lump sum for participation in a research program may itself be coercive, to the extent that it might cause the volunteer to feel trapped into cooperation during each subsequent stage.[71] Indeed, it may be the case that the person who typically volunteers himself as a research subject is more likely to need protection by the law against doing so before having fully considered all the risks and implications. A study at the Harvard Medical School revealed that 60 per cent of volunteers for research trials were seriously maladjusted to their social environment.[72] Certain categories of vulnerable subjects have been identified

---

[68] *Halushka v. University of Saskatchewa, supra*, n. 60. See Chapter 4, *supra*, pp. 111–115.
[69] Gray (1975), p. 205.
[70] According to Ayd (1972), hospitalised patients should be regarded as a vulnerable class for whom special rules ought to be developed if their consent to research is to be properly obtained.
[71] One suggestion is to adopt a pro rata payment system spread out over the entire research period: Hershey and Miller (1976), p. 65.
[72] Pappworth (1969).

with good reason as necessitating special protection—chiefly, prisoners and the mentally ill—and the ability of these within their particular context to give a free consent has been queried.[73]

Beyond the research setting, it would certainly be easier for a court to rule that the defendant's failure to disclose an inevitable consequence of the treatment constituted a misrepresentation: although non-disclosure of inevitable consequences may equally be unintentional, it is easier for a court to decide that this type of failure culminated in a battery.[74] Moreover, the courts sometimes appear willing to *construct* an intention not to disclose a particular *risk*, and the implied basis upon which it will do so is more or less whether the risk was a probable and therefore *foreseeable* one. According to Mosk in *Cobbs v. Grant*, battery should apply to situations where a doctor performs a treatment which is not that to which consent was given since "the requisite element of intent to deviate from the consent is present", but it should not apply where a doctor has failed to disclose a risk of "low probability" since that does not represent an intentional deviation from consent.[75] This implies that risks of higher probability must be disclosed as part of the consent process. A similar view was expressed in *Kelly v. Hazlett*, where Morden J. ruled that the "more probable the risk the more it could be said to be an integral feature of the nature and character of the operation. Further, even if a risk is truly collateral, but still material, it could be said that its disclosure is so essential to an informed decision to undergo the operation that lack of such disclosure should vitiate the consent."[76]

Thus it is that the distinction between information required by battery law and information required by negligence law depends for the greater part on *degree*. In many cases, the distinction distils down to a crude, impressionistic division between *collateral* risks governed by negligence and *integral* risks governed by battery. This echoes a similarly troublesome distinction made by the criminal law between non-disclosure of the nature of the act and non-disclosure of an issue collateral to the act. The criminal law has tended to interpret non-disclosure of an integral element (necessary to convey an understanding of the nature of the act about to be performed) as amounting to

---

[73] See: Appelbaum, Lidz, and Meisel (1987) p. 231; Bach-y-Rita (1974); Capron (1973); Fromer (1981); Martin, Arnold, Zimmerman *et al.* (1968); and Sabin, Bronstein and Hubbard (1975).
[74] Sommerville (1981), p. 750.
[75] *Cobbs v. Grant* 502 P. 2d 1 (1972) at 8.
[76] *Kelly v. Hazlett* 75 D.L.R. (3d) 536 (1976) at 559.

fraudulent behaviour or misrepresentation, thereby vitiating the consent that was apparently given. In *R v. Flattery*, a 19-year-old woman's consent to sexual intercourse was vitiated by the defendant doctor's misrepresentation that "breaking nature's strings" was necessary to cure her ailment.[77] By contrast (in a pre-AIDS culture), it was decided in *R v. Clarence* that the defendant's failure to disclose that he had a venereal disease did not vitiate the plaintiff's consent to sexual intercourse.[78]

The collateral distinction has understandably attracted criticism. Giesen argues that "it appears quite unreasonable to maintain artificial procedural differences which can only be explained in terms of legal history", and that the collateral risk divide is a distortion of reality which is likely only to frustrate reasonable expectations of how the law works.[79] By way of reform, Tan Feng proposes a widening of the rules governing liability in battery, thereby avoiding the necessity of transforming the tort of medical negligence.[80] However, unless the battery action is dramatically reconstructed by the judges (which is unlikely), this proposal seems implausible, for an amplification of its present scope simply would not match clinical reality or accord even broadly with principles of fairness to defendants. It is the highly elusive and impractical modifiers employed by the courts—collateral, real, probable, material, significant, general, *etc.*—which place doctors in peril of legal uncertainty. Undoubtedly, doctors are under a positive legal duty to *know*, as far as is known, what risks are broadly attached to particular forms of treatment; this duty must surely be nourished by the increased availability of medical data.[81] Doctors may be better served by following guidelines which have been approved in advance by the medical and the legal professions or by following a statutory code detailing necessary items of disclosure for the proper obtaining of a patient's preliminary consent to specified treatments.[82]

---

[77] *R. v. Flattery* [1887] 2 Q.B.D. 410.
[78] *R. v. Clarence* (1888) 22 Q.B.D. 23: approved in the medical context in *Sidaway v. Bethlem Royal Hospital* [1984] 1 All E.R. 1018 at 1026 *per* Donaldson M.R. and 1029 *per* Dunn L.J., CA. Similarly, in *Hegarty v. Shine* [1878] Cox C.C. 145 at 150, the Irish Court of Appeal decided that consent to sexual intercourse—albeit in an "illicit" affair—was not vitiated by the defendant's "reckless" or "deceitful" concealment of a venereal disease unless, according to Palles C.B., "a duty be shown to communicate the fact concealed to the party who has been deceived."
[79] Giesen (1988), p. 351.
[80] Feng (1987), pp. 160–162.
[81] As proposed by Waltz and Scheuneman (1970), p. 631.
[82] This direction has been adopted by numerous States in America: see Chapter 4, *supra*, p. 101.

Clearly, such a project would be time-consuming and costly, and would ultimately require a structured alliance between the medical and legal professions. Yet it has much to recommend it, at least for certain forms of invasive or high-risk procedures.

The historical lineage which informed consent law shares with the battery action is a fact which continues to obscure the issues surrounding it. In its identification of risks which must be disclosed (because they are material to a patient's right to make an informed consent), the doctrine of informed consent arguably moves closest to its origins in the simple analysis of disclosure, consent, and authorised interference[83]—providing an opportunity for some to argue that the chief differences between the two lies in statistical degree of risk.[84] This proposition, if indulged further, would strip informed consent law of its intended effects on the doctor-patient relationship, beyond the neutral provision and acceptance of medical data. Informed consent doctrine is concerned with more than the disclosure of statistically more probable risks. Its raison d'etre is that risks and alternatives—which together may more fruitfully be referred to as *options*[85]—are presented to each patient in a manner which is calculated to engage the patient in a discussion as to which option best serves him in the light of the patient's own values, preferences, and goals. Currently, it is submitted, informed consent law (howsoever named) functions best as a complement to the proper taking of preliminary consents. This is chiefly because the informed consent analysis (within which expert testimony of professional general practice is less determinative), or at any rate the ordinary negligence analysis, gives the court far more flexibility to balance the nuances of each case (which in disclosure trials tend to be highly subtle, usually fraught by inconclusive evidence). The court is not restricted, as it is in battery actions, to grave derelictions of duty, nor to the leaden concepts of fraud, misrepresentation, or the failure to obtain *real* consents. It is free to consider to what extent the doctor failed to involve the patient sufficiently in a vital decision-making process and with what consequences.

---

[83] Indeed, this historical propinquity with matters of consent and battery provides one explanation for the largely unchallenged rule that it is the treating doctor who must disclose the relevant medical information to the patient. See Chapter 9, *supra*, p. 275.

[84] Feng (1987) p. 160.

[85] Appelbaum, Lidz, and Meisel (1987), p. 55.

Chapter 7

Causation in Malpractice Trials

The Causation Requirement

To succeed in his action, the plaintiff must do more than prove that the defendant was negligent. He must further prove that the defendant's negligence *caused* his injury or loss. The legal notions of cause and causation share little with their counterpart words of common currency. Causation is in this context a legal device to determine liability within the institutional parameters of fault liability. It draws variously but never exclusively from a variety of sources that include: *viva voce* testimony in court by medical experts and by witnesses to the event; the court's interpretation of the relative merits of viewpoints testified to by witnesses (in the light of objective facts and a subjective impression of the credibility and demeanour of witnesses); physical evidence; scientific fact and probability; legal principle; judicially acknowledged public policy interests; and the application of justice and common sense.

For personal injuries generally, causation is often a self-evident fact. In a case, for instance, against an employer for injuries sustained after a fall from hazardous scaffolding, the dominant issue will tend to be the level or standard of owe owed by the employer to his employee, and little time if any will be spent assessing whether or not the injuries were "caused" by the defendant's breach of duty. This, however, is otherwise for injuries sustained in the health care context. Though it is difficult to prove that a doctor breached the appropriate standard of care, plaintiffs face a much more difficult challenge (in many cases, a dead end) when they come to prove causation. Medical causation presents peculiar difficulties, not least because in each medical negligence action, numbered in the range of potential causes of the plaintiff's injury is the disease or illness from

191

which the patient originally suffered. This renders each instance a case of *multiple* causation, a case complicated by at least two competing causes, the patient's disease and the doctor's breach of duty.[1]

The causation analysis has evolved as a two-pronged process.[2] First, the plaintiff must establish *cause-in-fact*: that as a matter of fact, the defendant can be said to have caused the injury. Second, the plaintiff must establish *cause-in-law*; that the law *ought* to hold the defendant liable. The legal test is "attributive", being concerned with assigning liability consequences to the cause-in-fact. This segregation between factual and legal cause transmits a misleading sense that the first test is neither attributive nor evaluative when in truth it is both. In most cases of medical causation, there can be no conclusive scientific knowledge of how precisely the various causes took effect and led to the plaintiff's injuries. The court is forced to speculate according to degrees of probability, and ultimately to state a preference for one proposition over another. Fact, in this sense, is a statement of belief.

That is to say that cause-in-fact is a legalistic concept which is dependent from the outset upon the production of testimony and evidence, and further on interpretation, definition, and evaluation of terms.[3] Where the courts distinguish between substantial causes and minimal causes, they employ values that reflect the extent to which legal liability should lie for certain causes or factors leading up to the outcome. The fact that medical science is fraught with uncertainty, and that it must be decoded by experts trained in it, means that cause-in-fact must be established by medical experts who are usually reluctant to do more than express conjectures. The medical expert does not examine particular phenomena in the abstract but in his role as physician: "He cannot escape forming associations between events that will comport with the purposes of his profession, for this is the only way in which a causal relationship can be meaningful to him."[4] This may entail a comparative analysis between which of two particular routes a doctor may have taken; indeed, where the defendant's alleged negligence involves an omission to act, the court may decide to rely on expert evidence of customary medical practice as a means of deciding what further course of action would probably

---

[1] Stauch (1997), p. 214.
[2] See Atiyah and Crane (1993), pp. 96–105.
[3] Malone (1950).
[4] *ibid.*, p. 63.

have been taken had the defendant not initially failed to act.[5] Analysis of cause-in-fact has enjoyed something of a belated ascendancy in modern critiques of causation and fault liability. This is largely due to a more sophisticated understanding of the limitations of earlier legal concepts of cause and the wider social implications of definition for compensation and accountability. Distribution of the burdens of proof, the proper scope of *res ipsa loquitur*, the standard to which the plaintiff must prove cause-in-fact, have emerged as the pertinent issues, and much of the jurisprudence available to us has been wrought on the anvil of medical injury.

Under the legal test of causation, the court ascertains finally whether liability should as a matter of law attach for the injuries, which is another way of asking whether the plaintiff is permitted to recover damages from the defendant for this type of injury. In doing so, the court will usually ask whether the damage was a reasonably foreseeable consequence of the defendant's conduct, or whether the risk of injury was remote. Alternatively it may reason that the defendant's conduct was not the "real" or "proximate" cause (the *causa causens* or the *causa sine qua non*). The first test may produce different results than the second: that is to say, "an event may be the proximate cause of an unforeseeable result."[6] Indeed, the courts may instead choose to be influenced by the magnitude of the plaintiff's potential injury. Much, it is submitted, depends upon the court's instinctive sense of reasonableness in the context of the factual and legal issues arising from the case. If the magnitude of potential loss for the plaintiff is great or specific to that plaintiff, the courts are likely to incorporate this fact into its final assessment of whether or not the defendant should reasonably have foreseen the plaintiff's injury.[7]

---

[5] *Bolitho v. City & Hackney Health Authority* [1998] A.C. 232: approved in *Joyce v. Merton, Sutton & Wandsworth Health Authority* (1996) 7 Med. L.R. 1.

[6] Atiyah and Crane (1993), p. 101.

[7] In *Rogers v. Whitaker* (1992) 109 A.L.R. 625, the Australian High Court decided that the defendant was liable for non-disclosure of a statistically remote risk (1 in 14,000) on the basis that the potential injury was severe and specifically material to the plaintiff (spread of blindness from one eye to the other). In *Walsh v. Family Planning Services* [1992] I.R. 497 at 521, McCarthy J. for the Irish Supreme Court decided that a risk of loss of sexual capacity (described as "extremely rare") should have been disclosed before the plaintiff decided to undergo a vasectomy, since "remote percentages of risk lose their significance to those unfortunate enough to be . . . critically concerned with that risk".

These various principles must be seen to coalesce in the cherished principle that permeates the concept of *fault* liability—that a defendant should not be held liable for injury which was not reasonably foreseeable. Understood in this light, we see that "the legal concept of cause reflects ideas about personal responsibility . . . [and] to say that a person's negligence was not the legal cause of another's loss may be a disguised way of saying that the loss was 'not really that person's fault'."[8]

Recovery may be denied or indeed permitted on grounds of public policy, though this residual common law discretion is as a matter of practice reserved to claims for new types of recovery which raise sensitive issues of public controversy.[9] The presence of policy may also be glimpsed in what has come to be known as the "eggshell or thin skull" rule. This reasons that a victim's pre-existing condition or susceptibility to injury is not a bar to the defendant's liability, and should only be taken into account when assessing damages (otherwise stated as the principle that a wrongdoer must take his victim as he finds him).[10] The thin skull rule greatly qualifies the general principle articulated in the *Wagon Mound* decision, according to which the test of recoverability is whether the injury was of a reasonably foreseeable type.[11] It was tested recently in *Page v. Smith*, where the plaintiff had been suffering from ME (chronic fatigue syndrome) at the time the defendant's car crashed into him.[12] The crash caused his condition to become chronic and permanent. The Court of Appeal ruled that since the plaintiff's psychiatric illness did not arise from any physical injury but was precipitated by the nervous shock sustained during the crash, the injuries were unforeseeable. The House of Lords disagreed in a decision which ruled out the view that the thin skull principle does not apply where the damage is psychiatric; on the facts of the case, it found that the negligent driver

---

[8] Atiyah and Crane (1993), p. 105.
[9] In recent years, the obvious example has been the evolving actions for wrongful life, birth, and conception: see chapter 5, *supra*, pp. 155–156.
[10] *Bournhill v. Young* [1943] A.C. 92; *Smith v. Leech Brain & Co.* [1962] 2 Q.B. 405; *Robinson v. Post Office* [1974] 2 All E.R. 737; *Brice v. Brown* [1984] 1 All E.R. 997.
[11] *Wagon Mound* [1961] A.C. 388. Subsequent precedents have explained that it is not necessary to establish the foreseeability of the mechanism by which the injury occurred, nor foreseeability of the specific accident or extent of injury, but that it suffices to show that it was broadly foreseeable that injury and harm would result: *Draper v. Hodder* [1972] 2 Q.B. 556; *Stewart v. West African Terminals Ltd* [1964] 2 Lloyd's Rep. 371.
[12] *Page v. Smith* [1995] 2 W.L.R. 644.

had to be taken to have foreseen that physical and/or psychiatric injury could flow from his careless driving.

The Burden of Proof and *Res Ipsa Loquitur*

The scope of *res ipsa loquitur* doctrine, within and beyond the tort of medical negligence, is still anything but clear: as a legal proposition phrased in Latin, it "achieves the beauty of conciseness at the cost of leaving to be understood what it is that the res says."[13] At its simplest, the doctrine permits the court in exceptional cases to draw an inference of negligence at an early stage in the trial on the basis of circumstantial evidence of a highly suggestive nature. The presumption relieves the plaintiff, at least temporarily, of proving that the defendant's negligence caused his injuries. Where the causation issue is very difficult to prove or disprove, the presumption is likely to lead to a verdict in the plaintiff's favour. Because of this rather drastic interference with the normal distribution of the burden of proof throughout the trial, the courts have consistently restricted *res ipsa loquitur* to exceptional cases, deferring to the rule stated by Erle C.J. in *Scott v. London and St Katherine Docks Co.* where the event which causes injury to the plaintiff "is shown to be under the management of the defendant or his servants, and the accident is such as in the ordinary course of things does not happen if those who have the management use proper care, it affords reasonable evidence, in the absence of explanation by the defendant, that an accident arose from want of care."[14]

The courts usually require evidence of an extraordinary event. In the medical setting, past examples have included causing the patient's heart to stop for over thirty minutes following anaesthetic;[15] causing injury to a healthy part of the patient's body;[16] mistakenly extracting the wrong teeth;[17] causing the plaintiff to enter a deep coma during

---

[13] *Nominal Defendant v. Haslbauer* (1967) 117 C.L.R. 448 at 462, *per* Kitto J.
[14] *Scott v. London and St Katherine Docks Co.* (1865) 3 H. & C. 596 at 601. Applied in *Mahon v. Osborne* [1939] 2 K.B. 14, where a swab had been found in the plaintiff's body two months after an operation, ultimately leading to his death. A majority of the court was satisfied that the operation had been an event under the management and control of the defendant, that the plaintiff had limited means of knowledge, and that the event was out of the ordinary.
[15] *Saunders v. Leeds Western Health Authority* [1985] C.L.Y. 2320.
[16] *Arnold v. Bonnell* 55 N.B.R. 2d 385 (1984).
[17] *Gagnon v. Stornini* 4 O.R. 2d (1984).

the course of a regular operation to remove an appendix.[18] The requirement of an out-of-the-ordinary event or outcome is a sensible (if inevitably vague) one. As a rule of evidence, *res ipsa loquitur* is very much an exception to the well-entrenched rule that the party who takes the legal action, and who requests the court to take action on its behalf, must bear the legal burden of proving his claim from start to finish. Literally, *res ipsa loquitur* means "the acts speak for themselves", so it is natural that it be restricted, particularly in the medical sphere, to those few cases where it would be churlish in the circumstances not to demand an explanation from the defendant. In this, common sense and ordinary logic have been perceived to play an important role. Fleming put it that the "maxim contains nothing new; it is based on common sense, since it is a matter of ordinary observation and experience in life [that] sometimes a thing tells its own story."[19]

In cases of medical injury, the courts have often defended the use of *res ipsa loquitur* on the basis that the defendant possesses, and the plaintiff lacks, the means of knowledge necessary to explain the injuries.[20] In some cases, the doctrine has been deployed as a means of "loosening the defendant's tongue"—in one case to penetrate a "conspiracy of silence" amongst the defence and its medical experts when evaluating how the plaintiff came to suffer an external shoulder injury during an appendectomy.[21] As a rule of evidence which may give rise to exceptional implications throughout the course and conduct of the hearing, it is right that the courts should consider its applicability in the light of the respective ability of either side to explain or prove what caused the injuries.[22] Means of, or access to, the relevant knowledge has often influenced courts in the past when deciding whether to put the defendant to proof.[23]

---

[18] *Lindsay v. Mid-Western Health Board* [1993] I.L.R.M. 550.

[19] Fleming (1987) p. 291. Endorsed by the Irish Supreme Court in *Lindsay v. Mid-Western Health Board, ibid.* at 555.

[20] According to the Irish Supreme Court in *Lindsay v. Mid-Western Health Board, ibid.* at 554: "Disparity between the situation of the respective parties is crucial" to *res ipsa loquitur.*

[21] *Ybarra v. Spangard* 25 Cal. 2d 486 (1944), 154 P. 2d 687 (1944).

[22] In *Farrell v. Snell* (1990) 72 D.L.R. (4th) 289 at 300, the Supreme Court of Canada justified its application in the medical context on the basis that often the details of the medical accident are known only to the defendant doctor. See, however, *supra*, p. 197, n. 32.

[23] According to Stephen: "In considering the amount of evidence necessary to shift the burden of proof, the Court has regard to the opportunities of knowledge with respect to the fact to be proved, which may be possessed by the parties respectively"

However, the fact that the defendants are in a *better* position than the plaintiffs to explain how the injuries occurred has never, and should never, be sufficient to ground this inference of negligence. It is dangerous and unjust to presume in all hard cases of extraordinary medical injury that the defendant exclusively possesses the means of proof. It may well be that the cause of the plaintiff's injuries cannot satisfactorily be proved within the current limitations of medical science.[24] Indeed, it is due to the ongoing inexactitude of medical science—also, undoubtedly, out of an attempt to restrict malpractice litigation—that *res ipsa loquitur* was at one time thought inapplicable to cases of medical negligence.[25] Thus, the better view of *res ipsa loquitur* is that it gives rise to an inference of negligence in circumstances where the fact of the accident without more points strongly to the defendant's negligence, but that in considering whether or not it arises in the case, the court will have regard to the means of knowledge on either side, and whether or not the defendant exercised control of the event that gave rise to injury.

There is little agreement amongst courts or indeed jurists on how specifically the doctrine affects the burdens of proof throughout the trial of the action. It should be clear that once the maxim has been deemed to apply, the plaintiff has effectively discharged his early burden of making out a *prima facie* case sufficient to entitle his case to be decided by the court. It should also be clear that the maxim causes *a* burden of proof to shift to the defendant, who is asked to rebut the inference that the patient's injury was caused by a negligent want of care on his part. It is not always clear, however, what *type* of burden

---

(Stephen's *Digest, Evidence Act 1896*, as cited in *Cummings v. City of Vancouver* (1911) 1 W.W.R. 31 at 34). Peculiar knowledge has, in the past, caused the legal burden of proof to shift to the defence in criminal trials: *R. v. Turner* [1814–23] All E.R. Rep. 713; *Minister for Industry and Commerce v. Steele* [1952] I.R. 301. It has since fallen out of favour – criticised by the Court of Appeal in *R. v. Edwards* [1975] Q.B. 27— though may still be employed to cause evidential burdens to shift or to decide whether enough evidence has been raised to discharge either a legal or evidential burden of proof: Heydon (1991), p. 18.

[24] According to Kelleher J. in *Wilkison v. Vesey* 295 A. 2d 676 (1972) at 691, the *res ipsa loquitur* doctrine is rarely applied in the medical scenario because "medicine is recognized as an inexact science from the practice of which serious complications can arise that cannot, without proof of some negligent act, be charged to the physician."

[25] The Canadian courts refused to apply the doctrine of *res ipsa loquitur* against doctors for this reason until the 1953 case of *Holt v. Nesbitt* [1953] 1 D.L.R. 671, overruling *Clark v. Wansborough* [1940] O.W.N. 67. According to Denning M.R. in *Whitehouse v. Jordan* [1980] 1 All E.R. 650 at 658, CA, the doctrine does not apply to cases concerning medical treatment of a high-risk nature.

has been caused to pass to the defendant. One can identify this only in terms of understanding the consequences of the defendant's failure to rebut the inference. Two types of burden may be affected, either an evidential burden or the legal burden of proof. In civil cases, the legal burden lies on the party who asserts the founding propositions, and who requires the court to alter the status quo and to take action on his behalf. However, the incidence of the legal burden is not immutable, and may be altered by statute or by common law principle. We recognise that the legal burden has been affected where (1) a burden of disproof of the facts-in-issue (the defendant's negligence) has shifted to the defence, *and* (2) the consequence of the defendant's failure to rebut the inference and discharge the burden is that the court is obliged to rule in the plaintiff's favour.

In some English cases, the courts have treated *res ipsa loquitur* as a compelling presumption—one that obliges the court to find the defendant negligent where he has failed to exonerate himself by presenting the court with an explanation of the accident which is consistent with no negligence on his part.[26] This approach envisages *res ipsa loquitur* as a distinct rule of law which compels an inference in appropriate circumstances, causing the legal burden of proof to pass from plaintiff to defendant.[27] It reflects the view that in some cases it would be unfair and unjust to require the plaintiff to prove what he cannot, where the defendant possesses or has access to the relevant means of knowledge.[28] Technically speaking, it means that the plaintiff is entitled to a verdict, even where the defendant has not offered rebuttal evidence, and perhaps even where the court is left doubting the existence of negligence (though if the inference of negligence was judged exceptionally compelling in the first place, the court will usually not be left doubting it).[29]

On the whole, however, the common law appears to favour the view that, since *res ipsa loquitur* is a presumption which arises from circumstantial evidence, it is not sufficient to cause a legal burden of

---

[26] *Henderson v. Henry E. Jenkins & Sons* [1970] A.C. 282; *Colvilles Ltd v. Devine* [1969] 1 W.L.R. 475.
[27] Atiyah (1972), p. 337.
[28] *Byrne v. Boadle* (1863) 2 H. & C. 722.
[29] Atiyah (1972) at 337.

proof to shift to the defence.[30] According to this view, the maxim permits but does not compel the court to find in the plaintiff's favour where the defendant has failed to discharge the inference of negligence.[31] This *permissive* approach looks on *res ipsa loquitur* as an evidential practice and not a fixed rule of law, and seems to be rooted in a judicial unwillingness to pin liability on a defendant for something that he has not been proved to have caused, or for something which cannot now but may one day be properly explained.[32] The Privy Council seemed to favour the permissive approach in *Ng Chun Pui v. Lee Cheun Tat*, though its choice of words fell somewhat short of achieving this.[33] The appeal was fought dominantly on the applicability and effect of *res ipsa loquitur* in a case where the plaintiffs argued that evidence of a road accident between a bus and a coach was sufficient to justify an inference of negligence. According to Lord Griffiths, where the plaintiff is allowed to rely on the circumstances surrounding the accident to ground an inference of negligence, against which rebuttal evidence is then tendered, the court must evaluate the rebuttal evidence to see if it is reasonable that the inference of negligence still stands. However, if the defendant adduces no rebuttal evidence, "the plaintiff will have proved his case."[34] This may seem to suggest a compelling presumption, though it is clear that Lord Griffiths did not intend it. His words are better interpreted to reflect the reality that if a strong inference of negligence was judged to arise in the first place, and the defendant has made little attempt to rebut it, the plaintiff must be taken to have proved his case. In his closing remarks, Lord Griffiths observed that resort to the burden of proof "is a poor way to decide a case", and at

---

[30] *Nominal Defendant v. Haslbauer, supra*, n. 13 at 461–463; *Fitzpatrick v. Walter E. Cooper Property Ltd* (1935) 54 C.L.R. 200; *Piening v. Wanless* (1968) 117 C.L.R. 498; *Crits v. Sylvester* [1956] 1 D.L.R. (2d) 502; *Rietze v. Bruser (No. 2)* [1979] 1 W.W.R. 31, 50ff; *Schanilec Estate v. Harris* (1987) 39 C.C.L.T. 279; *White v. McCool* 395 So. 2d 774 (1981); *Lloyd v. West Midlands Gas Board* [1971] 2 All E.R. 1240; and *Barkway v. South Wales Transport Co Ltd* [1950] 1 All E.R. 392.

[31] *Crits v. Sylvester, ibid.; Sweeney v. Erving* 228 U.S. 233 (1913).

[32] In *Lindsay v. Mid-Western Health Board, supra*, n. 18 at 556, O'Flaherty J. of the Irish Supreme Court commented that: "It has often been said that medical science is not an exact one and it is safe to prophesy that medical science and its technology will advance past frontiers which are not within anyone's contemplation at this time and so matters at present not amenable to explanation will be capable of resolution."

[33] *Ng Chun Pui v. Lee Cheun Tat* [1988] R.T.R. 298.

[34] *ibid.* at 301.

the end of the day the court remains free to evaluate all the evidence and decide whether negligence is established.[35]

The courts have consistently emphasised in this way that at the end of the day, the court still retains a discretion to evaluate whether or not the inference has been successfully rebutted. How it does so is important. If the court decides that the inference has been rebutted by the defendant, the plaintiff is once more on proof, which may prove difficult if the plaintiff was forced to rely on the presumption in the first place. In theory, the defence is not required by way of rebuttal to prove *how* the plaintiff's injuries occurred, only that the defendant exercised reasonable care and skill and did not himself cause the injuries.[36] It is likely, however, that in some cases (depending on the facts), the defendant will be judged to have failed to disprove the inference of negligence if he does not explain how the injury could have been sustained without negligence on his part.[37] The courts have been far from uniform on this point—a fact which recently prompted the Canadian Supreme Court to propose the abolition of *res ipa loquitur*.[38] In *Moore v. R Fox & Sons*, the Court of Appeal reasoned that the defendants could not be taken to have rebutted the *res ipsa* inference by establishing that the explosion which killed the workman was inexplicable, or by establishing a range of possible causes of the explosion, but that they had to additionally show a cause which ruled out negligence on their part. By contrast, in *Brazier v. Ministry of Defence*, McNair J.'s view of the law was that a defendant did not have to rebut the inference by affirmatively establishing the absence of negligence, but that he would have to present an explanation of how the injury *could* have occurred without negligence.[39] This was discharged in the case by showing that proper

---

[35] *Ng Chun Pui v. Lee Cheun Tat, supra,* n. 33 at 301.

[36] *Lindsay v. Mid-Western Health Board, supra,* n. 18 at 556; *O'Shea v. Tilman Anhold* Irish Supreme Court, unreported, October 23, 1996. In *Nominal Defendant v. Haslbauer, supra,* n. 13, at 462, Kitto J. reasoned that the defendant is required at most to counter the inference by establishing that "no specific negligent act or omission on his part has been proved as a cause of the damage" and that "it is no longer logical to infer that some unidentified negligence on his part was such a cause."

[37] This view was evident in *Cassidy v. Ministry of Health* [1951] 2 K.B. 343 at 366, where Denning M.R. attached importance to the fact that the defence had "nowhere explained how [the injury] could happen without negligence. They have busied themselves in saying that this or that member of their staff was not negligent. But they have called not a single person to say that the injuries were consistent with due care on the part of all the members of their staff."

[38] *Fontaine v. Loewen Estate* (1997) 156 D.L.R. (4th) 181.

[39] *Brazier v. Ministry of Health* [1965] 1 Lloyds Rep. 26, CA.

surgical procedure had been followed, and that the surgical needle probably broke due to a latent defect in the shaft of the needle.

Non-Disclosure of Risks and Alternatives

For medical disclosure actions, the plaintiff must establish both *injury* causation (that an undisclosed risk materialised, causing him injury) and *decision* causation (that if the doctor had disclosed the necessary information, the plaintiff would have chosen to forego the recommended treatment). In the bulk of disclosure cases, injury causation does not raise special concerns. Negligence law generally requires proof of physical injury; it permits recovery for mental distress in some cases, nervous shock in still fewer cases, and pure economic loss for negligent advice in circumstances that do not include medical negligence. Thus the requirement that the plaintiff show that the risk in question actually materialised and caused him injury is not contentious, beyond the larger debate that has grown up around the doctrine of loss of chance.[40] The unfortunate fact that a risk materialised during the course of treatment, and that it caused the plaintiff's injuries, is often self-evident. Where it is not, it is usually in the defendant's interests to claim that the injuries were caused by one such risk and not instead by negligence in the course of treatment.

It may, however, be asked whether the undisclosed risk must be the risk that materialised. Where the law requires disclosure of risks A and B, yet only risk A was disclosed and only that risk materialises, may the plaintiff recover where he can satisfy the court that if both risks had together been disclosed he would not have undergone the treatment? The answer to this depends on whether, in assessing causation-in-fact, the court treats each risk separately or cumulatively. Since each operation carries with it a bundle of risks, from the general to the specific, it is submitted that the cumulative assessment accords more with clinical reality. Common sense would suggest that the statistical weighting of the risks is also likely to bear on this issue. Where before treatment a doctor discloses a 2 per cent risk of injury but not a 0.5 per cent risk, and either risk materialises, it will be more difficult to establish that the patient would not have undergone treatment had the 0.5 per cent risk been disclosed, given that he

---

[40] See *infra*, p. 224–226.

submitted to treatment having been warned of a higher, more pressing risk than that which in the event materialised. This is otherwise, of course, where the doctor fails to disclose a higher risk that actually materialises. The cumulative approach was adopted recently by Lord Caplan in *Moyes v. Lothian Health Board*, where the patient had been informed of the 0.02–0.03 per cent risk of stroke but not that that risk doubles where the patient suffers from hypersensitive reaction.[41] Ultimately, however, the court was not persuaded by the plaintiff's causation submissions, given that she had undergone the procedure in the belief (wrongly, as it turned out) that it carried a much higher risk of 5 per cent.

It may also be queried whether there is to be a set-off of risks, by which for example a 10 per cent risk of death inherent in the treatment is off-set by a 10 per cent risk of death if the treatment is foregone. The answer to this question is likely to depend on whether the governing test is informed consent or the professional standard. Informed consent doctrine emphasises the patient's right to decide what is to be done to his body. It reflects this in a rigorous approach to the standard of disclosure owed by doctors (though as we will see, this is severely undercut by the application of an objective test of decision causation). Nevertheless, it is more likely to take into account, in rejecting such a set-off, that the risks could have materialised at different times, that the patient might have obtained a second opinion, and that the plaintiff might for instance have wished to brave the risk of death in favour of the risk of paralysis.[42]

Proof of decision causation is altogether more complicated. The court is asked to determine one way or the other whether the plaintiff would have decided at the time to undergo the recommended treatment having been given information which it was the doctor's duty to disclose to him. Evidence that the plaintiff's treatment would be necessary at some point in the future is not generally a defence to liability, though where the plaintiff's circumstances were urgent, it is likely to affect the court's assessment of damages. Nor does such evidence automatically disprove causation, though proof that without the treatment the plaintiff's condition would have deteriorated rapidly will cast doubt on the plaintiff's testimony that he would not have undergone the treatment knowing

---

[41] *Moyes v. Lothian Health Board* (1990) 1 Med. L.R. 463.
[42] Sommerville (1981), p. 758.

its full risks.[43] For instance, in *Stamos v. Davies*, Krever J. of the Ontario High Court found that the defendant should have disclosed the risk inherent in a lung biopsy of puncturing the patient's spleen, but that since the plaintiff had turned down other forms of treatment and since he suffered from a life-threatening condition, no reasonable person in the patient's position would have rejected the therapy even if informed.[44]

A recent decision by the Australian High Court breaks boldly from this tradition. In *Chappel v. Hart*, the defence's pivotal argument on appeal was that the patient would inevitably have had to undergo the treatment which in the event had led to injury to her vocal cords and voice loss.[45] It further argued that the injury suffered was caused by a random occurrence, the materialisation of a risk to which she would inevitably have been exposed if not then, in the foreseeable future. In rejecting these propositions, Gaudron J. reasoned that the degree (as opposed to nature) of risk is not the same for every doctor who performs an operation, even where performed competently by each: in this respect, the plaintiff was entitled to assert that she would have deferred treatment until it could be performed by a more experienced doctor. Further, the damage upon which plaintiffs base their claims in medical disclosure actions is not exposure to risk but rather exposure to physical injury: to say that she would inevitably have been exposed to this risk of injury is not the same as to say that she would inevitably have suffered this harm.

Whether or not the informed patient would have undergone the treatment at the relevant time requires an answer to a hypothetical question, centring on a point in the past now impossible to revisit.[46] The answer is by this stage critical to the outcome of the action. Yet the courts have differed significantly between and within jurisdictions on the formulation and application of the appropriate principles. Chief amongst their problems is the extent to which the court should accept at face-value the subjective claims made in hindsight by the injured and aggrieved patient. United States decisions prior to

---

[43] See *Reibl v. Hughes* (1981) 114 D.L.R. (3d) 1 at 16, *per* Laskin C.J.C.; and *Smith v. Barking, Havering, and Brentwood Health Authority* (1994) 5 Med. L.R. 285.

[44] *Stamos v. Davies* 21 D.L.R. (4th) 507 (1985).

[45] *Chappel v. Hart* [1998] H.C.A. 55.

[46] In *Diack v. Bardsley* (1983) 25 C.C.L.T. 159 at 170, McEachern C.J. considered it appropriate to construct an imaginary dialogue between plaintiff and defendant in which they discussed the pros and cons of the treatment options. The learned judge concluded that the plaintiff was not "one of those patients who would refuse or decline to follow the specific advice he received although .. some patients do."

Canterbury v. Spence had adopted battery as the cause of action for non-disclosure, and in keeping with orthodox battery analysis, the plaintiff's subjective testimony tended to be accepted.[47] Many commentators presumed that a subjective test would equally apply once negligence was adopted as the appropriate cause of action. Anything less, it was felt, would negate informed consent's doctrinal pledge to safeguard a patient's right to self-determination, rendering the action worthless.[48] However, the *Canterbury* court opted for an objective assessment of whether or not the negligent non-disclosure caused the plaintiff to submit to treatment he would otherwise have foregone. Robinson J. reasoned that this was necessary to guard physicians from "the patient's hindsight and bitterness", and the court from having to accept a speculative answer to a hypothetical question, subjectively expressed by the patient-witness and shadowed by the occurrence of the undisclosed risk.[49] The rationale for this objective assessment was developed further by the Supreme Court of California in its influential decision in *Cobbs v. Grant*:

> "The patient-plaintiff may testify on this subject but the issue extends beyond his credibility. Since at the time of trial the uncommunicated hazard has materialized, it would be surprising if the patient-plaintiff did not claim that had he been informed of the dangers he would have declined treatment. Subjectively he may believe so, with the 20/20 vision of hindsight, but we doubt that justice will be served by placing the physician in jeopardy of the patient's bitterness and disillusionment".[50]

The objective test of causation has elicited stern criticism from proponents of informed consent doctrine, which, it is argued, pledges to protect the right of each patient to make his own health care decisions whether rationally or not.[51] Under an objective causation test, the plaintiff is compelled to prove that the reasonable patient duly informed would not have undergone the recommended treatment.

---

[47] See *Shetter v. Rochelle* 409 P. 2d 74 (1965).
[48] See: Waltz and Scheuneman (1970); and Plante (1968).
[49] *Canterbury v. Spence* 464 F. 2d 772 (1972) at 790. All states except Oklahoma and Oregon apply an objective test of causation: Shuck (1994), p. 919.
[50] *Cobbs v. Grant* 502 P. 2d 1 (1972) at 11–12.
[51] See: Giesen D (1988), pp. 298–299; Katz (1984), pp. 71–76; Seidelson (1976), pp. 320–326.

It is not all clear from the case-law whether informed consent is constructed to *enable* a patient to make a *rational* decision, or to *ensure* that he does so, or whether the aim instead is to provide the patient with information which he is free to *rationalise* and then to base a decision on, even though the decision seems *irrational*. Though the latter approach seems to have been intended,[52] there lies a grave contradiction at the heart of informed consent law as articulated by *Canterbury v. Spence*. Robinson J. acknowledged that "the objective of risk-disclosure is preservation of the patient's interest in intelligent self-choice on proposed treatment, a matter the patient is free to decide for any reason that appeals to him."[53] At the causation stage, however, this right yields to an objective test of reasonableness that reflects the fact that "at a post-injury trial", the question of what the patient would have done is "purely hypothetical".[54] Taken to its logical conclusion, the informed consent model will anomalously protect each patient's freedom to commit to one of numerous possible choices, only to the extent that it happens to coincide with a hypothetical decision by the *reasonable* patient to do likewise. A system of this kind inevitably discriminates between patients who have successfully asserted their rights in the clinical environment to be involved at the crucial decision-making stage (where they may *irrationally* decide to forego a particular treatment in favour of another) and those patients whose rights to decision-making have not been honoured and who then face the prospect of having to prove what they would have done by aligning themselves with static standards of reasonableness. The idiosyncratic patient, thus, is afforded no *post hoc* protection.[55]

Under this system, the plaintiff patient will find it difficult if not impossible to rebut the assumption that reasonable people do not refuse operations and procedures which have been recommended by their doctors. That is, under a purely objective assessment, the sheer fact of the doctor's medical recommendation sometimes determines cause-in-fact against the plaintiff. In this respect, informed consent

---

[52] See Chapter 4, *supra*, pp. 128–131.
[53] *Canterbury v. Spence, supra*, n. 49 at 790.
[54] *ibid.*
[55] This indeed has been judicially recognised in America. See *Scott v. Bradford* 606 P. 2d 554 (1979) at 559: "To the extent the plaintiff, given an adequate disclosure would have declined the proposed treatment and a reasonable person in similar circumstances would have consented a patient's right to self determination is irrevocably lost."

has suffered for the loss of its moorings in the battery analysis. In addition to respecting the patient's subjective testimony on matters of causation, the battery action offers some compensation for dignitary infractions of one's right to bodily integrity in the absence of direct physical injury.[56] By contrast, under the negligence model, the plaintiff must establish that the defendant's breach of duty has directly caused the physical harm of which the plaintiff complains.[57]

In response to these conceptual and practical difficulties, *Reibl v. Hughes* advocated a hybrid test of causation which instead assesses *the reasonable person in the patient's position*. This is essentially a "subjectified objective" test. That it was intended to be dominantly objective is clear from the court's qualification that "the patient's particular concerns must be reasonably based".[58] These, the court felt, might include financial considerations such as the impairment of one's ability to work, or the loss of work-related entitlements. Laskin C.J.C. attempted to assuage objections that might reasonably be levelled against this objectification, and insisted that it would not leave the question of causation in the hands only of doctors: "Merely because medical science establishes the reasonableness of a recommended operation does not mean that a reasonable person in the patient's position would necessarily agree to it, if proper disclosure had been made of the risks attendant upon it, balanced by those against it."[59]

Notwithstanding Chief Justice Laskin's cautions, causation has proved to be a substantial stumbling block for Canadian plaintiffs in the wake of *Reibl v. Hughes*, and ironically the impediment seems to

---

[56] *Stewart v. Stonehouse* (1926) 2 D.L.R. 683. In the U.S., the courts have tended to reason that emotional distress caused by an offensive battery may itself form the basis of a battery action as the infliction of personal injury: *Brown v. Stauffer Chemical Co.* (1975) 539 P. 2d 374; *Kissinger v. Mannor* (1979) 285 N.W. 2d 214.

[57] See *Stamos v. Davies, supra*, n. 44, where Krever J. of the Ontario High Court found that the defendant breached a duty to disclose the fact that the patient's spleen had been punctured, but the plaintiff had failed to establish a causal connection between this breach and the damage to and eventual removal of his spleen. He also rejected a plea of fraudulent concealment on the basis that no additional damage had been sustained. This reluctance to recognise dignitary infractions has given rise to much criticism. See Goldstein (1975), where it is argued that the omission of a material medical fact constitutes a dignitary harm to the patient to the extent that his power to choose is thereby weakened.

[58] *Reibl v. Hughes, supra*, n. 43 at 17.

[59] *ibid.* at 16.

be the sheer fact that the treatment was medically recommended.[60] According to Professor Osborne, amongst the post-*Reibl* cases, "the degree to which personalized factors are incorporated into the reasonable person test is extremely variable. Moreover this variable application can be productive of unfairness because the selection of personal factors is largely arbitrary."[61] Some courts have devoted the causation analysis entirely to objective criteria, chiefly the pros and cons of the treatment, and the extent to which in medical terms the treatment was necessary or simply prudent.[62] Other courts have consciously considered a number of personal factors by way of modification of its objective assessment. In two cases, this notably worked to the plaintiff's disadvantage. In *Zimmer v. Ringrose*, the Alberta Court of Appeal was influenced by evidence that the plaintiff had been anxious to avoid hospitalisation so that she could take care of her new born baby at home; the procedure recommended by the doctor was the only one which would have enabled her to accomplish this.[63] Similarly, in *Mang v. Moscovitz*, the court decided that the following subjective factors disproved the plaintiff's claims at the causation stage: she had been stubbornly determined to have an abortion as soon as possible; in doing so, she had ignored a threat of divorce by her husband, and had gone against the advice of her doctor; further, she had wished to return to work as soon as possible, and was determined to complete the abortion by the time her brother returned from Hong Kong.[64]

It might tentatively be said that there exists a third possible model in the "pure subjective" assessment, though the purity of this standard and its workability within the adversarial system may seriously be questioned. It found favour in *Ellis v. Wallsend District Hospital*, a decision by the New South Wales Court of Appeal.[65] The

---

[60] See Osborne, "Causation and the Emerging Canadian Doctrine of Informed Consent to Medical Treatment" 33 C.C.L.T. 131; Robertson (1991); and Dugdale 1984.

[61] Osborne, *ibid.*, p. 139.

[62] In *Haughian v. Paine* (1987) 37 D.L.R. (4d) 624 at 645, Sherstobitoff J. A. of the Saskatchewan Court of Appeal ruled in favour of the plaintiff on causation even though the plaintiff had led testimony on the issue, since the causation test "is largely an objective one, that of whether or not a reasonable person, in the circumstances of this case, would have proceeded with the operation in the face of full disclosure". See also: *Bickford v. Stiles* (1981) 128 D.L.R. (3d) 516; and *Videto v. Kennedy* (1984) 31 C.C.L.T. 66.

[63] *Zimmer v. Ringrose* (1981) 124 D.L.R. (3d) 215.

[64] *Mang v. Moscovitz* (1982) 37 A.R. 221.

[65] *Ellis v. Wallsend District Hospital* 2 Med. L.R. 103 (1990).

court expressed a reluctance to put a premium on what might have been deemed *medically* prudent in the patient's circumstances, which it felt any objective test must inevitably entail. Samuels JA asserted that he would "more readily accept the threat of hindsight than adopt medical practice as the determinant".[66] He further explained that the court will be influenced by not only what the plaintiff testifies to, but also her demeanour and credibility in court, and "her capacity, assuming that she was endeavouring to be honest, to restore herself in recollection to the situation in which she stood when the critical decision had to be made."[67] The court went further, and suggested that if the plaintiff's testimony is not challenged on cross-examination, the court may be obliged to accept it as true unless it is "inherently incredible" or "inherently improbable".[68]

The English courts ostensibly apply a subjective test; though after the full weight of the professional standard approach to due disclosure has been brought to bear on the claim, the analysis only occasionally reaches this point. It did so at first instance (though not on appeal) in *Gold v. Haringey Health Authority*, where Schiemann J. accepted the plaintiff's testimony that if she had known the respective failure rates for female sterilisations and male vasectomies, she would have foregone treatment in favour of vasectomy of her husband, and would not have conceived a child.[69] In this, the plaintiff's claim was not prejudiced by the birth of another unwanted child—evidence which suggested the absence of a causal link between the negligent non-disclosure and the birth of her penultimate child—after the plaintiff satisfied the court that her husband had not since been vasectomised for financial reasons.

Other English cases, however, point more realistically to some need for objectification of the plaintiff's testimonial assertions. In *Chatterton v. Gerson*, Bristow J. claimed to adopt a subjective test, saying that the appropriate question to ask was whether the *particular* patient would have undergone the treatment.[70] Ultimately, however, the learned judge objectified the plaintiff's assertion that if informed, she would not have consented, concluding that the "whole picture on the evidence was of a lady desperate for pain relief."[71]

---

[66] *Ellis v. Wallsend District Hospital, supra*, n. 65 at 119.

[67] *ibid.* at 122.

[68] *ibid.* at 121–122.

[69] *Gold v. Haringey Health Authority* (1989) 5 P.M.I.L.L. No. 4.

[70] *Chatterton v. Gerson* [1981] 1 All E.R. 257.

[71] *ibid.* at 267.

In *Smith v. Barking, Havering and Brentwood Health Authority*, Hutchinson J. was invited to select between the *Reibl* test (which was described as objective) and the subjective test as traditionally applied in England. In an honest and telling analysis, Hutchinson J. noted the "peculiar difficulty . . . in this sort of case—not least for the plaintiff herself—in giving, after the adverse outcome is known, reliable answers as to what she would have decided before the operation had she been given proper advice as to the risks inherent in it."[72] For this reason the judge ruled that an objective assessment must be given weight:

> "If everything points to the fact that a reasonable plaintiff, properly informed, would have assented to the operation, the assertion from the witness box, made after the adverse outcome is known, in a wholly artificial situation and in the knowledge that the outcome of the case depends on the assertion being maintained, does not carry great weight unless there are extraneous or additional factors to substantiate it. . . . [such as] religious or other firmly held convictions; particular social or domestic considerations . . ."[73]

On the facts of the case, the judge gave weight both to objective and subjective criteria in deciding that the plaintiff, even if fully informed of the risk of paralysis, would still have undergone the treatment: chief amongst these were the remoteness of the risk, the urgency of the treatment, the speed at which the patient's condition was deteriorating, and the fact that the patient had been "temperamentally disposed to follow the advice of her doctors" with whom she had already had a long association.[74]

An interesting scenario arose in *McAllister v. Lewisham and North Southwark Health Authority*, where it was the plaintiff who candidly attempted to objectify the answer to the question of what she would have done if informed of the undisclosed risk.[75] She testified that as the job had been very important to her, she would definitely have waited until its probationary period was over, but that beyond that time it was impossible for her to tell what she would have done,

---

[72] *Smith v. Barking, Havering, and Brentwood Health Authority, supra*, n. 43 at 289.
[73] *ibid.*
[74] *ibid.* at 290.
[75] *McAllister v. Lewisham & North Southwark Health Authority* (1994) 5 Med. L.R. 343.

especially in the light of what had recently transpired. Notwithstanding, Rougier J. felt that the "fact that the plaintiff herself, fully conscious of the distortion to her thinking likely to be caused by hindsight, is reluctant to hypothesize, should not of itself preclude a judge from the attempt, provided there exists sufficient material upon which he can properly act."[76] After having had "even fourth thoughts", he decided that she "would have continued to decline the operation", given that: (1) she was a "sensible and independent-minded woman . . . who could be expected to make a rational judgment"; (2) her condition was not advancing rapidly; (3) the chance, even if slight, of the deficit (her condition) arresting itself remained; (4) her job and independence were precious to her; and (5) it was one of the most important decisions of her life, and she would have sought a second opinion which may reasonably have made her more aware of the dangers inherent in the operation.[77]

What, then, is the best way forward? Let us revisit first the objective standard, and the problems which it presents. In its purest form, it is difficult to see how an objective test can function properly as a device to prove cause-in-fact. Establishing that the objectively reasonable patient would not have declined the treatment does not prove that the plaintiff similarly would not have declined.[78] According to Robertson, the only way in which such a model can work as a test of causation is where it rests on an irrebuttable presumption that the plaintiff would have acted in the same manner as the reasonable person, thus rendering much of the evidence of the plaintiff's character and past actions irrelevant—a logic the courts would be reluctant to develop.[79] According to Giesen, to "make the me-thinketh of third parties the judicial yardstick by which to measure the individual patient's informational needs is blunt paternalism which is no more excusable when exercised by the courts than by the medical profession."[80]

It has been argued that the law should strive to accommodate the patient's right to self-determination, rather than expect the patient to fit the law, and that the hypothetical reasonable man is far more problematic than the testimony of a patient with hindsight.[81] An

---

[76] *McAllister v. Lewisham & North Southwark Health Authority, supra*, n. 75 at 353.
[77] *ibid.*
[78] Robertson (1984), p. 79.
[79] *ibid.*
[80] Giesen (1988), p. 299.
[81] See: Gochnauer and Fleming (1981); and *McPherson v. Ellis* 287 S.E. 2d 892 (1982) at 897.

objective assessment, no less than a subjective one, requires a speculative answer to a hypothetical question. The ironic result is that the doctor is presumed to be better able to predict how a fictitious reasonable patient would act on the basis of certain information, than how the immediate patient (who is in a professional relationship with the doctor) would act.[82] The defendant's claims in this respect are, let us remember, formulated and articulated in the context of an adversarial dispute.

An ostensibly pure subjective assessment presents equally pressing concerns. Severe injury alters the most robust of minds; an uncritical submission to views expressed subjectively and retrospectively by the plaintiff on his past hypothetical behaviour is no less artificial, and certainly more dangerous, than the attempt to objectify a hypothetical behaviour. It is natural that courts should want to consider the severity of the plaintiff's original illness, the options medically open to that plaintiff, and the pressure under which the plaintiff acted in the circumstances.

Hybrid tests have been explicitly favoured in Canada and England. Clearly, these are designed to mitigate the inherent unworkability of a purely subjective test and the undesirability of a purely objective test. These widely straddle a middle-ground which recognises the weight both subjective and objective factors naturally carry in this type of action. The courts should never consciously adopt a model of law that demeans the status or weight of the plaintiff's evidence on this issue, by rendering it inadmissible or by type unreliable. Nor should a court deny itself the right to critically evaluate the plaintiff's subjective answer to the hypothetical question. It ought to consider the plaintiff's original illness and prognosis, the treatment that was recommended, and the consequences for the patient if he chose not to undergo treatment at the relevant time. It ought not, however, be bound (as it may be under a purely objective test) by evidence that a majority of patients in similar circumstances would have undergone the treatment.

The hybrid test requires the court to consider whether *both* the plaintiff patient and the hypothetical reasonable patient would have undergone the treatment.[83] However, it seems likely that, whether in name or not, the courts will in most cases consider an assortment of subjective and objective factors before reaching its decision; indeed,

---

[82] Seidelson (1976), p. 326.
[83] *ibid.*, p. 332.

they may not have to consciously apply one test over another. It is not particularly surprising that many United States cases after *Canterbury* applied an objective test in name only. In *Holt v. Nelson* for instance, Callow J. decided that, independent of proof that the reasonable patient would have declined treatment, a "physician need not have informed the patient of the risk of the procedure if the doctor can establish the defense that *the [instant] patient* would have proceeded whether he had been informed of the risks or not."[84] Nor is it any more likely that a subjective test could ever realistically avoid considering some objective criteria to temper the plaintiff's claims. Many of the problems anticipated by the courts could be softened by a recognition, or in jury trials careful directions, that certain parts of the plaintiff's evidence may be prejudiced by hindsight, but that the plaintiff's testimony "should be allowed as a part of the totality of evidence even though self-serving".[85] Another way to mitigate the severity of an inevitable objectification of the plaintiff's testimony may be to insist that the plaintiff's testimony be heard after the defendant's, so that it becomes "possible to ensure that the questions to which [the plaintiff] addressed herself were, in fact, the relevant ones."[86]

The disclosure action clearly suffers from a significant epistemological and evidential gap, caused by the impossibility of knowing factually what the patient would have decided under different conditions at a point in time lost forever to the past. This is not a new phenomenon, and the common law is far from unaccustomed to deciding one way or the other how plaintiffs, defendants, and third parties would probably have acted in hypothetical settings.[87] In cases of this nature, usually omissions to act, the court must consider a range of evidence, and permit the scales of justice to fall on the side of the more credible version.

A loss of chance assessment of causation—which I consider further on—would give the court greater flexibility in attaching broad percentile degrees of belief to the versions pushed by plaintiff and defendant. It would also enable the court to award damages to a

---

[84] *Holt v. Nelson* 523 P. 2d 211 (1974) at 219 (emphasis added).

[85] *ibid.* at 216, *per* Callow J.

[86] As proposed by Hutchison J. in *Smith v. Barking, Havering, and Brentwood Health Authority, supra,* n. 43 at 290.

[87] *Chaplin v. Hicks* [1911] 2 K.B. 786; *Kitchen v. Royal Air Force Association* [1958] 1 W.L.R. 563, [1958] 2 All E.R. 241; *Allied Maples v. Simmons & Simmons* [1995] 1 W.L.R. 1602.

plaintiff notwithstanding that he has not proved cause-in-fact on the balance of probabilities. The level of proof that the plaintiff has been judged to attain (say, 40 per cent) would under a loss of chance analysis be reflected in the damages the plaintiff is due, by contrast with the orthodox torts rule that the plaintiff is entitled to full damages for his injuries from the defendant once he has established that it is more likely than not that the defendant caused them. Loss of chance has found favour in some United States states, but was recently rejected by the House of Lords.[88]

Alternative methods of compensating plaintiffs for non-disclosure exist within the orthodox model of fault liability. It is interesting to observe an emerging practice at first instance in England to award damages for mental distress precipitated by non-disclosure, where the plaintiff has failed to make out a full case for negligent liability.[89] In *Goorkani v. Tayside Health Board*, the plaintiff was easily able to establish that the defendants were negligent in failing to warn him of the risk of infertility caused by long-term use of an immuno-suppressant, since the consultant physician admitted that he ordinarily disclosed this risk.[90] Although the court accepted that disclosure would have prompted the plaintiff to pre-emptively bank his sperm, it could not accept that he would have foregone use of the drug, given that it had been prescribed to prevent a condition that might lead to permanent loss of his sight. Lord Cameron, however, awarded £2,500 for "the loss of self-esteem, the shock and anger at the discovery of his infertility together with the frustration and disruption which ignorance and the sudden shock of discovery brought to the marital relationship".[91] Similarly, in *Smith v. Barking, Havering and Brentwood Health Authority*, £3,000 in general damages were awarded for shock and depression caused by the negligent non-disclosure of the substantial risk of tetraplegia, in circumstances where the court felt it could not hold that the plaintiff would have foregone this operation to potentially halt an ever deteriorating condition.[92] These awards were made to compensate psychological and emotional trauma suffered as a direct result of not being informed in time to cope with the risk if and when it materialised; because it was coupled with physical injury (through crystallisation of

---

[88] See *infra*, pp. 224, 226–230.
[89] See *infra*, p. 226.
[90] *Goorkani v. Tayside Health Board* (1991) 3 Med. L.R. 33.
[91] *ibid*. at 39.
[92] *Smith v. Barking, Havering, and Brentwood Health Authority*, supra, n. 43.

the risk), there was no question of limiting the trauma to the narrow range of nervous shock recognised by the common law for the purpose of founding an independent cause of action.[93] Though the precise legal basis for these awards may be queried (damages recovered despite the plaintiff's failure to fully prove negligence), the motives behind them are commendable and perhaps reflect the sense that damages for negligent non-disclosure should be more proportionate to the wrong.

The Standard of Proof

Proof in the trial of a civil action is generally established *on the balance of probabilities* as being something more probable or more likely than not. This preponderance or 51 per cent standard applies at each stage of proof of negligence liability. It is reflected in the "but for" test of causation, which requires the plaintiff to prove that but for the defendant's negligence the damage would not have occurred (in other words, that the defendant's negligence was a necessary condition of the plaintiff's loss). In cases that do not present any special evidential difficulties, this test was and remains useful. For instance, in *Barnett v. Chelsea & Kensington Hospital Management Committee*, the court could conclude that, though a casualty officer had negligently failed to examine the deceased after he had presented himself at casualty complaining of stomach cramps and vomiting, the plaintiff had failed to prove that but for this negligence the patient would not have died, since at the relevant time the poison had advanced its way through the patient's body and nothing could have halted it.[94]

However, the "but for" model is mischievously limited in its focus. It can tell us whether a factor is a cause, but not that it is *not* a cause; in other words, as a rule it is helpful when it is least needed.[95] In the medical context, the "but for" test is even less productive since it presumes a neutral background free of competing risks. In difficult cases of multiple medical causation, where causes act sequentially and often inexplicably, it is an arrant guide, cutting off a lot of meritorious claims notwithstanding that breach of duty has already been

---

[93] Jones (1994).
[94] *Barnett v. Chelsea & Kensington Hospital Management Committee* [1969] 1 Q.B. 428.
[95] Weinrib (1975).

established.[96] Further, it tends to overcompensate the few plaintiffs who manage to establish fault by the preponderance rule. Under negligence law, once causation is established, the defendant is liable for all ensuing damage so long as the damage was reasonably foreseeable.[97] The plaintiff is compensated in full. Even where the probability of a causative link is much less than 100 per cent and closer to 50 per cent, the law under this model presumes that the link is factually established.[98] The effects of the test can be callous for plaintiffs. In *Stacey v. Chiddy*, for instance, the plaintiff established that the defendant had been negligent in failing to detect malignant cancer growths before they developed fourteen months later, but could not establish to the court's satisfaction that that failure caused the development of the cancer.[99]

The all-or-nothing approach to causation has understandably attracted pronounced criticism from legal scholars. According to one view, it "subverts the deterrence objectives of tort law by denying recovery for the effects of conduct that causes statistically demonstrable losses. . . . A failure to allocate the cost of these losses to their tortious sources undermines the whole range of functions served by the causation-valuation process and strikes at the integrity of the torts system of loss allocation."[1] The crudity and unfairness of the all-or-nothing or "but for" models has placed considerable pressure on judges to reformulate the standard of proof and bend other rules of evidence such as *res ipsa loquitur* by way of mitigation.

Developments in English law have been at the forefront of this debate, receiving much publicity in other jurisdictions. The first significant judicial attempt to alleviate proof of causation for plaintiffs emerged with a rule that where the plaintiff has established that the defendant breached a statutory duty owed to him, and the plaintiff "is injured in a way which could result from the breach, the onus of proof shifts on to the employer to show that the breach was not the

---

[96] *e.g. Cooper v. Sisters of Charity* 27 Ohio St. 304 (1938), 13 N.E. 2d 242 (1938). The plaintiff boy had suffered a fractured skull in a road accident. Surgery which might have saved his life was not performed. Despite a positive finding that this constituted a negligent breach of duty, recovery was denied on the basis that the plaintiff had failed to establish on the balance of probabilities that the failure to perform the operation (and not the original accident) was *the* cause of his death.

[97] *The Wagon Mound, supra*, n. 11.

[98] *Falcon v. Memorial Hospital* (1990) 462 N.W. 2d 44 at 47, *per* Levine J.

[99] *Stacey v. Chiddy* (1993) 4 Med. L.R. 345.

[1] King (1981), p. 1377. This view is shared by many English torts scholars, including: Stapleton (1988), Price (1989), and Foster (1995).

cause."[2] The rule survived for 10 years, until it was rejected in *Bonnington Castings v. Wardlaw*, where the House of Lords insisted that for breach of common law duty and equally for breach of statutory duty, the onus remains on the plaintiff to prove causation.[3] However, the House further reasoned that when proving causation, the plaintiff need only establish that the fault complained of caused or *materially contributed* to the injury, unless provided otherwise by statute. Materiality, according to Lord Reid, is a question of degree: "A contribution which comes within the exception de minimus non curat lex is not material, but I think that any contribution which does not fall within that exception must be material. I do not see how there can be something too large to come within the de minimus principle, but yet too small to be material."[4]

Bonnington presented a difficult case of multiple causation, with an evidential gap that was impossible to fully bridge. The plaintiff had contracted pneumoconiosis through inhaling silica dust in the air where he worked. The main source of the dust came from pneumatic hammers (at a time when there was no known means of neutralising or avoiding the dust); some of the dust, however, was due to the defendant employer's failure to keep his dust-extraction ducts free from obstruction contrary to statute. It was impossible to tell to what extent the latter caused or contributed to the injuries. On the other hand, the disease could be said to have been caused "by the whole of the noxious material inhaled and, if that material [came] from two sources, it [could not] be wholly attributed to material from one source or the other."[5] The House firmly rejected the trial judge's verdict that the court must establish which was the *more probable* source of the disease. The court should instead ask "whether the dust from the swing grinders *materially contributed* to the disease."[6]

Bonnington was the first in a series of decisions that bravely attempted to modernise our causation laws. The second was *McGhee v. National Coal Board*, where the House of Lords held that when the plaintiff cannot prove that *but for* the defendant's breach of duty the plaintiff would not have sustained his injury, but when he can establish that the defendant's breach *materially increased the risk* of injury (in other words, that it reduced the chance of the plaintiff

---

[2] *Vyner v. Waldenberg Bros* [1946] 1 K.B. 50 at 55, *per* Scott L.J.

[3] *Bonnington Castings v. Wardlaw* [1956] 1 All E.R. 615.

[4] *ibid.* at 618–619.

[5] *ibid.* at 618.

[6] *ibid.* (emphasis added).

avoiding the injury), the burden of proving causation is initially discharged and the inference passes to the defendant to refute.[7] It has been said that this went far beyond the usual principles justifying *early* reversal of proof, which on grounds of policy had lent "against allowing defendants to exploit the very fact of their multiplicity [or] compelling the plaintiff to satisfy an onus that the defendant has made impossible".[8] For in *McGhee*, the defendant was not responsible for the impossibility of ascertaining to what extent his failure to provide washing facilities had caused the plaintiff's dermatitis. Though the decision has since courted considerable controversy, it is difficult not to see it as another way of saying what the Court of Appeal had said in *Bonnington*, that the plaintiff need only prove that the defendant materially contributed to his injury. Its controversial nature perhaps lay in Lord Wilberforce's choice of terminology, his reformulation in terms of risk creation, which brought the causation analysis close to a loss of chance one. According to Lord Wilberforce, the plaintiff faced an "inherent evidentiary difficulty" of proof; on the other hand, the defendant was "the creator of the risk who ex hypothesi, must be taken to have foreseen the possibility of damage, [and] who must bear its consequences".[9] The significance of this step was heightened by Lord Reid's earlier observations in *Bonnington*, that a contribution is material when it is not minimal. In the light of this, *McGhee* was seen as authority for the principle that the magnitude of risk created by a defendant is no longer relevant once breach of duty and injury are together established, but that once the plaintiff establishes that the risk of his suffering injury was greater after the defendant's negligent act, the burden of proof of causation has been discharged and the defendant must disprove causation.[10]

The emerging if undelineated principle in *McGhee* was applied to the medical context in *Clark v. MacLennon*.[11] The patient had suffered from stress incontinence shortly after the birth of her child. When conservative treatments failed, her consultant recommended surgery which carried a normal success rate of 33.33 per cent. It was general practice that gynaecologists did not perform the operation until at least three months after birth to ensure against haemorrhage. This precaution was not followed, and haemorrhage occurred which two

---

[7] *McGhee v. National Coal Board* [1973] 1 W.L.R. 1.
[8] Weinrib (1975), p. 527.
[9] *McGhee v. National Coal Board, supra,* n. 7.
[10] Robertson (1984); Weinrib (1975).
[11] *Clark v. MacLennon* [1983] 1 All E.R. 416, QBD.

subsequent operations failed to reverse or mitigate. Approving Lord Wilberforce in *McGhee*, Peter Pain J. ruled that "where there is a situation in which a general duty of care arises and there is a failure to take a precaution, and that very damage occurs against which the precaution is designed to be a protection, then the burden lies on the defendant to show that he was not in breach of duty as well as to show that the damage did not result from his breach of duty."[12] He further endorsed the view of Lords Simon and Kilbrandon that it is artificial in cases of this type to distinguish between breach of duty and causation, where the taking of a particular precaution demanded by law made it more likely that injury would occur.

The *McGhee* principle is of enormous benefit to plaintiffs, and will continue to be so. It survived a bruising in the case of *Hotson v. East Berkshire Health Authority*, where it became entangled in an attempt by the Court of Appeal to incorporate elements of the loss of chance analysis into conventional causation laws.[13] In *Wilsher v. Essex Area Health Authority*, the House of Lords sought to clip its wings by emphasising that, as a general rule, where there are multiple possible causes of an injury, of which the defendant's negligence is but one, the combination of breach of duty and injury does not give rise to a presumption of causation in the plaintiff's favour. Lord Bridge interpreted *McGhee* as resting on a "common sense" inference from evidence of cumulative causes that the defendant's fault not merely increased the risk of injury but contributed an effect which formed an inextricable part of the total effect.[14] Once this inference could be drawn, the plaintiff had satisfied the orthodox test that on the balance of probabilities the defendant caused a portion of the injuries. According to Sopinka J. in *Farrell v. Snell*, courts have vacillated between following Lord Wilberforce's early reversal of onus in *McGhee* or the subsequent inference interpretation of *McGhee* by the House of Lords in *Wilsher*.[15] The learned judge expressed the view that it makes no practical difference which line is chosen: the plaintiff must be taken to have established a *prima facie* case or inference of causation once he has shown a breach of duty, the creation of a risk, and the occurrence of injury within the area of that risk.

---

[12] *Clark v. MacLennon, supra,* n. 11 at 427.
[13] *Hotson v. East Berkshire Area Health Authority* [1987] 1 All E.R. 210, CA; [1987] 1 A.C. 750, HL. See *infra*, p. 224.
[14] *Wilsher v. Essex Area Health Authority* [1988] 1 All E.R. 871, HL.
[15] *Farrell v. Snell, supra,* n. 22 at 299.

In *McGhee* the defendant enhanced a pre-existing risk, and exposure to the risks was cumulative; whereas in *Wilsher* the defendant increased the number of risks, and exposure to the risks was consecutive.[16] The Court of Appeal in *Wilsher* seemed to attach importance to the distinction between enhancing an existing risk and adding to other risks. Yet if in both cases the defendant increased the risk of injury to the plaintiff, why did the court infer causation in one and not the other? This may be because in *McGhee* the two possible causes acted in combination to cause the injury, whereas the court could not know in *Wilsher* that the defendant's breach of duty had any effect on injury. According to one view, the *Wilsher* case was very similar to *McGhee*, the chief difference being the number of potential causes: where in *McGhee* there were two, in *Wilsher* there were five possible causes one of which might have been the defendant's negligence. It may well be that the greater the number of competing causes, the more reluctant the court will be to infer that the defendant's breach was causative of injury.[17] It is Fleming's contention that the *Wilsher* decision may best be justified on the basis that the plaintiff's injuries were possibly caused by innocent means without fault by any of those involved in the event. By contrast, in *Fitzgerald v. Lane*—decided before their Lordships' rulings in *Wilsher*—it was impossible to tell which of two cars (or to what extent each) caused the plaintiff's injuries during a road accident.[18] The Court of Appeal invoked *McGhee*, and held both drivers liable. This, then, was a case where the plaintiff potentially fell between two guilty tortfeasors, and would have failed to obtain any compensation for his losses if the court had not invoked a mitigating rule.[19]

Wilsher asserts that both policy and principle demand that the plaintiff suffer the consequences of the evidentiary gap and continue to shoulder the full burden of proof. This conservative treatment of causation undoubtedly reflects an unspoken reluctance to keep the floodgates closed to medical malpractice actions.[20] Yet since *McGhee* was approved of in *Wilsher*, a material increase of risk can in certain circumstances establish causation. Lord Bridge did not limit that case to instances where the defendant fails in breach of duty to take specific precautions to avoid a risk, or to cases where medical knowledge

---

[16] Khan and Roberts (1997), p. 176.
[17] Stauch (1997), p. 215.
[18] *Fitzgerald v. Lane* [1989] A.C. 328.
[19] Fleming (1989), pp. 671–672.
[20] Boon (1988), p. 513.

cannot precisely explain the causes of a particular medical injury. The Court of Appeal recently reaffirmed the *McGhee/Bonnington* development. In *Page v. Smith*, the plaintiff had been suffering from ME (chronic fatigue syndrome) at the time the defendant's car crashed into him.[21] The crash caused his condition to become chronic and permanent. The trial judge had phrased the test as whether or not the accident, on the balance of probabilities, caused or materially contributed or materially increased the risk of his condition (where "material" did not include the "minimal" or "trivial" or "insignificant"). The Court of Appeal affirmed this approach, at least for cases of multiple causation with troublesome evidential gaps, "in which other causes *could have played a part* in the causation of the plaintiff's exacerbated symptoms".[22] Referring to *McGhee* as "difficult', Bingham M.R. showed great reluctance to be drawn into a loss of chance discourse (as the Court of Appeal had done before in *Hotson*): "In the present case, the question is not whether the plaintiff was exposed to an increased risk of exacerbation of his existing symptoms, but whether the accident did in fact have that result. It was not, in my view, a case concerned with risk at all."[23]

The onus on the plaintiff to prove breach of duty and causation may come to be reversed at an earlier stage in the trial, according to how the court formulates the standard of proof that he must meet. In practical terms, an early reversal of onus to the defendant achieves much the same effect as *res ipsa loquitur*, and it would seem that both devices are equally grounded in a sense that in some cases it is unfair that the plaintiff bear the full burden of explaining how he came to be injured. This was evident in *Cook v. Lewis*, where the gun shot that caused the plaintiff to lose an eye could have come from either of two hunters who had fired simultaneously in the direction of the plaintiff.[24] The court decided that where a single injury has been caused by one of two negligent defendants, the onus shifts (after proof of their negligence) to each defendant to show on the balance of probabilities that he was not the injurer. The decision would seem to be grounded in a sense of fairness to an innocent third party vis-a-vis two negligent defendants.[25]

---

[21] *Page v. Smith No. 2* [1996] 1 W.L.R. 855, CA. See also *Fitzgerald v. Lane, supra*, n. 18.
[22] *ibid*. at 858 (emphasis added).
[23] *ibid*. at 858.
[24] *Cook v. Lewis* [1951] S.C.R. 830, [1952] 1 D.L.R. 1. See also: *Summers v. Tice* 33 Cal. 2d 80 (1948), 119 P 2d 1 (1948); and *Fitzgerald v. Lane, supra*, n. 18.
[25] Fleming (1989), p. 665.

For much the same reason, but with wholly different effect, the doctrine of loss of chance has been canvassed as an alternative. It amounts to a reformulation of the *interest* whose infringement may be sued upon, enabling a plaintiff to obtain damages when he proves that the defendant has caused or increased the chance of a certain outcome, or decreased the chance of avoiding the outcome (whether or not the defendant's contribution to the outcome was less than 50 per cent). It operates a form of *discounted liability*, whereby the defendant is required to pay compensation only to the degree to which he has been found to have caused or contributed to the injury.

Loss of Chance Doctrine

The doctrine of *loss of chance*, or "la perte d'une chance", is of French civil law extraction.[26] In recent years, its possible incorporation into the common law has begun to be seriously debated by courts and legal scholars. The doctrine permits a plaintiff to sue for the loss of a chance of avoiding a result rather than merely for the result itself; the loss of chance is the injury which grounds the plaintiff's cause of action. This has the advantage of enabling a court to award damages where the plaintiff can establish a less than 50 per cent contribution by the defendant to his injuries. It also gives the court a wider measure of flexibility in cases where it is difficult to commit to a categorical decision on subjective, objective, and mixed assessments of how the plaintiff would have acted at a hypothetical point in the past. It also honours the principle that where a defendant has caused the disappearance of the means of proof (by denying a plaintiff the opportunity to have acted in a certain way), it is unfair that the plaintiff should bear the full brunt of the evidential gap by being required to prove a certain hypothetical proposition as something more probable than not.[27]

Loss of chance theory diverges from a well-entrenched common law rule that once the plaintiff proves on the balance of probabilities

---

[26] See generally: Boon (1988); Reece (1996); Robertson (1984); Stapleton (1988); and Weinrib (1975).

[27] Weinrib (1975) at 525. Before *McGhee v. National Coal Board, supra,* n. 7, the reversal of the burden of proof was limited to instances where the absence of proof was somehow the doing of the defendant: for example in *Gardiner v. National Bulk Carriers* 310 F. 2d 284 (1962), the captain of a ship had refused to turn back, thus making it impossible to tell whether a seaman could have been saved. In *McGhee,* medical science and not the defendant was responsible for the evidential gap.

that the defendant caused or contributed to his loss—even where that contribution to injury is only marginally greater than 50 per cent—he is entitled to damages in full from that defendant. The compensation to which the plaintiff is entitled under a loss of chance model is proportionately assessed according to the approximate degree by which the defendant reduced the plaintiff's chance of avoiding the injurious outcome. Thus the chief strength of the loss of chance model is seen to lie in the fact that it does not insist that the defendant's contribution be the greater cause, and that it is constructed to provide a more accurate and just valuation of the impact of the defendant's conduct on the plaintiff. It thus promises justice both to plaintiffs (since more plaintiffs are entitled to recover damages, though these will be reduced to reflect the degree of the defendant's contribution) and to defendants (since they are required to pay damages only in approximate proportion to their causal contribution to injury).

Loss of chance reasoning has been applied in the medical context in numerous American states[28] and by some English decisions prior to the House of Lords' tide-stemming decision in *Hotson*. In *Clark v. MacLennon*, Peter Pain J. invoked the decision in *McGhee*, but went one step further in allowing recovery for the loss of a one in three chance of a successful outcome; the learned judge then proceeded to assess damages according to the degree (33 per cent) to which the operation might have succeeded for the plaintiff.[29] In *Herskovits v. Group Health Cooperative*, the defendant's negligent diagnosis reduced the plaintiff's chances of survival from lung cancer by an approximated 14 per cent.[30] The Supreme Court of Washington deemed this a proximate cause of the plaintiff's injuries, and allowed recovery for loss directly caused by a premature death. In *Sutton v. Population Services Family Planning Programme*, the plaintiff's cancer was again

---

[28] See also: *Falcon v. Memorial Hospital, supra*, n. 98; *Aasheim v. Humberger* 215 Mont. 127, 695 P. 2d 824 (1985); and *DeBurkarte v. Louvar* 393 N.W. 2d 131 (1986). To facilitate a loss of chance analysis, some US states approved a standard of proof that requires the plaintiff to prove only that the defendant's negligence increased the risk of harm; the plaintiff could recover where the chance lost was a "substantial factor" in causing the harm: Restatement (Second) of Torts #323 (1965). See decision by the Pennsylvania Supreme Court in *Hamil v. Bashline* 392 A. 2d 1280 (1978) at 1286. In *Quinlan v. Brown* 419 A. 2d 1274 (1980) at 1278, the same court restricted this development to situations where "the nature of the case inhibits proof of causation to a reasonable degree of medical certainty." See Smith (1985).

[29] *Clark v. MacLennon, supra*, n. 11.

[30] *Herskovits v. Group Health Co-operative* 664 P. 2d 474 (1983).

detected at a negligently late stage, and again the cancer would ultimately have caused the plaintiff's death, though onset would have been delayed by approximately four years.[31] The trial judge awarded damages for the loss of those four years.

The recent debate surrounding loss of chance owes its fervour to a bold chain of developments in England that began with the case of *Hotson v. Fitzgerald*.[32] For the first time, a version of loss of chance analysis in torts cases was expressly endorsed at first instance and by the Court of Appeal, before it was ultimately overturned by the House of Lords.[33] The plaintiff patient had claimed that the defendants' negligent failure to diagnose his injury five days earlier materially increased his risk of contracting necrosis leading to permanent disability. Evidence was accepted that without the delay, the plaintiff would have had a two in three chance of avoiding the injury.

At first instance, Simon Brown J. questioned the decision in *Clark v. MacLennon* to invoke *McGhee* as an onus shifter once it had been established that there was a 2 in 3 chance of recovery had the operation been performed at the right time. In *McGhee*, the court had been unable to assess the degree by which the defendant's breach of duty increased the risk of injury. According to Simon Brown J., in cases of this type where the defendant's contribution to injury cannot properly be ascertained, the plaintiff should be required to establish a higher degree of materiality of risk or chance, though he is then entitled to full damages (so that the issue is causation and not quantification of damages). But where, as in the present case, the court is able to roughly assess the extent by which the defendant's conduct increased the risk, and that risk is not insubstantial (proposing a less than 25 per cent risk), causation has been made out, and the issue becomes one of apportioning damages accordingly. The judge admitted that the case before him, successful under this empirical analysis, would have failed under the orthodox balance of probabilities test. The decision was a surprising one, given that it consciously bypassed proof of causation, which must be established

---

[31] *Sutton v. Population Services Family Planning Programme, The Times*, November 7, 1981.

[32] *Hotson v. Fitzgerald* [1985] 3 All E.R. 167, QBD.

[33] Loss of chance analysis had already been employed in contractual lost chance cases: e.g. *Chaplin v. Hicks, supra*, n. 87; and *Kitchen v. RAF Association, supra*, n. 87. The Australian High Court has recently recognised that recovery lies for the tortious loss of a commercial opportunity: *Poseidon Ltd v. Adelaide Petroleum NL* (1994) 68 A.L.J.R. 313.

before the court is entitled to proceed to consider what damages may be recovered.[34]

The Court of Appeal adopted a more faithful loss of chance analysis. According to Dillon L.J., the court had to ask what damage or loss the plaintiff had suffered—what he was permitted to sue for.[35] In his lordship's opinion, this was the loss of a chance of avoiding his present injuries, and not those injuries *per se*. The court refused to accept that the categories of actionable loss are closed and incapable of extension.[36] Where the plaintiff could establish on the balance of probabilities that the defendant's breach of duty caused damage to the plaintiff, and the loss of a chance or benefit could be identified and valued, the plaintiff was entitled to recover on that basis so long as the loss of chance was not minimal or speculative. The novelty of the Court of Appeal's decision in *Hotson* has been interpreted to lie in its formulation of the *gist of the action*—not in terms of necrosis outcome but in terms of a loss of chance of avoiding that outcome.[37] That is, it relied on the orthodox assessment of causation by the balance of probabilities, but mitigated its effects by redefining the interest which was destroyed by the defendant.

In a decision rightly described as striking for its "analytic poverty and legal cowardice",[38] the House of Lords nipped this emerging innovation in the bud. According to Lord Bridge, it rested on a superficially attractive analogy between obvious cases of lost chance and the avoidance of personal injury.[39] In his view, if a plaintiff has proved that the defendant materially contributed to his injury, no principle can justify a reduction in damages according to the degree by which the defendant's actions caused the injury. Both Lords Bridge and Mackay, however, qualified their findings so as to not to utterly overrule *McGhee*. According to Lord Mackay: "Material increase of the risk of contraction of dermatitis is equivalent to material decrease in the chance of escaping dermatitis."[40]

Loss of chance is designed to compensate for the loss of chance of avoiding a result rather than the result itself. At its purest, this loss is the injury that grounds the cause of action; as such, it is not

---

[34] Price (1989), p. 745.
[35] *Hotson v. East Berkshire Area Health Authority, supra*, n. 13 at 219, CA.
[36] *ibid.* at 217, *per* John Donaldson M.R.
[37] Stapleton (1988).
[38] Foster (1995), p. 229.
[39] *Hotson v. East Berkshire Area Health Authority, supra*, n. 13 at 782 HL.
[40] *ibid.* at 786.

consequential on proof of existing physical or economic loss. This aspect of loss of chance doctrine has elicited most objection from the judges. The House of Lords' deliberations in *Hotson* overtly reveal the fears that this will compel compensation for plaintiffs who have yet suffered no tangible damage, and will in turn lead to a flood of speculative and pre-emptive actions. These fears are overstated. The English courts have rarely imposed liability for future injury, though notably the House of Lords did so in its controversial decision in *Anns v. Merton London Borough Council*, where damages were awarded against a local authority and builder for a claim founded on possible future damage caused to the plaintiffs by defective foundations in their home.[41] The House's emphasis on property damage, as opposed to economic loss, may suggest that it recognised recovery for creation of risk and apprehension of danger for both personal and property actions.[42]

Orthodox torts law differs from the loss of chance model in its conception of the actionable interest upon which the plaintiff may sue. In a case, for instance, concerning premature death by cancer, the court would insist that the plaintiff prove on the balance of probabilities that the defendant caused the patient's death—not whether the defendant negligently deprived him of a chance or opportunity of living longer. This was the conclusion reached by the Supreme Court of Canada in *Lawson v. Lafferiere*, where it rejected loss of chance doctrine as it applies at least to past injuries.[43] In the main, the common law . chooses to restrict its enquiry within temporal deterministic limitations, permitting recovery only for injury or loss that has already occurred. As Donaldson M.R. said in *Hotson* (where nonetheless he supported loss of chance), if the loss suffered is nil "only nominal damages will be recoverable".[44] Many common law courts unfavourably disposed to changing over to a loss of chance model have begun to mitigate the severity of the all-or-nothing approach by awarding damages for mental distress and

---

[41] *Anns v. Merton London Borough Council* [1978] A.C. 728, [1977] 2 All E.R. 492. The House of Lords explained later in *Murphy v. Brentwood District Council* [1991] 1 A.C. 398 that in cases of latent structural defect, the damage is economic and not physical, and therefore this development does not require a broadening of the basis of torts liability.

[42] Fleming (1989), p. 678. This interpretation was rejected subsequently by their Lordships in *D. v. F. Estates* [1989] A.C. 177, [1988] 2 All E.R. 992.

[43] *Lawson v. Lafferiere* (1991) 78 D.L.R. (4th) 609.

[44] *Hotson v. East Berkshire Area Health Authority, supra* n. 13, CA.

psychological suffering.[45] This direction has been chosen in a few English first instance decisions in the context of the disclosure action, where the plaintiff has established a negligent breach of duty to disclose but has not satisfied the court on the balance of probabilities that he would not have undergone the treatment had full disclosure been made.[46]

The common law may continue to insist upon proof of actual as opposed to potential outcome, and still adopt a loss of chance analysis within that limit, as Donaldson M.R.'s observations in *Hotson* suggest. Yet it must be questioned whether recovery should automatically be precluded for future injury or death which the defendants' conduct has made more likely or imminent. The loss of chance argument will continue to haunt the law of torts, particularly in the context of injury caused by exposure to toxic substances, involving long latency periods between exposure to risk and manifestation of injury.[47] Modern technology has caused these problems; it would be an unpleasant irony if science and technology were not permitted a freer hand when the court evaluates causative contribution and in turn entitlement to compensation. In *Hotson*, the House of Lords was clearly disinclined to employ statistics to assess hypothetical probability in torts cases, even where it has become impossible to establish or prove the relevant past facts.[48] In defence of this stance, Hill argues that the statistical analysis tells us what tends to occur but not what occurred in the instant case: in other words, the House of Lords refused to be influenced by *statistical* chance on the basis that it cannot be taken to connote *personal* chance.[49] This is a fact which loss of chance advocators do not dispute. It is, after all, epistemologically impossible to determine whether the patient would have fallen within one statistical category over the other. The orthodox approach to causation in torts rests upon a misconception that the law *must* continue to require that a plaintiff prove by direct evidence, when he cannot, that he was one of the number of patients

---

[45] *e.g. Lawson v. Laferriere, supra,* n. 43, where the plaintiff was instead awarded damages for the better quality of life and comfort he would have enjoyed, had the defendant informed him more promptly.

[46] See *supra,* p. 213.

[47] See: Gold (1986); Notes (1998).

[48] *Hotson v. East Berkshire Area Health Authority, supra,* n. 13, HL: Lord Mackay (at 785 and 789) on the basis that the court must assess "past facts" and not the "hypothetical". Lord Bridge (at 782) was tentative on this point and Lord Ackner did not directly address it.

[49] Hill (1991), p. 512.

who would have benefited from the treatment, when instead it could require the plaintiff to establish, where he can do so, that there was a particular chance that he would have so benefited.

Throughout the common law, the torts system has traditionally favoured proof of causation by *particularist* evidence from the mouths of witnesses, of a direct, anecdotal, and non-statistical character.[50] For this reason, its balance of probabilities standard is intended to facilitate a fairly impressionistic evaluation of the evidence. This may or may not entail the search for some crude 51 per cent plus approximation of probability: one research study concluded that in practice it leads courts to look for something like 75 per cent likelihood that the defendant caused the plaintiff's injuries.[51] Whichever side it favours, it encourages in all cases a lack of transparency and clarity in its conclusion of support for one proposition over another. By contrast, scientific epistemology has for a considerable time abandoned the comparatively simple Newtonian belief in physical causation, preferring instead to employ hypothesis, inductive testing, and probabilistic assessments.[52] Loss of chance doctrine reflects these advances, giving greater effect, in terms of proof and distribution of liability, to a probabilistic assessment of each agent's contribution to injury on the basis of known statistical information. It may well be the case that the probabilistic assessment is the only tenable one to apply in medical negligence cases. The precise pathogenesis of many diseases is unknown. Many disease processes culminate in unsuccessful outcomes despite the best medical treatment, so that "the best any patient can achieve is to show that he lost the opportunity of being cured."[53]

Ironically, the common law tends to avoid minute scientific enquiries, despite giving free reign—particularly in medical negligence cases—to the views of experts, loosely expressed in the discourse of medical science. The inevitable reluctance of scientific experts to make precise conclusions must in many cases have caused the court to feel that the plaintiff had failed to prove his case—a fact recognised by Sopinka J. in *Farrell v. Snell*, where he asserted that, on the contrary, the courts' "power to draw the inference . . . [is] not impaired by the failure of any medical witness to testify that it was in

[50] Fleming (1989), p. 662.
[51] Simon and Mahan (1970–1971).
[52] Brennan (1987–1988).
[53] Scott (1992), p. 521.

fact the cause. Neither can it be impaired by the lack of unanimity as to the respective likelihood of the potential causes . . . or by the fact that other potential causes of the aggravation existed and were not conclusively negated by the proofs."[54] In the learned judge's opinion, if Lord Wilberforce had recognised this in *McGhee*, he would not have perceived the evidential gap he did, nor would he have felt it necessary to reverse the onus of proof. What this leaves us with is a system that permits but does not actively encourage scientific or statistical analysis of causation. Expert witnesses are allowed to formulate their weighty opinions in terms that exploit the multi-shaded minutia of science in the context of proof by a preponderance of probability. What results is instinctive guess-work, a wholly inexact and unempirical process that in many cases turns on the credibility and demeanour of court-room witnesses. By contrast, statistics are "derived systematically from our previous experience of similar cases", and they "provide us with a very accurate probability-weighting for each candidate" or potential cause.[55]

In turning to statistics as a benchmark for the distribution of loss, the loss of chance model, to its credit, seeks to minimise the very uncertainty that the traditional model ultimately accentuates. The "use of statistics . . . minimises such uncertainty by telling us over a range of similar cases how frequently the unknown conditions appear: in *Hotson*, 75 per cent of the time".[56] It does not, nor ought it, deprive the court of giving weight to factors that are personal to the parties to the action, such as the size or location of the plaintiff's heart, which if relevant ought to be considered alongside any statistical data that is accepted.[57] Statistics, if relied upon for no more than what they indicate, should serve to focus the court's attention more efficiently and more accurately to culpability and contribution to risk creation and injury.

It may be argued that loss of chance doctrine would be highly useful to courts in evaluating the plaintiff's propositions in disclosure claims. Whether or not he would have undergone the treatment had disclosure been made is a notoriously difficult question begging at best a speculative answer to a hypothetical question.[58] Yet the point in

---

[54] *Farrell v. Snell, supra*, n. 22, at 299, citing *Sentilles v. Inter-Caribbean Shipping Corp* 361 U.S. 107 (1959) at 109–110.
[55] Stauch (1997), p. 219.
[56] *ibid.*, p. 218.
[57] Lunney (1995), p. 12.
[58] See *supra*, pp. 203–214.

time when the plaintiff could have been able to make an informed decision is gone, the chance is lost, due to the defendant's negligent breach of duty. On the one hand, the plaintiff's pronounced belief that he would have foregone treatment had disclosure been made is retrospectively coloured by the actual outcome, his injuries. On the other hand, the defendant's proposition that the majority of patients (ergo the reasonable man) would have undergone the treatment in the circumstances, does not prove that the individual patient would have so acted; to attach unequal weight to this type of proposition would be to hand a blank cheque to medical paternalism. The courts do not sufficiently identify that often one of a number of *reasonable* decisions may be made by a patient in response to a variety of factors which it is difficult with hindsight to identify—personal circumstances, his symptoms, the treatment that has been medically recommended, the alternatives open to him, etc. A plaintiff should be entitled to recover where he can establish that a decision to forego the treatment *might* reasonably have been a decision the reasonable man would have made: that is, that such a decision was at least *a* and not necessarily *the* reasonable thing to do. For this reason, a purely statistical approach to disclosure claims is dangerous: the fact that 70 per cent of patients informed of the risk would still submit to treatment does not mean that the plaintiff patient would have acted similarly.[59] The common law should empower itself, by utilising a wider scale of degrees of belief in competing propositions, so that where it feels that the plaintiff's proposition attracts approximately a 30 per cent likelihood, damages may be awarded to reflect that extent.

The application of loss of chance theory to the medical context will always prove controversial, given that it carries the prospect of opening the floodgates to more numerous malpractice claims. A variety of possible directions face the common law. If it chooses to adopt a full loss of chance model (which at present seems unlikely), its decision would necessitate a reformulation of the cause of action or interest upon which plaintiffs can sue. Alternatively, it could continue to apply a lower standard of proof in hard cases of multiple causation, in the manner of *Bonnington* and *McGhee*. Instead it could adopt the innovative hybrid model advanced at first instance and before the Court of Appeal in *Hotson*. That model joins features of the *McGhee* test to one aspect of loss of chance doctrine, by

---

[59] Stauch (1997), p. 222.

proposing a reformulation of the standard of proof (material contribution to injury) and then assessing damages in proportion to the degree of causation proved against the defendant. The advantage of this latter approach is that it does not necessitate a radical departure—only an innovative one—from rules deeply embedded in the common law. It promises to achieve a more proportionate vindication of rights (in terms of damages), and a useful deterrent, socialising effect. In its absence, the common law's traditional test of causation seems to represent a symbolic and practical compensatory inequity, which can only serve to heighten the calls for more radical changes such as transition over to a no-fault compensatory scheme.[60]

---

[60] See chapter 8, *infra*, pp. 231–240. The propinquity between no-fault and the loss of chance model is suggested by an observation of Riley C.J. in *Falcon v. Memorial Hospital, supra*, n. 98 at 67–68: "Rather than deterring undesirable conduct, the rule imposed only penalizes the medical profession for inevitable unfavourable results."

Chapter 8

Reviewing the System

Fault Liability

The primary aim of fault liability is to compensate victims of accidental loss where shown to have been caused by the defendant's negligence. As a compensation-provider, it therefore discriminates between victims of accidental injury "not according to their deserts but according to the culpability of the defendant" so that "legal fault does not entirely coincide with moral fault."[1] The adversarial process of proof employed by the common law was cannily described by one medical expert as "a variant of hand to hand combat of selected gladiators" whose weapons are words.[2] By its nature, this process encourages ranks on each side of the law suit to close at the earliest possible date.[3] The unequal means of knowledge (or access to that knowledge) which the patient initially suffers is sealed, and the possibility of meaningful dialogue and explanation between doctor and patient is for practical reasons abruptly foreclosed.

Despite this, it is the plaintiff (as the party who makes the assertion and requests the court to take action on his behalf) who bears the heavy burden of proving all components of the medical negligence claim. Proof that the defendant positively breached a standard of care owed in the circumstances to the patient is peculiarly onerous for plaintiffs: it is difficult to persuade expert medical witnesses to

---

[1] James (1950), p. 778.
[2] Lucire, "The Expert Witness Self-Examined", in Winfield (1989), p. 89.
[3] To mitigate this effect, English and Irish law now provide for the mandatory exchange of reports prior to the hearing of personal injury actions: Annual Practice Current Rules, Ord. 38, rr. 37–38 (Eng); and Courts and Courts Officers Act 1995 (Ir). See further: Carolan (1995); and O'Neill (1997).

condemn the actions of the defendant as something which no reasonable or prudent practitioner would have done in similar circumstances; yet once the defendant has established expert testimonial support for his actions, suggestive of an approved medical practice, only in the scarcest of cases will the negligence claim against him succeed. Far more complicated is proof of causation. A deeply ingrained policy on the part of the courts to minimise claims against the medical profession has served to restrict attempts to alleviate the plaintiff's burden of proof on this issue.[4] In many cases the court must consider an elaborate range of possible agents that singly or in combination acted to cause the plaintiff's present injuries. Despite unbridgeable evidential gaps, the common law for the time being continues to require the plaintiff to prove that the defendant caused or contributed to his injury to the extent at least of 51 per cent (that is, on the balance of probabilities). Generally, the defendant who has breached a duty of care, but contributed to the plaintiff's injuries somewhat less than 51 per cent, escapes liability. By contrast, the defendant who is shown to be at least 51 per cent responsible for the plaintiff's injury is required to compensate the plaintiff for all the reasonably foreseeable consequences of his actions.

This all-or-nothing approach to compensation has rightly attracted much criticism for its lack of proportionality, its inefficiency, and its inequity. The common law manifests a clear preference for full or no compensation, a culture that has been absorbed by legislators in the bulk of common law jurisdictions, blocking ongoing calls for systemic reform. Common law judges and lawyers rarely pause to consider whether a policy of generously awarding the few and ignoring the bulk of accidental personal injuries is necessarily a sound one. Aside from the obvious inequity of this incidental discrimination (flowing from the requirement that the defendant must be shown to be legally at fault), one may query the common law's assumptions underpinning compensation, its effects, and the motives of those who seek it. According to one view, "[b]asic economic theory teaches us that generously rewarding pain and accompanying misery creates a strong incentive for suffering . . . How better to document one's suffering than by prolonged absence from work and repeated trips to the doctor?"[5] In this light, the results of a study on the effect of the no-fault option (for neurological injury caused to children during

---

[4] See Chapter 7, *supra*, pp. 219, 224–230.
[5] O'Connell (1985), p. 900.

childbirth) in Florida and Virginia prove interesting.[6] No-fault and tort claimants differed in their reasons for claiming.[7] No-fault claimants tended to be far more concerned with practical financial issues, lost income, and medical costs; by contrast, tort claimants were more motivated by blame and retribution, seeking to find out what caused their injuries and who was responsible. It may well be that blame has become confused with a superior entitlement to "full" compensation. The payment of compensation by lump sum—as opposed to periodically reviewable payments—is perceived to be another weakness of the present system, along with the common law's refusal to reduce the award to reflect payments already received by the plaintiff from a different source in respect of the same injuries (the collateral sources rule).[8]

The simplistic view that torts is solely concerned with compensation has given way in the latter part of this century to a shrewder appreciation of its indirect socialising effects, its potential for deterrence, and its implicit attempts to transmit precedential warnings to members of society. At a general level, the fault system is often accused of having lost its deterrent teeth, to the extent that the contemporary availability of insurance has transformed many private law suits into disputes between insurance companies, thereby complicating tort law's potential for behavioural control.[9] In the medical sphere, this is not quite the case. Each professional practitioner's most valuable but vulnerable asset is his reputation. The frequency with which medical defence unions are thought to settle claims stems partly, one suspects, from a desire to minimise bad publicity for individual practitioners as well as the medical community in general. The devastating effects for the doctor, personally and professionally,

---

[6] Fla. Stat. chs 766.301–316 (1997); Va. Code Ann. 38.2–5000 to 5021 (Michie 1994). In the U.K., strict statutory liability was created for congenital disabilities caused by the negligence of obstetricians or obstetric attendants, under the Congenital Disabilities (Civil Liability) Act 1976. Disability is defined by section 4(1) as "any deformity, disease or abnormality including predisposition (whether or not susceptible of immediate prognosis) to physical or mental defect in the future". This is subject to the "doctor's defence" under section 1(5), that the obstetrician "took reasonable care having due regard to then received professional opinion applicable to the particular class of case."

[7] Sloane, Whetten-Goldstein, Entman, Kulas, and Stout (1997), p. 50. The survey found that torts claimants were ten times more likely to be motivated by retribution.

[8] Reversed in a number of U.S. states (Colorado, Connecticut, Florida, Idaho, Kansas, Minnesota, and Utah): Scheid (1997), p. 14.

[9] Sugarman (1985), p. 573.

of a finding of negligence against him suggest that the current model may be as inequitable to defendants as it is to plaintiffs.

Only very recently has some degree of attention been devoted to the plight faced by hospital doctors. According to Teff, the ingredients for negligent treatment have already been built into the system: "The combination of budgetary constraints, overworked and sometimes inexperienced medical staff under pressure to cut waiting lists, and continued growth in the number of referrals is a recipe for litigation."[10] Stress incurred by hospital doctors must contribute significantly to the substance abuse which reportedly exists within the medical profession.[11] George McNeice, chief of the Irish Medical Organisation, recently concluded that hospital doctors are working in a state of near collapse, creating an "insane hazard" for patients: "It would be unthinkable to allow a pilot to fly under the same circumstances."[12] In this charged, volatile environment, the ability of the law to improve professional concentration and care is limited.[13] It may well be the case that to be genuinely deterrent, the law should encourage doctors to refuse to treat patients once they suspect that they cannot do so competently whether because of sleep deprivation or personal stress.[14]

Alternative Systems

Under the fault liability rule, a wrong is corrected by shifting the loss to the party who is shown to be at fault. This loss is by necessity internalised or absorbed by the activity of which the tortfeasor is a member (typically via the insurance mechanism). Alternative proposals to fault liability tend to spring from a more sophisticated

---

[10] Teff (1994), p. 19. In this regard, it is interesting to note that in *Johnstone v. Bloomsbury Health Authority* [1992] Q.B. 333, the plaintiff doctor succeeded in his argument that his contract of employment with the defendants was unlawful for infringing an implied contractual duty to take reasonable care not to injure his health. The plaintiff testified to having worked up to 100 hours some weeks, and up to 88 hours most weeks, which caused him to suffer stress, depression, and thoughts of suicide.

[11] The British Medical Association recently estimated that some 1 in 10 doctors is addicted to drugs or alcohol—a rate assessed to be seven times higher than for other professions: *The Sunday Times*, May 18, 1996.

[12] So said at an Irish Medical Organisation conference, April 19, 1996.

[13] Abraham and Weiler (1994), p. 412.

[14] Brazier (1992), p. 220.

understanding of the interaction between the various targets and the intended social effects of the fault liability rules for accidental personal injury. Numerous calls have been made to encourage the judiciary to consider when determining liability how best the type of loss suffered by the plaintiff may be borne by society in general. The belief that accidental loss should be distributed as opposed to shifted has been the mainstay of economic theories of torts law for four decades now.[15] In the medical context, law and economics studies have for some time pushed the no-fault liability rule as a more equitable and efficient alternative, and on occasion members of the judiciary have expressed a similar preference.[16]

The no-fault model accepts the fact of medical accidents as a social phenomenon, and directs its attention to how best it should spread existing and future resources, and how best the health care service may absorb the resultant loss (though not necessarily in an economic sense alone). No-fault theory typically reasons that certain types of compensation claims should be redirected from the courts to independent tribunals who are equipped with the expertise to process the claims more efficiently and equitably than tort rules currently permit. Medical no-fault schemes have operated in New Zealand and Sweden for years, to apparently significant levels of success.[17] Generally, members of the tribunal have access to all relevant medical records and information, assisted where necessary by independent and impartial medical experts hired by the tribunal. The tribunal's enquiry is inquisitorial as opposed to adversarial. Compensation awards are drawn from a central fund established by the state or through private insurance.

In New Zealand, a comprehensive no-fault system operates for all species of accidental personal injury.[18] It is committed to the principle of replacing financial loss; to this end, it differs from a social welfare goal of ensuring minimally adequate living standards.[19] Benefits are

---

[15] *e.g.* Calabresi (1961, 1968, 1970); Coase (1960); Fletcher (1972); Landes and Posner (1987); and Posner (1992).

[16] According to McCarthy J. of the Irish Supreme Court, the "case for a no-fault system of compensation for those who suffer injury as a result of medical treatment seems so strong as to be virtually unanswerable" (*Hegarty v. O'Laughran* [1990] I.L.R.M. 403 at 418). See also *Koerber v. Kitchener-Waterloo Hospital* 62 OR. (2d) 613 (1987) at 632.

[17] Gellhorn (1988); Ison (1980); McGregor Vennell (1989); Oldertz (1983); Oliphant (1996); Palmer (1979); Saks (1992); Sappideeen (1993); Sugarman (1985).

[18] As established by the Accident Compensation Act 1972.

[19] Fleming (1987), p. 375.

not flat but earnings-related. Decisions are made by the Accident Corporation, which may within one month review its own verdict. An appeal lies to the Accident Compensation Appeal Authority, further to the High Court of New Zealand, and ultimately on a point of law to the Court of Appeal.[20] A claim which falls under the terms of the scheme is barred from common law adjudication (which remains only for claims that do not fall within the scheme).[21] The scheme extends itself to "medical, surgical, dental or first aid misadventure".[22] This has been more recently defined as "bodily or mental injury or damage in the course of, and as part of, the administering to that person of medical aid, care or attention, and such injury or damage is caused by mischance or accident, unexpected and undesigned, in the nature of medical error or mishap."[23]

Recent legislative amendment has restricted recovery to severe disability and rare occurrences, mainly for cost reasons.[24] Similarly, the courts have limited the application of the scheme to adverse consequences which are rare and severe, beyond that which is normally and reasonably contemplated as within the risks attached to the administering of medical treatment. According to Speight J., "misadventure" connotes "ill luck" or "bad fortune".[25] As such, the legislators intended to embrace a wide variety of accidental occurrences, but not a test based on the consequences of medical negligence. Misadventure could not be said to exist where the unsatisfactory outcome "can be classified as merely within the normal range of medical or surgical failure attendant upon even the most felicitous treatment".[26] To this end, the New Zealand courts have consistently emphasised that the scheme covers "mishandling" of a plaintiff's illness, and that it subsumes medical negligence and non-negligent errors which lead to results that could have been avoided.[27] The Act has also been interpreted not to include injury

---

[20] Accident Compensation Act 1982 (No. 181), ss. 101, 103, 106, 111.

[21] *ibid.*, s. 27.

[22] Accident Compensation Act 1972 s. 2, as amended by Accident Compensation Act 1974.

[23] Accident Rehabilitation and Compensation Insurance Act 1992, s. 5(1), as amended by Accident Rehabilitation and Compensation Insurance Amendment Act (No. 2) 1993.

[24] Accident Rehabilitation and Compensation Insurance Act 1992.

[25] *Accident Compensation Commission v. Auckland Hospital Board* [1981] N.Z.A.C.R. 9.

[26] *ibid.* at 13d–g.

[27] *Green v. Mattheson* [1989] 3 N.Z.L.R. 564 at 572–573; *Childs v. Hillock* [1994] 2 N.Z.L.R. 65 at 72.

suffered as a result of participation in experimental or research-based treatment, on the basis that in the research context it is foreseeable that risks may materialise.[28] Where a known (but undisclosed) risk inherent in treatment materialises, there is no "medical misadventure"; so informed consent may prove to be an important avenue of relief outside of the scheme.[29]

The effect of no-fault liability is to shift the law's focus from proof of fault to proof of causation. This is intended to increase the pool of potential claimants. Additional cost is usually offset by a saving in administrative costs through simplification of the compensation process and a lowering of compensation levels. Critics of no-fault have tended to argue that the savings in administrative costs for *medical* no-fault liability are inevitably far less than for other types of injury; further that proof of causation must still be faced by plaintiffs (in establishing that the injury is iatrogenic), a burden which is likely to be as difficult for plaintiffs to discharge as proof that the defendant breached the appropriate standard of care. Danzon argues that making causation the rule might actually increase the administrative costs: "Basing compensation on medical causation rather than negligent performance will reduce average litigation expense per case only if the demarcation between medically-caused and non-medically-caused adverse outcomes is clearer than the demarcation between negligent and non-negligent care."[30] This has not been the experience of no-fault jurisdictions. The task of distinguishing between an iatrogenic injury and progression of an original illness is already simplified by the fact that the claim is being *investigated*, and to a much greater extent is freed from the obvious constraints placed by the adversarial process.[31] It is also so that eliminating the need to prove that the defendant's fault caused the injury is bound to simplify the process (and avoid the difficulties faced in the recent *Bolitho* case in England, where the House of Lords accepted that customary and approved practice may be considered when assessing whether an omission to act caused the injury). Though it is an undeniable fact that proof of medical causation represents a formidable challenge for plaintiffs, the assumption that it is the most difficult component of proof was rebutted recently by a Harvard Medical Practice Study,

---

[28] *Re Kishor Bava: Decision No. 1022* [1983] N.Z.A.C.R 669.
[29] *MacDonald v. Accident Compensation Corporation* [1985] 5 N.Z.A.R. 276. See also Mahoney (1985), p. 123.
[30] Danzon (1985), p. 215.
[31] Brazier (1992), p. 218.

which concluded that scientific judgments of medical causation are only about one-quarter as difficult to make as judgments about medical fault.[32] Evidence compiled of the New Zealand experience allays fears that administrative costs would not significantly be reduced. Giesen records that the New Zealand no-fault model has proved to be a needs-oriented success, whose administration costs have consistently hovered at around 10 per cent of its income.[33]

The common law's response to the dilemma posed by proof of medical causation has been to tamper incrementally and often confusingly with orthodox rules, for instance by recognising early discharges of the plaintiff's burden of proof (forcing defendants to disprove any inferences that have been judged to arise) or lowering the standard of proof required on the causation issue.[34] By contrast, no-fault tribunals have tended to avoid problems associated with the burdens of proof and the balance of probabilities.[35] In most cases, the injury is permitted to speak for itself, and it is only when the injury "is not obviously brought about by some identifiable external incident that the Corporation will examine the sequence of events to decide whether injury by accident has in fact occurred."[36]

Whilst the no-fault model generally aspires towards a more equitable spread of compensation to victims of accidental medical injury, it remains a model of *liability*. Though the effect of liability is less stigmatising—given that more claims are processed—incentives remain to prompt health care practitioners and institutions to avoid accidents, since the former are implicated in the plaintiff's injuries and the latter are deemed liable for them. Indeed, the schematic decision to award compensation for injuries caused by medical misadventure, but not for disabilities caused by the progression of a patient's initial illness, suggests that incentive to avoid further accidents is inbuilt in the no-fault model. It is noteworthy that the Royal College of Physicians in England, in expressing its support for a no-fault scheme for medical injuries, recommended that it be accompanied by a parallel mechanism to investigate each claim to ensure that the appropriate level of professional care was not transgressed, on the basis that where substandard care is discovered,

---

[32] Weiler, Hiatt *et al.*, *A Measure of Malpractice* (1993): cited in Abraham and Weiler (1994), p. 433.
[33] Giesen (1988), p. 541.
[34] See Chapter 7, *supra*, pp. 214–230.
[35] Blair (1983) pp. 41–42.
[36] *ibid.*, p. 41.

parallel disciplinary action should be taken against the practitioner.[37] Clearly, the existing grounds for internal disciplinary action would need to be broadened greatly by statute to provide a more viable conduit for deterrence concerns.[38]

No-fault was considered and rejected in England by the Pearson Commission in 1978.[39] The report drew attention to the many practical obstacles facing any overhaul of fault liability—emphasising the causation analysis—without rigorously assessing the benefits to be gained. Conservatism has thus far impeded any rigorous consideration at executive level in England or Ireland of the desirability of no-fault, alongside opposition by the insurance industry to same. A decision to substitute no-fault for existing laws would of course be costly, time-consuming, and potentially unpopular (particularly where it entails a lowering of compensation levels). However, there remains the possibility of introducing no-fault on a limited basis for "designated compensable events" such as outcomes which more often than not are associated with medical negligence.[40] If this, however, was restricted to the type of case that would normally settle (that is, to cases already involving low administrative costs), the burden of financing and running the twin systems would be in vain.[41] There would also be the problem of proving that the injury comes under the partial no-fault model, and the more haunting possibility that doctors would become less likely to perform certain procedures which if unsuccessful would give rise to liability under one model and not the other, or would charge higher fees for such procedures.

An unsuccessful attempt was made by the Clinton Administration in 1993 to abolish the individual liability of doctors under negligence law and replace it with a model of enterprise medical liability under which statutorily identified health care plan organisers would bear and channel the loss.[42] Abraham and Weiler spear-headed and

---

[37] *Report of the Royal College of Physicians*, 1990.

[38] Jones (1996), p. 14.

[39] *Royal Commission on Civil Liability and Compensation for Personal Injury* Cmnd. 7054 (1978).

[40] Havighurst and Tancredi (1974). This was recently advocated on a twin-track basis by the Prichard Report (1990) in Canada: *Report of the Federal/Provincial/Territorial Review on Liability and Compensation Issues in Health Care* (1990), pp. 28–30). The Report targets "significantly avoidable health care injuries".

[41] Danzon (1984), p. 117.

[42] See Abraham and Weiler (1994). The proposal was ultimately defeated after intense lobbying from insurance groups and the American Medical Association who, according to the authors, had belatedly begun to fear exchanging the threat of lawyers for the threat of insurers.

continue to support the scheme. They identify the following weaknesses of the existing medical negligence model. Insurance costs are based on actuarial projections per specialty, so that

"inevitable changes in the frequency or severity of claims against a particular specialty in a particular state—changes that might result in modest rate changes for the members of a large risk pool—have an exaggerated effect on a small pool . . . These shocks in the market for malpractice coverage produce not only economic effects, but also political repercussions that generate ill-designed tort reform of various sorts."[43]

Whereas fault liability is concerned with individual rather than institutional responsibility, under enterprise liability the individual doctor is primarily a member of a larger team of medical personnel. Enterprise liability holds out more promise for injury prevention. Where the institution is made responsible to assimilate losses, it is better placed to ensure that channels of communication between doctors, nurses, and paramedics are improved, that medical equipment is updated, and that management of hospital health care is competent and efficient. The causation enquiry would be greatly simplified where the plaintiff is not required to identify which member of staff was responsible for the medical injury: "In short, once the current regime's obsession with individual fault is replaced by a system-wide focus through the adoption of EML, shifting from a fault-based to a no-fault-based regime is likely to seem far more natural than it does at present."[44] Abraham and Weiler conclude that

"enterprise medical liability could prove to be something of a half-way house between the current malpractice regime and a dramatically different no-fault alternative. Making hospitals and other health care enterprises liable for all malpractice-related injuries suffered by their patients would fit comfortably within the current fault-based tort regime, which makes virtually all other business enterprises responsible in tort for negligently inflicted injuries resulting from the enterprise's activities."[45]

Various other alternative dispute resolution proposals have been floated. One is the creation of a forum for arbitration and conciliation, under which a qualified arbitration panel would process claims

[43] Abraham and Weiler (1994), *supra*, n. 42, p. 402.
[44] *ibid.*, p. 434.
[45] *ibid.*, p. 435.

more efficiently and conclude with a determination binding on both parties.[46] A variant of this proposal would involve a mediator whose purpose is to bring about compromise and agreement between both sides, but whose determination is not legally binding on either side.[47] Agreements in advance to refer if necessary to arbitration raise special concerns. The patient may feel compelled to sign such a form on a "take it or leave it" basis as a precondition for admission into hospital or for treatment.[48] It is likely that any agreement which deprives the patient of a meaningful opportunity to decide whether or not to relinquish his constitutional right of access to the courts would fall foul of the law.[49]

The latest development of note in England is the publication of Lord Woolf's *Access to Justice*, which must be applauded for its pragmatic assimilation of loss distribution ideas.[50] Lord Woolf proposes the establishment of a special court to hear medical negligence claims, and the training of a specified number of judges in medico-legal issues. He also proposes a "fast track" judicial system for personal injury claims under £10,000, with a shorter timetable for resolution, one expert chosen by both parties, one lawyer representing each party, and with a fixed limit of costs of £3,500. Alternatively, it suggests a procedure tailored to the specific case with a budget agreed in advance, an 18 month time-scale, and a joint expert who would act as adviser to the court. It is also proposed that there be a contingency legal aid fund for multi-party actions, initially financed by government and then by levies on successful actions. It is contemplated that such a fund would be generally available, and not only to those who would ordinarily be entitled to legal aid.

As a proposal, the creation of court experts has begun to gain momentum. To the extent that it is designed to minimise the element of surprise associated with the adversarial process, it complements recent changes requiring each side of the dispute to disclose reports prepared by expert witnesses in advance of the trial.[51] Rendering experts neutral, non-adversarial, and at the service of the court rather than one particular side, marks a move towards a more inquisitorial model. A direction of this nature would enable the court

---

[46] This was recently considered in England by the Department of Health. See Jones (1992).
[47] See Easterbrook (1996).
[48] Giesen (1988), p. 506.
[49] *Gale v. Providence Hospital* 325 N.W. 2d 439 (1982).
[50] Woolf (1996).
[51] See *supra*, p. 231 (n. 3).

to appoint an expert from a panel of approved experts, who is obliged to produce a report which then becomes a single and authoritative document for the trial. This is intended to avoid the type of bias and partiality which naturally emerges (whether consciously or not on the part of medical experts) in adversarial contexts; it also attempts to remove the restrictions on experts giving testimony freely, to minimise unfairness caused to the under-resourced party to the dispute, and to ensure quality control of expert testimony.[52]

The traditional response by common law judges to the perceived threat of a boom in malpractice claims has tended to favour the medical community. This is especially so in England and Ireland, where the courts have sought to restrict the future evolution of this tort by distinguishing it as one which requires the courts to consider a range of *public policy interests* unique to medical negligence claims. The presence of policy in torts evaluations has been keenly felt in recent years, more obviously in the cautious development of the nervous shock action, and judges have begun to admit with more candour that in addition to the individual proofs recognised by the law of negligence, the common law reserves the power to consider whether as a matter of public policy it would be just and reasonable to hold the defendant liable.[53] On one view, expressed by Lord Scarman, this should rarely occur, and only where the court's development of *principle* "entails a degree of policy risk . . . leaving policy curtailment to the judgment of Parliament."[54] On another view, expressed by Lord Justice Griffiths, in "any state of society it is ultimately a question of policy to decide the limits of liability".[55] According to Lord Diplock, the judge's sense of policy is governed by his or her "cumulative experience . . . of the actual consequences of lack of care in particular instances."[56] Though this may be so, policy

---

[52] For a somewhat imbalanced criticism of this model, see Howard (1991), p. 101 where it is argued that witnesses already run the risk of exposure of their fallacies in public: "The picture of the suave cross-examiner leading an unwary expert witness into supporting in the witness box the scientific thesis advanced by the opposite party is an attractive one; but it does not accord with reality." Against this, see Chapter 3, *supra*, pp. 74–76.

[53] *Caparo Industries plc v. Dickman* [1990] 2 A.C. 605. See Chapter 3, *supra*, pp. 84–85 and Chapter 6, *supra*, p. 180.

[54] *McLoughlin v. O'Brien* [1983] 1 A.C. 410 at 430, HL.

[55] *McLoughlin v. O'Brian* [1981] Q.B. 599 at 611, CA.

[56] *Home Office v. Dorset Yacht Co* [1970] 2 All E.R. 294 at 324. Judges, however, are generally loath to reveal the process behind their exercise of judicial discretion The frustrating reality of this was vividly experienced by a team of Oxford criminologists,

must be informed and updated, if it is to reflect the experiences and expectations of society. It is disheartening to observe that a fuller expression of the tort of medical negligence has constantly been impeded by a range of unsubstantiated and undeveloped judicial *idées fixées*, which are allowed to transform each specific allegation of medical negligence into a paradigm case fraught with sensationalised implications.[57]

It has been said that the deepest ideological struggle currently facing the law of torts is not between fault liability and strict liability; instead it concerns whether the court should direct itself solely to the claims and interests arising from the instant case, or whether it should also strive to reach a decision which serves the present and future interests of society.[58] In adopting the latter approach, the courts may implicitly assess how the particular loss (or losses in general) should best be absorbed or distributed by society and by the activity that gives rise to the risk of injury in question. In Hoffman's view, "the courts have never brought themselves to admit to the tension, in common law principles of negligence, between the policy of resting liability upon moral responsibility and the policy of redistributing loss on more general grounds of social justice and economic benefit."[59] The reasonable man device, employed by the common law in various guises to shape the standard of care owed by the defendant to the plaintiff, is designed to "fudge" these issues. Though contemporary demands seem to be for more individualised justice,[60] the courts when handling medical negligence cases tend to surrender to vague policies, all evocative of the floodgates fear.

---

led by Professor Ashworth, who attempted to gain the co-operation of the judiciary in an attempt to rationalise the means by which sentencing discretion is applied by the judiciary: Ashworth, Gedners, Mansfield, Peay, and Player (1984).

[57] *e.g. Roe v. Ministry of Health* [1954] 2 All E.R. 131 at 137 & 139, *per* Denning L.J.; *Sidaway v. Bethlem Royal Hospital* [1984] 1 All E.R. 1018 at 1035, CA, *per* Browne-Wilkinson L.J.; and *Edwards v. Jenkins* Irish High Court, unreported, January 20, 1989, *per* O'Hanlon J.

[58] Fletcher (1972), p. 540.

[59] Hoffman (1995), p. 134. Where the reasonable man imposes a standard beyond the actual mental or physical abilities of the defendant, it becomes an instrument for the redistribution of loss. Hoffman contrasts the hands-off approach taken to medical negligence with solicitors negligence, and observes that this makes little sense in terms of moral responsibility.

[60] Gleeson (1995), p. 432. Gleeson observes a trend in the law as a whole towards discretionary powers tailored to permit judges to meet the exigencies of individual cases. In the torts sphere, it is evident in a heightened reliance on broad concepts of reasonableness, a willingness to dissolve mechanistic distinctions and categories, and a preference to analyse claims under tort rather than contract.

English judicial policy has been rooted for some time in the instinctive fear that liberal medical negligence laws will generate a litigation boom with disadvantageous consequences for both the financing and practice of health care. The specific policy interests which more frequently intrude into these claims were summarised as follows by Lord Denning in *Whitehouse v. Jordan*:

> "[T]ake heed of what has happened in the United States. "Medical malpractice" cases there are very worrying, especially as they are tried by juries who have sympathy for the patient and none for the doctor, who is insured. The damages are colossal. The doctors insure but the premiums become very high; and these have to be passed on in fees to the patients. Experienced practitioners are known to have refused to treat patients for fear of being accused of negligence. Young men are even deterred from entering the profession because of the risks involved. In the interests of all, we must avoid such consequences in England."[61]

Interrogating the Policies

The spectral fear of a malpractice crisis relative in scale to the American experience of the 1970s is frequently advanced to justify the courts' refusal to soften the application of strict medical negligence rules. A fair deal of critical attention has been directed in recent years to the causes of the U.S. crisis. The conclusion which seems to have gained the widest acceptance is that it arose from a complicated interaction between a range of diverse factors, but chiefly the legal process, the insurance industry, and shifts in cultural expectations and demands.[62] This is suggested by the fact that despite fears to the contrary, the so-called medical malpractice crisis failed to spread to

---

[61] *Whitehouse v. Jordan* [1981] 1 W.L.R. 246. See also *Dunne v. National Maternity Hospital* [1989] I.R. 91 at 110, where Finlay C.J. proposed that the "development of medical science and the supreme importance of that development to humanity makes it particularly undesirable and inconsistent with the common good that doctors should be obliged to carry out their professional duties under frequent threat of unsustainable legal claims."

[62] Danzon (1984); Giesen (1988), p. 507; Katz (1984); Picard and Robertson (1996), p. 422; Robertson (1991); Scheid (1998); Teff (1985 a); and Terry (1986).

Canada or to other common law jurisdictions.[63] Doctors have been accused of wilfully exaggerating their own plight by drawing parallels with the position in the United States in an attempt to make the problem seem worse than it actually is.[64] This stands at odds with evidence that doctors are aware that the present operation of fault liability in England is unfair to patients.[65]

In 1974 and 1975 the medical insurance crisis erupted in the United States, when insurers in many states sought premium increases of up to 500 per cent. Between 1976 and 1981, the average malpractice claim rose from \$192,344 to \$840,396, to which obstetricians were most vulnerable.[66] In some states the crisis of cost became a crisis of insurance availability, leaving practitioners with the choice of forming their own insurance companies or going without cover. In response, most states legislated to require the mandatory provision of insurance at reasonable rates to medical practitioners as a precondition to the lawful offering of insurance.[67]

The willingness of juries to award ever higher levels of compensation for medical injuries stands out as an obvious cause of the panic that spread through the insurance industry.[68] This trend seems to continue in the United States, and the statistics suggest that it might be a response to the fact that few malpractice suits are seen to

---

[63] According to recent estimates by the MDU in England, the rate of increase in claims against doctors is currently at 15%—an unremarkable increase, given the comparatively recent development and publicity surrounding the action: as reported in *Law Society Gazette*, May 7, 1998, p. 4.

[64] Jones (1987), p. 45. In the U.K., doctors pay less for unlimited cover than other professionals do for limited cover: doctors pay 0.5–3.5% of pre-tax income, architects 5–15%, solicitors 2–4%, and surveyors 7–10%: Medical Protection Society (1986) 293 B.M.J. 512.

[65] 56% of 161 surveyed doctors expressed a belief that the present compensation system is unfair to patients; only 54% believed it unfair to doctors: Jones and Morris (1989), p. 41.

[66] An out-of-court settlement for a child who was born blind and deaf through meningitis could be expected to receive \$120 million if she lived to the age of 78. 25% of Florida's obstetricians stopped their practice in the wake of this trend: Note (1984). See also Terry (1986).

[67] 50 U.S. states legislated in response to the escalating problem. Some states established voluntary arbitration procedures (*e.g.* Alaska); others restricted the limitation periods within which patients could sue (Indiana); but the bulk of states responded by purporting to place caps on damages (by 1987, 27 states): see Rasor (1993) and Ross (1997).

[68] Danzon (1984); Note (1984). The Prichard Report (*supra*, n. 40, p. 17) found that less than 10% of patients with viable malpractice claims receive compensation in Canada. It further noted that claims for compensation under \$100,000 are routinely discouraged by lawyers (Appendix A, p. 104).

succeed. It was recently estimated that about 70 per cent of all medical malpractice cases are found in favour of the defendant.[69] For those cases that reach trial, the defendant's success rate rises to 81 per cent.[70] But in cases where the court finds in favour of the plaintiff, the jury tends to levy substantial awards of compensation.[71] In the light of this evidence, it seems unrealistic to blame the crisis on the American judges' liberalisation of malpractice rules. It is true that the courts from time to time were moved to manipulate technical distinctions in the plaintiff's favour, and it would seem that this was motivated by a sense that the rules worked an injustice.[72] However, the significant developments of the law in the years preceding the malpractice boom—chiefly, the abolition of charitable immunity and the locality rule[73]—were timely and natural ones, and have been adopted without fuss throughout the common law since.

A range of other factors have been identified as possible causes: the expansion of medical liability insurance; contingency fee arrangements between lawyers and clients; a growth in money spent by Americans on health care services; a greater consumer awareness of medical advances; a sense that market justice demanded a liberalisation of malpractice rules[74]; a general increase in personal injury claims; a growth in the number and complexity of medical treatments; and a break-down in the doctor-patient relationship due to an increase in professional specialisation.[75] The natural litigiousness of American society, and the indomitable writ-peddling of American lawyers, tend to be presented as self-evident causes, though they are begotten more of stereotype than hard fact. Each assumption has

---

[69] "Marketplace: Will Medical Liability Outlays Boost Total Health Care Costs?" (1997), cited in Scheid (1998), p. 5.

[70] *ibid.* According to other findings, the proportion of patients who receive compensation for viable claims is closer to 2%: Brennan (1992).

[71] *e.g.* between October 1995 and September 1996, the average award for Cook County, Illinois was $3,423,425: "Summary & Category Index, Vol. MM" (1996) Cook City Jury Verdict Report, cited in Scheid (1998), p. 5.

[72] See Chapter 4, *supra*, pp. 94–95, 97.

[73] The locality rule enabled physicians to be judged according to the standard that prevailed in their particular locality. The rule was eventually abolished throughout the U.S. in the 1960s: see, *e.g. Brune v. Belinkoff* 235 N.E. 2d 793 (1968).

[74] According to which, "people are entitled only to those valued ends such as status, income, happiness, etc., that they have acquired by fair rules of entitlement, eg, by their own individual efforts, actions or abilities. Market-justice emphasizes individual responsibility, minimal collective action and freedom from collective obligations except to respect other persons' fundamental rights": Beauchamp, "Public Health as Social Justice" in Jaco (1979), pp. 444–445.

[75] Danzon (1984); Note (1984); Project (Various) (1971), pp. 940–942.

been questioned, lawyers on the basis that the malpractice action is a comparably unattractive option,[76] and litigiousness on the basis of available data.[77] Numerous sources accuse the insurance industry of manipulating and perpetuating the sense of crisis. Richard Gerry, acting as President of the Association of Trial Lawyers in America ("ATLA"), observed that the crisis was "artificial", and that insurance companies had grossly inflated their charges to the medical profession on the basis of exaggerated, worst-case-scenario predictions for the late 1970s and the 1980s, which in turn generated escalating health care costs and charges without any corresponding upsurge in the costs of litigation.[78]

Though there have been some recent indications of a mounting willingness in the lower English courts to mitigate the severity of current medical negligence rules,[79] the superior courts in England continue to act defensively and protectively in the interests of the medical profession. Though this stems partly from the fear of a malpractice boom, it is also motivated by a rather pronounced sympathy for the professional reputation of doctors. Lord Denning once tellingly observed:

> "The courts have no hesitation in holding that mistakes made by car drivers or employers are visited by damages; but they make allowances for the mistakes of professional men. They realise that a finding of negligence against a professional man is a serious matter for him. It is not so much the money, because he is often insured against it. It is the injury to his reputation which a finding of negligence involves."[80]

The courts are right to recognise that the professional person is vulnerably reliant on cultivating and maintaining a good reputation. It

---

[76] Hawkins (1985), p. 246 draws attention to the views of American attornies who do not particularly welcome being involved in malpractice claims as they are expensive and time-consuming to prepare, are to a large extent out of their hands since heavily dependent on experts, and carry only a 1 in 4 chance of winning.

[77] It was estimated in a recent survey in America that about 27% of medical injuries to patients were due to negligence, but that only 1 in 8 such victims sued and only 1 in 16 obtained damages (a conclusion which seems to contradict the stereotypical assumption that American society is radically litigious): Harvard Medical Practice Study, summarised by Harris in Cane and Stapleton (1991), p. 289.

[78] ATLA publication Trial, June 1982, at 6, as quoted by Giesen (1988), p. 508.

[79] See Chapter 3, supra, p. 145 and Chapter 5, supra, pp. 213–214.

[80] Foreword to Eddy (1955). In Hatcher v. Black [1954] C.L.Y. 2289, The Times July 2, 1954, Denning L.J. likened attacks on the professional reputation of doctors to daggers through the body.

is not entirely clear, however, why the common law treats the reputation of doctors more sensitively than it does the reputations of solicitors, accountants, or engineers which repeatedly withstand successful litigious challenges against them. In the few instances where plaintiffs have succeeded or come close to succeeding in their claim against a doctor, the presiding judges have demonstrated remarkable semantic dexterity in cushioning any sense that the doctor has fallen from grace. In *Whitehouse v. Jordan*, Donaldson L.J. took care to remark: "There are very few professional men who will assert that they have never fallen below the high standards rightly expected of them. That they have never been negligent. If they do, it is unlikely that they should be believed. And this is as true of lawyers as of medical men. If the judge's conclusion is right, what distinguishes Mr. Jordan from his professional colleagues is not that on one isolated occasion his acknowledged skill partially deserted him, but that damage resulted."[81] In *Clark v. MacLennon*, Peter Pain J. commented: "Counsel for the defendant has referred to Professor Turnbull's Olympian reputation. I hope Professor Turnbull will take comfort in the thought that even Apollo, the god of healing, and the father of Aesculapius, had his moments of weakness." [82]

In consciously impeding the natural evolution of the tort of medical negligence, the courts have frequently voiced the policy fear that an increase in malpractice suits will lead to a corresponding increase in defensive medical practice.[83] In executing their duties, doctors would be prompted to act or omit to act primarily out of fear of legal consequences. This policy tends to refer to the experience of the malpractice crisis in the United States, often in misguidedly sensational terms.[84] There is no hard evidence that this in fact

---

[81] *Whitehouse v. Jordan* [1980] 1 All E.R. 650 at 666, CA.

[82] *Clark v. MacLennon* [1983] 1 All E.R. 416 at 433.

[83] See: *Whitehouse v. Jordan, supra*, n. 81 at 659, CA, per Lawton L.J.; *Roe v. Ministry of Health, supra*, n. 57 at 139; *Sidaway v. Bethlem Royal Hospital, supra*, n. 57 at 1031, CA, per Dunne L.J., at 1035 per Browne-Wilkinson L.J., and [1985] 1 All E.R. 643, HL, at 653 per Lord Scarman, at 657 per Lord Diplock; and *Wilsher v. Essex Area Health Authority* [1986] 3 All E.R. 801 at 810, per Mustill L.J.

[84] See, *e.g. Hughes v. Staunton* Irish High Court, unreported, February 16, 1990, at 52–53, where Lynch J. observed that: "[i]t would certainly be inconsistent with the common good if a state of affairs was reached where . . . a patient attending a hospital for a sprained ankle could not be discharged until a detailed examination of his entire anatomy and physiology had been carried out together with a battery of tests lest he might also be suffering from some abstruse disease not producing any adverse symptoms at the time and the hospital might be sued for discharging him without warning him of it."

occurred for reasons that were not more naturally linked to the privatisation and specialisation of American health care.[85] One high-profile attempt to assess the impact of defensive practice ultimately served more to reveal the difficulties facing any attempt to empirically test this phenomenon.[86] The responses revealed a significant disagreement amongst doctors as to the medical benefits of a wide range of procedures. In only two of the questionnaire's hypothetical scenarios did more than 60 per cent side with the procedure on a cost-benefit analysis. Even though more Californian than North Carolina doctors gave the threat of malpractice suit as their reason, more North Carolina doctors selected to follow the defensive procedure.

Some element of defensive practice is inevitable, whether or not motivated by real threat. Evidence of it exists in the way hospitals tend to treat patients with head injuries: the excessive taking of x-rays; admission to hospital of patients with minor head injuries; and the over-cautious reading of radiographs.[87] The fallacy at the heart of the defensive practice argument is that doctors are presumably well aware that if they perform invasive techniques and procedures on patients which are not strictly necessary, the duty of care they owe to the patient is likely to become correspondingly higher.[88] A doctor who acts responsibly and adheres to standards approved by a body of competent professional opinion is more likely to be sheltered from liability. Of course, general medical practice may itself become defensive over time: unfortunately, much of the *expert* testimony in medical trials involves merely the witness' assessment of the proportion of doctors who are likely to have acted in a similar manner to the

---

[85] The Prichard Report (*supra*, n. 40 at 19) found that some defensive medical practice occurred in Canada, but that the problem had been greatly exaggerated. It concluded that potential liability in negligence had exerted a positive effect on health care, particularly in reducing the risks posed by health care injuries of a recurring type.

[86] Project (Various, 1971): surveyed 100 doctors from each of 10 different specialities in both California (with a high rate of malpractice claims) and North Carolina (with a significantly lower rate) to assess the extent of positive defensive action. Some of the scenarios assumed by the researchers to represent defensive conduct could easily have been justified as a matter of routine necessity. For example, psychiatrists were asked whether they kept detailed records of their examination and treatment of paranoiac patients, as well as retaining any correspondence with them. Attaching any importance to the response that such measures were taken out of a fear of malpractice (the second most popular response) makes little sense given that the most popular response was, sensibly, "to facilitate future treatment".

[87] See Filed (1976) and Jennett (1976).

[88] Jones and Morris (1989), p. 40; Giesen (1988), p. 128; Tribe and Korgaonkar (1991), p. 3.

defendant. Approved medical practice may not be as stable or perceptible as the professional standard model is wont to presume (though the *Bolam* test reflects the uncertainty which may exist in clinical practice by implying that there may be numerous practices which are approved within the medical community). Approval is likely to be all the more splintered where concerned with the wisdom of utilising a range of diagnostic tests and procedures.

In the context of information and disclosure, the courts have eagerly condemned defensive formalism on the basis that it subverts the policies which underpin rules such as the requirement of consent,[89] though the English courts have thus far failed to promote heightened communication between doctor and patient in the hospital context, and instead continue to subject the disclosure action to the professional standard assessment of due care.[90] It has been suggested that defensive clinical responses to disclosure and consent may generate more reliable note-taking and accordingly, more concrete trial evidence.[91] It is also possible that the fear of legal consequences by itself may precipitate higher standards of disclosure as a general practice. Interestingly, in a recent survey of 400 English doctors, 92 per cent of general practitioners and 76 per cent of hospital doctors agreed with the proposition that a "doctor *must* ensure that the patient *fully understands* and consents to *all aspects* of his treatment."[92] It is also possible that enhanced communication with patients will reduce the suspicion which prompts defensiveness in doctors, which proposition has often been recognised by the courts.[93] It is to this concern I finally turn.

---

[89] *e.g. Chatterton v. Gerson* [1981] 1 All E.R. 257 at 265, *per* Bristow J. See Chapter 6, *supra*, pp. 181–182.

[90] See Chapter 5, *supra*, pp. 134–149.

[91] Tribe and Korgaonkar (1991), p. 5.

[92] *ibid.*, p. 4 (emphasis added).

[93] According to the German Federal Constitutional Court: "What is necessary is a responsibly conducted dialogue between physician and patient and, thus, a sharing of responsibilities between them, lest the difficult and often risky work of the medical profession becomes unbearable and develops into some kind of defensive medicine which no longer fulfils the social task the profession is there for" (Bundesverfassungsgericht, July 25, 1979 Entscheidungen des Bundesverfassungsgerichts 52, 131 at 170 and 179). Similar views were voiced in *Wilkinson v. Vesey* 295 A. 2d 676 (1972) at 690, *per* Kelleher J.; and *White v. Turner* (1981) 120 D.L.R. (3d) 269 at 290, *per* Linden J. See chapter 9, *infra*, pp. 251–252.

Chapter 9

Doctor-Patient Communication:
A Pre-emptive Strike?

It has been observed that in medical malpractice suits, the blame factor tends to be higher and the sympathy of society more pronounced.[1] Though there may be many complex reasons for this, not all of them in the law's capacity to redress, it is possible to identify one source in the communication and rapport that exists between doctors and patients. If it is the case that disappointment is proportionately related to expectation, and accusation to the loss of trust, it is equally so that patients who are made to feel estranged from the health care process, and permitted only a minimal amount of explanation and involvement, are more likely to be aggrieved and accusative in the event of an unsuccessful outcome. The disclosure action in many ways exemplifies this dynamic, particularly where it is not anchored to an allegation that the doctor was negligently responsible for the unsuccessful outcome. On the other hand, where patients are encouraged to commit to choice, to assume some responsibility for the palliative management of their illness, they are less likely to extricate themselves from the therapeutic process or to blame the medical profession when through no fault something goes wrong. Some few judges have recognised the primary importance of communication and rapport. Linden J. memorably proposed in *White*

---

[1] "Firstly, there is always human drama—invariably a loved one is snatched away or horribly disabled. Secondly, in all the best myths, a small man fights against almost insuperable odds: gunned down, he battles against the might of doctors, the intransigence of lawyers, penury, and his own dreadful afflictions. Usually he loses, but just sometimes the cavalry of the media takes an interest and he triumphs. The media enjoy being the saviours of the small man, and it is indeed one of their essential functions": Smith (1983), p. 1433.

251

v. Turner that: "the doctor-patient relationship should be improved greatly by the better communication between doctors and their patients. The high level of trust Canadians now have in their doctors should be even higher. Another beneficial consequence may be even fewer malpractice actions than are now instituted in this country."[2]

Over the following pages, I discuss those facets of the doctor-patient dynamic which set it apart from others and merit careful attention by those responsible for developing and shaping the law. I close with the argument that the benefits to be gained from encouraging enhanced dialogue between doctor and patient greatly outweigh the perceived disadvantages, and that the law ought to promote communication, rapport, and patient satisfaction as a primary public policy interest.

Obstacles to Communication

Various psychological analyses—based on observation of doctor-patient behaviour, intuitive reasoning, and the application of well entrenched principles of psychology—have sought to explain why it is that medical paternalism has succeeded for so long as a legitimate health care strategy, with what consequences, and what this tells us about the respective needs and anxieties of patients and doctors. Much has been written about the *infantalisation* of patients and the aggrandising of the doctor when illness brings a person to hospital for relief from pain and illness.[3] This inherent inequality in status has occasionally been recognised by the judiciary. McLachlin J. of the Supreme Court of Canada, for instance, recognised that "the doctor-patient relationship shares the peculiar hallmark of the fiduciary relationship—trust, the trust of a person with inferior power that another person who has assumed superior power and responsibility

---

[2] *White v. Turner* (1981) 120 D.L.R. (3d) 269 at 290. See also *Wilkinson v. Vesey* 295 A. 2d (1972) 676 at 690, where Kelleher J. of the Rhode Island Supreme Court recognised that informed consent may promote a mutuality of interest between doctor and patient, ultimately capable of therapeutic benefit and reduced blame, for if the patient has been made aware of risks he is less likely to be shocked subsequently if they materialise, and "if patient-rapport is high, [he] is much less likely to sue his doctor in the first instance", quoting Morris and Moritz, *Doctor and Patient and the Law* (5th ed., 1971).

[3] Parsons (1951), p. 465; Ssasz and Hollander (1956); Ssasz (1977), p. 2; and Tagliacozzo and Maukscl, in Jaco (1979), p. 196.

will exercise that power for his or her good and only for his or her best interests."[4] There are many intricate factors that conspire to preserve this inequality, particularly in the hospital context. It is worthwhile to identify these, as they often seem to precipitate the destruction in specific cases of doctor-patient rapport.

The relationship into which the patient enters is one of the least ideal in an economics sense.[5] Demand greatly outweighs the supply of medical services. Patients are infrequent consumers of the health care service, and typically become party to a relationship they wish greatly to avoid. Patients rarely possess enough information to make informed health care judgments, and it is difficult for them to adequately appraise the quality of the service before and after treatment. Whereas in the "ideal type of commercial relationship one is not A's customer to the exclusion of other sources of supply for the same needs",[6] it is institutionally quite difficult and often impractical for a patient to obtain other medical advice once he has agreed to be a particular doctor's patient.[7] The doctor's assessment and treatment can not guarantee to be perfect; to this extent, he becomes a joint bearer of the risk of an adverse outcome by necessity and under pressure so to do by the patient.

The plaintiff's loss of control over his body, and ignorance of its cause, contrasts starkly with the doctor's power to illegitimise the patient's negotiating power by diagnosing cancer, AIDS, depression, schizophrenia, and an array of other discrediting traits.[8] Anderson and Helm present the case that it is "through language that social realities are constructed, and through the expression of language that realities can be negotiated".[9] Thus, the "physician gains in power through his or her access to and control over the 'legitimate' language of health

---

[4] *Norberg v. Wynrib* (1992) 92 D.L.R. 4d 449 at 486.
[5] See: Arrow (1963); Fuchs (1966); Mooney and McGuire, "Economics and medical ethics in health care: an economic viewpoint", in Mooney and McGuire (1988), pp. 8–14); and Newdick (1995), pp. 77–78.
[6] Parsons (1951), p. 465.
[7] Traditional medical ethics requires that a doctor not give a second opinion where the first doctor is unaware that the patient is seeking one. Some inroads into these restrictions have been attempted recently under the banner of patients' rights. For instance, under the Declaration of Lisbon (to which Ireland and the U.K. subscribed), "the patient has the right to choose his physician freely": World Medical Association, *Declaration of Lisbon: the rights of the patient*, reprinted in the British Medical Association's *Handbook of Medical Ethics* (London: British Medical Association, 1984), p. 72.
[8] Anderson and Helm, "The Physician-Patient Encounter: A Process of Reality Negotiation", in Jaco (1979), p. 269.

and illness."[10] Language and discourse are powerful controlling tools which are sometimes employed by doctors, whether consciously or subliminally, to affirm their own expertise, and to mystify, depersonalise, desexualise, or intimidate patients. According to Gillet, how a doctor appears may colour his words; his "demeanour and apparent level of concern may influence the patient's perception of how much she is being informed and consulted about her treatment."[11] When things go wrong, the patient will tend to enquire specifically about his condition and treatment; and memory, being "an often reliable but sometimes shifty servant of the mind", will tend to reconstruct this according to what had been discussed with him, so that the doctor's "warmth, courtesy, brusqueness, apparent callousness or whatever will be brought to centre-stage in the patient's reconstruction of the information which raised hopes that are now shattered . . . [and] fed by pain and anxiety."[12]

Doctors are often accused of patronising their patients, particularly those they perceive to be less educated and more working class.[13] In a survey of 739 randomly selected recent patients, Cartwright drew the following observations and opinions of the doctors involved.[14] They didn't say much, speaking only to other doctors, students, or nurses, but instead observed the patient, sometimes nodded, and appeared "rather like gods" at the foot of the bed. They seemed to forget about the patient after walking five yards from the bed, making them feel like a numbered prisoner. They seemed to find out what was wrong with a patient by elaborately and cryptically discussing him very openly with others (such as students). When a patient asked what was wrong, the response was that of a paternalist to a child: "you're doing very well. We'll have you out in no time." They were "aloft", "remote", "abrupt", "superior" seeming, and sometimes "sarcastic", making numerous patients feel "embarrassed", "hypochondriac", or a "nuisance" for asking questions, some patients reporting having felt abashed into silence or inarticulateness by the doctor's cursoriness, confidence, and, occasionally, sarcasm. Doctors tended overwhelmingly not to divulge their names, and patients usually ascertained them from each other or from the ward sister and nurses. In

---

[10] Anderson and Helm, *supra*, n. 8 at 266.
[11] Gillet (1989), p. 119.
[12] *ibid*.
[13] Faulder (1985), p. 114 criticises the lack of training given to doctors in psychology and doctor-patient relations, and the frequently off-putting nature of doctors' body language.
[14] Cartwright (1964), pp. 88–90.

response to this Cartwright observes: "If you know a person's name this helps to identify the person and to create a more personal relationship. Normally middle-class people are introduced, or introduce themselves, with whom they have a relationship which is at all personal. That hospital doctors largely ignore this convention in their dealings with patients suggests that they do not regard the relationship as a particularly personal one."[15] The fact that doctors should sometimes feel this is curious on one level, given that it suggests a more business-like approach to health care, the consumer rights or contractual implications of which have been traditionally resisted by the profession.

The propensity of codes of medical ethics to demand, and individual physicians to expect, trust in the medical relationship, which typically does not reciprocate this veracity or confidence, is said to breed dependency in the patient.[16] Ssasz argues that "much of what passes for "medical ethics" is a set of rules the net effect of which is the persistent infantilization and subjugation of the patient."[17] He draws a comparison with the master's treatment of the negro slave in the South, where kindness was used to pacify and subjugate. Patronising sentiments of kindness for the *poor patient* serve to accomplish an equivalent social effect.

James Bridie, the Scottish playwright and qualified doctor, writes that "there is a temptation for any creature who seems obviously to be doing the work of the Almighty to imagine himself a god. This is particularly so in medicine, and an almost unavoidable error in the hospital physician or surgeon. He is surrounded by respectful and adoring acolytes, and he holds the power of life and death over helpless patients".[18]

That this should often result is hardly surprising. The time honoured deification of the physician from ancient mythology on, and the investment in him of superior moral and social sensibilities, have in effect swathed the physician in some of the noblest symbolic garments possessed by man. Our healers may have indulged this process, but they were never exclusively responsible for it. Man has always tended to mystify knowledge—in equal measures dazzled and terrified by it. Myths through the ages reveal that dire consequences

---

[15] Cartwright (1964), p. 95.
[16] Jones (1984), p. 359.
[17] Ssasz (1984), p. 18.
[18] As quoted by Strauss (1969), p. 384.

are feared and suspected to flow from acquiring deep knowledge of man's inner nature and life. The Greek myths of Aesculapius[19] and Prometheus,[20] and of course the Biblical conception of the Fall of Man through Original Sin, continue to tower as symbols of man's anxious ambivalence towards stealing power through knowledge and of thinking thoughts too great for man.[21] The common thread to these myths would seem to be man's fear of losing those few things he feels certain of, and of attracting punishment for stealing knowledge of that which lies beyond his control. In more modern settings, it is reflected in a panoply of images and adages: the proverbial suspicion that too much reading could lead to insanity; the image of the artist and inventor, all the lonelier and more hermitic for the insights he is privy to; the fear in governments that knowledge is dangerous, encouraging rebellion or dissension; and the widespread insistence of organised religions that blind faith is the key to understanding and redemption, and that rationality or intellectualism lead one to hopeless ruination.

At a more localised psychological level, there is in man, according to Freud, a dread fear of self-knowledge, which he claimed was the greatest cause of psychological illness and neurosis.[22] Defensively, we avoid certain issues and questions, repressing them through *denial*, assuaging them through *transference*, so that we may cling to self-esteem, fearful of despising ourselves through knowledge. Indeed, one of the consequences of this fear of discovery, which mythology shows to be an invariable constant throughout the history of man, is the greater likelihood of *transference*. This phenomenon has been defined in the medical context as:

---

[19] Discussed in Chapter 1, *supra*, pp. 8–9.

[20] According to Greek legend, as set down by Aeschylus in *Prometheus Bound* (trans. 1961), Prometheus was consumed by an extreme greed (*pleonexia*), and in unbounded and insubordinate presumption (*hubris*) trespassed beyond the limits of man (*aitia* and *mesotes*) by stealing fire from the heavens. As *nemesis* from the Gods, he was chained in iron to a Caucasian rock where all day long an eagle fed upon his liver; his punishment, typically reserved for demigods, was directly proportionate to his *hubris*. Mary Shelley's *Frankenstein: Prometheus Unbound* is a more modern reworking of this myth.

[21] This theme is resumed throughout the Bible: in *Ecclesiastics* (i 18), for instance, it is written: "In much wisdom is much grief: and he that increaseth knowledge increaseth sorrow". Interestingly, in *O'Keefe v. Cody*, Irish High Court, unreported, March 11, 1994, at 7, Lynch J. responded to the patient's efforts to research her medical condition by quoting Alexander Pope: "a little learning is a dangerous thing/ Drink deep, or taste not the Pierian spring:/ There shallow draughts intoxicate the brain/ And drinking largely sobers us again."

[22] Maslow (1963) pp. 119–120.

"the attribution to the physician of significances to the patient which are not "appropriate" in the realistic situation, but which derive from the psychological needs of the patient. For understandable reasons a particular important class of these involves the attributes of parental roles as experienced by the patient in childhood. Transference is most conspicuous in "psychiatric" cases but there is every reason to believe that it is always a factor in doctor-patient relationships."[23]

Indeed, at the dawn of organised health care, Hippocrates sagely observed that a patient would think a doctor the worst in the world "if he does not promise to cure what is curable and to cure what is uncurable."[24] In this light, it might valuably be queried whether instead the reason for the survival so long of medical paternalism is that "health care professionals are paternalistic in response to social expectations."[25]

According to Comaroff, placebos are often employed by physicians to enable them to manage patients, to control initial clinical uncertainty, and at the same time to fulfil patient's expectations of the doctor "doing something": they can be viewed "primarily as a function of the way in which doctors have come to use the prescription, and its attendant ritual, to solve fundamental problems inherent in their social situation and in their relations with their patients."[26] Others are of the view that rather than ushering in transparency and objectivity, the scientific revolution of medicine may instead have whetted the public's trust in cures and its acquiescence to the transferred omnipotence of *the other*. Kennedy argues that: "[s]cience has destroyed our faith in religion. Reason has challenged our trust in magic. What more appropriate result could there be than the appearance of new magicians and priests wrapped in the cloak of science and reason? Please understand that it is we, all of us, who have hitched our wagon to the wrong star, scientific medicine."[27]

This psychological reconstruction of the doctor, the composition of unfathomable personal and universal longings, finds obvious expression in the concept of *paternalism*. As a word and strategy of

---

[23] Parsons (1951), p. 453.
[24] As quoted by Katz (1984), p. 6.
[25] Childress (1982), p. 46.
[26] Comaroff (1976), p. 96.
[27] Kennedy (1983), p. 25.

benign control, it is founded variously upon the metaphor of the father-figure in its biological, social, and political manifestations.[28] Varieties of this root metaphor can be glimpsed in images of the doctor as captain of a crew or navigator of a ship. The *transfiguration* of the doctor in this way is evident in numerous accounts, for instance by the world's second heart transplant recipient who documented his conversations with the innovative and legendary Professor Chris Barnard.[29] The patient was in urgent need of intervention and on the verge of death. He described drowsily awakening to see Barnard for the first time: how he "sensed" someone at the foot of the bed, who turned out to "tall, young, good-looking . . .. [whose] hands were beautiful; the hands of a born surgeon . . . He inspired me with the greatest confidence, an invaluable asset in the relations between a surgeon and his patient. I felt somewhat better. Here was a man to whom I would willingly trust my life." The patient next saw Dr Barnard after the first heart transplant patient had died of pneumonia. The doctor looked "haggard . . .. more a martyred Christ." When he was told that the first attempt had failed, the patient responded thus: "I want to go through with it now more than ever—not only for my sake but for you and your team".[30]

Transformations are inevitably fragile, fickle affairs. Where greatness has been vested, failure tends to attract correlatively more intense disappointment and blame. This is evident in the history which surrounds one of the first attempts to implant a wholly artificial heart into a patient in 1969.[31] The patient's wife issued statements through the hospital's publicity office, eulogising the team behind the attempt as gifted "God-given" saviours; after the attempt failed she vented considerable spleen, arguing that her husband had been wantonly exploited and misguided.

Throughout the course of the doctor-patient relationship, the doctor is equally likely to undergo distinct psychological processes which are not always healthy or beneficial. It is possible that a *countertransference* may arise, whereby various unconscious anxieties in

---

[28] Childress (1982), p. 4. At p. 9, he writes that the "image of father in paternalism clearly antedates changes in family structure in this century" so that *parentalism* is now a preferable alternative.

[29] Katz (1984), p. 131–140, drawing from Blaiberg (1968).

[30] Blaiberg, *ibid.*, pp. 65–66.

[31] See: Capron (1974), p. 431; Fox and Swazey (1974), p. 152; and *Karp v. Cooley* 493 F 2d 408 (1974).

the doctor are projected defensively on to the patient.[32] Katz recognises this in Dr Barnard's sense of deflation when his first heart transplant patient died. The doctor responded to the predicament by investing in the deceased various goals and qualities he latterly assumed him to have possessed.[33] This was apparent in Dr Barnard's confusion of identity, and in his reference to salvaging "Washkansky's dream" of a successful heart transplant operation, which Katz interprets to have arisen from his personal guilt and sadness over the death and his wish to resurrect him "intrapsychically". Dr Barnard may also have displayed an inbuilt anger at the patient for abandoning him through death, causing the doctor to leave his second patient waiting for 10 days while he faced the nation.

Others couch this countertransference in terms of the doctor's psychological need to maintain power in the relationship. Anderson & Helm write that the manner in which doctors typically carry out their duties—detached and cool, even in the face of disaster—"may facilitate distance, control, and self-preservation and enable them the psychic energy necessary to face the varied problems of the typical workday."[34] Menninger writes:

> "[T]he doctor has too much narcissistic investment in his power position vis-a-vis the patient. Many of us have developed subtle but disguised ways of maintaining that power position, all in the name of "good treatment." The fact is that medicine, as many of us practice it, encourages a patient's dependency. It does not encourage a more desirable goal, namely the establishment of a kind of parity in the relationship that promotes a greater responsibility by the patient for his own treatment."[35]

What results from these psychological processes is, according to Katz, a therapeutic *autocracy* instead of a therapeutic *alliance*: "Indeed, the longer I reflect upon the idea of informed consent, the more

---

[32] This dynamic may be suggested by evidence that since 1986, almost 100 doctors in England have been called before the disciplinary committees of the General Medical Council accused of improper sexual or emotional affairs with their patients, 15 of whom were struck from the register (as reported in *The Sunday Times*, June 23, 1996).

[33] Katz (1984), p. 139. Based on Bernard and Pepper (1969).

[34] Anderson and Helm, in Jaco (1979), p. 269.

[35] Menninger (1976), p. 537.

convinced I become that professionals' unrecognized coun-
tertransferences are a greater impediment to its meaningful imple-
mentation than are patients' transference."[36]

This possibility is worth considering, as it seems to be borne out
by observations drawn from clinical experience. It may well be the
case that in some instances non-disclosure springs more from the
doctor's unwillingness and less from a fear of adverse emotional
consequences for the patient. It has been observed that doctors often
retreat "in the face of the inexorable progression of [an] illness",
when in fact they have a lot to offer the patient about coping with
that illness.[37] Oken found an overwhelming reluctance (almost 90 per
cent) amongst surveyed surgeons, doctors, and interns to disclose
cancer diagnoses to patients.[38] Almost all of them had resorted to
falsification of diagnosis or evasion a few times, especially where the
cancer was at an advanced stage. The typical justification was that the
patient if informed would have lost all hope and become depressed,
possibly even suicidal. In the most extensive survey of American
doctors and patients, undertaken by the President's Commission,
doctors were asked what they would tell a patient who had fully
confirmed lung cancer at an advanced stage, and the responses
received were the most divisive of all questions asked: 13 per cent
said they would give a straight statistical prognosis; 33 per cent would
tell the patient that it was impossible to say how long he would live
but that it could be for a substantial period of time; 28 per cent
would tell the patient that it was impossible to say how long he'd live
but that most people live no longer than one year; and 22 per cent
would not speculate on how long the patient might live.[39]

Many of the reasons given for withholding disclosure of fatal
illness presume a single permanent impact on the patient. Yet it is
believed that coming to terms with death has different stages, and

[36] Katz (1984), p. 148.
[37] Appelbaum, Lidz and Meisel (1987), p. 162, citing Stetten, "Coping with
Blindness".
[38] Oken, "What to Tell Cancer Patients: A Study of Medical Attitudes", in Lockwood
(1985), p. 112. Depending on the study, 60–90% of doctors favour withholding
disclosure of terminal illness: see Glaser, "Disclosure of Terminal Illness", in Jaco
(1979), p. 227, where the authors cite a range of empirical research from 1964 to
1970. There is, however, some evidence which strongly suggests a change in practice
amongst American doctors. According to Novak et al. (1979), approximately 97% of
doctors surveyed said they preferred disclosing diagnosis to cancer patients.
[39] President's Commission, Vol. 2 (1982), p. 246, Tables 8–8. This study was made of
seven different wards in four different hospitals.

that these can be worked out by chaplains, nurses, family members, and counsellors.[40] Further, the prevailing justifications largely presume that the patient will not already have guessed the truth. Kubler-Ross claims that most terminally ill patients are likely to realise that they are dying in the absence of being told.[41] Oken observed that most surveyed doctors who reported problematic responses to disclosure could only give "vague accounts from which no reliable inference could be drawn . . . Instances of depression and profound upsets came quickly to mind when the subject was raised, but no one could report more than a case or two, or a handful at most. . . . The same doctors could remember many instances in which the patient was told and seemed to do well."[42] Against a backdrop of evidence which suggests that an overwhelming amount of patients wish to be disclosed the truth of terminal illness,[43] the reluctance of doctors so to do may valuably be probed.[44]

The efforts to master the body and mortality in pressurised circumstances naturally strain a doctor's psychological and emotional reserves. Carmichael identifies a constant *dualism* that emerges as a meta-narrative in historical representations of healing and medicine: "good vs. evil, myth vs. science, magic vs. experimentation medicine man vs. herb woman, physician vs. quack".[45] Although terms have changed, this dualism may be distilled down to the observation that "[b]eating back the forces of darkness the larger story of medicine is

---

[40] Abrams (1966) observed that before diagnosis is expressed, cancer patients typically express a desire to know the truth. Following diagnosis, doctors and patients tend to engage in a meaningful exchange of information relative to the arrest and cure of the disease. As the cancer advances, however, patients tend to state that they prefer detailed information but rarely ask further questions. During the terminal stage, communication dwindles to a minimum.

[41] Kubler-Ross (1969).

[42] Oken, in Lockwood (1985), pp. 112–113.

[43] In the surveys conducted by the President's Commission (Vol. 2, 1982), pp. 136, 137, and 244, Tables 4–3, 4–4, and 8–6: 94% of the general public replied that they would wish to be told everything about their medical condition even if unfavourable, and there was negligible difference in response between people of differing health statuses; 96% of the public replied that they would like to be informed by their doctor if they had cancer; and 85% replied that if they had a cancer which was expected to prove fatal within a year, they would prefer if their doctor gave them a realistic estimate of life expectancy. A Gallup opinion poll in 1978 indicated that 82–92 % of the population would want to be told if they had a fatal illness: see Childress JF (1982 at 146).

[44] The need to train doctors in how to break bad news has only recently been acknowledged. See Vaidya *et al.* (1999).

[45] Carmichael and Ratzan (1991), p. 14.

the triumph of true knowledge over error and chaos."[46] Yet at root, and despite the glorious promises made by science and modern technology, medicine remains "a science of uncertainty and an act of probability".[47] Uncertainty and disagreement may frequently arise over the correct diagnosis, etiology, and treatment. Further, the efforts of medical science to master mortal illness are inevitably complicated by the unscientific presence of the human as *person* rather than machine, and the thin line which persists between the physical and the somatic: for, in "the practice of medicine as well as in psychiatry, "therapy *is* diagnosis." Curing the patient and determining the truth about his condition can never be entirely separated."[48]

It has been observed by those trained in psychology that there exists in man a periodically manifest tendency to flee defensively from the chaotic, the uncertain, and the irrational.[49] This is expressed in his tendency, which is both adaptive and maladaptive, to substitute certainty for uncertainty. Lidz, Meisel, *et al.* reported to the U.S. President's Commission that they saw "behind the scenes" how medical staff frequently tended to disagree, and how they were reluctant to convey this uncertainty to patients.[50] It has further been suggested that *specialisation*, though adaptively necessary (since medicine can no longer be mastered in its entirety), may partly be a flight from uncertainty.[51]

Death, the constant social taboo, arguably presents the most problems, emotionally, psychologically, and behaviourally for those who must witness its process.[52] It is also the starkest reminder of the limitations to medical science. According to Waitzkin and Stoeckle, who write in the sociological tradition, a "physician's disclosure of fatal illness is equivalent to a declaration of his own powerlessness."[53] In this sense, the often defensive opposition by health care providers to the withdrawal of extraordinary artificial treatment from vegetative

---

[46] Carmichael and Ratzan (1991), p. 14.
[47] Sir William Osler, as quoted in Bean (1961).
[48] Ramsay, "Freedom and Responsibility in Medical and Sex Ethics: A Protestant View", in Various (1956), p. 1191.
[49] Katz (1984), p. 174.
[50] Lidz, Meisel, *et al.*, "Informed Consent and the Structure of Medical Care", in President's Commission, Vol. 2 (1982), p. 374.
[51] *ibid.* at 188. At 189, the authors write: "Contemporary medicine is not a unitary profession but a federation of professions with differing ideologies and senses of mission."
[52] Encapsulated well by Leo Tolstoy in "The Death of Ivan Ilyitch" (1902).
[53] Waitzkin and Stoeckle (1972), p. 189.

patients[54] may be likened, in the language of Dylan Thomas, to a "rage against the dying of the light".[55] Waitzkin and Stoeckle continue that, apart from palliative therapy and supportive care, "the physician's technical ability to cure has vanished, and admission of this fact implies loss of power."[56] They draw support for this theory from a survey by Glaser and Strauss who discovered that in the cancer wards of a Veterans Administration hospital, where poor patients received free care, doctors had no hesitation in disclosing terminality immediately: "Since the captive lower class patients cannot effectively threaten the hospital or the doctors, the rule at this hospital is to disclose terminality regardless of the patient's expected response."[57] Their observations are similar to those reached via the psychological analysis, but for different reasons. They argue that "a physician's ability to preserve his own power over the patient in the doctor-patient relationship depends largely on his ability to control the patient's uncertainty."[58] This in turn will determine the level and nature of information he conveys. However, where the patient's experience and knowledge of medical matters is more sophisticated and developed, he is more likely to resist renouncing control to the doctor.[59] Appelbaum and Roth discovered, in their study of refusals by patients in seven wards of four different hospitals, that non-compliant patients would either feel angry with their doctors or guilty and apologetic for wanting more information about their treatment.[60] Some would cry, explaining that it was not the case that they were being uncooperative. Some panicked, fearing they would be thrown out of the hospital. The Commission also found that when the medical staff backed off after a refusal, the patient was left feeling bewildered and fearful of having made a disastrous choice. In other cases, when doctors backed off, patients were inclined to

---

[54] See Chapter 1, *supra*, p. 36–38.

[55] As identified in Kennedy (1983), p. 198.

[56] *ibid*.

[57] Glaser and Strauss, *Awareness of Dying* (1965), as quoted by Waitzkin and Stoeckle (1972), p. 189. For doctors' fear of death, see also: Feldman (1992), pp. 1–3; and White (1969).

[58] Waitzkin and Stoeckle (1972), p. 187.

[59] Roth, "Information and the Control of Treatment in Tuberculosis Hospitals", in Friedson (1963). On this point, Anderson and Helm, in Jaco (1979), p. 261 argue that science "mystifies" the doctor; but that when he is demystified, the doctor-patient relationship more properly becomes a negotiation of realities, which adds greatly to the uncertainty which characterises this relationship.

[60] Appelbaum and Roth, "Treatment Refusal in Medical Hospitals", in President's Commission, Vol. 2 (1982), pp. 417–472.

believe that the doctor's proposal had not been necessary in the first place. The investigators were surprised by how often doctors would refer to certain patients as "angry", "difficult", or "uncooperative" given that they found that all bar one of the refusing patients were very willing to talk about the causes of their malaise.

It is difficult to resist the conclusion that a more realistic appraisal of the doctor-patient dynamic, and a more sophisticated understanding of its irrational elements, would improve therapeutic decision making and lessen the subsequent impulse to blame. Unresolved irrationalities inbuilt within the doctor-patient relationship serve to exacerbate relations when health care for one reason or another fails to reach a fortunate conclusion.[61] It has been observed that doctors tend to formulate their treatment recommendations *after* the diagnosis process, and not before actively consulting the patient to ascertain his preferences.[62] It is through the workings of transference that patients, in this way, come to accept or, in a minority of cases, reject the doctor's recommendation, in a way "that later may come to haunt the physician-patient relationship. Particularly in the case of acceptance, agreement and surrender may imperceptibly blend in patients' minds, and subsequently become affected by doubts and even convictions that it was solely the doctor's judgement that led to the treatment."[63] Thus may arise a wrong sense that the doctor

---

[61] Katz (1984), p. 154: "Unless patients' regressive manifestations are moderated through conversation, they should not serve as justification for imposing doctors' authority on the final decision, if only because coercion in the name of psychological health can easily run wild." This view is shared by the editors of the Yale Law Journal, who in 1970 (Vol. 79), pp. 1551 & 1553 observed that when a patient refuses to comply with what their doctor recommends, the doctor tends often to feel personally threatened, causing him to label the patient's decision unreasonable. This "[i]nsistence on the 'irrationality' of patients precludes any attempt to understand the patient's state of mind or lack of motivation. . . . Abandonment of authoritarianism in favour of sharing decision-making power with patients would provide the contemporary doctor with the chance to make more personalized decisions which maximize contemporary technical benefits."

[62] Maslow (1963).

[63] Katz (1984), p. 101. In vivid contrast, Robert Burt (1979), p. 112 controversially argues for a return to medical paternalism and the shamanistic laying on of hands, and interprets the scientific rationalisation of medicine as misguided in its attempt to eradicate the placebo effect and the emotional bond and psychological merging of interests that formerly existed between healer and patient: "The earlier physician who relied on his capacity to soothe his patient as a mother could not invariably predict that his curative ambition would succeed. He did not understand the source of his healing power any more than the patient might understand it; and, more than this, the physician's healing capacity appeared to depend on a reciprocal response

coerced the decision. It could also be the case that enhanced dialogue between doctor and patient may prove psychologically beneficial to the doctor when he later confronts the fact that treatment has failed. It has, for instance, been suggested that complete disclosure in the research context, and the fostering of a collaborative relationship between researcher and subject (wherein the subject appreciates the good he is doing for future patients), may appease the sense of guilt which researchers are apt to feel when they have compromised the subject or patient's immediate health.[64]

The emergence of blame is responsible not only for breeding a general bitterness and resentment against the medical profession; it also seems at a personal level to provoke defensive responses by health carers, which may work counter-productively to fan rather than quench the proverbial flames. There has been some internal acknowledgment of this phenomenon. Arnold Simanowitz, the director of Action for Victims of Medical Accidents ("AVMA") in Britain, wrote that his experience of doctors was that they "regarded any patient who dared to suggest that there had been no accident as their enemy. The hospitals seemingly abounded with people who were just waiting to launch opportunistic legal claims against the doctors who, if they were unable to defend themselves against this threatening avalanche, would soon be driven to emigrate, or give up the practice of medicine altogether."[65] By contrast, Simanowitz has estimated that some 70 to 80 per cent of patients who come to the AVMA seek *satisfaction* rather than financial compensation:

> "They want to know what happened. Why, for example, all their friends recovered fully from their hysterectomy within anything from two months to six months, whereas they are still suffering from pain and incontinence some two years later. They want a clear explanation which does not smack of a cover-up and an admission of wrong doing if that is appropriate. And, finally, they want, almost above all, an apology—not the sort of apology that I keep hearing from the profession—'I am sorry that the result of your operation was not expected and for the awful suffering that you have undergone, but you know all operations involve risk and you were just unlucky".[66]

from the patient."
[64] Epstein and Janowsky (1969) and Park, Covi, and Uhlenhuth (1967).
[65] Simanowitz (1986), p. 109.
[66] *ibid.* p. 106.

Benefits of Enhanced Communication

Enhanced disclosure and communication between doctor and patient need not be justified exclusively by recourse to autonomy principles. Research findings strongly suggest that disclosure, if sensitively made, is likely to be of therapeutic benefit to the patient; and it is worth noting that 56 per cent of doctors surveyed for the U.S. President's Commission expressed the conviction that increasing the patient's role in decision-making would improve the quality of medical care.[67] According to Egbert: "Absence of preoperative fear, and consequently the occurrence of postoperative psychological disturbance, is largely attributed to a lack of information about the impending stresses of surgery."[68] Park *et al.* found that patients in a nonblind placebo trial showed more symptomatic improvement than did patients in a double-blind study, and concluded on this basis that "[p]erhaps attempts to keep secrets from patients, such as the research nature of a treatment, in conjunction with obvious clues that the treatment is research, can leave patients uneasy and unclear about what is really going on."[69] Preoperative counselling has been shown to reduce anxiety and complications at the convalescence stage,[70] and to make childbirth and the treatment of cancer more bearable.[71] These reports tend to conclude that information forces patients to confront the reality of their illness, and in this way to emotionally fortify themselves. It renders expectations more realistic, whilst allowing patients to inhabit a role in shaping their own recovery or confronting and planning according to what may be an inevitable outcome.[72]

Levinson *et al.* discovered a direct link between lack of communication and litigation.[73] This view is supported by evidence that the bulk of cases against doctors centre on breakdowns in communication instead of professional competency,[74] and further by evidence that (where possible) patients tend to leave doctors who do not

---

[67] Simanowitz (1986), p. 282, Table 9–12: 22% believed that it would have no effect on health care, and 16% that it would reduce the quality.
[68] Egbert *et al.* (1964).
[69] Park *et al* (1967), p. 353.
[70] Wilson (1981).
[71] Levy *et al.* (1960).
[72] Brazier (1987), p. 176.
[73] Levinson *et al.* (1997).
[74] Richards (1990).

involve them in treatment decisions.[75] Research findings clearly demonstrate that patient satisfaction often depends upon the extent to which patients have been informed and involved at the pre-treatment stage.[76] Some even report positive effects on the patient's progress and recovery to the extent that a correlation between communication and physical health cannot be dismissed.[77]

It has been proposed, on the basis of clinical research, that involving patients more in their health care decisions significantly increases their compliance with prescriptions and regimens, thereby minimising loss to health care resources.[78] It may also be the case that strengthening the notion of disclosure as *duty* may serve to promote more detailed history-taking and medical records. The medical negligence cases suggest that medical records tend to record clinical observations and therapeutic measures but little of what has been disclosed, thus creating problems later over what exactly was said, by whom it was said, and how it was absorbed by the patient.[79]

The disclosure issue offers an opportunity to repersonalise the medical relationship, mitigating the effects of the ongoing scientific and technological rationalisation of health care which, it is widely felt, has caused doctors to increasingly neglect the human aspect of their skill. More commonly criticised are the effects science has wrought for the selection and training of doctors, and its tendency to precipitate its own development.[80] Technologically "new methods for

---

[75] Kaplan *et al* (1996).

[76] Ong *et al*. (1995). See also Turner *et al*. (1996), where a survey of 165 patients with Hodgkin's disease found that irrespective of the risk to which patients were exposed, and irrespective of treatment outcomes, patients who were satisfied that they had been given adequate information were correlatively happier with the overall process.

[77] Stewart (1995).

[78] See: Davis (1967); Dimatteo and DiNicola (1982); Morris and Kanouse (1982); and Stone (1979), p. 54. However, some studies yield contradictory results. One found that a formal relationship increased compliance: Donabedian and Rosenfeld, "Follow-up study of chronically ill patients discharged from hospital", as cited in Francis *et al*. (1969), p. 535. Another found that a warm friendly relationship increased compliance: Charney *et al*. (1967). Francis *et al*. (1969), p. 538 differed from those surveys by dealing with short-term complaints and relationships with doctors. They found that while "friendliness or warmth on the part of the doctor as perceived by the patient did not in itself result in increased compliance . . . in cases in which the mother stated that the doctor did not *seem* friendly, there was a significant reduction in compliant behaviour". However, "highly satisfied patients were significantly more compliant (53.4%) than those who were grossly dissatisfied with their clinic visit (16.7% compliance)."

[79] Waitzkin and Stoeckle (1972), pp. 183–184. See Chapter 5, *supra*.

[80] It is significant that the U.S. President's Commission (Vol. 1, 1982), p. 131 accepted

diagnosis and treatment . . . [have] tended to become ends in themselves",[81] whilst doctors have been encouraged to view themselves as scientific problem solvers.[82] It has been said that the amalgamation of primary sciences into the university curriculum, and the emphasis and weight devoted to pure science, has divorced *health* care from its origins in holism under which illness was treated both psychologically and somatically.[83] The past lack of serious instruction in psychology, behavioural sciences, and community medicine may have transmitted a particular cultural sensibility, an orthodox scepticism of the psychological with the consequent relegation of non-somatic sources as last options suggestive of personality dysfunction.

It is often disingenuously argued against optimal disclosure in specific cases that too much information of a pessimistic nature would have engendered fear and anxiety in the patient.[84] It is improbable that a modern hospital doctor would acquaint himself sufficiently with the patient to ascertain if distress is genuinely likely to accompany disclosure. A conclusion of this nature might require "a profound knowledge of the most intimate details of the patient's life history, his characteristic ways of coping with personal crises, his personal and vocational commitments and aspirations, his feelings of obligation toward others, and his attitude toward the completeness or incompleteness of his experience."[85] Notwithstanding, the doctor

---

after extensive research that the prevailing selection policy results in a disproportionate emphasis on memorisation rather than observational skills; ultimately this draws "applicants who are least likely to espouse a humanitarian view of the medical enterprise—individuals who are tough, competitive, single-minded, and narrowly focused in the 'hard' biological sciences."

[81] Bloom, "Some Implications of Studies in the Professionalization of the Physician", in Jaco (1958), p. 315.

[82] See Kutner, "Surgeons and Their Patients: A Study in Social Perception", in Jaco (1958), p. 395.

[83] For an account of holism in ancient Greek and Chinese medicine, see Kao (1976), p. 181, where it is proposed that the "key to health and maturity is wholeness, balance and harmony."

[84] Clifford Hawkins (1985), p. 191, Fig. 33, reproduces a parody consent form drafted by American physicians, which includes the following possible risks: "Large artery may be cut and I may bleed to death. . . . Clot may develop in these veins which will loosen when I get out of bed and hit my lungs, killing me. . . .I may slip in hospital bathroom. I may be run over going to the hospital. The hospital may burn down." This is followed by a statement that the patient now understands "the anatomy of the body, the pathology of the development of hernia . . . the physiology of wound healing", etc.

[85] Buchanan (1978), pp. 381–382. At 382, he writes: "In a society in which the personal physician was an intimate friend who shared the experience of families under his

must do more than *predict* the effects of disclosure, he must *evaluate* whether it is *best* for the patient that he remain ignorant of certain information.[86] Beliefs that information is likely to endanger fear in the patient are permitted to revolve around a small cluster of sensational cases and clinical anecdotes which have few firm roots in clinical and psychological reality.[87] Indeed, the President's Commission concluded that the therapeutic privilege—which vests in doctors a limited discretion not to disclose some information in their patient's best interests—has been vastly overused as an excuse for not informing patients of facts they are entitled to know; further, that doctors should explain far more precisely what they mean when they refer to terms like "harmful", "negative", "upsetting", and "anxiety", to ground this type of defence.[88]

Sometimes it is argued, particularly against informed consent doctrine, that patients in general lack the capacity to meaningfully understand medical information or to base their decisions reliably upon it.[89] Research suggesting that this is so has been widely criticised on the grounds that it does not demonstrate that patients *cannot* understand the material, merely that they *did not* in the circumstances.[90] This conclusion was reached by the U.S. President's Commission: 48 per cent of surveyed doctors stated that in their experience, 90 to 100 per cent of their patients understood most aspects of their treatment and procedures if sufficient time was spent explaining it; 34 per cent believed that 70 to 80 per cent of patients could understand the information to this extent.[91] Empirical findings for and against patient-understanding tend to be inconsistent.[92] They are often discredited for lacking scientific credibility, in particular for failing to study appropriate control groups, and for disingenuously employing "an operational definition based on the patient's ability to use information, and to use it in a specific way, namely, to make the

---

care, it would be somewhat more plausible to claim that the physician might possess such knowledge. Under the present conditions of highly impersonal specialist medical practice it is quite a different matter."

[86] *ibid.* p. 382.
[87] See: Kaplan *et al.* (1977); Katz (1977); and Appelbaum, Lidz, & Meisel (1987), p. 96.
[88] President's Commission, Vol. 1 (1982), p. 96.
[89] See Ingelfinger (1972).
[90] See: Appelbaum, Lidz and Meisel (1987), pp. 138–140; and Meisel and Roth (1983).
[91] President's Commission, Vol. 1 (1982), p. 59.
[92] For instance, Elling R *et al.* (1960) found that low education was linked to poorer understanding and diminished co-operation in patients suffering from rheumatic heart disease. Yet Davis and Eichhorn (1963) found the reverse for cardiac patients.

very decision for which it was initially provided."[93] Meisel and Roth sensibly propose that disclosure law policy should instead be based "largely on values, informed but not dictated by sound social science inquiry"; and moreover that informed consent should be interpreted to govern the *manner* in which medical decisions are made rather than its *outcome*.[94] In this way, understanding and recall would not be prerequisites to making a proper informed consent. Praising *informed consent* as a label on the grounds that it avoids cumbersome overlaps with "understanding" and "competence", they point out that many patients simply don't want to make decisions when sick, and that this could be for a variety of reasons rooted in their dependency and consequential wish to be passive participants in the process.

There is the additional problem that a legal requirement of understanding may serve in practice to undermine a patient's decision where it diverges from the medically prudent recommendation. Informed consent theory is of the view that patients ought to be given the opportunity to make their own decisions whether or not these appear prudent, and that patients possess "the right to take decisions based on factors other than pure reason, [which] embraces the right to take a *wrong* decision."[95] It does so in the knowledge that the "quality of life is intensely personal",[96] and that a patient, if given the opportunity, might wish to act upon values and preferences which are subjectively compelling only to that person. In one survey, about 20 per cent of patients expressed a preference for radiation treatment instead of surgery for the treatment of their throat cancer, because the former, though not as effective, was less likely to deprive them of speech.[97] The treatment of laryngeal cancer has been tested as another example of the necessity for autonomous choice. At stage T3 carcinoma of the larynx, a laryngectomy (partial excision of the larynx) will result in loss of normal speech; by contrast, radiation treatment will preserve speech. The first carries a 60 per cent rate of survival for the following three years, whereas the second carries a 30 to 40 per cent survival rate for the following three years. One study by the Harvard Medical School showed that, under these odds, 19 per cent would choose radiation and that 24 per cent would choose

---

[93] Meisel and Roth (1983), p. 296.
[94] *ibid.*, p. 340.
[95] Brazier (1987), p. 175.
[96] *ibid.*
[97] "What Are My Chances, Doctor?: A Review of Critical Risks" Office of Health Economics (1986), as cited by Brazier (1987), p. 175.

radiation if there was an option of a delayed laryngectomy.[98] More recently, research published in the British Journal of Cancer found that in terms of influencing choice of therapy, a majority of long-term survivors felt that short-term side-effects were more, or equally, as important as late morbidity.[99] Patients tended unpredictably to attach more weight to issues such as weight-gain and fatigue, and less to the prospect of infertility or risk of relapse, prompting the researchers to conclude that patients do not necessarily share their doctors' priorities in treatment decision-making.

Ultimately, enhanced communication between doctor and patient may engender a more softened exercise of professional paternalism and a sharing of the responsibility over what is to be done *for* rather than *to* the patient. Patients ought to be drawn into the decision-making stage to the extent that they are fully aware that they may *choose* to follow the course which the doctor in his expertise recommends ought to be taken; and equally, doctors ought to recognise that medically imprudent preferences may valuably reflect a patient's personal values. In this way, a doctor's professional advice should perceptibly become the "yardstick against which patients can measure their own inclinations and . . . a stimulus to further questioning and discussion if the recommendation is not one the patient agrees with."[1]

Promoting Disclosure and Communication

It is clearly in the best interests both of patients and health carers that patients be given the opportunity to grasp important information in a rudimentary manner. The most recurring stumbling block to understanding has been the manner in which medical information is conveyed. In a large-scale investigation of verbal interaction in a paediatric clinic, Francis, Korsch, and Morris found that there was a "tendency for the doctor, especially when faced with a child with gastrointestinal disturbance, to prescribe a fairly complex, graded feeding regimen with different strengths of formula at different points in time, with variously restricted menus and with detailed instructions. . . .. [s]ome of which were so complex that the research

---

[98] Beauchamp and McCullough (1984), p. 147.
[99] Turner *et al.* (1996).
[1] President's Commission, Vol. 1 (1982), p. 76.

workers found them hard to interpret and were not surprised to learn that parents had floundered."[2] In an assessment of five representative surgical consent forms, Grunder found that the readability for each was equivalent to standards required of upper undergraduates or graduates.[3] Four were written in the style and content of a scientific journal, and the other of a specialised academic magazine.

Various alternatives have been tested and proposed. Morrow, Gootnick, and Schmale tested 77 patients for their recall of seven types of information communicated to obtain an informed consent.[4] 37 patients were placed in an immediate group (who signed the consent after consultation and communication in the usual way) and 40 in a delayed group (who brought the informed consent form home to peruse, before signing it on their next visit one to three days later). Within 24 hours of signing the form, each patient was interviewed for 10 to 20 minutes. In terms of understanding the relevant procedures, purpose, and risks, the delayed group achieved almost 100 per cent success. Whereas about 70 per cent and 78 per cent of the delayed group properly understood alternatives and diagnosis respectively, only 40 per cent and 35 per cent of the immediate group did. Delaying decision making in this manner, where possible, has been advocated by the U.S. President's Commission and other investigators on the grounds that it gives the patient an opportunity to discuss the material and the options with family and friends.[5]

Informed consent need not be in any particular form. Disclosure necessary to an informed consent raises issues that have been deemed legally and ethically distinct (though related) from the need to obtain a basic consent. Disclosure in this sense is not a static legalistic undertaking, but should be tailored to the special qualities of the patient, his medical complaint, and the range of potential treatments. Nor must the information be precise or certain. One rather negative view might hold that *informed* consent is impossible whilst medical or scientific knowledge is uncertain.[6] Absolutism of this nature is unhelpful to the debate. It is at this stage taken as given, equally for lawyers as doctors, that uncertainty persists within medical science,

---

[2] Francis, Korsch, and Morris (1969), p. 539.
[3] Grunder (1980).
[4] Morrow, Gootnick, and Schmale (1978).
[5] President's Commission, Vol. 1 (1982), p. 126. See also Silberstein (1974), p. 156 and Stuart (1978), p. 74.
[6] Jenkins (1996), p. 83.

though in some areas more than in others. It is submitted that in instances where acute uncertainty exists, patients should be informed of this fact: indeed, there is a strong case to be made for disclosure across the board of the limits to medical judgment. Disclosure of a more pragmatic nature, if sensitively made, might serve to minimise the frustration of a patient's expectations, and to encourage him to view his treatment as a collaborative enterprise steered by the doctor's medical expertise.

Hawkins proposes the following.[7] To overcome patients' embarrassment and awkwardness, patients should be encouraged to ask questions or to write down issues for discussion on the next ward round. Ward rounds should be divided into two types: academic and personal (both devoted to talking with patients, preferably in a separate room and not the hospital ward). There should be a separate heading on the case-notes for communication, and this should be used to note any personal dimensions (such as marital difficulties, etc.). Written information is cheap, and junior doctors should be encouraged to prepare these for their seniors (also as a way of encouraging them to think in terms of patient communication). Doctors should be taught communication skills whilst in college. As it is, they are forced to learn these skills from their ward seniors:

> "Talking is not enough. In no other field of life is the written word so neglected: when buying a car or radio, brochures and pamphlets are provided—whereas someone undergoing a major operation is brushed off with a few words during a busy round. To expect anyone to understand and remember medical details after a brief talk is absurd. Lectures and seminars to medical students are supplemented by hand-outs and reading lists; seldom do they learn anything solely by listening, yet patients are hardly ever given anything in writing."[8]

It has been pointed out that "formal decision-analysis is unfamiliar to most patients, whereas physicians are trained in problem-solving. Thus, armed with adequate information about a patient's values, the physician may be in a better position to decide effectively what is best for the patient than the patient even if he has been informed of all the medical information and then makes his decision."[9] According to

---

[7] Hawkins (1985), pp. 282–286.
[8] *ibid.* p. 283.
[9] Weiss (1985), p. 186.

the U.S. President's Commission, if a doctor believes the patient's decision is the result of defective reasoning powers or a mistaken understanding of the facts, he should "work with the patient toward a fuller and more accurate understanding of the facts and a sound reasoning process" rather than declare the decision wrong.[10] Where a doctor believes the decision to be wrong, he should still balance the interests of self-determination and well-being. That balance will be affected by the consequences for the patient of the decision he has made. Where the consequences are more severe, scrutiny of the decision may be expected to be greater.

The Audit Commission has been critical of the steps taken by the NHS and hospitals to ensure patients are informed and make intelligent decisions:

> "[F]ifty per cent of the urologists and surgeons in [the survey] who treat men with benign prostratic hyperplasia do not mention the risks and complications associated with transuretheral resection of the prostrate in the out-patient clinic unless the patient asks about them. Instead, they leave that discussion to the junior doctor who interviews the patient on the ward, to obtain his signed consent just before the operation. This means that the patient first hears of the risks after the decision to operate has been made."[11]

According to Giesen, communication breakdown is most apt to occur "where the care is provided either by numerous personnel working shifts, or by teams of highly specialized professionals whose individual responsibilities may be defined less by the overall informational (and other) needs of the patient than by particular diseases or organ systems."[12]

The common law has consistently recoiled from imposing direct liability on hospitals for the breach of a non-delegable duty of care, beyond administrative duties and the provision of adequate or competent staff and equipment.[13] A majority of state courts have rejected attempts to impose non-delegable duties on hospitals to provide an informed consent, on the basis that the treating doctor

---

[10] President's Commission, Vol. 1 (1982), p. 60.
[11] Audit Commission (1993), para. 63.
[12] Giesen (1988), p. 372.
[13] See generally: Note (1979); Note (1983); and Chapter 2, *supra*, pp. 42–44.

possesses the expertise necessary to the discharge of that task.[14] The common law generally requires that the doctor who is to operate or treat the patient must be responsible for making disclosure, and this is equally the case whether the action is phrased in negligence, battery, or breach of contract.[15] It may be unwise to tamper with this rule. First, there is a close temporal link between disclosure of information necessary to the obtaining of a basic consent (which the law also requires must be conveyed by the treating doctor). Secondly, the doctor is best placed to know what risks and alternatives arise for advance consideration. Thirdly, if the defences of therapeutic privilege and emergency are to properly apply, disclosure must come from the party who is to treat, particularly where these relate to complications which arise during the course of treatment. Fourthly, a more communicative, sensitive exercise by doctors of their service might reduce the gulf traditionally perceived to exist between doctors and nurses in the administration of care.[16]

Fears that the implicit motive of informed consent doctrine was to open the floodgates to more numerous and successful malpractice claims, and indirectly to strict liability for a greater spread of unsuccessful medical treatment,[17] have proved naive in the light of empirical evidence that it has not and, more persuasively, in the light of the judicial rules and decisions themselves.[18] Indeed, judicial development of the doctrine of informed consent has been widely criticised on the basis that it does not achieve the goals to which it

---

[14] See *Roberson v. Menorah Medical Center* 588 S.W. 2d 134 (1979). However, some courts have recognised a direct duty on hospitals to ensure that an informed consent has been obtained by their doctors. See: *Magana v. Elie* (1982) 439 N.E. 2d 1319; and *Cooper v. Curry* 589 P. 2d 201 (1978).

[15] See in particular, *Considine v. Camp Hill Hospital* (1982) 133 D.L.R. 3d 11.

[16] The potential for conflict between doctors and nurses in matters of disclosure and communication can not be made light of. Significantly, the first code of the American Nurses Association in 1950 stressed the nurse's obligation to carry out doctors' orders, whereas the revised code of 1976 stressed the nurse's obligations to patients. The International Council of Nursing's code underwent a similar change in its 1973 revision. Indeed, there has been evidence of concern amongst the nursing staff in England over the lack of disclosure made by doctors to patients. See: Turton, "Wall of Silence" (1986) 82:15 *Nursing Times* 23; McGarr, "Final Knowledge" (1986) 82:14 *Nursing Times* 52.

[17] Meisel (1977).

[18] See Chapter 4, *supra*, pp. 103–105. The effect of *Reibl v. Hughes* (1980) 114 D.L.R. 3d 1 on Canadian law proved interesting. Trumpeted initially as a radical breakthrough, in much the same way as *Canterbury v. Spence* (1972) 464 F. 2d 772 had been in North America, its effects on the outcome of malpractice cases were demonstrated ten years later to have been minimal: see Robertson (1991).

aspires.[19] The ideology of informed consent law has inevitably been compromised by its context—personal injury arising from an unsuccessful medical outcome, subject then to the institutional parameters of an adversarial system of proof. The most significant hurdle for plaintiffs has been proof of causation, namely proof that the patient would have chosen not to undergo the treatment had due disclosure been made at the relevant time. North American courts have decided that this must be assessed objectively according to the *reasonable person in the patient's shoes*.[20] The potential constraints which such a scheme places on the supposed goals of informed consent are many and severe, since they minimise the opportunities to safeguard a patient's right to make a decision different to that which the reasonable patient may be presumed to favour. It is difficult to afford more rigorous protection wherever proof of decisional causation is required, insofar as testimonial answers to hypothetical questions which plaintiffs subsequently make at disclosure trials must, as a matter of common sense and legal policy, be treated by the court with some degree of caution.

It is also so that within informed consent, there is much scope for discretion in the assessment of *reasonableness*.[21] Despite their different wording and points of enquiry, the reasonable patient (informed consent) and reasonable doctor (professional standard) tests are broad enough to potentially yield the same result in many cases.[22] This is

---

[19] Of these, the most vehement critic is Jay Katz (1984), pp. 71–72, who argues that the "strong commitment to self-determination at the beginning of the [*Canterbury*] opinion gets weaker as the opinion moves from jurisprudential theory to the realities of hospital and courtroom life. By the end, the opinion has only obscured the issue it intended to address: the nature of the relationship between the court's doctrine of informed consent, as ultimately construed, and its root premise of self-determination " Katz in particular targets the failure of the common law to appraise disclosure under a battery analysis which would recognise that non-disclosure is inherently intentional, and the inability of current causation requirements to protect the right to make decisions which are not uniform or coincident with the reasonable person. See also Silverman (1989).

[20] See Chapter 7, *supra*, pp. 203–206.

[21] A reality which has caused Jay Katz (1977), p. 138 to bemoan that "[o]nly in dreams or fairy tales can 'discretion' to withhold crucial information so easily and magically be reconciled with 'full disclosure' ".

[22] Ultimately, this will depend upon the extent to which the court is willing to censure medical opinion. In the Irish Supreme Court decision of *Walsh v. Family Planning Services* [1992] 1 I.R. 496, advocators of the reasonable patient test (O'Flaherty J. and Hederman J.) and of the reasonable doctor test (Finlay C.J.) found in favour of the disclosure made, whilst McCarthy J. and Egan J., who were less willing to articulate general principles, dissented. One may further recall that in *Sidaway v. Bethlem Royal*

because each is a product of negligence law whose generality gives the court a wide berth in balancing fact and legal policy. Just as it is possible that "informed consents" can be smuggled in through the back-door of the reasonable doctor test (via provisos and qualifications to the defence of general practice), it is possible too that patients may fail to assert their rights to informed consent under that doctrine (where the court, for example, narrowly defines *material* risk or widely defines *therapeutic privilege*).[23] There are many reasons why the courts should retain a good measure of flexibility within the legal model it chooses. Admittedly, the use of vague signifiers to categorise risks—collateral, real, material, general, specific, special, etc.—is unlikely to advance the cause of legal certainty and predictability. Yet some generality is necessary, if the policy of encouraging disclosure is not to be defeated by bureaucratic obedience. The courts have consistently held that enhanced disclosure does not necessarily require "total" disclosure,[24] nor that doctors "give complicated seminars on medicine to all of their patients".[25] Rather, it requires "that patients should be treated as intelligent, mature and rational individuals" and that there be "better communication between doctors and their patients."[26]

Under traditional medical negligence rules, once the defence of general practice is sanctified in court by a defendant's professional seniors or peers, corralled by counsel as expert witnesses, it becomes the court's legal paradigm of reasonable care and skill. It is against this that the particular challenge must ordinarily be appraised, introducing to the proceedings, well in advance of judgment, an air of determinacy. In light of the many opportunities within the

---

Hospital [1985] 1 A.C. 871 HL, Lords Templeman and Bridge both advocated a reasonable doctor test, yet they respectively proffered as examples of risks which ought *clearly* to be disclosed, a 4% risk and a 10% risk of serious injury.

[23] See, *e.g. Arato v. Avedon* (1993) 23 Cal. Rptr 2d 131 at 144, where the California Supreme Court overturned a decision that the defendant doctor was under a duty to disclose statistical life expectancy data to a patient dying of pancreatic cancer. The court entertained, and was influenced, by evidence that it was not general practice to disclose this information unless asked for it. The court accepted that expert evidence of general medical practice is now subsidiary when a court is considering the duty to disclose; however, it acknowledged that in some cases, such evidence will be pivotal to the issue of due disclosure.

[24] According to Robinson J. in *Canterbury v. Spence, supra,* n. 18 at 786, cases which refer to "full" disclosure envisage something less than "total" disclosure, recognising that doctors are not required to "discuss with their patients every risk of proposed treatment—no matter how small or remote."

[25] *White v. Turner, supra,* n. 2, at 290, *per* Linden J.

[26] *ibid.*

negligence model to restrain the development of informed consent, and in light of the bad press which medical negligence continually receives for its willing deference to expert medical witnesses, it is perhaps surprising that informed consent is not more readily embraced as a concessionary symbolic move by the English and Irish courts. For, by distinguishing disclosure issues as something the court is not dependent on expert testimony to decide, the status and nature of expert medical testimony may ultimately benefit from an appreciation of its specific relevance. For some time now, the professional standard model has permitted rough speculative estimates of professional support for non-disclosure to discharge important decision-making functions of the court. Justice must be seen to be done in the courtroom. This means that reliance on experts ought to be at all times justifiable, lest the rationale for the professional standard be perceived to be a disinclination rather than inability of the courts to hold the reins when administering justice in cases of medical negligence.

The doctrine of informed consent does not necessarily serve to diminish the doctor's role within the medical relationship. Its definition of materiality of risk—in terms of *what the physician knows or ought to know what the reasonable patient would deem material*—may be understood to prod him to ascertain how the patient wishes to exercise his power of choice. The availability of a therapeutic privilege and emergency exception may be construed to enable doctors to fulfil their ethical priorities, but in such a way that these are more specifically used (since they may have to be justified at a later stage). The court, in turn, benefits from a more focused justification by the defendant as to why disclosure was not made in the particular case.

A decision to assess the standard of disclosure by the application of generic principles already employed throughout the law of negligence (via a reasonable person or patient test), would not necessarily mark an attempt to banish the views of medical experts from the court, as Lord Bridge mistakenly believed in *Sidaway*.[27] The court may yet be guided by expert medical testimony to establish: whether a risk is material (its statistical likelihood, its known consequences, its "character"—whether general or specific); how the reasonably prudent patient might have behaved; and whether or not non-disclosure

---

[27] *Sidaway v. Royal Bethlem Hospital, supra* n. 22 at 899, HL.

can objectively be excused in the given circumstances under a therapeutic privilege.

It cannot safely be said that a reasonable patient test is likely to be more unruly, less predictable than its counterpart. Indeed, as it is, disclosure trials tend to suggest much disparity between expert witnesses on *general* disclosure practices. More persuasively, as a matter of intuitive logic, there is unlikely to exist within the medical profession meaningful *general* disclosure practices. Non-disclosure which is later justified as inhering in an unwillingness to alarm or frighten a patient presupposes that some *specific* attempt has been made to ascertain the emotional make-up of the particular patient. By contrast, expert testimony of general disclosure practices tends ultimately to amount to the vouchsafing of mere *opinion* as to what the expert doctor would have said in similar circumstances. The artificiality of the professional standard, where medical experts seem to conspire to exonerate the defendant's impugned discretion, is perhaps most apparent when the analysis is on information and patient choice, an artificiality which no amount of tentative judicial provisos and qualifications can rewrite, and which is further exasperated by a pervasive sense that such a small amount of dialogue could have avoided so much subsequent legal difficulty.

What ultimately distinguishes the informed consent and the professional standard models is that each is guided, at least ostensibly, by different policies, by a distinct cultural *esprit* and focus, one which tends to couch as a doctor's duty what the other tends to couch as a patient's right. A reasonable patient test undeniably carries with it the possibility of significantly more rigorous and meaningful standards of disclosure. It is difficult to cavil with the acknowledgment by the U.S. President's Commission that "[g]reat advances in medical technology deserve to be matched by improvements in the human side of health care", and that the objective of repersonalising medical relationships may best be achieved by giving centrality to communication.[28] Whilst it is difficult to compel changes in human discourse when so much depends on the spirit in which it is conducted,[29] it is within the capacity of the law to affect social change indirectly and gradually. The law ought to transmit a signal to the medical profession which is firm but encouraging, beneficial, and likely to ultimately achieve the most legal clarity. To this extent the courts

---

[28] President's Commission, Vol. 1, (1982), p. 114.
[29] *ibid.* at 147.

should seek to pre-emptively avoid the prevarication which is likely to occur increasingly within its existing structures when fresh challenges are assayed by new or emerging concerns (such as elective treatment, inquisitive patients, research trials, experimental treatment and wrongful birth claims). Patients ought to be drawn into the decision-making process to the extent that they are made fully aware that they may *choose* to follow the course which the doctor in his expertise recommends; equally, doctors ought to recognise that medically imprudent preferences may valuably reflect a patient's personal values. Finally, promoting disclosure as a lever to engage the patient's trust and goodwill within the medical relationship may help to subdue the many tensions which have begun to emerge between duties and rights in the medical context, lessening, rather than enhancing, the prospect of medical negligence crisis.

Bibliography

Abraham, K.S. and Weiler, P.C. (1994), "Enterprise Medical Liability and the Evolution of the American Health Care System" 108 *Harvard Law Review* 381.

Abrams, R.D. (1966), "The patient with cancer—his changing pattern of communication" 274 *New England Journal of Medicine* 317.

Ackerman, T.F. (1982) 12(4) *Hastings Center Report* 14.

Aeschylus, *Prometheus Bound* (trans., Vellacott, P.) (London: Penguin, 1961).

Alfidi, R.J. (1975), "Controversy, Alternatives, and Decisions in Complying with the Legal Doctrine of Informed Consent" 114 *Radiology* 231.

Appelbaum, P.S., Lidz, C.W., and Meisel, A. (1987), *Informed Consent: Legal Theory and Clinical Practice* (New York: Oxford University Press).

Aristotle, *Politics* (London: Heineman, 1950).

Arrow, K.J. (1963), "Uncertainty and the Welfare Economics of Medical Care" 53 *American Economics Review* 941.

Ashworth A. Gedners, E. Mansfield, G. Peay, J. and Player, E. (1984), *Sentencing in the Crown Court: Report of an Exploratory Study* (Centre for Criminological Research, Oxford, Occasional Paper No. 10).

Atiyah, P.S. (1972), "*Res ipsa loguitur* in England and Australia" 35 *Modern Law Review* 337.

Atiyah, P. and Crane, P. (eds) (1993), *Atiyah's Accidents, Compensation and the Law* (5th ed. London: Butterworths).

Audit Commission (1993), *What Seems to be the Matter: Communication between Hospitals and Patients* (HMSO).

Ayd, F.J. (1972), "Motivations and rewards for volunteering to be an experimental subject" 13 *Clinical Pharmacology and Therapeutics* 771.

Bach-y-Rita, G. (1974), "The Prisoner as an Experimental Subject" 229 *Journal of American Medical Association* 46.

Bernard, C. and Pepper, C. (1969), *Christian Barnard: One Life* (New York: Macmillan).

Bawdon, F. (1996), "A crowded thoroughfare" 1996 *New Law Journal Supplement* 1742.

Bean, W.B. (ed.) (1961), *Aphorisms from his bedside teachings and writings* (2nd ed., Illinois: Charles C. Thomas).

Beauchamp, T.L. and Childress, J.F. (1983), *Principles of Biomedical Ethics* (2nd ed., New York: Oxford University Press).

Beauchamp, T.L. and McCullough, L.B. (1984), *Medical Ethics: The Moral Responsibilities of Physicians* (New Jersey: Prentice-Hall).

Becker, H.S. (1963), *Outsiders: Studies in the Sociology of Deviance* (New York: Free Press).

Beecher, H.K. (1966), "Ethics and Clinical Research" 274 *New England Journal of Medicine* 1354.

Belli, M. (1956), "An Ancient therapy Still Applied: The Silent Medical Treatment" 1 *Villanova Law Review* 259.

Bernstein, B. (1964), "Elaborated and Restricted Codes: Their Social Origins and Some Consequences" 66 *American Anthropology* 55.

Beyleveld, D. and Longley, D. (1998), "Informing Potential Participants of Local Research Ethics Committee Approval of Research Protocols" [1998] *Medical Law International* 209.

Binchy, W. and Craven, C. (1998), "Doctors in the Dock" *Law Society Gazette*, June 1998, 18.

Blaiberg, P. (1968), *Looking at My Heart* (New York: Stein & Day).

Blair, A.P. (1983), *Accident Compensation in New Zealand* (2nd ed., Wellington).

Bobinski, M.A. (1994), "Autonomy and Privacy: Protecting Patients from their Physicians" 55 *University of Pittsburgh Law Review* 291.

Bok, S. (1974), "The Ethics of Giving Placebos" 231 *Scientific American* 17.

Boon, A. (1988) "Causation and the Increase of Risk" 51 *Modern Law Review* 508.

Brandt, A.M. (1978), "Racism and Research: the case of the Tuskegee Syphilis Study" 8 *Hastings Center Report* 21.

Brazier, M.A. (1987), "Patient autonomy and consent to treatment: the role of the law?" 7 *Legal Studies* 169.

Brazier, M.A. (1992) *Medicine, Patients and the Law* (2nd ed., Harmondsworth: Penguin).

Brennan, T.A. (1988), "Causal Chains and Statistical Links: The Role of Scientific Uncertainty in Hazardous-Substance Litigation" 73 *Cornell Law Review* 469.

Brennan, T.A. (1992), "An Empirical Analysis of Accidents and Accident Law: The Case of Medical Malpractice Law" 36 *St Louis University Law Journal* 823.

Brody, H. (1985), "Autonomy revisited: progress in medical ethics" 78 *Journal of the Royal Society of Medicine* 380.

Bromberger, B. (1983), "Patient Participation in Medical Decision-Making" 6 *University of New South Wales* 1.

Brownell, K.D. and Stunkard, A.J. (1982), "The Double-Blind in Danger: Untoward Consequences of Informed Consent" 139 *American Journal of Psychiatry* 1487.

Buchanan, A. (1978), "Medical Paternalism" 7 *Philosophy & Public Affairs* 370.

Bullough, V.L. (1966), *The Development of Medicine as a Profession: The Contribution of the Medieval University to Modern Medicine* (New York: Karger Basel).

Burnham, J.C. (1982) "American Medicine's Golden Age: What Happened to it?" 215 *Science* 1475.

Burt, R.A. (1979), *Taking Care of Strangers: The Rule of Law in Doctor-Patient Relations* (New York: Free Press).

Byrne, D.J., Napier A. and Cushieri, A. (1988), "How informed is signed consent?" 296 *British Medical Journal* 839.

Calabresi, G. (1961), "Some Thoughts on Risk Distribution and the Law of Torts" 70 *Yale Law Journal* 499.

Calabresi G. (1968), "Does the fault System Optimally Control Primary Accident Costs?" 33 *Law & Contemporary Problems* 429.

Calabresi, G. (1970), *The Cost of Accidents* (New Haven: Yale University Press).

Callahan, D. (1984), "Autonomy: A Moral Good, Not a Moral Obsession" 14 *Hastings Center Report* 40.

Canadian Law Reform Commission (1980), *Consent to Medical Care.*

Cane and Stapleton (eds) (1991), *Essays for Patrick Atiyah* (Oxford (U.S.): Oxford University Press).

Caplan (1992), "Twenty Years After: the Legacy of the Tuskegee Syphilis Study" 22 *Hastings Center Report* 29.

Capron, A.M. (1973) "Medical Research in Prisons: Should a Moratorium be Called?" 3 *Hastings Center Report* 4.

Capron, A. (1974), "Informed Consent in Catastrophic Disease Research and Treatment" 123 *University of Pennsylvania Law Review* 340.

Capron, A.M. (1979), "Tort Liability in Genetic Counselling" 79 *Columbia Law Review* 618.

Carmichael, A.G. and Ratzan, R.M. (eds) (1991), *Medicine: A Treasury of Art and Literature* (New York: Hugh Lauter Levin).

Carolan, B. (1995) "Mandatory Disclosure of Medical Reports in Personal Injuries Actions: Irish, English and U.S. Law Compared" 1 *Medico-Legal Journal of Ireland* 105.

Carswell, R. (1964), "Professional Negligence—The Sword of Damocles" 48 *Northern Ireland Law Quarterly* 197.

Cartwright, A. (1997), *Human Relations and Hospital Care* (London: Routledge & Kegan Paul).

Cassileth, Zupkis, Sutton-Smith, and March (1980), "Informed Consent—Why Are Its Goals Imperfectly Realized?" 302 *New England Journal of Medicine* 896.

Charney, E. *et al.* (1967), "How well do patients take oral penicillin? Collaborative study in private practice" 40 *Paediatrics* 188.

Childress, J.F. (1982), *Who Should Decide? Paternalism in Health Care* (New York: Oxford University Press).

Clements, L.M. (1995), "Self Determination and 'Informed Consent' to Medical Treatment" [1995] *Professional Negligence* 136.

Cloninger and Guze (1970), "Psychiatric Illness and Female Criminality: The Role of Sociopathy and Hysteria in the Antisocial Woman" 127 *American Journal of Psychiatry* 303.

Coase, R. (1960), "The Problem of Social Cost" 3 *Journal of Law & Economics* 1.

Comaroff, C. (1976), "A Bitter Pill to Swallow: Placebo Therapy in General Practice" 24 *Sociological Review* 94.

Cotton, F. (1933), "Medicine, Ethics and the Law" 208 *New England Journal of Medicine*.

Coulter; H.L. (1973), *Divided Legacy. A History of the Schism in Medical Thought* (Washington DC: McGrath).

Curran, W.J. (1978), "Legal Liability in Clinical Investigations" 298 *New England Journal of Medicine* 778.

Danzon, P.M. (1984) "The Frequency and Severity of Medical Malpractice Claims" (1984), *Journal of Law and Economics* 115.

Danzon, P.M. (1985), *Medical Malpractice: Theory, Evidence, and Public Policy* (Cambridge, Mass: Harvard University Press).

Davies, M. (1996), *Medical Law* (London: Blackstone).

Davis, M.S. (1967) "Variations in patients' compliance with doctors' advice: an empirical analysis of patterns of communication" 58 *American Journal of Public Health* 441.

Davis, M.R. (1960–1961) "Duty of Doctor to Inform Patient of Risks to Treatment: Battery or Negligence?" (1960–1961) 34 *Southern California Law Review* 217.

Davis, M.S. and Eichhorn, R.L. (1963) "Compliance with medical regimens: panel study" 4 *Journal of Health & Human Behavior* 240.

Dimatteo, M.R. and DiNicola, D.D. (1982), *Achieving Patient Compliance: The Psychology of the Medical Practitioners role* (New York: Pergamon Press).

Diamond, B.L. (1974), "The Psychiatric Prediction of Dangerousness" 123 *University of Pennsylvania Law Review* 439.

Donnelly, M. (1996), "Legal Actions for Negligence Relating to Sterilisation" 2 *Medico-Legal Journal* 21.

Donnelly, M. (1997), "The Injury of Parenthood: The Tort of Wrongful Conception" 48 *Northern Ireland Legal Quarterly* 10.

Dugdale, A. (1984), "Diverse Reports: Canadian Professional Negligence Cases" 2 *Professional Negligence* 108.

Dunstan, G.R. and Shinebourne, E.A. (eds) (1997), *Doctor's Decisions: Ethical Conflicts in Medical Practice (New York: Oxford University Press)*.

Durkheim, E. 1897, *Le Suicide* (New York: Macmillan, 1952).

Dyer, C. (ed) (1992), *Doctors, Patients and the Law* (Blackwell Science).

Dyer, C. (1996), "GP Struck Off for Fraud in Drug Trials" (1996) 312 *British Medical Journal* 798.

Easterbrook, J. (1996), "Resolving Health Care Disputes" (1996) *Solicitors Journal* 140.

Editorial (1986), "The Bioethicist as Missionary" 13 Institute of Medical Ethics Bulletin 1.

Eddy, J.P. (1955), *Professional Negligence* (London).

Egbert, L.D., Battit, G.E., Welch, C.E. and Barlett, M.K. (1964) "Reduction of postoperative pain by encouragement and instruction of patents" 270 *New England Journal of Medicine* 825.

Elling, R., Wittemore, and Greene, M. (1960), "Patient participation in pediatric program" 1 *Journal of Health & Human Behavior* 183.

Epstein, R.S. and Janowsky D.S. (1969), "Research on the Psychiatric Ward: the Effects on Conflicting Priorites" 21 *Archives of General Psychiatry* 455.

Faden, R.R. and Beauchamp T.L. (1986), *A Theory and History of Informed Consent* New York: Oxford University Press).

Faulder, C. (1985), *Whose Body is It? The Troubling Issue of Informed Consent* (London: Virago).

Feldman, F. (1992), *Confrontations with the Reaper: A Philosophical Study of the Nature and Value of Death* (New York: Oxford University Press).

Feng, T.K. (1987), "Failure of medical advice: trespass or negligence?" 7 *Legal Studies* 149.

Field, M.G. (1953), "Structured Strain in the Role of the Soviet Physician" 58 *American Journal of Sociology* 493.

Filed, J.H., *A Study of the Epidemiology of Head Injury in England and Wales* (London: Department of Health & Security).

Fisher, S. and Todd (eds) (1983), *The Social Organization of Doctor-Patient Communication* (New York: Center for Applied Linguistics).

Fleming, J.G. (1987), *The Law of Torts* (7th ed, London: Sweet & Maxwell).

Fleming, J.G. (1989), "Probabilistic Causation in Tort Law" 68 *Canadian Bar Review* 661.

Fletcher, G.P. (1972), "Fairness and Utility in Tort Theory" 85 *Harvard Law Review* 537.

Foster, C. (1995), "A plea for a lost chance: *Hotson* revisited" (1995), *New Law Journal* 228.

Fox, R. and Swazey, J. (1974), *The Courage to Fail: A Social View of Organ Transplants and Dialysis* (Chicago: Chicago University Press).

Francis, V., Korsch, B.M. and Morris, M.L. (1969), "Gaps in Doctor-Patient Communication" 280 *New England Journal of Medicine* 535.

Frantz, L.B. (1978), "Modern Status of Views as to General Measure of Physician's Duty to Inform Patient of Risks of Proposed Treatment" 88 A.L.R. (3d) 1008.

Friedson, E. (1963), *The Hospital in Modern Society* (Glencoe: Free Press).

Freidson, E. (1970), *The Profession of Medicine* (New York: Dodd, Mead).

Freidson, E. and Lorber, J. (eds) (1972), *Medical Men and Their Work* (Chicago: Aldine).

Freud, S. (ed. Strachey, J.) (1981), *Complete Psychological Works of Sigmund Freud* (London: Hogarth Press & Institute of Psychoanalysis).

Fromer, M.J. (1981), *Ethical Issues in Health Care* (St Louis: CV Mosby).

Fromm, E. (1942), *The Fear of Freedom* (London: Kegan Paul, Trench).

Fuchs, V.R. (1966), "The Contributions of Health Services to the American Economy" 44 *Milbank Memorial Fund Quarterly* 65.

Fulford, K.W.M. (1989), *Moral theory and Medical Practice* (Cambridge: Cambridge University Press).

Gellhorn, W. (1988), "Medical Malpractice Litigation (U.S.)—Medical Mishap Compensation (N.Z.)" 73 *Cornell Law Review* 170.

Gerle, B. Lunden, G. and Sandlom, P. (1960), "The Patient with Inoperable Cancer from the Psychiatric and Social Standpoint" 13 *Cancer* 1206.

Gert, B. and Culver, C.M. (1976), "Paternalistic Behavior" 6 *Philosophical & Public Affairs* 45.

Giesen, D. (1988), *International Medical Malpractice Law: A Comparative Law Study of Civil Liability Arising from Medical Care* (2nd ed, London: JCB Mohr).

Gillet, G.R. (1989), "Informed consent and moral integrity" 15 *Journal of Medical Ethics* 117.

Gillon R., *Philosophical Medical Ethics* (Chichester: John Wiley & Sons).

Gleeson C.J., "Individualised Justice—The Holy Grail" 69 *Australian Law Journal* 421.

Gochnauer, M. and Fleming, D. (1981), "Tort Law—Informed Consent—New Directions for Medical Disclosure—*Hopp v. Lepp* and *Reibl v. Hughes*" 18 *University of British Columbia Law Journal* 475.

Gold, S. (1986), "Causation in Toxic Torts: Burdens of Proof, Standards of Persuasion, and Statistical Evidence" 96 *Yale Law Journal* 376.

Goldstein, J. (1975), "For Harold Lasswell: Some Reflections on Dignity, Entrapment, Informed Consent, and the Plea Bargain" 84 *Yale Law Journal* 683.

Gray, B. (1975), *Human Subjects in Medical Experimentation* (New York: John Wiley & Sons).

Grubb, A. (1984), "Medical Law—Doctor's Advice and the Reasonable Man: Do We Need a Second Opinion?" [1984] *Cambridge Law Journal* 240.

Grubb A. (1985), "Informed Consent to Medical Treatment: Who Decides, the Patient or the Doctor?" [1985] *Cambridge Law Journal* 199.

Grubb, A. (1985), "A Survey of Medical Malpractice Law in England: Crisis? What Crisis?" 1 *Journal of Contemporary Health Law & Policy* 75.

Grunder, T.M. (1980), "On the Readability of Surgical Consent Forms" 302 *New England Journal of Medicine* 900.

Guthrie, D. (1945), *A History of Medicine* (London: Nelson).

Guze, Tuason, Gatfield, Stewart and Ricker (1962), "Psychiatric Illness and Crime with Particular Reference to Alcoholism: A Study of 223 Criminals" 134 *Journal of Nervous & Mental Disorders* 512.

Guze, Goodwin and Crane (1969), "Criminality and Psychiatric Disorders" 20 *Archives of General Psychiatry* 583.

Haddad (1987), "Analysis of 2932 Workers' Compensation back injury cases" 12 *Spine* 765.

Hall, M.A. (1997), "A Theory of Economic Informed Consent" 31 *Georgia Law Review* 511.

Hall, M.A. (1994), "Rationing Health care at the Bedside" 69 *New York University Law Review* 693.

Harper, F.V. and James, F. Jr. (1956), *The Law of Torts* (Boston: Little Brown).

Harpwood, V. (1996), "Medical Negligence: A Chink in the Armour of the Bolam Test?" 64 *Medico-Legal Journal* 179.

Harris Survey (1976), *Yearbook of Public Opinion* (New York: Louis Harris and Associates).

Harris, N. (1992), "Medical Negligence Litigation: The Need for Reform" 60 *Medico-Legal Journal* 205.

Haug, M.R. (1975) "Deprofessionalization of Everyone?" 8 *Sociological Focus* 197.

Havighurst, C. and Tancredi, L. (1974), "Medical Adversity Insurance: A No-Fault Approach to Medical Malpractice and Quality Assurance" 613 *Insurance Law Journal* 69.

Hawkins, C. (1985), *Mishap or Malpractice?* (Blackwell Scientific).

Healy, J. (1995), "Failure of Doctors to Communicate Risks to Patients: at the Pre-Treatment Stage: A Case of Negligence or Medical Negligence?" 13(8)-(9), *Irish Law Times* 196 and 222.

Healy, J. (1998a), "Duties of Disclosure & the Elective Patient: A Case for Informed Consent" [1998] *Medico-Legal journal of Ireland* 13.

Healy, J. (1998b), "Duties of Disclosure & the Inquisitive Patient A Case for Informed Consent" [1998] *Medico-Legal Journal of Ireland* 69.

Hershey, N. and Miller, R.D. (1976), *Human Experimentation and the Law* (Germantown, Maryland: Aspens Systems Corporation).

Heuston, R.F.V. and Buckley, R.A. (1992), *Salmond and Heuston on the Law of Torts* (20th ed., London: Sweet & Maxwell).

Heydon, J.D. (1991), *Evidence: Cases & Materials* (3rd ed., London: Butterworths).

Hill, T. (1991) "A Lost Chance for Compensation in the Tort of Negligence by the House of Lords" 54 *Modern Law Review* 511.

Hinsdale (ed.) (1973), *A History of Liberal Theory* (Illinois: Dryden Press).

Hippocrates, *On Decorum xvi, in Hippocrates* trans. Jones, W.H.S. (Cambridge, Mass: Harvard University Press, 1923).

Hippocrates, *The Medical Works of Hippocrates*, trans. Chadwick, J. and Mann W.N. (London: Blackwell Scientific, 1950).

Hoffman, L. (1995), "Anthromorphic Justice: The Reasonable Man and his Friends" [1995] *Journal of Association of Law Teachers* 127.

Holmes, O.W. (1881), *The Common Law* (Boston: Little Brown).

Holmes, O.W. (1883), *Currents and Counter-currents* (Boston: Houghton Mifflin & Co.).

Hopper, K.D., TenHave, T.R. and Hartzel, J. (1995), "Informed consent forms for clinical and research imaging procedures: how much do patients understand?" 164 *American Journal of Roentgenology* 493.

Houston, W.R. (1938), "The Doctor Himself as a Therapeutic Agent" 11 *Annals of Internal Medicine* 1416.

Howard, M.N. (1991), "The Neutral Expert: a plausible threat to justice" [1991] *Criminal Law Review* 98.

Hughes, E.C. (1963), "Professions" 92 *Daedalus* 655.

Iglehart, J.K. (1994), "Physicians and the Growth of Managed Care" 331 *New England Journal of Medicine* 1167.

Illich, I. (1990), *Limits to Medicine: Medical Nemesis* (London: Penguin).

Ingelfinger, F. (1972), "Informed (but Uneducated) Consent" 287 *New England Journal of Medicine* 465.

Ison, T. (1980), *Accident Compensation: A Commentary on the New Zealand Scheme* (London: Croom Helm).

Jackson, R.M. and Powell, J.L. (1987), *Professional Negligence* (London: Sweet & Maxwell).

Jaco, E.G. (ed.) (1958), *Patients, Physicians and Illness: A Sourcebook in Behavioral Science and Health* (New York: Free Press).

Jaco, E.G. (ed.) (1979), *Patients, Physicians, and Illness: A Sourcebook in Behavioral Science and Health* (3rd ed., New York: Free Press).

Jaeckel, L.B. (1975), "New Trends in Informed Consent?" 54 *Nebraska Law Review* 66.

James, F. (1950), "Accident Proneness and Accident Law" 63 *Harvard Law Review* 769.

Jenkins, D. (1996), "Consent: A Matter of Trust not Tort" [1996] *Medico-Legal Journal of Ireland* 83.

Jennett, B. (1976), "Some medicolegal aspects of the management of acute head injury" *British Medical Journal* 1383.

Johnson, J (1991), "A Proposal to Adopt a Professional Judgment Standard of Care in Determining the Duty of a Psychiatrist to Third Parties" 62 *University of Colorado Law Review* 237.

Jones, J.H. (1981), *Bad Blood* (New York: Free Press).

Jones, M.A. (1984), "Doctor Knows Best" 100 *Law Quarterly Review* 355.

Jones, M.A. (1987), "The Rising cost of medical malpractice" 3 *Professional Negligence* 43.

Jones, M.A. (1990), "Saving the patient from himself" 6 *Professional Negligence* 107.

Jones, M.A. (1992), "Arbitration for Medical Claims in the NHS" 8 *Professional Negligence* 142.

Jones, M.A. (1994), "Failure to warn: establishing the causal link" 10 *Professional Negligence* 24.

Jones, M.A. (1996), *Medical Negligence* (London: Sweet & Maxwell).

Jones, M.A. and Morris, A.E. (1989), "Defensive medicine: myths and facts", *Journal of the Medical Defence Union*, Summer 1989.

Kao, C.L. (1976), "Maturity and Paternalism in Health Care" 3 *Ethics in Science & Medicine* 179.

Kaplan, S.H., Greenwold, R.A. and Rogers, A.J. (1977), "Neglected Aspects of Informed Consent" 296 *New England Journal of Medicine* 1127.

Kaplan, S.H., Greenfield, S., Gandek, B., Rogers, W.H. and Ware, J.E. (1996), "Characteristics of physicians with participatory decision-making styles" *Annals of International Medicine* 497.

Katz, J. (1977), "Informed Consent—A Fairy Tale? Law Vision" 29 *University of Pittsburgh Law Review* 137.

Katz, J. (1984), *The Secret World of Doctor and Patient* (New York: Free Press).

Kennedy, I. (1983), *The Unmasking of Medicine* (London: Granada).

Kennedy, I. (1988), *Treat Me Right: Essays in Medical Law and Ethics* (Oxford: Clarendon Press).

Kennedy, I. and Grubb, A. (1989), "Testing for HIV infection: the legal framework" (1989) 15 *Law Society Gazette* 30.

Kennedy, I. and Grubb, A. (1994), *Medical Law: Text with Materials* (2nd ed., London: Butterworths).

Kenny, A. (1983), "The Expert in Court" (1983) 99 L.Q.R. 197.

Keown, J. (1989), "The Ashes of AIDS and the Phoenix of Informed Consent" 52 *Modern Law Review* 790.

Keown, J. (1989), "Easing the Burden on Medical Plaintiffs" [1995] *Cambridge Law Journal* 30.

Kett, J. (1968), *The Formation of the American Medical Profession: The Role of Institutions, 1780–1860* (New Haven: Yale University Press).

Khan, M. and Roberts, M. (1997), *Medical Negligence* (London: Cavendish).

King, J.H. (1981), "Causation, Valuation, and Chance in Personal Injury Torts Involving Preexisting Conditions and Future Consequences" 90 *Yale Law Journal* 1353.

King, L.S. (1958), *The Medical World of the Eighteenth Century* (Chicago: University of Chicago Press).

Kirby, M.D. (1984), "Negligence and the Physician" (1984) 14 *Australian & New Zealand Journal of Medicine* 867.

von Klein, C.H. (1905), "The Medical Features of the Eber's Papyrus." 45 *Journal of the American Medical Association* 26.

Konald, D.E. (1962), *A History of American Medical Ethics 1847–1912* (Madison: State Historical Society of Wisconsin).

Kubler-Ross, E. (1969), *Death and Dying* (New York: Macmillan).

Lancher, M.J. (1981), "Physicians and Patients as Obstacles to a Randomized Trial" 2 *Clinical Research* 287.

Landes, W.M. and Posner, R.A. (1987), *The Economic Structure of Tort Law* (Cambridge, Mass: Harvard University Press).

Leach, G. (1972), *The Biocrats: Implications of Medical Progress* (Harmondsworth: Penguin).

Lee, S. (1985), "Operating under Informed Consent" 101 *Law Quarterly Review* 316.

Levinson, D.F. (1987), "Toward Full Disclosure of Referral Restrictions and Financial Incentives by Prepaid Health Plans" 317 *New England Journal of Medicine* 1729.

Levinson W., Roter, D.L., Mullooly, J.P., Dull, V.T., Frank, R.M. (1997), "Physician-patient communication: the relationship between malpractice claims among primary care physicians and surgeons" [1997] *Journal of the American Medical Association* 553.

Levy, J.M., McGee, R.K. (1975), "Childbirth as Crisis: A Test of Janis' Theory of Communication and Stress Resolution" 31 *Journal of Personality and Social Psychology* 171.

Linden, A. (1975), "The Negligent Doctor" 11 *Osgoode Hall Law Journal* 31.

Lock, S. (ed.) (1996), *Fraud and Misconduct in Medical Research* (2nd ed, London: BMJ).

Lockwood, M. (ed.) (1985), *Moral Problems in Medicine* (New York: Oxford University Press).

Lunney, M. (1995), "What price a chance?" 15 *Legal Studies* 1.

McCoid, A.H. (1957), "A Reappraisal of Liability for Unauthorized Medical Treatment" 41 *Minnesota Law Review* 381.

McDonald, B. and Swanton, J. (1996), "Issues in Medical Negligence" 70 *Australian Law Journal* 688.

McGraw, D.C. (1995), "Financial Limits to Limit Services: Should Physicians be Required to Disclose These to Patients?" 83 *Georgia Law Journal* 1821.

McGregor Vennell, M.A. (1989), "Medical Injury Compensation under the New Zealand Accident Compensation Scheme: an Assessment Compared with the Swedish Medical Compensation Scheme" (1989) *Professional Negligence* 141.

McHale, J., Fox, M. and Murphy, J. (1997), *Health Care Law: Text, Cases and Materials* (London: Sweet & Maxwell).

McKeown, J. (1998), "Reining in the *Bolam* test" [1998] *Cambridge Law Journal* 248.

Mahohey, R. (1985), "Informed Consent and Breach of the Medical Contract to Achieve a Particular Result: Opportunities for New Zealand's Latent Personal Injury Litigation to Peek out of the Accident Compensation Closet" 6 *Otago Law Review* 103.

Malone, W.S. (1950), "Ruminations on Cause-In-Fact" 9 *Stanford Law Review* 60.

Martin, D.C., Arnold, J.D., Zimmerman, T.F., *et al.* (1968), "Human Subjects in Clinical Research—A Report of Three Studies" 279 *New England Journal of Medicine* 1426.

Maslow, A.H. (1963), "The Need to Know and the Fear of Knowing" 68 *Journal of General Psychology* 111.

Mason, J.K. (1990), *Medico-Legal Aspects of Reproduction and Parenthood* (Hants: Dartmouth).

Mason, J.K. and McCall Smith, R.A. (1994), *Law and Medical Ethics* (4th ed, London: Butterworths).

Megargee, E.J. (1976), "The Prediction of Dangerous Behaviour" 3 *Criminal Justice & Behavior* 3.

Meisel, A. (1977), "The Expansion of Liability for Medical Accidents From Negligence to Strict Liability" 56 *Nebraska Law Review* 51.

Meisel, A. (1979), "The Exceptions' to the Informed Consent Doctrine Striking a Balance between Competing Values in Medical Decisionmaking" [1979] *Wisconsin Law Review* 413.

Meisel, A. and Kabnick, L.D. (1980), "Informed Consent to Medical Treatment: An Analysis of Recent Legislation" 41 *University of Pittsburgh Law Review* 407.

Meisel, A. and Roth, L.H. (1983), "Toward an Informed Discussion of Informed Consent: A Review and Critique of the Empirical Studies" 25 *Arizona Law Review* 265.

Meltzer, M. (1975), *Never to Forget: The Jews of the Holocaust* (New York: Harper & Row).

Mencken, H.L. (ed.) (1956), *A Mencken Chrestomathy* (New York: Alfred A Knopf).

Menninger, R. (1976), "Diagnosis of Culture and Social Institutions" 40 *Bulletin of Mellinger Clinic* 531.

Mill, J.S. (1956), *On Liberty* (New York: Liberal Arts Press).

Miller, B.L. (1981), "Autonomy & the Refusal of Lifesaving Treatment" 11 *Hastings Center Report* 22.

Mohr, J. (1993), *Doctors and the Law: Medical Jurisprudence in Nineteenth-Century America* (New York: Oxford University Press).

Monahon, J. (ed.) (1976), *Community Mental Health and the Criminal Justice System* (New York: Pergamon Press).

de Mondeville, H. (ed. and trans. Nicaise, E.) (1893), in *Chirurgie (Paris: Felix Alcan)*.

Mooney, G. (1980), "Cost-benefit analysis and medical ethics" 6 *Journal of Medical Ethics* 177.

Mooney, G. and McGuire, A. (eds) (1988), *Medical Ethics and Economics in Health Care* (Oxford: Oxford University Press).

Morris, L.A. and Kanouse, D.E. (1982), "Informing Patients about Side Effects" 5 *Journal of Behavioral Medicine* 363.

Morrow, G., Gootnick, J. and Schmale, A. (1978), "A simple technique for increasing cancer patients' knowledge of treatment" 42 *Cancer* 793.

Myers, M.J., "Informed Consent to Medical Malpractice" 55 *Californian Law Review* 1396.

National Commission for the Protection of Human Subjects of Biomedical and Behavioural Research (1978), *The Belmont Report: Ethical Guidelines for the Protection of Human Subjects of Research* (DHEW Publication No. (OS) 78–0012, Washington: US Government Printing Office).

Newdick, C. (1985), "The Doctor's Duties of Care under *Sidaway*" [1985] *Northern Ireland Law Quarterly* 243.

Newdick, C. (1995), *Who Should We Treat?: Law, Patients and Resources in the NHS* (Oxford: Clarendon Press).

Note (1976), "The Limits of State Intervention: Personal Identity and Ultra-Risky Actions" 85 *Yale Law Journal* 826.

Note (1979), "Hospital Corporate Liability: An Effective Solution to Controlling Private Physician Incompetence? "32 *Rutgers Law Review* 342.

Note (1983), "Patient Recovery—A Poor Prognosis for Hospitals? The Expanding Scope of Hospital Liability" 10 *Ohio New University Law Review* 519.

Note (1984), "Malpractice problem continues to grow" [1984] *Pediatrics* 73.

Notes (1998), "Latent Harm and Risk-Based Damages" 111 *Harvard Law Review* 1505.

Novak, D.H. *et al.* (1979), "Changes in physicians' attitudes toward telling the cancer patient" 241 *Journal of the American Medical Association* 897.

O'Connell, J. (1985), "A 'Neo No-Fault' Contract in Lieu of Tort: Preaccident Guarantees of Post Accident Settlement Offers" 73 *Californian Law Review* 898.

O'Neill, D. (1997), "Disclosure in Personal Injuries Actions" 2 *Bar Review* 77.

Oldertz, C. (1983), "The Swedish Patient Insurance System—Eight Years of Experience" 52 *Medico-Legal Journal* 43.

Oliphant, K. (1996), "Defining 'Medical Misadventure': Lessons from New Zealand" 4 *Medical Law Review* 1.

Ong, L.M., de Haes, J.C., Hoos, A.M. and Lammes F.B. (1995), "Doctor-patient communication" [1995] *Society of Scientific Medicine* 903.

Ormrod, R. (1989), "Is Consent Really Necessary?" 29 *Medicine, Science, & Law* 4.

Palmer, G. (1979), *Compensation for Incapacity: A Study of Law and Social Change in New Zealand and Australia* (Oxford University Press).

Pappworth, M.H. (1969), "Ethical Issues in Experimental Medicine", in Cutler, D.R. (ed.), *Updating Life and Death* (Boston: Beacon Press).

Park, L.C., Covi, L. and Uhlenhuth, E.H. (1967), "Effects of Informed Consent on Research Patients and Study Results" 145 *Journal of Nervous and Mental Disease* 349.

Parsons, T. (1939), "The Professions and Social Structure" 17 *Social Forces* 458.

Parsons, T. (1951), *The Social System* (New York: Free Press).

Pellegrino, E.D. (1979), "Toward a Reconstruction of Medical Morality: The Primacy of the Act of Profession and the Fact of Illness" 4 *Journal of Medicine and Philosophy* 32.

Picard, E. (1981), "*Reibl v. Hughes* casenote" 1 *Oxford Journal of Legal Studies* 441.

Picard, E.I. and Robertson, G.B. (1996), *Legal Liability of Doctors and Hospitals in Canada* (3rd ed., Ontario: Carswell).

Pincus, R.C. (1993), "Has informed consent finally arrived in Australia?" 159 *Medical Journal of Australia* 25.

Plante, M.L. (1968), "An Analysis of Informed Consent" 36 *Fordham Law Review* 639.

Plato, *Laws* (Law 720), Bury, R. (trans.) (1926) (New York: Putnams).

Posner, R.A. (1992), *Economic Analysis of Law* (4th ed Boston: Little Brown).

Postema, G.J. (1980), "Moral Responsibility in Professional Ethics" 55 *New York University Law Review* 63.

Pratt, L. Seligmann, A. and Reader, G. (1957), "Physicians' views on the level of information among patients' 47 *American Journal of Public History* 1277.

President's Commission for the Study of Ethical Problems in Medicine and Biomedical and Behavioral Research (1982), *Making Health Care Decisions: A Report on the Ethical and Legal Implications of Informed Consent in the Patient-Practitioner Relationship, Vols 1–2* (Washington: U.S. Government Printing Office).

Price, D.P.T. (1981), "Causation—the Lords Lost Chance?" 38 *International & Comparative Law Quarterly* 735.

Project (Various) (1971), "The Medical Malpractice Threat: A Study of Defensive Medicine" [1971] *Duke Law Journal* 939.

Ramsay, P. "(1977), "Children as Research Subjects: A Reply" 7 *Hastings Center Report* 40.

Rasor, D.J. (1993), "Mandatory Medical Malpractice Screening Panels: A Need to Re-Evaluate" 9 *Ohio State Journal on Dispute Resolution* 115.

Reece, H., "Losses of Chance in the Law" 59 *Modern Law Review* 188.

Report of the Federal/Provincial/Territorial Review on Liability and Compensation Issues in Health Care (Chairman, J.R.S. Prichard) (1990), *Liability and Compensation in Health Care* (Toronto: Toronto University Press).

Richards, T. (1990), "Chasms in communication" [1990] *British Medical Journal* 1407.

Roberts, P. (1997), "The Philosophical Foundations of Consent in the Criminal Law" 17 *Oxford Journal of Legal Studies* 391.

Robertson, G.B. (1978), "Civil Liability Arising from 'Wrongful Birth' Following an Unsuccessful Sterilization Operation" 4 *American Journal of Law & Medicine* 131.

Robertson, G.B. (1981), "Informed Consent to Medical Treatment" 97 *Law Quarterly Review* 102.

Robertson, G.B. (1984), "Overcoming the Causation Hurdle in Informed Consent Cases: The Principle in *McGhee v. NCB*" 22 *University of West Ontario Law Review* 75.

Robertson, G.B. (1987), "Fraudulent Concealment and the Duty to Disclose Medical Mistakes" 25 *Alberta Law Review* 215.

Robertson, G.B. (1991), "Informed. Consent Ten Years Later: The Impact of Reibl v. Hughes" 70 *Canadian Bar Review* 423.

Ross, J. (1997), "Will States Protect Us, Equally, from Damage Caps in Medical Malpractice Legislation?" 30 *Indiana Law Review* 575.

Sabin, A.B., Bronstein, A.J. and Hubbard, W.N. (1975), "The Military/The Prisoner" in *Experiments and Research with Humans: Values in Conflict* (Washington: Academy Forum).

Saks, M. (1992), "Do We Really Know Anything about the Behaviour of the Tort Litigation System—and Why Not?" 140 *University of Pennsylvania Law Review* 1147.

Samuels, A. (1982), "What the Doctor Must Tell the Patient" 22 *Medical Science Law* 41.

Sappideeen, C. (1993), "No Fault Compensation for Medical Misadventure" 9 *Journal of Contemporary Health Law & Policy* 311.

Lord Scarman (1986), "Consent, Communication and Responsibility" 79 *Journal of the Royal Society of Medicine* 697.

Scheid, J.H. (1998), "1998 American Statutory Responses to the Medical Malpractice Crisis" [1998] *Medico-Legal Journal of Ireland* 3.

Scorer, G. and Wing, A. (eds) (1979), *Decision Making in Medicine: the practice of its ethics* (London: Edward Arnold).

Scott, W. (1992), "Causation in Medico-Legal Practice: A Doctor's Approach to the 'Lost Opportunity' Cases" 55 *Modern Law Review* 521.

Seidelson, D.E. (1976), "Medical Malpractice: Informed Consent Cases in 'Full-Disclosure' Jurisdictions" 14 *Duquesne Law Review* 309.

Shah, S. (1978), "Dangerousness: A paradigm for exploring some issues in law and psychology" 33 *American Psychologist* 224.

Shaw, J.W. (1972), "Annotation: Recovery Against Physician on Basis of Breach of Contract to Achieve Particular Result or Cure" 43 A.L.R. 3d 1221 (1972).

Shuck, P.H. (1994), "Rethinking Informed Consent" 103 *Yale Law Journal* 899.

Silberstein (1974), "Extension of Two-Part Consent Form" 291 *New England Journal of Medicine* 155.

Silverman, W.A. (1989), "The myth of informed consent: in daily practice and clinical trials" 15 *Journal of Medical Ethics* 6.

Simanowitz, A. (1986), "Action for Victims of Medical Accidents", address at meeting of The Royal Society of Medicine 54 *Medico-Legal Journal* 104.

Simon, R.J. and Mahan, L. (1976), "Quantifying Burdens of Proof" 5 *Law & Society Review* 319.

Skegg, P.D.G. (1974), "A justification for Medical Procedures Performed Without Consent" 90 *Law Quarterly Review* 512.

Skegg, P.D.G. (1988), *Law, Ethics and Medicine: Studies in Medical Law* (Oxford: Clarendon).

Sloane, F.A., Whetten-Goldstein, K. Entman, S.S., Kulas, E.D. and Stout, E.M. (1997), "The Road from Medical Injury to Claims Resolution: How No-Fault and Tort Differ" 60 *Law & Contemporary Problems* 35.

Smith, H.W. (1942), "Antecedent Grounds of Liability in the Practice of Surgery" 14 *Rocky Mount Law Review* 233.

Smith, D.H. (1985), "Increased Risk of Harm: A New Standard for Sufficiency of Evidence of Causation in Medical Malpractice Cases" 65 *Boston University Law Review* 275.

Smith, J. (1991), "Preventing Fraud" 302 *British Medical Journal* 362.

Smith R. (1983), "Medicine and the Media" 286 *British Medical Journal* 1433.

Smith, R.G. (1994), *Medical Discipline: the Professional Conduct, Jurisdiction of the General Medical Council 1858–1990* (Oxford: Clarendon Press).

Sommerville, M.A. (1980), *Consent to Medical Care* (Ottawa: Law Reform Commission of Canada).

Sommerville, M.A. (1981), "Restructuring the Issues in Informed Consent" 26 *McGill Law Journal* 740.

Ssasz, T.S. and Hollander, M.H. (1956), "A Contribution to the Philosophy of Medicine: The Basic Models of the Doctor–Patient Relationship" 97 *Archives of Internal Medicine* 585.

Ssasz, T.S., *The Theology of Medicine* (Louisa State University Press).

Ssasz, T.S., *The Myth of Mental Illness* (New York: Harper Collins).

Stapleton, J. (1988), "The Gist of Negligence, Part 2: The Relationship Between 'Damage' and Causation" 104 *Law Quarterly Review* 389.

Starr, P. (1982), *The Social Transformation of American Medicine* (New York: Basic Books).

Stauch, M. (1997), "Causation, Risk, and Loss of Chance in Medical Negligence" 17 *Oxford Journal of Legal Studies* 205.

Stevens, R. (1971), *American Medicine and the Public Interest* (New Haven: Yale University Press).

Stewart, M.A. (1995), "Effective physician-patient communication and health outcomes: a review" [1995] *Canadian Medical Association Journal* 1423.

Stone, G.C. (1979), "Patient and the Role of the Expert" 35 *Journal of Social Issues* 34.

Strauss, M.B. (ed.) (1969), *Familiar Medical Quotations* (London: J & A Churchill).

Stuart (1978), "Protection of the Right to Informed Consent to Participate in Research" 9 *Behavioral Therapy* 73.

Sugarman, S.D. (1985), "Doing Away with Tort Law" 73 *California Law Review* 555.

Swan, N. (1991), "Australian Doctor Admits Fraud" 302 *British Medical Journal* 1421.

Symmons, C.R. (1987), "The problem of 'informed consent' in the 'wrongful birth' cases" 3 *Professional Negligence* 56.

Taylor, J.P. (1931), *Treatise on the Law of Evidence* (12th ed, London: Sweet & Maxwell).

Teff, H. (1985a), "Consent to Medical Procedures: Paternalism, Self-Determination 101 *Law Quarterly Review* 432.

Teff, H. (1985b), "The Action for 'Wrongful Life' in England and the United States" 34 *International & Comparative Quarterly* 423.

Teff, H. (1994), *Reasonable Care* (Oxford University Press).

Teff, H. (1998), "The Standard of Care in Medical Negligence—Moving on from Bolam?' 18 *Oxford Journal of Legal Studies* 477.

Temkin, O. and Temkin, C.L. (eds) (1967), *Ancient Medicine: Selected Papers of Ludwig Edelstein* (Baltimore: John Hopkins University).

Terry (1986), "The Malpractice Crisis in the United States" 2 *Professional Negligence* 145.

Thomasma, D. (1985), "Autonomy in the Doctor-Patient Relation" 5 *Theoretical Medicine* 1.

Thomson S. (1825), *A Narrative of the Life and Medical Discoveries of Samuel Thomson* (2nd ed, Boston: EG House).

Tolstoy, I. (1902), "The Death of Ivan Illich" in *The Death of Ivan Illyitch and Other Stories* (trans. Garnett, C., London: William Heinemann).

Tomkin, D. & Hanafin, P. (1995), *Irish Medical Law* (Dublin: Roundhall).

Tribe, D. and Korgaonkar, G. (1991), "The impact of litigation on patient care: an enquiry into defensive medical practices" 7 *Professional Negligence* 2.

Tulley, P. (1992), "Towards a wider view of informed consent to medical treatment" 8 *Professional Negligence* 74.

Turner, E.G. (1982), *History of the British Medical Association* (London: BMA).

Vaidya, V.U., Greenberg, L.W., Patel, K.M., Strauss, L.H. and Pollack, M.M. (1999), "Teaching physicians how to break bad news" 153 *Archives of Pediatrics & Adolescent Medicine* 419.

Various (1956), "Symposium: Morals, Medicine and the Law" 31 *University of New York Law Review* 1161.

Various (1968), *Life or Death: Ethics and Options* (Seattle: University of Washington Press).

Vincent, J.L. (1998), "Information in the ICU: are we being honest with our patients?" 24 *Intensive Care Medicine* 1251.

Wadlington, W. and Wood III, W.J. (1991), "Two 'no-fault' compensation schemes for birth defective infants in the United States" 7 *Professional Negligence* 41.

Waitzkin, H. and Stoeckle, J.D. (1972), "The Communication of Information about Illness" 8 *Advanced Psychosomatic Medicine* 180.

Waltz, J.P. and Scheuneman, T.B. (1970), "Informed Consent to Therapy" 64 *Northwestern University Law Review* 628.

Weinrib, E.J. (1975), "A Step Forward In Factual Causation" 38 *Modern Law Review* 518.

Weiss, G.B. (1985), "Paternalism modernised" 11 *Journal of Medical Ethics* 184.

Weit, T. (1998), "Suicide in Custody" [1998] *Cambridge Law Journal* 241.

Welborn, M.C. (1977), "The Long Tradition: A Study in Fourteenth-Century Medical Deontology", in Burns, C.R., *Legacies in Ethics and Medicine* (New York: Science History Publications).

White, L.P. (1969), "The Self Image of the Physician and the Care of Dying Patients" 164 *Annals of New York Academic Science* 822.

Wilkinson, T.M. (1996), "Dworkin on Paternalism and Well-being" 16 *Oxford Journal of Legal Studies* 433.

Wilson, I.F. (1981), "Behavioral Preparation for Surgery: Benefit or Harm" 4 *Journal of Behavioral Medicine* 79.

Winfield (1926), "The History of Negligence in the Law of Torts" 42 *Law Quarterly Review* 184.

Winfield, R. (ed.) (1989), *The Expert Medical Witness* (Sydney Federation Press).

Woolf, L. (1996), *Access to Justice* (London: HMSO).

Index